THE FINANCIAL TIMES

GUIDE TO

USING THE FINANCIAL PAGES

FOURTH EDITION

ROMESH VAITILINGAM

FINANCIAL TIMES

Prentice Hall

An imprint of **Pearson Education**

London · New York · San Francisco · Toronto · Sydney · Tokyo · Singapore
Hong Kong · Cape Town · Madrid · Amsterdam · Munich · Paris · Milan

PEARSON EDUCATION LIMITED

Head Office:
Edinburgh Gate
Harlow CM20 2JE
Tel: +44 (0)1279 623623
Fax: +44 (0)1279 431059

London Office:
128 Long Acre
London WC2E 9AN
Tel: +44 (0)207 447 2000
Fax: +44 (0)207 240 5771

Website: www.business-minds.com

First published 1993
Second edition 1994
Third edition 1996
Fourth edition published in Great Britain in 2001

© Pearson Education Limited 2001

The rights of Romesh Vaitilingam to be identified as Author
of this Work has been asserted by him in accordance
with the Copyright, Designs and Patents Act 1988.

ISBN 0 273 65263 X

British Library Cataloguing in Publication Data
A CIP catalogue record for this book can be obtained from the British Library

This publication is designed to provide accurate and authoritative information
in regard to the subject matter covered. It is sold with the understanding that
neither the author nor the publisher is engaged in rendering legal, investing,
or any other professional service. If legal advice or other expert assistance is
required, the service of a competent professional person should be sought.

The publisher and contributors make no representation, express or implied,
with regard to the accuracy of the information contained in this book and
cannot accept any responsibility or liability for any errors or omissions that it
may contain.

10

Designed by Claire Brodmann Book Designs, Lichfield, Staffs
Typeset by Pantek Arts Ltd, Maidstone, Kent
Printed and bound in Great Britain by Biddles Ltd, Guildford & King's Lynn.

The Publishers' policy is to use paper manufactured from sustainable forests.

About the author

Romesh Vaitilingam is a media consultant and writer. He is the author of numerous articles and several successful titles in finance, economics and public policy, including *The Ultimate Investor: The People and Ideas that Make Modern Investment* (with Dean LeBaron) and *The Financial Times Guide to Using Economics and Economic Indicators*. As a specialist in translating economic and financial concepts into everyday language, Romesh has advised a number of top management consultancies and investment managers, as well as various UK government agencies. His work also involves media consultancy for the international economic research community, notably advising the Royal Economic Society and the Centre for Economic Policy Research on the management and development of their public profile.

Contents

Contents

Foreword

'I don't read the financial pages,' friends sometimes tell me. 'I'm not interested in stocks and shares.'

They don't know what they are missing. Information carried each day in the business press sheds light on – and helps to explain – issues which range far beyond the stock exchange. Movements in bond and commodity prices provide sensitive indicators to trends in business activity. Economic statistics give a whole series of snapshots of the health of nations. They do not only show what has happened in the past: they also provide early signals of what is likely to happen in the future.

The markets have developed enormous political importance as well. They have become global in character, and in the process have imposed severe curbs on individual governments' freedom of action. A finance minister who behaves in what the international financial markets believe to be an imprudent way will find it very difficult to manage his national budget, and to sustain his currency.

The French found this to their cost in the early 1980s, and had to reverse their policies as a consequence.

As one of President Clinton's aides famously observed: 'I used to think that if there was reincarnation, I wanted to come back as the president or the pope. But now I want to be the bond market: you can intimidate everybody.'

But it is true that financial pages all too often have an uninviting appearance: great slabs of numbers, impenetrable columns of jargon-ridden prose. Business editors have tried hard in recent years to make their pages more accessible, but the results can still look daunting to the uninitiated.

This is why I welcome the *Financial Times Guide to Using the Financial Pages*. It will certainly be of practical help to stock market investors. But it also provides a valuable service to a much wider group of readers, by explaining the way in which information published in the financial pages can provide insights into the workings of the economy as a whole.

Why publish a new edition? There are two main reasons. The first is that the financial pages themselves are changing, as a result of competition and technological development. Business sections have expanded considerably over the past decade, as rival titles have tried to capture a larger share of readers and advertisers. Newspapers have also had to face competition from electronic news services and a whole host of specialist newsletters. The result is that financial editors have given a lot of time to refining and improving their pages. Many of the tables in the FT have been enhanced for this reason in recent years. Moreover, technology makes it possible to be much more ambitious than in the past. In the old days, the FT managed to calculate a price index for a group of 30 leading shares just once a day. Now, the power of the computer makes it possible for us to work out an index for 600 companies on a minute-by-minute basis.

The second reason for producing a new edition is that markets themselves are changing, and so are the ways of reporting on them. Features appearing for the first time in this fourth edition include sections dealing with new financial markets across the world, the impact of the euro on business and investment, and electronically delivered financial information of the kind available at www.ft.com. Of course, the internet has had an extraordinary impact on business and investment over the past few years, and nowhere is this more evident than for publishers of financial information.

For obvious reasons, I read the FT carefully every day. But I have still managed to learn new things from this guide. It will stay within arm's reach of my desk.

Richard Lambert
Editor, *Financial Times*

Introduction

Money and the financial markets, as reflected in the television or radio news or the financial pages of a newspaper like the *Financial Times*, may often seem to be a different world, something well beyond the experience of most people. But the global movement of capital, the constant shifting of what are often vast amounts of money, does have a connection with our daily lives. Everyone has some contact with the financial system: through having a bank account; through contributing to a pension fund; through buying an insurance or life assurance policy; or through taking out a mortgage or running up an overdraft. And despite its appearance as a foreign country accessible to only a favoured few, and dealing in a baffling language of numbers and jargon, its basic workings are fairly simple to grasp.

The markets are simply a huge clearing house where the different financial needs of individuals, companies and governments can be brought together and matched through appropriate pricing mechanisms. They might be actual places or they might be networks of computers. Either way, they address two fundamental needs: what is variously known as saving, lending or investing – the use of funds excess to spending requirements to secure a return; and borrowing – the demand for funds over and above those already owned, to put to work in various ways.

The players in the financial markets and in the wider economy can be classified into four broad groups:

- **Investors** who have money to spare to spend on assets and, indirectly, lend it to the issuers of those assets. This includes individual investors, though nowadays the bulk of investment is done by large investing institutions such as pension funds and insurance companies.

- **Companies** that want to borrow money in order to buy capital goods or increase the scale of their business.

- **Financial institutions** (banks, building societies, brokers, dealers, marketmakers, etc.), which act as intermediaries, bringing together the borrowers and lenders in various marketplaces.

- **Governments**, which act as both borrowers and lenders, but also regulate the markets and attempt to monitor and influence the state of the economy through fiscal and monetary policy and various "supply-side" measures.

The role and behaviour of each of these players are examined in the first four chapters of this book. The second part of the book looks at the different markets in which they operate: the stock markets, bond markets, international capital markets, foreign exchange and money markets, futures and options markets, and commodity markets. Each chapter takes the relevant charts and tables from the *Financial Times* and explains how they work, what their significance is, and how they might be read and employed by private individuals, professional investors or business managers. The third part broadens the picture, examining the UK, European and world economies, and the effects that key economic indicators have on the financial markets.

The final chapters of the book move beyond the financial pages to explore other sources of financial information: the variety of newspapers, magazines, newsletters and other publications, and how to read between the lines of their financial reporting; the new electronic markets and online sources of financial information; and how to use company reports to find the key performance ratios. Readers who are unfamiliar with the *Financial Times* may want to start here: Chapter 20 gives a brief synopsis of the newspaper's contents. Lastly, two appendices reiterate the key ratios for easy reference and list the constituent companies of the leading market indices in the United Kingdom and the United States.

This book is intended for anyone who reads or needs to read the financial pages of a newspaper. It aims to provide a simple guide to understanding the statistics and the language of modern finance. Right from the first chapter, tables of figures with explanations are introduced to accustom the reader to the ease with which the numbers (as well as the reports and comments) can be interpreted and used with just a little background.

Much of the importance of the statistics lies in the ratios between numbers rather than in the actual numbers themselves. It is the relationship between the figures, both across companies, industries, sectors and economies, and over time that is critical. It is these ratios that investors, companies and the finance types that "make" the markets pore over to identify past patterns, future trends, and present opportunities and dangers.

The tables and charts of the financial pages are reference points, published every day as a snapshot of the state of the markets. But the markets themselves are dynamic, constantly in flux and, in some cases, trading 24 hours and across the globe. For readers needing immediate, real-time data, there are the more sophisticated sources of financial information of the internet age, web-based services providing information and analysis (such as ft.com) as well as online trading facilities and other financial intermediaries. These are discussed in Chapter 19.

Nevertheless, FT figures are a globally used reference point and the newspaper plays an important institutional role in the financial markets. It has pioneered such industry standards as the FTSE 100 index (known as the "Footsie"), used widely as an indicator of the state of the UK stock market, and as a benchmark for the performance of investors' asset portfolios. Furthermore, its pages fulfil the obligation of unit trusts to publish data on the value of their funds.

Although this is the *Financial Times* guide to using the financial pages, the map it provides to understanding that newspaper's financial and economic reports, comments, tables and charts is equally applicable to other papers, and indeed to other media. The newspaper is merely the most detailed and widely used of the non-specialised media. Indeed, other papers frequently provide information on many of the leading indicators that the *Financial Times* has developed, such as the Footsie and its derivative products.

Before turning to the markets and their statistical analysis, some basic and recurring mathematical concepts might be valuable:

- **Average:** a single number used to represent a set of numbers. It can be calculated variously as: a mode, the number that occurs most frequently in a set of numbers; a median, the number with 50 per cent of the rest lying below it and 50 per cent above, or if there is an even quantity of numbers, the average of the middle two; the arithmetic mean, the total sum of the numbers divided by the quantity of them; and the geometric mean, the figure that derives from multiplying the numbers together and taking their nth root, where n is the quantity of numbers.

- **Index:** a number used to represent the changes in a set of values between a base year and the present. Index numbers blend many different ingredients into a single index, and measure changes in it by changes in its parts. This involves giving appropriate weighting to the components according to their importance in what is being measured. A weighted average is usually calculated as an arithmetic mean, either using the same weights throughout (a base-weighted index) or adjusting the weights as the relative importance of different components changes (a current-weighted index). Base-weighted indices may have the base shifted periodically.

- **Inverse and positive relationship:** the connection between two numbers. Numbers with an inverse relationship move in opposite directions; those with a positive relationship move together. This is the mathematical explanation of why, for example, bond prices and yields move in opposite ways; if x is equal to y divided by z, and y is constant, then as x rises, z falls or vice versa. But if x or z is constant, x and y or z and y will rise or fall together. The two pairs are in a positive relationship.

- **Percentage:** the proportion that one number represents of another or the change in a number from one period to another. To calculate the proportion or percentage of y that x represents (whether x is another number or the difference between one number over two periods), x is divided by y. The result will be a fraction of 1, and to convert it into a percentage figure, it is simply multiplied by 100. Movements of a percentage figure might be mentioned in terms of points (one point is 1 per cent) or basis points (one basis point is one hundredth of 1 per cent). Percentage points or basis points are different from percentage changes.

With these simple tools and developments of them explained in the text, the reader should be well equipped to negotiate the figures of the *Financial Times'* financial pages, analysed in what follows.

All tables and figures are reproduced by kind permission of the *Financial Times*. Thanks go to *Private Eye* for permission to reproduce the Nick Whitmore cartoon on p. xviii. I would like to thank those members of staff at the *Financial Times* who have contributed their time and assistance in the preparation of this book over its four editions, particularly Adrian Dicks, Emma Tucker and Keith Fray. I would also like to thank all the staff (past and present) who have worked on the book at Pearson Education, notably Mark Allin, Sally Green, Helen Pilgrim and Richard Stagg. Thanks also to Stephen Eckett of Global-Investor.com for advice, and especially to Annemarie Caracciolo and Skanda Vaitilingam.

"Heard the latest?"

PART 1

Identifying the players

"To avoid having all your eggs in the wrong basket at the wrong time,
every investor should diversify."

Sir John Templeton

"Remember that time is money."

Benjamin Franklin

1

Investors

- **Buying assets** – the important considerations: risk and return; liquidity and time; portfolio diversification; hedging and speculation

- **Comparing investments** – how to make comparisons between the prospects for different assets: the markets on which they are traded; asset prices and the role of interest rates

- **Using the financial pages** – how to navigate the markets: stock markets; bond markets; commodity markets; derivative markets; foreign exchange markets; money markets; managed funds

Most people have a weekly or monthly income – remuneration for the work they put in at their job. Once their basic needs (food, drink, clothing, accommodation) are taken care of, the choices for what they do with what is left over, if anything, are essentially two. They can spend it on more "luxurious" items, such as holidays, music and books. This, together with the basic needs expenditure, is known as consumption. Alternatively, they can save it for future spending by them or their heirs, as a precaution against unanticipated future needs, or to generate future income.

Investors are people who have a surplus of money from their income that they want to save for any of these reasons. They can do this by keeping it in cash, or by putting it in a bank account or building society, the traditional meaning of savings. Alternatively, they can buy something that they expect at least to maintain its value, that might provide a flow of income, and that can be resold when needed. Any of these is an asset. How investors decide on the assets that they buy and own is the subject of this chapter.

■ Buying assets

Assets come in many shapes and forms: cash, bank and building society deposits, premium bonds, securities (that is, ordinary shares in a company or gilt-edged stocks, bonds issued by the government), life assurance policies, works of art and antiques, gold or foreign currencies, and houses and flats. Each type of asset has different characteristics, and the investor's preferences between those characteristics will determine which assets are bought.

The first characteristic of an asset that an investor might consider is its annual return: does ownership of it entitle the investor to receive any further income and, if so, how much? Obviously, for hard cash, the answer is no, but if that cash is placed in a building society account, the investor will earn monthly, quarterly or annual interest at a specified rate. Similarly, a premium bond does not pay its owner any interest (though it offers the regular chance of winning a prize), but a gilt-edged bond will pay a guaranteed fixed amount each year. And ownership of ordinary shares (equities) will generally mean that the investor gets a dividend, a slice of the profits made by the company over a six- or 12-month period.

Investors typically consider the return on an asset as an annual percentage of its value. This is the rate of return or yield, and is calculated by dividing the return by the asset's value. For example, if a building society adds £5 to every £100 deposited with it for a year, the return is that £5 and the rate of return is 5 per cent. In this case, of course, it is known as the interest rate. Similarly, the yield on fixed interest securities like gilts is the fixed amount each pays, known as the coupon, as a percentage of the current price quoted in the bond market.

> The basic rate of RETURN on an asset is the income received as a percentage of the price paid for it

The basic rate of return on a share, the dividend yield, is calculated in a similar way: the dividend paid by the company is divided by the price of the share as quoted on the stock market. Of course, unlike bonds or indeed bank deposits, the dividend payment is by no means guaranteed. The company may, for whatever reason, decide not to pay out a dividend. But with shares, there is another way of receiving a return and that is the second important characteristic of an asset, its potential for capital appreciation.

Capital appreciation or capital growth is an increase in the value of invested money. For example, money in building society and some bank accounts earns interest, but that is the only way in which it can gain in value. In fact, if inflation is high, higher than the rate of interest, money will lose value in terms of its purchasing power, that is, how many goods can be bought with it. Gold and houses, in contrast, do not earn interest, but they can appreciate in value, their prices can rise. When inflation strikes, gold has often been a good asset to protect or hedge against loss of purchasing power. Houses, too, generally maintain their real value at these times.

Ordinary shares possess both characteristics: they can earn a dividend as well as appreciate in value. A share bought at a price of 100 pence might receive a dividend of 5 pence for a year, and it might also increase in price to 110 pence. In this case, the profit or capital gain is 10 pence, the total return on the asset is 15 pence and the overall rate of return is 15 per cent. Of course, the share might also fall in price in which case the return might be negative. In this example, if the price dropped to 90 pence, the capital loss is 10 pence, and the share is said to have depreciated in value by 10 per cent. Because of the dividend, the overall loss is only 5 pence, but this still means that the overall rate of return is negative at minus 5 per cent.

> The TOTAL RETURN on an asset comprises income plus capital growth; for a share, TOTAL RETURN is the dividend yield plus any change in its market price

Risk and return

The possibility of loss on an asset is the third characteristic an investor will look at. Different assets have different degrees of risk, and these usually relate to their potential for appreciation or depreciation. Bank deposits, for example, cannot appreciate or depreciate in price and, hence, are virtually risk free: their level remains the same apart from the periodic addition of interest. Unless the bank goes under, a rather rare occurrence nowadays, the investor's money is safe. The interest rate may drop so that the annual return is lower, but the basic capital is protected from any loss except for the loss of value caused by inflation.

Gilt-edged securities, in contrast, can fall in value. However, since they are sold and therefore backed by the government, they do still guarantee to pay that fixed amount, the coupon. But ordinary shares carry the risks of both falling prices and falling yields. Not only might declining profits lead to share prices declining in the market, but they might also lead to a company deciding it cannot afford to pay as big a dividend as a proportion of the share price, or even to pay one at all. Thus, while equities offer attractive potential rewards and often a relatively safe haven from inflation, the uncertainty over the future movements of their prices makes them a risky proposition.

Clearly, some assets are riskier than others, and some offer potentially better returns, both in terms of yield and capital growth. These characteristics of risk and return that all assets possess are intimately related, and this relationship is the foundation of investment decision-making. Portfolio theory, the body of ideas that attempts to explain why investors select and organise their assets in portfolios in the way they do, has at its core the connection between risk and return, between safety and yield. And all investors should ask themselves the question: how much of my capital am I prepared to risk on an uncertain future, and how much should I ensure gets a safe, solid return?

Portfolio theory can provide a guide to making these kinds of decision, suggesting that the greater the riskiness of an asset, the greater the potential return. If an asset like a bank deposit earns a fairly certain yield, that yield will be lower than the uncertain return on an asset like an ordinary share. The owner of the riskier asset is compensated for taking on greater risk by the possibility of much higher rewards. The appropriate aphorism to encapsulate this concept might be: "Nothing ventured, nothing gained".

In practice, this risk/return relationship appears to be true: the yield on a government bond is usually more than the interest rate on a bank deposit while the return on a share can be far more than both. While the dividend yield on shares is usually low compared to gilt yields, the potential for capital gain can more than make up for it. At the same time, the risk of loss is higher than for either the bond or the bank deposit. Thus, there is a trade-off between risk and return, and the investor will choose assets on the basis of his or her attitude to risk. Risk aversion means that the primary consideration is safety: the investor will prefer owning assets that cannot fall in price. Ideally, these assets should also avoid the possibility of falling in value, but unfortunately the assets that best do that, gold and shares, run the risk of price falls. It is also desirable for the safer assets to offer a reasonable rate of return, but again a relatively poor yield may be the cost of safety. The investor can merely select the best return among the assets that carry the maximum level of risk he or she is prepared to take on.

> Different assets have different degrees of RISK; generally, the more RISK of loss, the higher the potential return

■ Liquidity and time

Having weighed up the risk/return trade-off, the investor will probably want to consider how easy it will be to convert an asset into ready money in the event that it is needed. This is known as the liquidity of an asset, its fourth characteristic, and it too relates to the return on an asset. Generally, the more liquid an asset is, the lower its return. The easier it is for an investor to give up ownership of an asset without undue loss, the higher the price paid in terms of forgone return. Notes and coins, for example, the most liquid of assets, earn no interest and do not appreciate in value.

Liquidity is also used in a slightly different sense as a term to describe the nature of the markets in which assets are bought and sold. An asset that is in a liquid market can be bought or sold in a substantial quantity without the transaction itself affecting its price. The most liquid markets are those with a large amount of trading, a high turnover of assets. These generally include the currency and gilt markets, discussed in detail in Chapters 11 and 12.

> LIQUIDITY is the ease with which an asset can be converted into cash; the more LIQUID an asset, the lower its return

Asset liquidity and asset values are also affected by time, and this time value might be called an asset's fifth characteristic. For example, the longer money is tied up in a bank account, the more illiquid it is, and the higher the return it earns. Because of uncertainty about the future, especially about inflation, money today is worth more than money tomorrow. To bring their values into balance, and to encourage saving/investing rather than spending, the longer money is unavailable in the present, the more it needs to be rewarded. In addition, since the returns on other assets might change for the better over that period of time, the investor receives compensation for being unable to enjoy them. This is the second aphorism of portfolio theory: "Time is money".

Another example in which time value affects asset value is the time to maturity of an asset with a finite life, such as a gilt. The nearer a gilt is to its redemption date (the time that the government will redeem it for its face value), the more likely it is to be priced at or close to its redemption value; the further out it is, the more uncertainty and time value come into play and the further the price can be from the gilt's redemption value. In the latter case, depending on investor expectations about the future, the price might be at a premium to (above) the redemption price or at a discount (below).

With other assets as well as gilts, uncertainty, expectations and time all combine to influence their risk/return characteristics. The interaction of these factors can have dramatic effects on asset prices, and it is important for investors to understand them when evaluating an asset's prospects for yield and capital appreciation.

> TIME has an important effect on asset values: because of uncertainty, money today is worth more than money tomorrow

■ Portfolio diversification

In selecting an asset, an investor will look not only at its own various characteristics, but also at those of other assets he or she owns or intends to purchase. The whole collection of assets an investor owns is known as a portfolio, and the risk/return relationship of any given asset can be tempered by adding assets with different risk/return characteristics to the total portfolio of assets. For example, a portfolio comprising only cash in a bank account offers a safe but unspectacular return, while a portfolio made up solely of shares might perform very well but may also fall dramatically in value.

A portfolio that contains a combination of stock and cash, say with money allocated 50/50 between the two, provides a risk/return trade-off somewhere in between. In the extreme case where share values fall to zero, the total portfolio still maintains half of its value, in contrast with both an all-stock portfolio, which becomes worthless, and an all-cash portfolio, which holds its value. At the same time, if shares double in price, the total portfolio only makes half the profits of the all-stock portfolio, but still significantly outperforms the all-cash portfolio.

With investment objectives that seek a certain degree of safety, but also some potential of higher rewards, it makes sense to own a balanced portfolio, a range of different assets with varying degrees of risk and potential returns. These might include shares, gilts and cash plus some of the more exotic assets discussed in later chapters, such as options and Eurobonds. This is the principle of portfolio diversification, and the third aphorism of investment decision-making: "Don't put all your eggs in one basket".

> The different risk/return profiles of assets in a portfolio combine to generate its overall risk and potential return; the principle of PORTFOLIO DIVERSIFICATION demands a balance of stocks, bonds, cash and/or other assets

■ Hedging and speculation

When weighing up which assets to buy or which to hold, investors will keep returning to the degree of risk involved. The more risk-averse ones will want as much protection of their assets' value as possible and once they have taken the first step into the unknown of investing in assets more uncertain and riskier than a building society deposit, there are various means of achieving that.

The basic strategy is called hedging, and it is a version of the strategy of portfolio diversification: the investor holds two or more assets whose risk/return characteristics to some degree offset one another. One example might be simply to hold a low risk and low but solid return asset for every high risk and high potential reward asset. A more precise way to hedge is to use derivatives, the range of securities whose price depends on or derives from the price of an underlying security. A put option, for example, gives its owner the right, but not the obligation, to sell a share at a fixed price (the striking price) on or by a certain date. Owning one with the share itself means that the investor's potential capital loss is limited to the loss implied should the share fall to the striking price. If it falls further, the investor can use the option and sell the share at the striking price.

On the other side of the hedger's trading is the speculator, someone who is prepared to take on the extra risk that the hedger wants to avoid. Speculators are in the markets for the express purpose of making as large a profit as possible. They typically believe that they know the future prospects for asset prices better than the majority of investors, and hence are prepared to take bigger risks. The key characteristics of speculators are that they are prepared to leave themselves unprotected from possibly adverse market moves, and that they like to trade often and in substantial amounts. This behaviour is beneficial to other investors since it allows the more efficient management and transference of risk, and it gives the market greater liquidity.

With a put option, the speculator aims to make a profit from the premium paid by the hedger. He or she anticipates that the price of the underlying share will not fall to its striking price, and hence that the hedger will not need to exercise it. Of course, the risk taken on is substantial since, if the share price does fall below the striking price, the potential loss is unlimited: the speculator is obliged to buy the share at the striking price and can sell it only at whatever price it has fallen to.

The nature of the derivatives, or futures and options markets is discussed in more detail in Chapters 13 and 14. For the moment, it is merely important to note that these derivatives can be used for the complementary aims of hedging and speculation across a wide range of markets, including future movements of interest rates, exchange rates, commodity prices and security prices.

Both hedgers and speculators "go long" in the assets they expect to increase in value, that is, quite simply, that they invest in them. But they can also "go short": this means that they expect an asset to fall in value, and hence sell it on the expectation of buying it back in the future and realising a capital gain. It is quite possible for investors to short assets they do not own by borrowing them with the intention of returning them once the expected profits have been made. Of course, this is usually a highly speculative activity since the shorted assets may rise in value. It may be used by hedgers when the shorted asset offsets a long asset, for example, where selling a future (a contract to buy a certain asset at a fixed price on a fixed future date) protects against a fall in the price of the underlying asset over that period.

Investors, whether hedgers or speculators, who expect a rise in a particular asset price or in the market as a whole are known as bulls, while those who are pessimistic about future price prospects are known as bears. And it is quite possible to be bullish and bearish at the same time if contemplating contrasting assets or markets. For example, risk-averse investors wary of UK stock market prospects might view gilts as good buys, while ambitious speculators might short the pound or the dollar and go long in gold or property.

Comparing investments

It is important to clarify one potential source of confusion early on and that is the use of the words "investor" and "investment". Popularly, and especially in financial markets, an investment is an asset purchased by an investor with a view to making money, either through its yield or its appreciation in price. But this kind of investment involves only a transfer of ownership. No new spending has taken place: in the language of economics, the "investor" is actually saving. It might be better called financial investment.

Economists, by way of contrast, define investment as spending by companies or the government on capital goods: new factories or machinery or housing or roads or computer networks. This is capital investment. Generally, it is funded by borrowing from savers, perhaps through the issue of stocks or bonds. Thus, investment in this sense is the other side of the market from saving; it is borrowing rather than lending, spending rather than saving.

The financial pages of a newspaper may well use the words in both senses, though generally they will mean financial investment. Usually, though, the context will make it quite clear which is intended. In each case, the cost of the investment is determined in the markets for assets. The price of a stock or bond is, on the one hand, what an investor will have to pay to own it; on the other hand, it is what a company or government can expect to receive for the issue of a similar security.

■ Markets

Assets are bought and sold in markets, but what are these markets exactly? Essentially, they are institutions that allow buyers and sellers to trade assets with one another through the discovery of prices with which both parties are satisfied. They might be physical places where traders meet to bargain, but in an age of technology they do not need to be: generally, nowadays, they operate through electronic networks. Open outcry is the term for an actual gathering of traders offering prices at which they are prepared to buy and sell. But a very similar process is happening when they list their desired prices on the internet.

In each case, what is taking place is a form of auction. For example, a trader might have ten lots of an asset to sell. If there are too many or too few buyers at his or her suggested price (more or less than ten), the trader will lower or raise the price until there are exactly ten buyers. In effect, investors wishing to buy an asset are looking for sellers offering it at a price they find acceptable; sellers are doing the reverse. If neither side finds a counterparty willing to trade at that price, the buyers will raise the price they are prepared to pay, while the sellers will lower their acceptable price. Eventually, a compromise price is reached, and that becomes the current market price.

In the language of economics, this process is the balancing of demand and supply. The price of an asset moves to the level where demand and supply are equal. And since demand and supply continually shift with the changing patterns of investors' objectives and expectations, the price is continually moving to keep them in balance. In this environment of constant flux, it should, in principle, be possible for a seller to extract an excessive price from an unwary buyer if that buyer is kept unaware of the market price. Hence, another angle on the nature of a market is that it is a means for providing information. The more widely available that information, the better that market will operate.

Aggregating from the market for an individual asset produces a market in the recognised sense, an institution providing and generating prices for a range of assets with similar properties, and typically with an aggregate indication of which way prices are moving. In much financial reporting this market is personified as having an opinion or sentiment. What this means is that the bulk of the traders in a market consider it to be moving in a particular direction: if buyers overwhelm sellers, it will be up, while if more traders are trying to leave the market than to come in, it will be down.

Financial markets can be classified in different ways. One basic distinction is between primary and secondary markets: in the former, new money flows from lenders to borrowers as companies and governments seek more funds; in the latter, investors buy and sell existing assets among themselves. The existence of the secondary market is generally considered to be essential for a good primary market. The more liquid the secondary market, the easier it should be to raise capital in the primary market by persuading investors to take on new assets. The secondary market allows them to sell, should they decide it is not an asset they want to hold.

Markets may also be classified by whether or not they are organised, that is, whether or not there is an overarching institution setting a framework of rules and ready to honour the contracts of a failed counterparty. For example, London's Stock Exchange is an organised market while the over-the-counter derivatives market is not. Similarly, markets might be physical places like the New York Stock Exchange, screen-based computer networks like Nasdaq, or networks of telephones and electronic communication, such as those between the speculators and traders of foreign currencies.

And, of course, markets can be classified by the assets that are traded on them: stocks, bonds, derivatives, currencies, commodities and so on. Although these are all distinct markets, and the analysis in later chapters examines them each separately, there are very strong connections between them, connections that grow stronger as increasing globalisation and improved technology allow better flows of information. Investors do not simply choose one category of asset – they can select a mix. This means they can constantly compare the potential returns (yields and price changes) on a variety of assets. Hence, the markets are all linked by the relative prices of assets traded on them, and by the most important price of all, the rate of interest.

Prices and interest rates

Interest rates are prices for the use of money. An investor holding cash rather than depositing it in an interest-bearing bank account is paying a price, the forgone interest. Once the money is deposited, it is the bank that pays the price for the funds it can now use, again the interest payable on that account. Lastly, when the bank lends the money to a company, the company is paying a price for being able to borrow – the interest the bank charges for loans, which is normally higher than the rate it pays the investor, so it can make a profit.

At any one time, there are different rates of interest payable on different forms of money. For example, money deposited long-term receives more interest than a short-term deposit. Similarly, money loaned to a risky enterprise earns more than that in a risk-free loan. Thus, an alternative view of the rate of interest is as the price of risk: the greater the risk, the higher the price.

All of these rates are intimately related: if one changes, they all do. This works by the same process as the changing prices of assets, that is, the rebalancing of demand and supply. If, for example, the rate of interest payable on short-term deposits were to rise, money in long-term deposits would flow into short-term deposits. The sellers or suppliers of long-term deposits would be fewer, and to attract them back, the price, the interest rate would need to rise in line with the short-term rate.

A rise in interest rates has a beneficial effect on investors with cash deposits in interest-bearing accounts. On the other side of the market though, the buyers of money or the borrowers face increased costs since the price has gone up. This would be the experience of companies borrowing to finance new investment, or of homeowners with monthly mortgage payments to make. But a change in interest rates also has effects on the prices of other assets, notably bond and gilt prices, equity prices and the prices of currencies.

The relationship between bond prices and interest rates is an inverse one: as one goes up, the other goes down. This is because a bond pays a fixed amount which, when calculated as a percentage of its market price, is the yield, equivalent to the rate of interest. If rates go up, the relative attractiveness of a deposit account over a bond increases. Since the coupon is fixed, for the yield on the bond to rise to offer an interest return once again comparable to that on the deposit account, the price of the bond must fall.

The relationship between bond prices and interest rates is simple and certain; that between equity prices and interest rates is more complicated and less predictable. As with bonds, the relative dividend yield of shares will be less attractive than the interest rate on a deposit account if interest rates rise. The yield will also be less attractive than that on the bond with its adjusted price. Furthermore, the yield may become even less desirable because the rate rise will raise the company's interest costs, reduce its profitability and perhaps lead it to cut the dividend. However, much of the return sought on shares is from their potential for capital growth and an interest rate rise need not affect that.

Interest rates tend to rise and fall in line with the level of economic activity. In a recession and the early stages of a recovery, they will generally be low and falling to encourage borrowing, while in the subsequent boom, they will rise as the demand for money exceeds the supply. Thus, a recession should be good for bond prices and a boom less positive. For shares, the rising interest rates of a boom might be bad, but the rising economy should be advantageous because of its opportunities for enhanced profitability. In the long term, the prospects for the latter tend to have more of an influence on share prices than interest rates.

The last significant market influenced by interest rates is that for currencies. Exchange rates are in part determined by the relative rates across countries. If these change, by one country perhaps raising its rates, deposits in that country will become more attractive. To make the deposits, its currency will be bought and others sold, pushing up its price in terms of the other currencies. The higher value of a country's currency might also make its stocks and bonds more attractive relative to other international assets. Of course, a higher currency value makes exports more expensive, weakening the country's competitive position and potentially reducing exporters' profits. This may lead to equity price declines.

Each of these effects of changed interest rates could conceivably come before the change is actually implemented. This is because of the expectations of investors: if a rate rise is anticipated, bond owners will probably sell in the expectation of being able to buy the bonds back at the new lower price. This will cause prices to fall automatically because of surplus supply. Markets often discount the future in this way, building into the prices of the assets traded on them all past, present, and prospective information on their future values. Expectations of company profits can influence the current price of a share just as much as actual announced profits, sometimes more so.

Using the financial pages

How do all these concepts work out in practice in the financial pages of a newspaper? And how does the investor check on the prices of assets owned or considered for purchase? The second part of this book covers the entire range of market information carried by the *Financial Times*, providing details on the background and operations of the various markets as well as a guide to how to read the daily charts and tables.

Saturday's newspaper is the issue that focuses most on the interests of the individual investor in its personal finance pages. One table, for example, provides details on the best options available for depositing money in various kinds of accounts at major banks and building societies. The table lists the names of the financial institutions and accounts, telephone numbers, the notice periods for withdrawing funds from the account, the minimum deposits, and the interest rates and frequency at which they are paid.

Neighbouring tables provide details for a variety of mortgages, personal loans, overdrafts and credit cards: the lenders, their telephone numbers, and such key features as the period the quoted rate will last for and the maximum amount that will be lent in the case of mortgages. In a sense, the deposit rates table gives an indication of what is called the opportunity cost of an investment, the benefits lost by not employing the money in its most profitable alternative use. These rates of return represent the best alternative use of money invested elsewhere, and, of course, they are relatively risk-free investments as well. When making selections of assets, they serve as valuable benchmarks.

The concept of benchmarks is one that is repeated throughout this book: many of the figures provided by the *Financial Times* fulfil this purpose of enabling both investors and borrowers to make comparisons. This is particularly the case with indices, which provide investors with the guidelines for passive portfolio management. If the objective is to perform as well as, and no worse or better than the overall stock or bond market, the investor can simply buy the relevant index or mimic it by buying the equities or gilts whose values it measures. The converse of the passive approach is active management where the investor attempts to beat the market by following his or her personal philosophy of what moves asset prices.

Money markets

The money markets are the markets where highly liquid assets like money are traded. The term usually refers to the short-term markets in which financial institutions borrow from and lend to one another, as well as the foreign exchange markets. They are the short-term counterpart of the Stock Exchange's long-term investment market.

These markets are, for the most part, limited to a small number of institutional participants but they have the potential for enormous effects on the whole financial and economic system, and hence will be of interest to most investors and companies (see Chapter 12). They directly involve the individual investor in a more simple way, through their provision of places to deposit money safely and with a reasonable rate of return, the interest rate.

The *Financial Times* produces a daily table listing these money market bank accounts as part of its managed funds service, of which Figure 1.1 is a sample extract. Tables and charts with annotations, commentary and explanation like this appear frequently throughout the rest of the book, as a guide to financial pages everywhere, and particularly the *Financial Times*. They are intended to show how easy the interpretation and use of the financial pages really are once the basic principles and jargon have been understood. This table shows:

■ **Account name and amounts:** the first column lists the name of the account and/or the minimum/maximum that needs to be deposited in it to earn the interest rates indicated.

■ **Gross:** the second column shows the gross interest rate currently payable on money deposited in the account. Gross simply means the amount payable before deductions, in this case not allowing for deduction of income tax at the basic rate. As with all income, the interest received on an asset of this kind is liable to taxation and tax considerations will have an impact on all of the features of investment decision-making discussed earlier.

■ **Net:** the third column indicates the interest rate payable on the account net of income tax at the basic rate. Net is the converse of gross, the amount payable after deductions. Some accounts are tax exempt (for example, individual savings accounts or ISAs) under particular rules designed to shelter relatively modest savings. For these accounts, the gross and net rates are naturally the same.

■ **Gross AER:** the fourth column represents the gross annual equivalent rate. This applies to accounts where the interest is credited in periods more often than once a year. What happens here is that interest earned on the basic amount in the first period itself earns interest in succeeding periods, and so on. Hence the annual equivalent rate is more than the sum of the interest paid in each period. It is instead said to be compounded.

■ **Interest credited:** the last column supplies the detail on the frequency at which interest is credited to the account.

The early part of this chapter explained how the degree of risk affects the yield, with higher risk indicating higher potential return. Similarly, the time it takes to release money from an account, the notice period, affects its return. For example, savings accounts

Account type

Gross interest rate payable

Gross annual equivalent rate (gross AER)

Interest rate net of income tax

Frequency at which interest Is credited

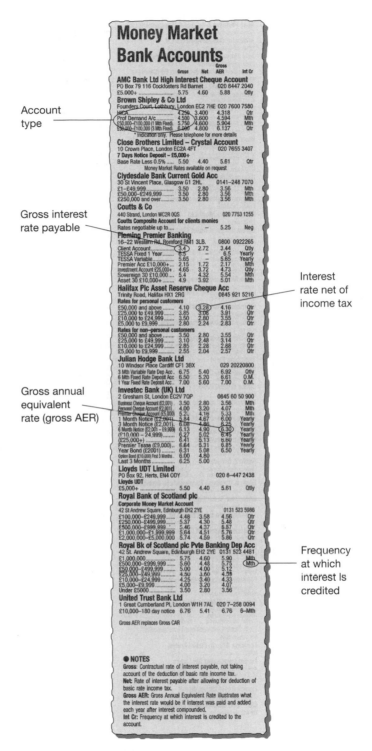

Fig. 1.1 Money market bank accounts

where the saver/investor is required to give 30 days' notice before withdrawing funds (or be penalised for early withdrawal) pay a higher rate of interest than those that allow immediate access. These tables indicate a third factor that affects return, namely the amount of money put into an asset. Generally, the more money an investor is prepared to tie up, the greater the return.

■ Major markets

The front page of the *Financial Times* carries a summary of values and changes in a number of key indicators across the broad range of world markets (see Figure 1.2):

Latest value of the FTSE 100 index of the 100 biggest UK companies by market capitalisation

Latest price for the 30-year US government bond, benchmark for long-term US interest rates

Closing price of the futures contract on a notional UK gilt maturing in June

Benchmark oil price

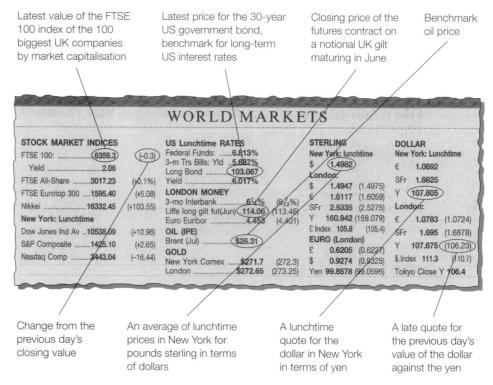

Change from the previous day's closing value

An average of lunchtime prices in New York for pounds sterling in terms of dollars

A lunchtime quote for the dollar in New York in terms of yen

A late quote for the previous day's value of the dollar against the yen

Fig. 1.2 World markets

- **Stock market indices:** equity performance indicators for the London, Tokyo and US exchanges, as well as an index for Europe. These are explored in more detail in Chapters 6, 7, 8 and 9.

- **US rates:** principal US interest rates and bond yields. These are explored in more detail in Chapters 11 and 12.

- **London money:** the London interbank market rate, the price of a future on the long UK government bond and a benchmark rate on the euro. These are examined further in Chapters 11 and 12.

- **Oil and gold:** prices of these two key commodities in New York and London. These are examined further in Chapter 14.

- **Sterling, euro and dollar:** rates for these three currencies in New York and London in terms of each other, Swiss francs and yen, as well as the value of sterling and dollar trade-weighted indices. These are the focus of Chapter 12.

Money watch

	Latest value	6 mths ago	Year ago
Retail Prices Index ♣ †	3.0	1.2	1.6
Halifax House Price Indx ⌘ †	14.2	10.8	4.4
Halifax mortgage rate (%)	7.74	6.85	6.85
Base lending rate (%)	6	5½	5¼
3-mth interbank mid rate (%)	6⅛	5⅝	5¼
10-year gilt yield	5.13	5.38	4.95
Long gilt/equity yld ratio (%)	2.20	2.45	2.14
$/£ exchange rate	1.5072	1.6015	1.6063
€/£ exchange rate	1.5964	1.5992	1.5588
Gold price ($ per oz)	280.25	283.13	265.05

⌘ All Houses index shown for Apr.   † Annual % change.
♣ RPI for April 2000: 170.1.

Fig. 1.3 Money watch

Saturday's newspaper also features a summary table designed to provide a snapshot of the previous week. Labelled "Money watch", it is carried on the back page of the Money section (see Figure 1.3). The table includes the latest values (plus comparable values for six months and a year previously) for a range of key economic and investment indicators: inflation rates, interest rates, yields, exchange rates and the price of gold. The significance of each of these indicators is discussed in the ensuing chapters.

The Money section provides an extensive range of articles, tables and charts relating to issues of personal finance and investment. Savers, borrowers and investors of all kinds can find valuable information in its coverage of companies, markets, saving and borrowing, investing for growth and for income, pensions, financial planning and unit trusts and investment trusts. A number of its key tables are examined in later chapters. Others include a table of top annuity rates (financial products that offer guaranteed income for life in return for a lump-sum investment) and a table of prices, coupons and yields for permanent interest-bearing shares (fixed interest securities in building societies).

"Stocks are usually more than just the abstract 'bundle of returns' of our models. Behind each holding may be a story of family business, family quarrels, legacies received, divorce settlements, and a host of other considerations. These stories may be too interesting and thereby distract us from the pervasive market forces that should be our principal concern."

Merton Miller

"I would rather see finance less proud and industry more content."

Winston Churchill

2

Companies

- **Presenting figures** – how to understand companies' key financial statements: profit and loss; balance sheets and cash flows; investment ratios; company financial news

- **Rewarding shareholders** – when companies issue information on their performance: results; dividends

- **Raising finance** – where companies find their sources of capital: equity; debt

- **Contesting corporate control** – the importance of bidders and targets: UK mergers and acquisitions; cross-border M&A activity

Companies are organisations established for some kind of commerce and with a legal identity separate from their owners. The owners are the shareholders who have rights to part of the company's profits, and who usually have limited liability. This means that the liability of the owners for company debts is limited to the amount paid for their shares. They can only lose what they invested.

Companies are often run by people other than the owners, although, in theory at least, the ordinary shareholders control the company. Management is expected to act in the best interests of the owners. Nonetheless, the ordinary shareholders are the last in the queue of claimants on a company: before they can receive anything, the demands of basic operating costs, interest payments and taxation must be met. This is especially evident when a business is wound up, and the owners become the final creditors to receive their stake.

Since this book is concerned with financial markets covered in the *Financial Times*, and in which, in principle, anyone can participate, the companies considered are typically public: this means that their shares are traded in a market, such as the London Stock Exchange for UK companies, and, for the most part, there are no dominant owners. The focus on companies in this chapter is on the features of corporate life over which the company has some direct control: its profitability, its dividend payments, its methods of raising new capital in the primary market, and its means of offence and survival in contests for corporate control. Chapter 5 focuses more on the secondary market, and the interplay of companies and investors in the context of the market for UK equities.

■ Presenting figures

The primary source for data and analysis of a company is its annual report and accounts. These give all the information on its business and financial affairs, and their publication is one of a company's legal obligations to its shareholders. They describe the current trading conditions of the company, what it has sold (its turnover, sales or revenues) and what it has paid out in wages and salaries, rent, raw materials and other inputs to the production of the goods or services it sells (its costs). They also indicate the company's profits or losses, the state of its assets and liabilities at the start and end of the financial year, and its cash flow.

Detailed explanations of the various financial statements published by a company and the ratios that can be used to analyse and interpret them can be found in numerous publications. This book aims merely to outline some of the relevant figures and ratios. Readers seeking greater depth of analysis are referred to Ciaran Walsh's *Key Management Ratios: How to Analyse, Compare and Control the Figures that Drive Company Value* (Financial Times/Prentice Hall) for a management perspective, and to Wendy McKenzie's *Financial Times Guide to Using and Interpreting Company Accounts* (Financial Times/Prentice Hall) for an investor's perspective. They should also turn to Chapter 18, which explores some of the key ratios from the perspective of both manager and investor over the course of a company's history.

There are essentially three financial statements in a company's annual report: the profit and loss account, the balance sheet, and the cash flow statement. From these three can be calculated all the significant ratios needed for companies to practise sound financial management of their business, and for investors to interpret corporate performance relative to the share price and the market more generally.

Profit and loss

A company's profit and loss account is a statement of the final outcome of all its transactions, all revenues and costs during a given period, usually a year. It shows whether the company made any money in the previous year, how it did it, and what it did with the profits, if any. It also allows comparison with previous years' performances and with other companies.

The total value of all goods sold by the company is known as its sales or turnover. Deducting from that figure the cost of achieving those sales either directly or indirectly (for example, either the raw materials in the sold products, or staff salaries paid for work on these and other products) gives the company's operating or trading profit. Deducting from that figure, in turn, the cost of interest payments made on loans from banks or in the form of corporate bonds, gives the company's pre-tax profit. This is the most widely quoted figure in financial reporting on company results and profitability.

The next deduction is tax: first, corporation tax is paid by the company on profits after all costs have been met except for dividends paid out to ordinary shareholders; and second, advance corporation tax, income tax paid on behalf of shareholders on their dividend income, is paid. The latter is paid at the lowest rate of income tax and can be reclaimed or supplemented by the shareholders depending on their tax bracket. Companies can also partially offset tax payable on dividend distributions against mainstream corporation tax.

Money left once taxation demands have been met is known as after-tax profit or equity earnings. This is now at the disposal of the company for distribution as dividends or ploughing back into the business as retained earnings. The allocation will depend on the conflicting aims of maintaining the level of dividends so that investor confidence in the share price remains solid, and having access to the least expensive source of funds for investment in further developing the business. The conflict corresponds to the dichotomy an investor faces between income and capital gain. The two do not preclude one another, but an appropriate balance needs to be struck.

The profit and loss account quantifies revenue and cost flows over a given period of time. In a sense, it links two versions of the second key financial statement, the balance sheet, one at the beginning of the year and the other at year end. The third document is the cash flow statement, which depends on a combination of the two balance sheets and the profit and loss account.

The basic profit and loss account:

Sales or turnover or revenue

minus cost of sales (direct costs)

minus overheads

= operating/trading profit or earnings before interest and tax (EBIT)

minus net interest paid

= pre-tax profit

minus tax (corporation tax and advance corporation tax)

= after tax profit, net profit or equity earnings

minus dividends

= retained earnings

■ Balance sheets and cash flows

The balance sheet is a snapshot of a company's capital position at an instant in time. It details everything it owns (its assets) and everything it owes (its liabilities) at year end. The two sides of a balance sheet, by definition, balance. They are merely two different aspects of the same sum of money: where it came from and where it went. Essentially, liabilities are sources of funds while assets are the uses to which those funds are put.

A company's assets are made up of two items: fixed or long-term assets, such as land, buildings and equipment; and current or short-term assets, such as stocks of goods available for sale, debtors or accounts receivable, and cash in the bank. Its liabilities are made up of three items, the first two being current or short-term liabilities, such as trade credit or accounts payable, tax, dividends and overdrafts at the bank; and longer term debt, such as term loans, mortgages and bonds.

The third form of liability is that of ordinary funds, and this in turn divides into three forms: revenue reserves or retained earnings – the company's trading profits that have not been distributed as dividends; capital reserves – surpluses from sources other than normal trading such as revaluation of fixed assets or gains due to advantageous currency fluctuations; and issued ordinary shares.

Ordinary shares have three different values: their nominal value, the face or par value at which they were issued and which may have no relation to the issue price or current trading price; their book value, the total of ordinary funds divided by the number of shares in issue; and their market value, the price quoted on a stock exchange. For the purpose of reading the financial pages, the last value is the one of primary significance.

The basic balance sheet:

Assets (fixed or long-term assets + current or short-term assets)

Liabilities (long-term debt + current or short-term liabilities + ordinary funds)

Ordinary funds or shareholders' funds = retained earnings + capital reserves + issued ordinary shares

The cash flow statement details the amount of money that flows in and out of a company in a given period of time. Cash flows into a company when a cheque is received and out when one is issued. This statement tracks the flow of the funds in those cheques: how much has flowed through the accounts, where the funds have gone to and where they have come from.

The balance sheet is a check of a company's financial health, and the profit and loss account an indicator of its current success or failure. Together they can be used to calculate a number of valuable ratios, and the cash flow statement can be used to understand what lies behind short-term movements in these ratios.

Financial ratios

Numerous ratios can be calculated from a company's financial statements, many of which are covered in detail in the Ciaran Walsh and Wendy McKenzie books, and in Chapter 18. For the purposes of a reader of the financial pages, some of the most useful are pre-tax profit margins, net asset values and the return on capital employed. Each of these allows valuable insights into corporate value and performance from the point of view of both investor and company manager.

The pre-tax profit margin is simply the pre-tax profit divided by the turnover for the period. Profit margins vary considerably between industrial sectors but can certainly be used to compare company performance within an industry. There are often rule-of-thumb industry standards.

$$\text{Pre-tax profit margin (per cent)} = \frac{\text{pre-tax profit} \times 100}{\text{turnover}}$$

Net asset value (NAV) is the total assets of a company minus its liabilities, debentures and loan stocks. This is the amount that the ordinary shareholders will receive if the business is wound up, the sum left for the last claimants on a defunct company's assets. It is also known as shareholders' interests or shareholders' funds, and is effectively the total par value of the shares in issue plus all historic retained earnings.

Net asset value per share is calculated by dividing net assets by the number of shares in issue. This has varying degrees of significance depending on the nature of the business. For example, the net asset value of a company whose performance depends primarily on its employees will not be important since its tangible assets are few. In contrast, a business heavily built on assets, such as investment trusts or property companies, will find its share price considerably influenced by its net asset value per share. The share price might be at a premium or a discount to the net asset value per share (see Chapter 10).

Return on capital employed (ROCE) is a ratio that indicates the efficiency of a business by showing to what effect its assets are used. It is calculated as the pre-tax profit divided by the shareholders' funds and any long-term loans. The resulting figures enable comparison between one company and another within the same sector; for the investor, they can also be used to compare across different sectors.

> Capital employed = ordinary funds + long-term debt
>
> $$\text{Return on capital employed (per cent)} = \frac{\text{pre-tax profit} \times 100}{\text{capital employed}}$$

Some other important ratios, including earnings per share, dividends per share and the debt/equity ratio, are explained later in this chapter and in Chapter 18. First, though, it is important to see how all these results and ratios feature in the pages of the *Financial Times*.

■ Company financial news

The Companies & Finance UK pages of the newspaper contain details of the financial results of all quoted UK companies, and a handful of those without quotations. There may only be space for a sentence or two on the results of the smaller companies, but larger ones will be given a substantial news story as well as a separate comment in the Lex column on the results. The comment, clearly separated from the news, gives the newspaper's views on why the results are as they are, what the company's prospects might be, and whether its shares are rated appropriately by the market. These pages also report fully on rights and other share issues and large takeover bids. They include briefer items on many smaller acquisitions.

A typical news report on a company's results looks like this, with remarks on the underlying determinants of a company's performance and prospects, and the sometimes unpredictable impact on the share price:

Scottish & Southern Energy, the power utility, yesterday said it wanted to spend up to £3bn on acquiring a UK electricity company and would expand its internet and telecommunications activities this year. The announcement came as the group unveiled a 14 per cent jump in pre-tax profits to £525.8m on turnover of £3.12bn. Earnings per share were 47.5p and the final dividend is 19.2p for a total of 27.5p, up 7 per cent. The shares fell 8p to 521p. (*Financial Times*, 1 June 2000)

In addition to the day-to-day reporting, the *Financial Times* publishes an annual list of the top 500 UK companies, a ranking of companies quoted on the Stock Exchange as measured by market capitalisation (the number of a company's shares in issue multiplied by their market price). This analyses a range of key figures on the companies, including their turnover, profits, return on capital employed and employee numbers. The newspaper also ranks and analyses the top 500 European companies.

■ Rewarding shareholders

Saturday's newspaper contains a table of company results due in its Money section. This includes all the companies expected to announce results in the following week, their sectors and announcement dates, the interim and final dividends paid the previous year and any interim dividend this year.

■ Results

Saturday's newspaper also lists recently announced statements of interim results and preliminary results (see Figure 2.1). The latter are actually the full year's results made to the Stock Exchange, to be fleshed out in the annual report a little later. The table shows:

■ **Name, sector and year to:** company details and the period covered by the results (half or full year) are given.

■ **Pre-tax profits:** these are figures both for this year and the same period of last year (the figure in brackets) in millions of pounds. The letter L indicates a loss.

■ **Earnings per share (eps):** this measures a company's total net return earned on ordinary share capital. It is calculated by first deducting tax, depreciation, interest and payments to preference shareholders (leaving after tax profit), and then dividing by the number of ordinary shares in issue. The figures given allow a comparison with the previous year.

■ **Dividends per share:** the total dividend net of tax divided by the number of shares in issue. Again, the figures allow a comparison with the previous year.

The value of earnings per share is one of the most widely quoted statistics in discussion of a company's performance and share value. The growth and stability of this ratio are a good indicator of how much a company is increasing profits for its shareholders. But it is sometimes difficult to make comparisons across companies because of different methods of calculating earnings.

$$\text{Earnings per share} = \frac{\text{after tax profit}}{\text{number of shares}}$$

■ Dividends

In Monday's newspaper, the Markets Week page discusses company results to be announced that week, including analysts' forecasts for earnings and dividends. A daily chart lists all results announced on the previous day, particularly focusing on dividends (see Figure 2.2), showing:

■ **Company, dates, turnover, pre-tax profits and earnings per share:** details of the companies that announced results and dividends the previous day, the periods covered and three key indicators of size and profitability.

Pre-tax profit this year

Pre-tax loss last year

Year end

Sector classification, for example, Engineering & Machinery

Dividends per share this and last year net of tax

Earnings per share this and last year

Last week's preliminary results

Company	Sector	Year to	Pre-tax profit (£m)		Earnings* per share (p)		Dividends* per share (p)	
Anglian Water	Wtr	Mar	203.9	(227.1)	60.5	(81.0)	-	(43.0)
AorTech Intl	AIM	Mar	1.76L	(1L)	7.71L	(5.05L)	-	(-)
BFS Small Cos Div	IvCo	Apr‡	77.54	(-)	11.39	(-)	9.0	(-)
Baronsmead VCT 2	IvCo	Mar‡	119.59	(95.65)	3.36	(3.17)	3.2	(3.0)
Billam	AIM	Dec	3.4L	(1.03L)	210.1L	(63.5L)	-	(-)
Boots	GRtl	Mar	561.7	(170.3)	45	(2.6)	25.2	(23.8)
Bristol & West	AIM	Mar	0.524	(0.273)	1.8	(1.41)	-	(-)
British Land	Real	Mar	156.4	(55.3)	24.8	(10.1)	10.9	(10.3)
Caffyns	Dist	Mar	2.15	(1.86)	51.3	(46.7)	15.0	(14.5)
Castings	EngM	Mar	10.2	(11.9)	16.56	(18.68)	7.16	(6.82)
City of London PR	Med	Mar	0.707	(0.961)	8.01	(9.97)	6.74	(6.42)
Dresdner RCM Emerg	IvCo	Mar‡	150.5	(98.2)	1.26L	(0.48)	-	(0.45)
Elderstreet VCT	IvCo	Dec‡	125.1	(94.7)	2.68	(3.06)	2.5	(2.4)
Electrocomponents	Dist	Mar	107.3	(112.4)	17.1	(17.8)	12.0	(10.5)
EMAP	Med	Mar	157.3	(115.8)	33.8	(33.0)	18.3	(16.6)
Express Dairies	FdPr	Mar	7.1	(52.8)	0.2L	(12.5)	8.48	(8.4)
FKI	EngM	Mar	156.8	(161.3)	18.87	(19.02)	9.35	(8.5)
Fuller Smith	Rest	Mar	13.7	(14.4)	37.62	(39.17)	13.41	(12.42)
GWR	Med	Mar	18.8	(18.3)	12.5	(11.1)	5.0	(4.2)
Gartmore High Inc.	IvCo	Mar‡	68.8	(96.7)	7.27	(-)	7.2	(-)
Govett Asian	IvCo	Mar‡	224.81	(130.64)	1.26L	(0.09)	-	(-)
IWP Intl €	PCHP	Mar	26.7	(14.6)	24.82	(13.34)	9.02	(8.2)
Invensys	EngM	Mar	66.0	(295)	6.4L	(2.7L)	7.7	(6.175)
Latchways	SpSv	Mar	2.78	(2.3)	18.85	(15.44)	8.25	(7.5)
Macdonald Hotels	Leis	Apr	11.8	(11.8)	14.92	(15.27)	6.0	(5.5)
Millwall	Leis	Nov	2.27L	(3.1L)	0.2L	(0.3L)	-	(-)
Monotub Inds	AIM	Mar	0.705L	(0.118L)	6.7L	(1.5L)	-	(-)
Northern Foods	FdPr	Mar	74.8	(94.5)	9.62	(12.55)	7.25	(6.8)
Old English Inns	Rest	Apr	6.17	(7.28)	13.72	(17.25)	5.2	(4.5)
Orbis	SpSv	Mar	31.2L	(2.69)	22.21L	(1.11)	-	(1.65)
Peel Holdings	AIM	Mar	37.9L	(18.5)	54.53L	(14.88)	11.5	(10.0)
Peel Hunt	n/a	Mar	16.0	(3.17)	28.38	(5.81)	2.0	(1.4)
Penna Holdings	SpSv	Mar	6.6	(5.54)	27.9	(26.1)	3.2	(2.9)
Pilkington	CBld	Mar	52	(118)	0.4L	(5.0)	5.0	(5.0)
Plasmon	Info	Mar	4.09	(0.322)	10.29	(0.49)	-	(-)
Prelude	IvCo	Mar†	151.6	(107.0)	6.5L	(0.7)	-	(-)
Primar-E	Sftw	Nov	0.862L	(0.098L)	1.19L	(0.12L)	-	(-)
QXL.com	GRtl	Mar	75.8L	(2.05L)	27L	(2.6L)	-	(-)
Quintain Estates	Real	Mar	16.2	(9.16)	10.5	(8.7)	5.5	(4.5)
Railtrack	Tran	Mar	360.0	(428.0)	73.3	(84.0)	26.9	(26.3)
Reflex €	Sftw	Dec	0.196	(0.527)	0.69	(1.27)	-	(-)
Sainsbury (J)	FdRt	Apr	509	(888)	18.3	(31.4)	14.32	(15.32)
Scottish & Southern	Elec	Mar	525.8	(293.3)	47.5	(23.6)	27.5	(25.7)
Shanks	SpSv	Apr	36.1	(35.1)	10.8	(11.2)	5.25	(4.8)
South African Brew.$	Bev	Mar	764	(600)	64.3	(43.9)	25.0	(-)
Stentor	AIM	Mar	7.23L	(11.2L)	6.15L	(32.35L)	-	(-)
Sutton Harbour	AIM	Mar	0.795	(0.733)	7.97	(4.81)	4.0	(3.8)
10 Group	AIM	dec	1.4L	(0.589L)	0.43	(0.32)	-	(-)
365	Sftw	Mar	14.8L	(1.15L)	9.5	(1.7)	-	(-)
Tricorder Tech	AIM	Mar	2.9L	(1.9L)	12.53L	(11.71L)-	(-)	
Trinity Care	AIM	Mar	1.34	(1.28)	17.3	(18.4)	5.65	(5.6)
Vodafone AirTouch	Tele	Mar	1,127	(342L)	0.34	(3.64L)	1.335	(1.272)

Fig. 2.1 Last week's preliminary results

RESULTS

	Turnover (£m)		Pre-tax profit (£m)		EPS (p)		Dividends				
							Current payment (p)	Date of payment	Corresponding dividend	Total for year	Total last year
African Lakes .... 6 mths to Mar 31	15.1	(6)	0.504L♠	(0.006)	0.5	(0.22)	-	-	-	-	-
Allders .... 6 mths to Apr 1	281.9	(290.4)	13.3♥	(14.3)	11.1	(13.1)	3.4	Aug 3	3.4	-	8.4
Anglian Water .... Yr to Mar 31	878.5	(838)	203.9♠	(227.1♠)	60.5	(81)	nil#	-	30.2	nil#	43
Bristol & West Φ .... Yr to Mar 31	1.21	(0.659)	0.524	(0.273)	1.8	(1.41)	-	-	-	-	-
British Land .... Yr to Mar 31	443.7□	(375.6□)	156.4♥	(55.3♠)	24.8	(10.1)	7.5	Aug 25	7.07	10.9	10.3
Caffyns .... Yr to Mar 31	147.3	(151.6)	2.15	(1.86)	51.3	(46.7)	9.5	July 25	9	15	14.5
Eldridge Pope .... 6 mths to Mar 31	25.6	(32.6)	0.81♠	(2.59♥)	2.29	(9.15)	2.6	July 28	2.42	-	6.9
Electrocomponents .... Yr to Mar 31	761.4	(677.1)	107.3	(112.4)	17.1	(17.8)	8.3	July 25	7.25	12	10.5
Invensys .... Yr to Mar 31	9,034	(9,414)	66♠	(295♠)	6.4L‡	(2.7L)	5.2	Sept 12	4.69	7.7	6.175
IWP Intl € .... Yr to Mar 31	565.1	(476.1)	26.7	(14.6♠)	24.82†	(13.34)	5.3	Oct 5	4.825	9.02	8.2
Maclellan Φ .... 6 mths to Mar 26	18.1	(14.8)	0.138	(0.052)	0.4	(0.2)	-	-	-	-	-
Methven's Φ .... 6 mths to Mar 31	3.98	(3.64)	0.554L♠	(0.021L♠)	3.78L†	(0.2L)	-	-	-	-	-
Northern Foods .... Yr to Mar 31	1,339	(1,286)	74.8♠	(94.5)	9.62	(12.55)	4.5	Aug 25	4.2	7.25	6.8
Orbis .... Yr to Mar 31	55.6	(49.3)	31.2L♠	(2.69♠)	22.21L	(1.11)	nil	-	1.27	nil	1.65
Plasmon .... Yr to Mar 31 ★	70.3	(49.9)	4.09♠	(0.322♠)	10.29	(0.49)	nil	-	nil	nil	nil
Primar-E .... Yr to Nov 30	9.19	(11.3)	0.862L♠	(0.098L♠)	1.19L	(0.12L)	nil	-	nil	nil	nil
QXL.com .... Yr to Mar 31	6.89	(2.55)	75.8L♠	(2.05L)	27L†	(2.6L)	-	-	-	-	-
Reflex € .... Yr to Dec 31	4.19	(3.64)	0.196♥	(0.527♥)	0.69	(1.27)	-	-	-	-	-
Sainsbury (J) .... Yr to Apr 1 ☆	16.3	(16.4)	509♠	(888♥)	18.3	(31.4)	10.3	July 28	11.3	14.32	15.32
Scottish & Southern .... Yr to Mar 31	3,117	(2,843)	525.8	(293.3♠)	47.5	(23.6)	19.2	Sept 29	18	27.5	25.7
Shanks .... Yr to Apr 4	320.6	(263.9)	36.1	(35.1)	10.8†	(11.2)	3.5	Aug 7	3.2	5.25	4.8
Sutton Harbour Φ .... Yr to Mar 31	4.75	(4)	0.795	(0.733)	7.97	(4.81)	2.6	Sept 29	2.4	4	3.8
365 .... Yr to Mar 31 §	22.4	(2.59)	14.8L♠	(1.15L)	9.5†	(1.7)	-	-	-	-	-
Trinity Care Φ .... Yr to Mar 31	22	(17.6)	1.34♥	(1.28♥)	17.3†	(18.4)	3.9	Aug 8	3.9	5.65	5.6

Investment Trusts	NAV (p)		Attributable Earnings (£m)		EPS (p)		Current payment (p)	Date of payment	Corresponding dividend	Total for year	Total last year
Asset Management .... 6 mths to Mar 31	173.8	(105.4)	0.644	(0.294)	7.43	(3.4)	2	July 3	1	-	4.5
BFS Inc & Growth . 9 mths to Apr 30 ★	33.28	(96.57)	7.31	(6.9)	8.35†	(8.5)	2.5§§	June 26	2.5	-	10.4
Edinburgh W'wide . 6 mths to Apr 30 ★	322	(267.02)	0.394	(0.724)	0.8	(1.48)	0.5	July 7	0.5	-	2.2
Gartmore High Inc .... 13 mths to Mar 31	68.8	(96.7)	1.45	(-)	7.27	(-)	2.4	♦	-	7.2	-
L&G UK Select .... 6 mths to Apr 30 ★	193.3	(198.8)	0.487	(0.663)	1.36	(1.8)	0.9	July 14	0.865	-	2.9
Scottish .... 6 mths to Apr 30 ★	520.8	(463.3)	8.97	(10.8)	3.35‡	(8.8)	2.27	July 17	2.2	-	6.65

Earnings shown basic. Dividends shown net. Figures in brackets are for corresponding period. ♠After exceptional charge. ♥After exceptional credit. †On increased capital. #Distribution of redeemable shares equivalent to previous year's pay-out. ΦAim stock. □ Gross rental income. ‡On reduced capital. €Euros. ★ Comparatives restated. ☆ Comparatives for 56 weeks. §Comparatives for eight months. §§Third interim; makes 7.5p to date. ♦Already paid.

Fig. 2.2 Results

- **Dividends:** the current payment; the date of the payment; the corresponding dividend the previous year; and the totals for the current and previous year. Companies usually announce their dividends net of tax since they calculate them on the figure for after-tax profit.

Dividends are paid only out of earnings, but in order for companies to maintain some consistency in their payments, these need not necessarily fall into the same year as the dividends. Where there has been a loss, a company might choose to make dividend payments out of retained earnings. Some companies, notably newer ones in the technology sector, do not pay any dividends – in part because they may have, as yet, no earnings; and in part because they want to plough earnings back into the business.

■ Raising finance

From a company perspective, the financial markets exist to raise money through various financial instruments. The sources of capital are basically three: the permanent capital of shareholders (also known as equity capital, ordinary shares or, in the United States, common stock); ploughed-back profits (equity funds or shareholders' reserves); and various forms of debt or loan capital.

Corporate finance, the subject of how companies arrange their capital structure, tends to focus on the relative benefits of financing via debt or equity. The relationship between the two elements in a company's capital structure is known as its gearing, balance sheet gearing or debt/equity ratio (or leverage in the United States), and is commonly calculated as total debt (current plus long-term debt liabilities) divided by ordinary funds (shareholders' equity plus retained earnings). The more highly geared or leveraged a company is, the higher are its borrowings relative to its share capital or turnover.

Total debt liabilities = long-term debt + current or short-term liabilities

$$\text{Balance sheet gearing or debt/equity ratio (per cent)} = \frac{\text{total debt liabilities} \times 100}{\text{ordinary funds}}$$

Gearing, in a general sense, is any situation where swings between profits and losses can be caused by quite small changes in underlying conditions. In the case of gearing with debt and equity, a small change in interest rates can have a dramatic effect: with an increase in the rate of interest, a highly geared company suffers much more from the increased payments necessary to service its debt. The small change can have a substantial effect on profits.

Another prominent gearing ratio is income gearing, which indicates a company's ability to service its debt, that is, how much room there is between the interest payments it has to make on its debt and the operating profit it is earning. The ratio is calculated as total interest expense divided by operating profit. An alternative way to express this ratio is what is known as interest cover, the number of times interest could be paid out of operating profit. In this case, the calculation is the reciprocal, operating profit divided by interest expense.

$$\text{Income gearing (per cent)} = \frac{\text{interest expense} \times 100}{\text{operating profit}}$$

$$\text{Interest cover} = \frac{\text{operating profit}}{\text{interest expense}}$$

■ Equity

Equity finance is the capital that allows companies to take the risks inherent in business, embarking on risky new investment projects. It is limited in a private company, and this is the main reason why such a company would want to "go public". In "coming to the market", getting quoted on the Stock Exchange or the Alternative Investment Market (AIM), through a new issue, a company has access to significantly more money for investment in the business. The means by which this is done, and *Financial Times* reporting of new issues, are discussed in Chapter 5.

There are two common classes of equity capital: ordinary shares, which have no guaranteed amount of dividend payments, but which carry voting rights; and preference shares, which usually carry a fixed dividend and have preference over ordinary shareholders if the company is wound up, but which have no voting rights. There are also a number of variations, including cumulative preference shares and part-paid shares. These are also discussed in more detail in Chapter 5.

Companies already listed on the exchange and wishing to raise new equity capital would normally do so by a pre-emption rights issue. This means that existing shareholders have first option on the new shares or the right to sell that option. An increase in the number of ordinary shares in a company without a corresponding increase in its assets or profitability results in a fall in their value – what is known as a dilution of the equity.

To avoid immediate dilution of the shares in issue, a company might use an alternative financial instrument to raise capital, a convertible (also known as a convertible loan stock or a convertible bond). These are debt instruments that can be converted into ordinary or preference shares at a fixed date in the future, and at a fixed price. Their value to a company, besides avoiding dilution, is that, in exchange for their potential conversion value, they will carry a lower rate of interest than standard debt.

Another form of financial instrument that companies use to raise capital is the equity warrant. This is a security that gives the owner the right, though not the obligation, to subscribe cash for new shares at a fixed price on a fixed date. Warrants are themselves traded on stock markets and work in a way similar to options, which are discussed in detail in Chapter 13. Since the subscription price on a new warrant will exceed the current market price of the underlying stock, the warrant is a speculative asset, gambling on a price rise. They are popular with companies since they can be issued without including them in the balance sheet.

■ Debt

The alternative to share capital as a source of finance is loan capital. Debt finance is attractive to companies since it allows the business to be developed without giving up a stake in the ownership, and the consequent loss of a share of the profits and a degree of control. It is also often more readily available than new equity capital other than that from retained profits, and it can be built into a company's capital structure as both short-term and long-term debt.

Like equity capital, corporate debt takes a number of different forms. Long-term loans are usually raised by issuing securities: the most common form in the United Kingdom is the debenture. Most debentures offer a fixed rate of interest payable ahead of dividends in the queue of claimants; and they are often secured on specific company assets. They usually trade on the Stock Exchange, involve less risk than equities, but pay a lower rate of interest than other kinds of debt.

Other forms of industrial or corporate loans include fixed and floating rate notes, and deep discount and zero coupon bonds. These differ in how the interest or coupon is determined and paid. Fixed notes pay a specified amount whatever happens to interest rates generally, and hence their price in the secondary market varies inversely with interest rates in the same way as gilts. Bonds of this kind have been a central part of corporate finance in the United States for many years, and are becoming more significant in the United Kingdom and continental Europe as a consequence of shrinking government bond markets and the positive impact of the euro on fund-raising across borders.

Floating rate notes are more prevalent in the Euromarkets, the markets in which players lend and borrow Eurocurrencies (currencies deposited and available for use outside their country of origin). These instruments pay a rate of interest determined by some standard rate such as the LIBOR, an agreed rate for short-term loans between banks, discussed in Chapter 12. Deep discount and zero coupon bonds, in contrast, pay little or no interest. Instead, the issuer offers them at a significant discount to their redemption value so that the investor makes most of the return from a capital gain rather than periodic interest payments. Each of these kinds of debt is discussed in more detail in Chapter 11.

The most common form of short-term loan is the overdraft at the bank, where companies can borrow up to an agreed limit and only pay interest on the amount actually borrowed at any given point in time. Another form is the commercial bill, the short-term counterpart of bonds, where the issuer promises to pay a fixed amount on a given date a short time in the future, usually three months. The bills are generally "accepted" (guaranteed) by a financial institution, and sold at a discount ("discounted") to their face value to provide the buyer with an appropriate return and the issuer with immediate cash.

One of the most recent innovations in debt instruments is the junk bond, a form of finance developed and used primarily in the United States. This is a bond that offers a higher rate of interest in return for a higher than usual risk of default by the issuer. In the 1980s, junk bonds were used as a means of generating substantial amounts of finance for the takeover of large companies by relatively small ones. They became a focal point of controversies over leveraged buyouts and other supposedly unwelcome or undesirable takeover bids.

■ Contesting corporate control

One of the aspects of corporate life that features prominently in reporting on companies and the financial markets is the contest for corporate control. Mergers and acquisitions (M&A), bidders and targets, corporate control and corporate governance are issues that frequently make the headlines, and ones that often have an impact on the market far beyond the individual companies or sectors they involve.

The primary argument in favour of acquisitions is that they are good for industrial efficiency: without the threat of their company being taken over and, in all likelihood, the loss of their jobs, managers would act more in their own interests than those of the owners. In particular, this might imply an inefficient use of company resources and a lack of concern about the share price, the value of which is often a sign of a company's vulnerability to takeover. Certainly, a bid is frequently beneficial to the shareholders of the target company in terms of immediate rises in the share price. It can be argued, however, that the threat of takeover means that management takes too short-term a view: bolstering the share price where possible, investing inadequately for the future, and, where a company has been taken over in a leveraged buyout, perhaps burdening it with too high a debt/equity ratio. The demands of making enough profits to meet interest payments might mean it is managed solely for the short term.

Bids and mergers

Saturday's newspaper has a list of the takeover bids and mergers announced in the previous week and involving bidder and target companies primarily based in the United Kingdom (see Figure 2.3). The table shows:

- **Bids:** details of current takeover bids for publicly quoted companies, naming the bidder and target, the value of the bid per share, the current market price of the target's shares, the price before the bid, and the total value of the bid in millions of pounds.

Bids might be made in the form of a cash offer for all the shares in issue (the value of the bid per share), a paper offer where shares in the bidder are offered in exchange for those of the target, or a combination of the two. The bids might be agreed to by the management of the target, or they might be defended or contested. Hostile bids are normally settled through what are known as proxy contests, where shareholders appoint proxies to vote on their behalf, either for or against the bid. The battles over corporate control have generated a new vocabulary of company life: white knights (alternative bidders who are preferred by the existing management of the target) and poison pill defences (tactics that mean a successful takeover triggers something deleterious to the target company's value) are just two of the most popular.

Current takeover bids and mergers

Company bid for	Value of bid per share**	Market price	Pre bid price	Value of bid £ms**	Bidder
Alld London Props	125*	122	122	88.25	Arrow Property
Alld London 5¾% Pf	110*	106½	101	44.0	Arrow Property
BOC	1460*	1265	1387	7.15bn	Air Lqd&Air Prod
BTP‡	600*	595	527½	1.05bn	Clariant
Beechcroft‡	4.7*	4¾	5	8.87	John Laing Homes
Bickerton Group	54	45	40	8.26	Artisan (UK)
Blockleys‡	24	27½	37½	5.99	Ennstone
Blue Circle	420*	411	414	3.40bn	Lafarge
Border TV	1061¾	1162	902½	114.67	Scottish Radio
Boxmore‡	265*	264	206½	72.0	Chesapeake
Britannia Group	71*	68	62½	16.33	YJL
Burmah Castrol	1675*	1535	1245	2.22bn	BP Amoco
CPL Aromas‡	110*	107½	91½	14.41	Doubleforecast
Carlton Comms.	684½	770	554¼	4.30bn	Utd News & Media
Carlton 5½% Cv Prf	193	211	554¼	340.98	Utd News & Media
Carlton 6½% Cv Prf	192	199	554¼	316.25	Utd News & Media
City Technology	204¾	195	172½	99.75	First Technology
Coca-Cola Bevs.	117	116	127	1.25bn	Hellenic
Courtaulds Texts.	145*	143	62½	150.37	Sara Lee
Critchley Group	575*	740	412½	93.73	Brady Corp.
Critchley Group	750*	740	657½	122.25	Tyco
Druid Group‡	2387	2350	2037½	558.60	FI Group
Exel	347	346	263	1.83bn	Ocean Group
Fairfield Ents.	200*	198½	178½	19.4	Bobst
Farlake Group	657¾	707½	580	23.02	Talisman House
Finelist	192*	188½	179	158.4	Europe Auto
Flextech	2001½	1944	1298	3.16bn	TeleWest
Gerrard Group‡	670*	667½	639	524.6	Old Mutual
Goodhead	67½*	66½	61½	27.27	John Madejski
Greenway	39*	38½	33½	7.57	OSS Group
Holt (Joseph)	2300*	2300	1445	63.64	Inhoco
i.e. Group	115*	110½	104½	20.81	Misys
Mannesmann♣‡	€323	€348	€209	€125.8bn	Vodafone Airtch
Meristem	16½	19	21	6.12	Torday& Carlisle
Metroline‡	240*	235	196	73.68	Delgro
Meyer Intl.‡	515*	512½	427½	1.04bn	Comp St Gobain
Norwich Union	396	405	435½	7.67bn	CGU

Fig. 2.3 Current takeover bids and mergers

Cross-border deals

Monday's newspaper extends the coverage of M&A deals to international bids made in the previous week (see Figure 2.4):

CROSS-BORDER M&A DEALS				
BIDDER/INVESTOR	**TARGET**	**SECTOR**	**VALUE**	**COMMENT**
Sema (UK/France)	LHS (US)	Telecoms srvcs	$4bn	All-share deal
Nortel Networks (Canada)	Xros (US)	Telecoms eqpmnt	$3.25bn	Optical switch
National Grid (UK)	SEES (US)	Power	$3.2bn	US approves
Ford (US)	Land Rover (UK)	Cars	$1.85bn	BMW sale
Dexia (France/Belgium)	FSA (US)	Financial srvcs	$2.6bn	Core develops
General Motors (US)	Fiat Auto (Italy)	Cars	$2.4bn	Initial 20%
TXU Corp (US)	Hidro el Cantábrico (Sp)	Power	$2.3bn	Post-poll swoop
Intel (US)	Ciga (Denmark)	Telecoms eqpmnt	$1.25bn	High-speed move
Shanks (UK)	WMN (N'lands)	Waste managemnt	$328m	WMI recycling
NTL (US)	B2 (Sweden)	Telecoms eqpmnt	n/a	Broadband buy

Fig. 2.4 Cross-border M&A deals

- **Deals:** details of the bidder/investor, the target company, the industrial sector and the value of the bid in dollars (how much the bidder is offering to pay).
- **Comment:** a phrase analysing the essential feature of the deal – whether the bidder is offering cash or shares, whether it is seeking to diversify or expand market share, the influence of regulators and competitors, etc.

Charts that appear periodically in the FT's economics coverage (in Thursday's "The economy at a glance" and in Saturday's Money section) show the number and value of overseas acquisitions by UK companies and acquisitions in the UK by overseas companies over recent years (see Figure 2.5):

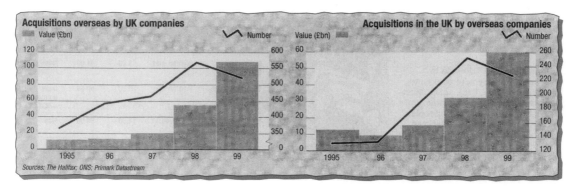

Fig. 2.5 Acquisitions

The total value of global mergers and acquisitions increased significantly through the late 1990s and into the new millennium, driven by the opening up of national economies and the booming stock markets of Europe and North America. The most significant to date was finalised in mid-2000, as reported in the newspaper:

> Mannesmann on Thursday night capitulated to a $186bn takeover from UK wireless rival Vodafone. It will throw open the corporate doors of Europe and pave the way for a wave of cross-border mergers and acquisitions. The merger is the largest takeover of all time, ranking above AOL's recently announced deal with Time Warner, and will generate the largest adviser fees, at almost $1bn. Vodafone's victory marks the first time a foreign company has succeeded with a hostile assault on a large German group. It demonstrates that there are no longer any no-go areas as European business embarks on a widescale restructuring. Vodafone – at $375bn – will emerge from the takeover as Europe's largest publicly traded company and the world's largest telecoms group. It will also rank as the fourth largest company in any industry behind Microsoft, General Electric and Cisco Systems. *(Financial Times, 26 June 2000)*

Information on recent patterns of domestic and transnational "corporate restructuring" like this can be enormously useful to investors thinking about exploring the relatively short-term investment opportunities in "special situations". What is more, these "recombinant techniques" of corporate finance often have an impact on the financial markets far beyond the individual companies and sectors they involve, so it is important to be sensitive to their likely impact.

The share prices of participating companies generally rise in response to announcements of M&A activity. Indeed, the whole market typically goes up if a really big deal hits the news. But do such events really benefit investors in either the buying or selling companies in the long term? The evidence seems to be clear that mergers ultimately do not pay off for either buyers or sellers. For acquirers, the impact can be very bad, reducing their profitability by as much as 15 per cent a year, especially if they have to use external funds to finance their takeovers. It seems to be better for investors to seek to buy potential targets rather than potential bidders – perhaps companies whose declining share prices make them vulnerable to takeover or whose businesses might appeal to overseas companies seeking to expand their global reach.

Throughout the 1980s and 1990s, the market for corporate control was the source of considerable financial innovation as well as a significant degree of controversy, notably in the United States. A new kind of arbitrage also became prevalent. Arbitrage is the technique of buying an asset at one price in a market and, almost simultaneously, selling it in another market for a profit.

Risk arbitrage dealt in the shares of companies targeted for takeover, buying before the announcement of a bid and selling when the usual price rise after announcement followed. At times it relied on inside information, and the practice of insider trading, compounded with other financial scandals, undoubtedly earned financial institutions a dubious reputation. The next chapter presents the much more positive side of these institutions: first, their provision of a marketplace for lenders and borrowers of money, and second, their advice and assistance to these two sides of the market.

"Some collective nouns: a gleam of bulls; a gloom of bears;

a roller-coaster of stock markets; a commission of brokers."

James Lipton

"The market is not an invention of capitalism. It has existed for centuries.

It is an invention of civilisation."

Mikhail Gorbachev

3

Financial institutions

- **Managing money** – how assets are distributed into the portfolios of investors: investing institutions and money managers; clearing banks

- **Financing industry** – how new securities are created to provide funds for borrowers: investment banks; securitisation

- **Making markets** – the provision of facilities for assets to be priced and traded: marketmakers and broker-dealers; stock exchanges; money, currency, and derivative markets

- **Moving prices** – demand, supply, and other key economic forces: short- and long-term determinants of share price movements; overall market movements

The most basic financial institution is a market – a place, not necessarily physical, where buyers and sellers can come together to trade. There are essentially four kinds of market in the financial system. The first type is the securities market where new capital is raised (the primary market) and where trading in existing shares and bonds takes place (the secondary market). Such markets include stock exchanges around the world, as well as the international capital markets. The other three kinds of market are: the money markets where highly liquid financial instruments are traded; the foreign exchange markets where currencies are bought and sold; and the futures and options markets where these derivatives can be used to hedge or speculate in future interest rate, exchange rate, commodity price and security price movements.

All of these markets are organised in the sense that they operate on well-established custom and practice, and direct access to them is limited to professional participants. Investors and borrowers usually gain access to the markets through intermediaries. Beyond the organised markets are the over-the-counter (OTC) markets – places or, more often, computer screen-based or telephone networks where securities are traded outside the recognised exchange. The biggest of them all is the foreign exchange market, although the OTC derivatives market is also growing dramatically.

There are three basic functions that have to be performed in a financial market: distribution of assets into the portfolios of investors who want to own them; creation of new ones in order to provide funds for borrowers; and "making" the markets, providing the means by which all of these assets can be easily traded. The first function relates more to investors, the second to companies, and the third is the central facilitating role to which all financial institutions contribute in one way or another.

One single financial institution might perform all three of these functions and do them across a broad range of markets. For example, many investment banks are involved in portfolio management of clients' investments as well as corporate finance, arranging deals, helping companies raise money through flotations, rights issues and bond issues, and advising them on takeovers. Furthermore, they often act as marketmakers, trading on their own behalf, especially in the foreign exchange, Eurobond and derivatives markets.

The performance of a range of different roles, and the contrast between acting as a principal on one's own behalf or as an agent on behalf of a client, throw up a number of conflicts of interest. Such devices as Chinese walls, notional barriers intended to deter valuable market information from being shared between parts of a company with conflicting interests, aim to prevent abuses. But this is still an area of considerable controversy. Apart from the benefits of specialisation, it is one of the reasons companies might focus on working different sectors and functions of the market.

■ Managing money

Chapter 1 explained the principles of investment on the premise that an individual investor is the dominant player on the saving/lending/investing side of the capital markets, making and implementing his or her own investment decisions. In reality, individual investors acting alone form only a small part of the investment community. Nowadays the bulk of investment is done by large investing institutions such as pension funds and insurance companies, operating on behalf of the millions of people who put money into them (see Figure 3.1). Furthermore, many individual investors rely on the services of a range of market professionals, intermediaries who offer advice on, and management of, their asset portfolios.

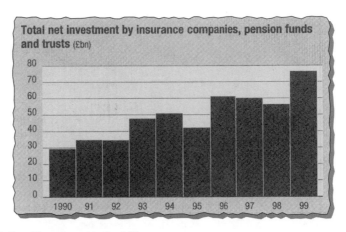

Fig. 3.1 Institutional investment in the UK

■ Investing institutions and fund managers

Many people save in occupational pension schemes. These savings are administered by pension funds, which have become the major players in equity and other markets, operating vast portfolios of assets on some of the basic principles outlined in Chapter 1. Annually, the *Financial Times* publishes a survey of pension fund management. This lists leading pension fund managers, the value of the funds under their management, and the number of clients for whom they provide these services, with comparative figures for previous years. This is a valuable guide to the performance of these institutions, and their relative weight in the investment community.

Life assurance and general insurance companies are also key players in securities markets. In common with pension funds, they manage their funds on the principle of matching the nature of the assets they hold with that of their liabilities. Thus, pension funds and life assurance companies often have liabilities that will only fall due in the long term. Hence, they typically have a preference for long-term assets, such as ordinary shares with good growth and capital gain potential. Insurance companies, whose liabilities might fall due much sooner, tend to prefer a portfolio containing some more liquid assets. In either case, the fund managers are bound to act prudently under their fiduciary obligations to the people who placed money in their care.

Unit trusts (known in the United States as mutual funds) are another form of managed investment. Investors buy units in a trust, and the trust manager invests the money in shares or any other assets laid down by the trust's investment objectives and its guidelines for decision-making. The advantage for investors is that relatively small amounts of money can be spread between a range of assets, securing the benefits of portfolio diversification: if invested well, the trust's capital grows and so does the price of its units. Unit trusts generally specialise in particular types of asset, such as equities of a certain industrial sector or a specific country or region.

Investment trusts are similar to unit trusts except that they have a limited size. Like unit trusts, they invest in equities and other assets, but whereas unit trusts are open-ended, with no limit on the amount of units that can be bought, investment trusts are closed-ended. In a sense, they are more like a regular company with a set number of shares in issue, and in fact their shares are usually listed on the stock market. Shareholders receive their income on investment trusts from dividends as well as any capital gains. Both unit and investment trusts are examined in more detail in Chapter 10.

Investing institutions will generally manage their asset portfolios themselves, but at times they will use the services of companies specifically set up to manage the portfolios of large institutional investors or wealthy individuals with substantial holdings. These are variously known as fund, asset, equity, capital or money management companies, and they will distinguish themselves both by the kinds of markets in which they operate, and by their investment philosophies. For example, certain companies may deal only in equity markets, others on such diverse principles as passive indexation, a preference for growth stocks, or the exploitation of market inefficiencies.

Pension funds and other investors, large and small, may also use the services of stockbrokers and other investment advisers. These brokers provide research to institutional and large individual investors for which they are paid by commission on business placed through them. They also provide market access for smaller retail clients, supplying a range of different services: relatively low cost trading; and advice on portfolio allocation, on particular transactions, and on tax issues. Stockbroking is often just one of the activities of a large diversified securities house or investment bank.

■ Clearing banks

The clearing banks' role in the management of money is very varied. Their key activity is as deposit-taking and loan-making institutions that make their money by borrowing (usually taking deposits, but also using wholesale funds from the money markets) at one rate of interest and lending at a higher one. Building societies operate in a similar way except that they specialise in lending for the purchase of property. But banks differ in that they also provide a range of other financial services, dealing directly with the public over matters from investment advice (both financial and capital) to foreign exchange needs for holidays or business trips abroad.

Banks also "create" money through what is known as the money multiplier. What happens is that a bank receives a deposit, some of which is kept in liquid form as a safeguard in case the depositor needs it back, with the rest being lent on. The borrower will then spend the money on an item, the seller of which will deposit it in a bank. Again, part of the deposit will be kept liquid with the rest lent on, and so the cycle continues. If it were not for the fact that the banks do not lend all that they receive in deposits, the process would continue indefinitely with the amount of money in the economy, the money supply, ballooning.

In fact, the proportion of their deposits not lent determines how much a given deposit eventually becomes within the whole banking system. If, for example, all banks keep back 10 per cent of their deposits, an initial deposit can expand tenfold: of a £100 deposit, £90 is lent and deposited, of which £81 is lent and deposited, and so on. The eventual total of bank deposits is £1,000.

As a result of the money multiplier, banks are highly geared companies, with a substantial proportion of their capital made up of borrowed funds. Since high gearing implies that small changes can have major effects, it is critical that they lend soundly or a large credit failure by one of their borrowers could have devastating consequences. This is why the monetary authorities attempt to influence, at times by decree, the various ratios (such as cash, liquidity and reserve assets ratios) banks employ to manage their finances. The other reason they do so is to control the expansion of the money supply, one of the most important determinants of inflation and the overall level of economic activity. Alternative means by which this might be done are discussed in the next chapter.

Financing industry

The provision of funds for industry is the role of the primary markets, where new securities are issued on behalf of clients. The aim of the financial institutions that perform this service on behalf of client companies is to attract cash for new capital investment, in the form of either equity or debt finance, from individual and institutional investors, banks and, in some cases, the Euromarkets.

Investment banks

When a company wants to raise new equity or debt finance, it will usually approach an investment bank for advice and assistance, and a broker to sponsor the issue. The bank is responsible for advising on the terms of the issue and, in particular, designing its key features. This is one of the most fertile areas for innovation as banks create the new and more exotic financial instruments discussed in Chapters 2 and 11. The bank will also arrange the mechanics of the issue, such as the various techniques for making new issues and rights issues discussed in Chapter 5.

New issues of equity capital require the publication of a prospectus to satisfy the regulations of the Stock Exchange, which is naturally concerned to protect its reputation and the interests of its investors. The issues also require underwriting by the issuing house, the investment bank. It must agree to subscribe for any shares not taken up by investors once the offer period has expired. The role of the sponsoring broker, which will be a member of the Stock Exchange, is to ensure that the Exchange's legal requirements are met, to pass on, if necessary, some of the risk of underwriting to sub-underwriters and to distribute the shares into the portfolios of willing investors.

As well as raising new capital, investment banks will usually be involved on one side or the other of the market for corporate control, advising on strategies. The *Financial Times* publishes an annual survey of corporate finance. This ranks investment bank corporate advisers by the value of their work in three areas: takeover bids, flotation of companies, and issues of shares by companies already with quotations. It is a valuable guide to how well the banks are performing against one another.

■ Securitisation

Of course, many companies might raise new capital through borrowing directly from a bank in the form of a loan. Nowadays, this has become less common owing to a process known as securitisation. This is the process that enables bank borrowing and lending to be replaced with the issue of some of the debt securities mentioned in Chapter 2: commercial bills, bonds, and floating rate notes. It creates attractive new securities for investors, and it has significant benefits for the companies. In particular, bank charges are reduced, and the cost of raising funds may be even less expensive if the markets turn out to be more efficient judges of the creditworthiness of companies than banks. Of course, investment banks will normally arrange the issue of these debt securities.

Securitisation also refers to the conversion of previously untradeable assets into securities that can be bought and sold. For example, an innovation of the 1980s was the mortgage-backed security. This is produced by converting the assets of a building society, the stream of payments due on its mortgages, into a tradeable security. Closer to the interests of the small investor is the certificate of deposit (CD), a very liquid, almost risk-free asset which pays a relatively low rate of return. It is analogous to an interest-bearing bank account, but it has the advantage that it can be traded; it is effectively a bank account that has been securitised.

■ Making markets

Marketmaking is the central function of financial institutions in the secondary markets where existing securities are traded. The role of the marketmakers is to determine security prices and to ensure that buyers and sellers can trade without having a significant impact on prices. Efficient marketmaking avoids substantial price shifts or undue volatility in response to individual buy or sell orders, providing liquidity and allowing dealing to take place on a large scale. It also ensures that the costs of trading are not too high.

Marketmakers and broker-dealers

The companies or branches of companies that are marketmakers buy and sell securities on their own account, acting as a principal. With the right to trade in this way goes the obligation to make the market. Hence, it is conceivable that at the end of a day's trading, marketmakers will be left with unwanted stocks or an undesirable shortage of stocks. They will therefore always be seeking to find a price that "balances their books". Their activities are an important influence on stock price movements.

When quoting prices at which they will buy or sell securities, marketmakers list bid (buying) prices and offer (selling) prices. The difference between the two figures is known as the spread. Since marketmakers naturally aim to profit from their transactions, the bid price is invariably lower than the offer price. This is comparable to a bank that takes deposits (borrows or "buys" money) at one rate of interest, and loans (sells) it at a higher price. Although the spread for the marketmaker or the rate differential for the bank may seem small, totalled over the huge amount of transactions they make, they are often able to make very considerable profits.

Stockbrokers or, as they are more commonly known nowadays, broker-dealers, are companies that act both as an agent for the investor, and as a principal, trading on their own behalf. Such companies face especially difficult conflicts of interest. But for the existence of Chinese walls, their marketmaking arm might be inclined to encourage their broking arm to advise client investors to take on securities the former is keen to unload. Similarly, they may also be inclined to the practice of "front running", buying promising securities or selling dubious ones ahead of clients, and potentially affecting the price adversely prior to the clients' trades.

Marketmakers and broker-dealers both thrive on activity: the more transactions they make or facilitate, the better their opportunities for profit or commission. Obviously, the benefit of the marketmakers' activity is to enhance market liquidity, but that of the brokers might not be so valuable. Again, there is a conflict of interest: the investor is aiming for return on assets; the broker is aiming partly for this (even if simply to ensure his or her services are retained), but also for commission on trades. The process of making trades frequently just to earn commission rather than for any long-term investment objective is known as churning.

Stock exchanges

The London Stock Exchange is the main securities market in the United Kingdom. This is the market for listed shares and gilts, plus debentures, convertibles and warrants. For all of these securities, it is both a primary and secondary market. The second tier of the Stock Exchange is known as the Alternative Investment Market (AIM). This market was established in 1995 to trade in shares not suitable for the main market. It enables smaller companies to "come to the market" to raise capital without having to satisfy the more onerous listing and disclosure requirements of the Stock Exchange. The equities listed on these markets and the indices that measure their overall performance are the focus of Chapters 5 and 6.

The most significant stock exchanges elsewhere in the world are in New York, Tokyo, Frankfurt and Paris. These are explored further in Chapters 7, 8 and 9. In terms of total market capitalisation, the sum of the "market cap" (the share price multiplied by the number of shares in issue) of all the securities listed on them, there are three that outrank the London Stock Exchange, which are the New York Stock Exchange, the Tokyo Stock Exchange and the US electronic exchange (the Nasdaq). The indices that evaluate them (in the United States, the Dow Jones Industrial Average, the Nasdaq Composite and the Standard & Poor's 500, and in Japan, the Nikkei) are some of the most important indicators of the state of the world's financial markets.

Until quite recently, trading on world stock exchanges was conducted in a physical setting, such as the City of London or Wall Street. The impact of technology has been that there are now fewer actual marketplaces. Instead, much trading is conducted through computer network systems, such as the National Association of Securities Dealers Automated Quotation (Nasdaq) system in the United States. These electronic trading systems tend to be quote-driven, with marketmakers and dealers quoting bid and offer prices on screen for other traders to select from. This contrasts with the older, order-driven system of trading where dealers listed their orders to buy and sell shares with the aim of finding a counterparty wanting to buy or sell that quantity at a price on which both parties could agree.

On top of technological advances, stock markets have also seen considerable deregulation in recent years – an easing of the restrictions on their operating methods. In the United Kingdom, the most notable event of this kind was the Big Bang of 1986. Prior to this deregulation, the two key institutions in the market were jobbers and brokers, each of whom operated in a single capacity. The jobbers were marketmakers who did not deal directly with customers, but only with brokers; the brokers placed their orders only through jobbers, and worked on behalf of customers but never dealt with them for their own account. The system protected investors from abuses of some of the conflicts of interest that arise from the principal/agent relationship, but it had a number of weaknesses.

The main problems of the pre-Big Bang Stock Exchange were that it operated as a cartel with fixed commissions on trades, it limited access to capital and new technology, and it constrained liquidity and the ability to make substantial trades without unduly influencing prices. The radical changes of Big Bang led to far more competition between financial institutions, a significant influx of outside capital as banks bought into the market, and the adoption of the screen-based trading system. Between them, these developments created a much more fluid market with information flowing more freely, liquidity enhanced, more and larger transactions made more feasible, and the costs of doing business, at least for the major players, notably reduced.

■ Money, currency and derivative markets

The money markets are markets where money and any other liquid assets such as Treasury bills and bills of exchange can be lent and borrowed for periods ranging from a few hours to a few months. Their primary function is to enable banks, building societies and companies to manage their cash and other short-term assets and liabilities, the short-term counterparts of the long-term capital markets. The main participants in these markets in the United Kingdom are: the banks; companies that issue short-term debt instruments; money market brokers; and the discount houses, which act as the market-makers for most of these assets. Discount houses are discussed in the next chapter.

The foreign exchange markets deal in currencies, for the most part the leading currencies of the developed world: the dollar, the euro, the yen, the pound and the Swiss franc. The main players are the marketmakers, primarily banks, who buy and sell currencies on their own account and deal with customers and other banks, and brokers who try to find trading counterparties for their clients. This is an over-the-counter market with business transactions conducted almost exclusively through a computer and telephone network. Both the money and currency markets are explored in more detail in Chapter 12, while the euro forms part of the subject of Chapter 16.

The derivatives markets deal in futures and options, and increasingly in more exotic financial instruments such as interest rate and currency swaps. Futures and options originated in the commodities markets, the markets for raw materials and primary products, as a means of protecting against seriously adverse price swings. They are still used today in such markets as the London Metal Exchange, but contracts and markets have also now evolved for a range of other securities, debt instruments and indices. In the United Kingdom, the focal point for this activity is the London International Financial Futures and Options Exchange, the LIFFE. There is also a growing market in over-the-counter derivatives, custom-built contracts between very large investors and borrowers usually created by the investment banks. The markets for futures and options other than those traded over the counter are discussed in Chapter 13, while the commodities markets feature in Chapter 14.

■ Moving prices

Chapter 1 examined how changes in interest rates might affect the prices of equities, bonds and currencies, but what other factors move the prices of individual assets and of whole markets? Obviously, supply and demand are the basic influences for an individual asset, but what are the underlying determinants of these economic forces, and what causes substantial broad market moves? These are questions surrounded in controversy, especially related to the stock market, and it is important to differentiate between various kinds of price movement.

In the stock market, there are essentially three kinds of moves: the long-term trend of the overall market as reflected in various indices; short-term moves around the trend; and the movements of individual shares and sectors. For the most part, individual sectors broadly follow overall market trends, though some may be growth industries, some may be mature or declining industries, or some may simply be the beneficiary or victim of a particular event with ramifications peculiar to that industry (for example, the oil industry and the Gulf War, or the technology, media and telecommunications (TMT) industries and the hype surrounding the potential impact of the internet). In those cases, sector values can diverge from the market trend.

The price movements of individual stocks are influenced by a range of factors specific to the business. Most of these are explored in Chapters 5, 6, 7, 8 and 9, but the more common include company profits, the growth of those profits, dividends, and takeover bids. These are the fundamentals of corporate life and fundamental analysis aims to uncover the truths about a company behind the figures to determine whether its shares are over- or underpriced. The way changes in company fundamentals actually cause price movements is not always obvious because of the market's capacity to discount future events. These are news events, the core of the forces that move individual stock prices, but expectations of future news events can be just as powerful.

The fact that prices move on account of expectations of the future, as well as being determined by historic and current knowledge of a company's performance, suggests that they incorporate all known information about the value of shares. This is the foundation of one of the most powerful theories of asset valuation, the efficient market hypothesis. The predictions of this theory are that no one can forecast future price moves consistently and that, over the long term, without inside information, no one can beat the market. The corollary is that stock prices follow what is called a random walk: at any point in an equity's price history, it is impossible to predict whether its next move will be up or down. Hence, investment strategies based on chartism or technical analysis, the study of past price trends, will not perform dependably.

■ Market movements

As well as causing individual equity price movements, news about particular companies can also have an impact on the whole market. This is especially the case with blue chip companies, the most highly regarded companies in the market and usually ones with substantial assets, a strong record of growth, and a well-known name. In recent times, the technology sector has had an important influence on the overall market, especially blue chip technology companies, like telecoms giant Vodafone. The following extract illustrates their importance as well as the influence of psychological market levels:

> It was another good day for London's equity market yesterday, with a burst of enthusiasm for TMT (technology, media and telecoms) stocks, driving all the FTSE indices sharply better. The power generated by the TMTs propelled the FTSE 100 back through the 6,600 level at the close, a move seen as demonstrating the market's willingness to take a run at the 7,000 level. Bulls took further comfort from another increase in turnover. Volume yesterday reached 154bn shares, boosted by another burst of trading in Vodafone. *(Financial Times, 31 August 2000)*

There is much dispute about what causes market moves like this. In this case, it is possibly a short-term move and these tend to be affected by such intangibles as sentiment, investor psychology and how the market is "feeling". Medium-term moves seem to be influenced by supply and demand factors, such as the weight of money moving into or out of stocks: there is also an element of that in this case as the market expects an increase in buying and selling activity following a summer lull.

It is probable that long-term moves depend on fundamental economic and political factors. The market often follows the broad patterns of economic activity, and certainly news about inflation, productivity, growth and the government's fiscal and monetary stance can have major effects on the level of the market. Hence the importance of understanding what the economic indicators mean and how they relate to the markets. These are the subjects of Chapters 4, 15, 16 and 17.

On occasion, stock prices can plummet in a way that appears to bear no relation to fundamentals, supply and demand or even, at least in its early stages, to market sentiment. Such an occasion was Black Monday and the stock market crash of 1987, when prices fell by record amounts in markets throughout the world. Much analysis of this event has been conducted and there is still no agreement on its root causes. Certainly, fundamental economic forces do not appear to have been critical, since most economies continued to grow reasonably well in its aftermath, and the downturn did not come until the very end of the decade. Part of this was due to the prudent economic policies of key governments, which avoided some of the disastrous policy mistakes made after the last major market meltdown, the crash of 1929. The central role of governments in financial markets and economic policy more broadly is the subject of the next chapter.

"The important thing for government is not to do things which individuals are doing already, and do them a little better or a little worse, but to do those things which at present are not done at all."

John Maynard Keynes

"There have been three great inventions since the beginning of time: fire, the wheel and central banking."

Will Rogers

4

Governments

- **Balancing the budget** – what the government gives and gets: fiscal policy; taxation and the budget deficit

- **Controlling the money supply** – government intervention in the money markets: Treasury bills and open market operations; interest rates and monetary control; central bank independence

- **Forecasting the economy** – the basis for government action: economic policy; credibility and the political business cycle

- **Regulating the markets** – the government's goals of preserving financial stability, promoting competition and protecting investors and depositors

Lenders/investors and borrowers/companies are the two sides of the interactions that meet in the financial markets, with financial institutions the third party, facilitating these transactions. The government is the fourth player in this picture. It typically acts as both borrower and lender but, in addition, it will frequently intervene, directly, through legislation or by persuasion, to regulate the markets.

Overarching all of these roles is the government's position as primary economic agent, attempting to monitor and influence the state of the economy. The principal means by which it does this are: fiscal policy, the budgetary balance between public spending and taxation; and monetary policy, essentially control of the money supply and manipulation of interest rates. Forecasting the future direction of the economy plays an important role in determining these policies. How they all impinge on the financial markets is the subject of this chapter. Further details on the economy feature in Part 3.

■ Balancing the budget

Governments spend money on a range of different goods, services, salaries, subsidies and other payments. These include defence, education, health, public transport, public infrastructure, public housing, the pay of public sector employees, social security and interest on government borrowings. To help pay for the services this spending provides and, to some extent, to redistribute incomes from the wealthier to the poorer, the government raises money, primarily through taxation. Some taxes are direct, levied on personal and corporate income; some are indirect, levied on sales, value-added, imports, and certain products such as petrol, cigarettes and alcohol.

The difference between public spending and taxation is known as the budget balance, the budget being the collective term for the government's annual decisions on how its tax and spending plans will be designed and implemented. It might be a balanced budget where revenues equal expenditure, a budget surplus where revenues exceed expenditure, or, most typically for the UK government, a budget deficit, where expenditure exceeds revenues – the public sector net cash requirement. Net income was the UK government's position for a brief period in the late 1980s and has been again since the late 1990s (see Figure 4.1). More commonly, there is a net outflow. The cumulative total of all public sector net cash requirements is known as the national debt.

Through the 1980s and 1990s, the UK government had one other source of revenue, namely the receipts from the sale to the public of nationalised industries, the process of privatisation. The influx of cash from "selling the family silver" had a very positive effect on government finances, and, naturally enough, through the issue of a   significant amount of new equities, aroused considerable interest in the financial markets. Many new investors were tempted to participate in the stock market, particularly with its "stag" opportunities, buying the privatised stocks in the primary market and selling them shortly afterwards at a premium in the secondary market. These matters are examined further in the next chapter.

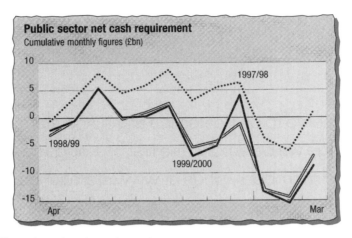

Fig. 4.1 Public sector net cash requirement

Fiscal policy

Fiscal policy is used by the government in a variety of ways: to provide services, such as education, health, defence and infrastructure, that might not be so well provided by the free market; to meet social goals of alleviating poverty and assisting the disadvantaged; to influence the behaviour of individuals and companies, encouraging desirable activities like investment and discouraging undesirable ones like smoking; and to manage the overall level of demand for goods and services in the economy, and hence the degree of economic activity and the rate of inflation. The government goal that may affect financial markets most significantly is that of influencing behaviour. For example, different tax treatment of different categories of assets will influence investment decision-making. Similarly, the tax treatment of corporate earnings will affect a company's dividend policy and its choice between raising capital through debt or equity. More broadly, government spending policy, perhaps in public procurement, might mean increased turnover and profitability for companies in the relevant industries. This might have a positive effect on their share prices. By the same token, excessive borrowing might drive up the costs of funds for all borrowers, perhaps resulting in a crowding out of private capital investment.

Achievement of the government ambition of demand management is generally attempted through countercyclical policy: the government aims to smooth out the more extreme patterns of the business cycle, damping demand in a boom and boosting it in a recession. This can be done in a boom either through raising taxes or cutting spending; in a recession, it may try lowering taxes or increasing spending. To some extent, there are built-in stabilisers, and this is what is meant by the cyclical effects of the business cycle. For example, in a recession people are earning and spending less, which means that the government's tax revenues fall. Of course, if the budget is already in deficit at that point, the deficit will expand even further. The government's problem then is to decide between raising taxes and cutting spending to ease the deficit, or the reverse to help pull the economy out of recession. At such a point, it may turn to monetary policy.

■ Taxation and the budget deficit

There is considerable controversy about the use of taxation and budget deficits to influence aggregate demand and incentives to work. The pursuit of higher output and lower unemployment, without overheating the economy and causing inflation, is Keynesian economic policy. Growth is pursued through increasing government spending or cutting taxes, creating or raising the budget deficit. Tax cuts, for example, increase demand through their beneficial effects on personal disposable income.

The question is, though, how far can the government manage demand in this way before running into inflationary bottlenecks. Furthermore, it is not clear that governments can make accurate enough assessments to judge exactly how much "pump-priming" or "deficit financing" is needed to "fine-tune" the economy to a non-inflationary growth path. Indeed, when demand should be restrained to avoid overheating, there are political reasons why governments might avoid raising taxes.

Increased spending or lower taxes as a means of demand management in times of recession are typically a politically centre-left policy. But tax cuts may also be advocated by centre-right politicians who view them as having a different economic effect. These politicians, and the economists who advise them, focus on the incentive and disincentive effects of taxation, arguing that lower taxes have a strong incentive effect, encouraging people to work harder, and thereby raising national output.

Certainly, taxation does affect incentives to some extent, but extreme believers in this position, who gained political power in the United States in the 1980s, took it a little too far. These supply-side economists claimed that cutting the tax rate significantly would have such powerful incentive effects that the level of tax revenues would actually rise. In reality, the result was a series of massive budget deficits.

Debates about taxation also focus on the appropriate form it should take. For example, progressive income tax is a way of redistributing income from richer to poorer sections of the population, creating a more equitable society. Supply-siders prefer the use of indirect taxes, such as value-added tax. These, they argue, are easier to enforce, and reduce the incentive to work by less than equivalent levels of income tax. The claim is that taxpayers experience "money illusion": if they pay taxes concealed in product prices, they notice it less than taxes taken out of their pay, and are thus prepared to pay more tax on goods than on income. This might have a number of political and economic benefits: if people feel less heavily taxed, they will behave accordingly.

Controlling the money supply

In order to finance their frequent budget deficits, and in common with any other individual or organisation that wants to live beyond its means, the government has to borrow in the financial markets. It does this by issuing securities with a range of different maturities, from the short, medium, long and irredeemable gilt-edged stocks traded on the Stock Exchange to three-month Treasury bills issued weekly in the money markets.

The government's agent for the sale of its debt instruments is the Bank of England, often known simply as the Bank. The stocks are first created by the Treasury's Debt Management Office and then the Bank arranges their sales, purchases and redemptions. New issues replace the ones that have matured in order to meet the government's continuing financing needs and the market's demand for a balance of differently dated stocks. Most are redeemable at some specified date, although a few, such as War Loan and Consols, are irredeemable.

Longer-term government debt takes the form of gilts. These are examined in detail in Chapter 11. For the present, it is merely important to distinguish gilts from fixed interest stocks generally. Not all gilts are fixed interest, nor are all fixed interest stocks gilts. For example, some of the corporate debt instruments discussed in Chapter 2 are fixed interest while some gilts are index-linked with their interest payments determined by the prevailing rate of inflation.

Treasury bills and open market operations

The means by which the Bank of England makes a public offering of stocks, where a minimum price is set and tenders invited, is most easily illustrated through the way the government's shortest-term debt securities, the Treasury bills, are issued.

Treasury bills are bills of exchange, short-term debt instruments issued by the Bank of England on behalf of the UK government. They have a three-month maturity but carry no interest, the total yield being the difference between the purchase and redemption prices. The bills are issued by tender each week to the discount houses in units of between £5,000 and £100,000, and every Monday the *Financial Times* contains a table with details of the tender (see Figure 4.2):

BANK OF ENGLAND TREASURY BILL TENDER

	Mar 17	Mar 10		Mar 17	Mar 10
Bills on offer	£100m	£100m	Lowest accepted yield	5.9000%	5.9300%
Total of applications	£945m	£795m	Ave. rate of discount	5.8418%	5.8436%
Total allocated	£100m	£100m	Average yield	5.9282%	5.9500%
Highest accepted			Offer at next tender	£100m	£100m
Yield	5.9300%	5.9300%	Min. accept. bid 28 days	-	-
Allotment at high level	93%	100%			

Fig. 4.2 Bank of England Treasury bill tender

- **Bills on offer, total of applications and total allocated:** the value of the bills on offer is £100 million and the value of the total applications to buy those bills is a measure of market enthusiasm for them. In this example, the later tender was much more oversubscribed than the earlier one. The factor by which an issue is oversubscribed is known as the auction's cover. Since there is almost invariably oversubscription, naturally the total allocated is the same as that offered.

- **Highest accepted yield and allotment at high level:** the former is the highest discount from face value accepted, implying the lowest accepted bid. The bid is lower than the redemption price so that the purchaser can make money on the difference. The allotment is simply the proportion of the bills sold at the highest yield; the rest would have been sold for higher prices (lower discounts).

- **Lowest accepted yield, average rates of discount and average yield:** the lowest accepted yield indicates the highest prices paid, with the average rate calculating in the discount on the bills sold for lower prices. The discount rates do not correspond exactly to the actual discount since they are presented as annual rates even though the bills mature in three months. Loosely speaking, these are the rates a buyer would earn for purchasing four consecutive bills. The discount rate is calculated as the difference between the purchase and redemption prices as a percentage of the latter. In contrast, the average yield is the difference as a percentage of the former. Thus, it corresponds to any other current yield, that is, annual return divided by current market price.

The discount houses have a special relationship with the Bank of England that is central to the implementation of the government's monetary policy. First of all, they act as marketmakers in the money markets and, as such, they are obliged to cover the amount of bills on offer in a Treasury bill tender as well as having a bid price for other bills of exchange and certificates of deposit. These then are their assets; their liabilities are deposits by banks of what is known as call money. This is money borrowed at interest rates lower than the discount houses earn on bills (again, as marketmakers, they are obliged to take the deposits), but which can be withdrawn at very short notice.

Discount houses can take on these obligations because the Bank stands behind them as the "lender of last resort". If they run short of funds, either because banks have withdrawn money or because they have been obliged to purchase other money market instruments, perhaps the weekly Treasury bill tender, they can go to the Bank. The Bank every day estimates the market's fund shortage and usually meets it by buying bills from the discount houses. In doing this it is injecting funds into the whole financial system; if instead it sells bills, it is withdrawing funds, effectively mopping up surplus money. This is known as open market operations and is one of the means by which the government controls the money supply.

■ Interest rates and monetary control

The extension of this control is how the Bank of England manipulates the level of interest rates. Since it deals actively in the bill markets through open market operations, it is in a position to create a shortage of cash when it wishes to. In that case, the discount houses are obliged to borrow, and as the lender of last resort, the level at which the Bank provides funds is an indication of the level of short-term rates of which it approves. These rates can then be used to influence rates across the whole economy.

As the previous three chapters made clear, the rate of interest, that is, the price of money, is one of the most powerful forces in the financial markets. Under the relatively free market approach of recent UK governments, interest rates have been allowed, for the most part, to be determined by market forces with the Bank's guidance. But with this system the Bank has to be careful to give only very subtle indications of where it wants rates to go: if it alerts the market to its intentions, the force of expectations will have immediate ramifications throughout the economy as traders discount the future. More recently, it has become quite directive in setting rates under the new monetary arrangements established in May 1997.

An alternative method of controlling the money supply is using direct controls on bank lending, aiming to limit money multiplier effects. This might be achieved by changing banks' reserve asset ratios, that is, the proportions they keep liquid from any given deposit, by imposing limits on total bank lending or consumer credit, or simply by persuading bankers to restrict their lending. A further technique, which was popular in the United Kingdom from the late 1970s to the late 1980s, is setting targets for monetary growth. One target was the monetary base, which consists of cash in circulation plus banks' deposits at the Bank of England.

The last way in which the Bank of England acts in the financial markets is with foreign exchange, where it may intervene to try to raise or lower the value of sterling. This again can be done through short-term interest rates: usually raising them attracts investors into buying sterling, while lowering encourages selling. The Bank might also work on the currency by using its official reserves of foreign currencies to buy pounds and, through the weight of its intervention, push up its value or at least hold it steady. But, nowadays, with the vast speculative volume of transactions in the foreign exchange markets, a successful intervention may need international cooperation. A government acting alone is no longer able to manage the financial markets or its national economy.

Central bank independence

Management of the economy through monetary policy used to be the preserve of monetarists, who focused on the importance of controlling the money supply as a way of keeping inflation in check. But monetary policy also affects growth: it is said to be neutral if the level of interest rates neither stimulates nor slows growth. If the interest rate rises, monetary policy might restrain consumer spending and encourage savings, hence reining in growth. Nowadays, the key roles of monetary policy in economic management of demand and inflation are almost universally acknowledged: the question is more one of who should control it, the government or independent monetary authorities.

The argument for central bank independence is that governments are poor at managing their economies, providing monetary accommodation not only for their own deficits, but also for wage claims, oil shocks and so on. This has caused inflation: since government control of the money supply is open to manipulation in response to political expediency, there is a built-in inflationary bias. The bias can only be removed by handing control over to the central bank, which will be free of political pressures. The central bank can then pursue its twin goals of monetary and financial stability, a sound money supply and a safe financial system.

The issue of central bank independence became particularly important in the United Kingdom as a result of the failure of the Conservative government's monetary policy in 1992. This policy, discredited by circumstances, was to control inflation and pursue economic convergence with fellow members of the European Union, by keeping the pound in the exchange rate mechanism (ERM) of the European Monetary System (see Chapter 16). After the collapse of this policy, the government aimed to restore its credibility in "the fight against inflation" by greater openness and an enhanced role for the Bank of England.

Following the election of the Labour government in May 1997, this role was extended with the Bank being given full operational independence to set short-term interest rates. Under the new monetary arrangements, the Chancellor of the Exchequer gives an annual remit to the Bank containing relatively precise objectives it is expected to pursue. That remit is an inflation target for the Retail Prices Index (excluding mortgage interest payments) of $2\frac{1}{2}$ per cent. Without prejudice to this target, the Bank is expected to set interest rates so as to support the general economic policies of the government (see Figure 4.3):

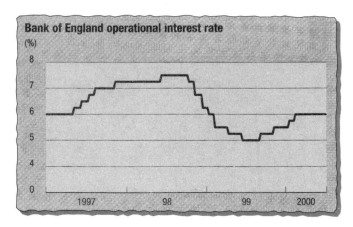

Fig. 4.3 Short-term interest rates

Interest rate decisions are taken monthly by a nine-member Monetary Policy Committee (MPC), five of whom are Bank officials and four of whom are "outside members", typically leading academic economists from Oxford, Cambridge or the London School of Economics. The MPC's inflation target is "symmetric", which means that inflation should never be more than one percentage point outside the target on either side. But reaction to MPC interest rate decisions tends to be anything but symmetric: plaudits flow in when rates are cut, but when they rise, out come the knives.

This adverse sentiment has been particularly strong because of a growing sense that the economy is returning to an era when low inflation is the norm rather than the exception. In recent decades, booms have always been followed by bust as the economy hits physical and human capacity constraints and prices and wages are bid up. Now though, it is widely argued, a combination of technology and global competition has increased capacity by raising productivity and potential growth as well as making it far more difficult for companies and workers to hike their charges.

MPC member DeAnne Julius is a leading "new economy" thinker and has consistently argued for lower rates than her colleagues. She explains the inflation benefits of globalisation: "In a more integrated global economy, it is the world output gap that matters for many prices, not domestic supply capacity. If there is spare world capacity in goods or services that can be transmitted actually or virtually across borders, then their prices will remain low or even fall. And supply bottlenecks at the global level are much less common."

Many new paradigm enthusiasts, particularly in the United States, translate their rosy view of global economic prospects into an equally positive prognosis for equity markets. But even if the world is moving into a new era of low inflation driven by technology and global competition, it is by no means clear that this is good news for market valuations. If companies face an increasingly tough time raising their prices, then this is likely to be bad for profit margins and ultimately for share prices. As former MPC member Professor Willem Buiter argues, while there will continue to be firms like Microsoft that dominate their markets and justify high valuations, there will be many more dogs with poor profitability prospects in both the short and long term.

Forecasting the economy

Forecasts play an important role in determining the policies of governments as well as companies and investors. These may be based on models of overall developments in the aggregate national or global economy: such models can be used to forecast shifts in demand across different markets, growth in total world trade, or changes in inflation, interest rates or unemployment. Or they might be models of parts of the economy: disaggregated forecasts may relate to developments in particular industrial sectors or regions of the world; while even more specific forecasts may relate to a single product or asset.

Basic approaches to forecasting simply extrapolate the past; they are merely a way of articulating present indications. More sophisticated models attempt to understand the source of past changes and build it into their forecasts. This requires a detailed knowledge of economic history and economic principles; even then, however, forecasting is by no means an exact science. But, while the accuracy of economists' predictions is frequently a target of jokes about the profession, forecasting remains an essential pursuit. As conducted at its most general level, by national governments and by global organisations on behalf of groups of countries, it drives all aspects of their economic policy.

Government forecasts are primarily concerned with forecasting the movement over time of key macroeconomic variables: output, inflation, unemployment, interest rates, and so on. They derive from large-scale macroeconomic models of the economy, and are usually produced every three to six months. In the United Kingdom, for example, the Treasury produces a central forecast at the time of its annual budget in March, which is then published again in revised form six months later.

Treasury forecasts include each component of the economy that contributes to overall growth: retail sales, manufacturing output and so on. But even models as detailed as that are more systems of managing information than accurate representations of real economies. Thus, while they can be expected to describe the present reasonably accurately, they cannot be relied on to forecast the future and get it right. Nevertheless, government forecasts are very much tied to the levers of economic policy, as well as the government's underlying beliefs about the way the economy works, and there can often be conflict between the ideas on which forecasts and policy are based.

A country's monetary authorities also typically produce an economic forecast, though it is not always published. The Bank of England, for example, is currently barred from publishing its full forecast in case it clashes with that of the Treasury. However, its quarterly inflation report does contain prognostications on current and future inflationary pressures. The more independent Federal Reserve ("the Fed") in the United States presents a half-yearly report containing its economic projections to Congress.

Central bank forecasts may well derive from models of the economy that are a little biased towards the levers of monetary policy, those over which the banks hold most sway. Such forecasts are sometimes criticised for being based on a view of the economy that focuses on a symptom (inflation) of poor economic performance, rather than deeper structural weaknesses, and which relies on monetary policy alone as a cure.

■ Economic policy

Treasury and central bank forecasts represent governments' views of the future. In conjunction with their stated economic goals, these form the basis for the planning and execution of economic policy. For example, the essence of the present UK government's ambitions can be encapsulated in the phrases "no return to boom and bust" and "raising national productivity, competitiveness and growth". The macroeconomic means by which it pursues these goals (in conjunction with the Bank) are monetary, fiscal and exchange rate policy, while the actual levers used to intervene in the economy are interest rates and decisions on taxation and public spending. These policies can have as important implications for the private sector as the forecasts.

The budget and short-term economic forecasting are intimately related, forming a central plank of overall economic policy. The macroeconomic task of the budget is to get the level of the surplus or deficit right: first, in terms of its effects on demand (will reduced taxes or increased spending boost demand and output?); and second, in terms of its effects on real interest rates (will an excessive debt ratio lead to a rise in interest rates, "crowding out" private investment?).

Monetary and exchange rate policy relate more to inflation and international competitiveness. They, too, are intimately related in that interest rates, the primary tool of both, can be used to target either the money supply or the exchange rate, but not both. From a manager's point of view, both goals are important, one in terms of the rate and predictability of inflation, the other in terms of the level and predictability of the exchange rate.

On the supply side of the economy, government policy can have direct effects on corporate and investor behaviour. For example, in the product markets, competition and regulatory policy, through government departments and such institutions of market regulation as the Competition Commission and the Office of Fair Trading, can be important in the provision of a stable business environment and the improvement of industrial performance. In the labour markets, tax incentives, education and training, and a host of other policies might boost productivity and competitiveness. The present UK government is particularly focused on the degree of competition in different industry sectors; the barriers to faster progress in electronic commerce and other aspects of the "new economy"; what can be done to address skill deficiencies in both the new technologies and elsewhere; and how to encourage greater levels of innovation, entrepreneurship and venture capital.

■ Credibility and the political business cycle

Economic policy is typically put together with a set of national objectives in mind: low inflation, full employment, no new taxes, and so on. Certainly, these goals are the slogans by which governments get themselves elected, or otherwise. For example, from 1979 to 1992, the UK Conservatives found that they could win elections by focusing on tax and inflation, and without a great deal of concern for unemployment. Elections have been won and lost on the basis of actual or distorted economics, such as the "Labour's tax bombshell" claim of the 1992 campaign.

But elections are also won and lost over the government's perceived management of the economy and its actual delivery on election pledges. Bill Clinton's 1992 campaign's frequent reminder, "it's the economy, stupid", for example, was a reflection of public perceptions of the failure of the Bush administration to ameliorate the recession, and the breaking of its promise not to raise taxes. Failure to deliver is often a result of politicians omitting to explain how difficult the fulfilment of economic ambitions might be when they are campaigning for office. This is most conspicuously the case in the former communist states where the fruits of market economic success will not be shared immediately by a large section of the population, as a result of which they often hanker for the old days.

Government economic credibility can also be strained when its policies are blown apart by events, as happened to the UK government with sterling's exit from the ERM. In this case, the government's primary objective was low inflation, and the means by which it was pursued, exchange rate policy through the ERM. Although inflation targets became a good alternative policy goal and relatively low inflation was maintained, Black Wednesday saw a sharp collapse in public confidence in the government's ability to handle the economy, a loss of credibility that eventually resulted in its devastating defeat at the 1997 election.

The importance of the economy to the electoral process has led to what is called the political business cycle, as governments attempt to achieve favourable economic circumstances at election time. For example, by engineering a boom before an election they might set the business cycle in motion, so that expansionary policies to boost incomes, reduce unemployment and maintain power must be followed by contractionary policies to limit inflation. For the present UK government, higher public spending on health and education has been the chosen course, but this could cause longer-term problems for the level of interest rates and inflation. Electoral success also requires the elusive "feelgood factor", and, most importantly, government credibility as an effective economic manager.

Credibility extends importantly to business and financial market confidence in the government's ability to achieve its objectives. For example, UK Treasury forecasts are often criticised for being as much an expression of what the government would like to see happen, as what they expect to happen; they are sometimes seen to be more akin to some companies' annual budgets, incorporating desirable rather than necessarily achievable targets. There is an element here of using forecasts as a means to the goal, perhaps trying to talk inflation down or maybe even keep recession at bay. The Treasury forecast for 1999, for example, was widely derided as optimistic at a time when many expected a recession; in the event, it undershot actual economic growth that year.

■ Regulating the markets

The overall objective of government economic policy is to secure sustainable economic growth and rising prosperity. This is primarily implemented through the macroeconomic policies outlined earlier, but the government also uses microeconomic policies, aiming to improve the efficiency of markets. In the context of the financial markets, this involves regulation through various measures to promote competition, to protect investors and depositors, and to preserve financial stability.

Financial services regulation plays a key role in securing market efficiency, but a competitive and versatile investment industry must be underpinned by adequate protection of investors and depositors. In setting the framework of regulatory rules, the government must aim to leave firms free to innovate and compete in an increasingly international market. At the same time, investor confidence requires open, free and fair markets in which all participants adhere to best practice.

The UK government, for example, encourages investors to follow five golden rules of investment to avoid being vulnerable to pressure selling of inappropriate financial products. These are that the buyer should always beware (*caveat emptor*); that investors should spread their investments; that they should seek good advice; read the small print; and recognise that authorisation by a government agency is not a guarantee. For companies and financial institutions, the government emphasises the need to provide full disclosure of all relevant material and to follow the codes of business conduct directed by such regulatory bodies as the Financial Services Authority (FSA) and the Competition Commission.

There are essentially two approaches to regulation: statutory regulation via legislation, and self-regulation where industry participants are encouraged to set their own rules and enforcement procedures. In the United States, the system of financial regulation is more orientated towards statutory regulation. It is primarily under the direction of the Securities and Exchange Commission (SEC), a government agency that closely monitors the activities of stockbrokers and traders in securities, and also monitors takeovers. If, for example, an individual or company acquires 5 per cent or more of the equity of another company, the SEC must be informed. There are also more specialised agencies such as the Commodity Futures Trading Commission, which oversees derivatives trading.

In the United Kingdom, the bias is more towards self-regulation within the framework of the 1986 Financial Services Act and the Financial Services and Markets Act currently being developed. Under their provisions, anyone involved in investment business has to be authorised by the FSA – until October 1997 known as the Securities and Investments Board (SIB) – an independent non-governmental body with statutory powers. The FSA Board is appointed by the Chancellor of the Exchequer and consists of an executive chairman, two managing directors, and 11 non-executive directors. The FSA has four main aims:

- to maintain confidence in the UK financial system;
- to promote public understanding of the financial system;
- to secure an appropriate degree of protection for consumers;
- to contribute to reducing financial crime.

In pursuing these objectives, the FSA bears in mind: the need to be efficient and economic in its use of resources; the responsibilities of regulated firms' own managements; the need to balance the burdens and restrictions placed on firms with the benefits of regulation for consumers and the industry; the desirability of facilitating innovation in the financial sector; the international character of financial services and markets and the desirability of maintaining the competitive position of the UK; and the value of competition between financial firms.

The main purpose of the new Financial Services and Markets Act is to provide a single legal framework for the FSA in place of the different frameworks under which the various regulators currently operate. As a result, most of its provisions represent consolidation of existing law or self-regulatory requirements. The main new provisions of the Act are: powers to impose financial penalties on those who abuse investment markets, for example by insider dealing or market manipulation; and the role of the UK listing authority, which will be undertaken under substantially the same powers as currently exercised by the London Stock Exchange.

The borrowing, asset-creating side of the market is also regulated by a combination of legislation and monitoring. Company behaviour falls under various Companies Acts enforced by the Department of Trade and Industry; while the provision of figures (and the requirement that companies give a "true and fair view" of their status) comes under the control of the Financial Reporting Council and the Accounting Standards Board. In the market for corporate control, the key institutions are the City Panel on Takeovers and Mergers, the Competition Commission and the Office of Fair Trading.

Banks are regulated under the 1987 Banking Act and supervised by the FSA. The Bank of England has general responsibilities to protect the stability of the financial system and to be the lender of last resort in the event of a liquidity crisis. But the FSA also has the specific role of supervisor of the UK banking sector with the power to regulate banks and protect depositors.

Beyond the United Kingdom, the single market in financial services requires common access and minimum standards throughout the European Union. This is achieved by vesting in member states responsibility for authorisation of investment business participants, and continuing prudential supervision. Providers of financial services are entitled to do business across the Union solely on the basis of their home authorisation.

Recent international scandals such as the collapses of Barings Bank and of the Bank of Credit and Commerce International have raised an important question about financial regulation: whether the globalisation of money, markets and information has put some companies and financial institutions beyond the reach of regulation. It seems clear that financial innovation, technology and the globalisation of investment have created a fragmented market for which the current rules may no longer protect investors. In particular, regulators fear that there may be gaps between the national and sectoral areas of supervision, and variations of standards that can give comparative advantage to one country's financial sector. Efforts to tackle the problem of "regulatory arbitrage", where companies can take advantage of different rules and governments are tempted to loosen domestic rules to gain advantage, focus on refining the rules on capital requirements (the ability of institutions to meet their creditors' needs), on increasing disclosure and on improving international cooperation.

PART 2

Interpreting the markets

"Information is the key input to the market. In an efficient market, prices immediately reflect all the available information."

Peter Bernstein

"Work the other side of the street! The nonpredictability of future prices from past and present prices is the sign, not of failure of economic law, but the triumph of economic law after competition has done its best."

Paul Samuelson

5

Stocks and shares

The UK equity markets

- **The London share service** – reading the figures for the London stock market and using the information: evaluating weekly performance; other share dealings; trading volume; rises and falls, highs and lows, main movers; winners and losers

- **Issuing new securities** – how new companies are launched (offers for sale, placings, introductions, rights issues, popular privatisation issues); how extra funds are raised for existing ones (rights offers)

- **Directors' dealings**

An equity is a stake in a company, a risk-sharing ownership of a part of a company's capital. The buyer of a share receives the rights to a probable flow of income in the form of dividends (which vary with the profitability of the company) and a potential capital gain.

The UK equity markets trade stocks across a wide spectrum of firms, ranging from established blue chip companies to higher risk ventures. The *Financial Times'* coverage of UK equities, the shares in UK companies that have a stock market quotation, consists of four main interlocking components:

■ A daily report of the most interesting trading features in the stock market.

■ The share prices of individual companies and various financial ratios based on those prices.

■ Detailed reports and comment in the news pages of the paper on events in company life.

■ A number of stock market indices, which chart the overall progress of equity share prices.

UK company news was explored in Chapter 2, while indices are the subject of the next chapter. This chapter focuses on *Financial Times* reporting on the market for UK equities, as reflected in its stock market reports and the London share service.

FT coverage of the UK equities market begins with reports on the London Stock Exchange on the back page of the second section. This is headed with an overview of the movements in the stock market indices of the previous day and possible reasons for them, as well as highlights of individual sectors that have moved significantly or that have been particularly prominent in trading. It also examines the main share price movements of the day in individual stocks, and suggests reasons for them. Particularly important movements are explored in separate stories further down the page.

The London share service

This is the most complete record of UK stock market statistics readily available to the public and covers around 3,000 shares. That is practically all of those actively traded in the London stock market, together with gilt-edged stocks, already mentioned in Chapter 4 and discussed in more detail in Chapter 11.

The London share service is divided into various geographical and industrial classifications, derived from the groupings used in the FTSE Actuaries All-Share index discussed in detail in the next chapter (see Figure 6.4). Categorisation in this way allows easy comparison of companies within the same industrial sector.

The share service covers not only companies that have a full stock market listing, but also those quoted on the Alternative Investment Market (AIM). The AIM has less onerous listing requirements than the main market and is designed to encourage smaller, fast-growing businesses to seek a quotation. Generally, there is less trading in AIM stock and, hence, shares may be less easy to buy and sell. In addition, the service incorporates many non-UK companies whose shares are traded in London, notably groups of shares classified as Americans, Canadians and South Africans.

The standard version of the share service is published on Tuesday to Saturday, inside the back page of the second section of the newspaper. Figure 5.1 features four sample industrial categories from the daily London share service, annotated with brief explanations of price, price change and year high and low, volume, yield and price/earnings ratio.

Reading the figures

- **Name and notes:** the first column lists the company name or its abbreviation, plus various symbols representing particular features of its shares. For example, a heart symbol indicates a stock not officially listed in the UK, for example many shares of overseas mining companies.

- **Market price:** the second column shows the average (or mid-price) of the best buying and selling prices (in pence) quoted by marketmakers at the 4.30pm close of the market on the previous trading day. Most prices are obtained from the Stock Exchange throughout the day via a direct computer link with the last transmission of data taking place at 4.45pm. If trading in a share has been suspended, perhaps because the company in question is involved in takeover negotiations, the figure shown is the price at suspension and this is indicated by a symbol. The letters "xd" following a price mean ex-dividend, and indicate that a dividend has been announced recently but that buyers of the shares will not be entitled to receive it.

- **Price change (plus or minus):** the third column gives the change in the closing price compared with the end of the previous trading day.

- **Previous price movements:** the fourth and fifth columns show the highest and lowest prices recorded for the stock during the past 12 months.

- **Volume:** the sixth column shows the number of shares traded the previous day rounded to the nearest 1,000. Dashes indicate either that no trade has taken place or that data is unavailable.

- **Dividend yield:** the seventh column shows the percentage return on the share. It is calculated by dividing the dividend by the current share price.

- **Price/earnings (p/e) ratio:** the last column is the market price of the share divided by the company's earnings (profits) per share in its latest 12-month trading period. Yields and p/e ratios move in opposite directions: if the share price rises, since the dividend remains the same, the dividend yield falls; at the same time, since the earnings per share are constant, the p/e ratio increases.

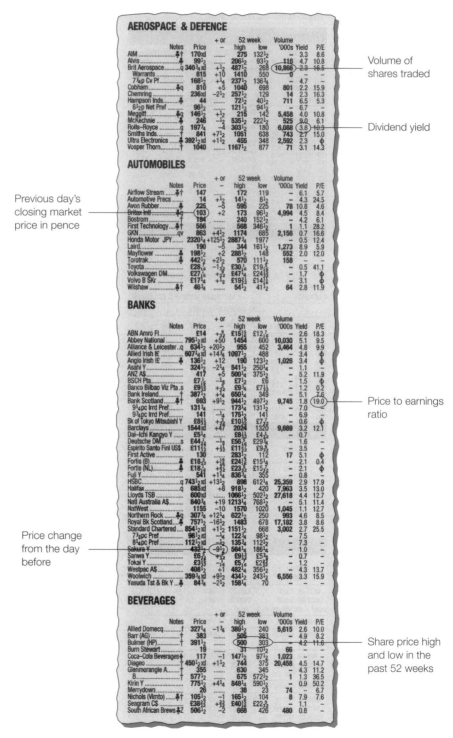

Fig. 5.1 London share service (daily)

Volume of shares traded

Dividend yield

Previous day's closing market price in pence

Price to earnings ratio

Price change from the day before

Share price high and low in the past 52 weeks

Using the information

The first indicator to look at in a share is its price. This is a reflection of the discounted value of future dividend payments plus a premium for the risk that the company may not pay dividends in the future and/or go under. On its own, though, it conveys minimal information since it needs to be seen in the context of its history and possible future.

The figures for high and low provide some of the historical perspective on the share price. If, for example, the present price is a long way below its high point for the past 12 months, and performing against the market trend, the indications are that the market is expecting trouble. The reverse is true in the case of a share that is pushing up strongly to new points when the market or its sector is not. The difference between the high and low also gives an indication of the price volatility of the stock.

The prices quoted are mid-prices between the bid or buying price and the offer or selling price at which marketmakers will trade. The difference between bid and offer is known as the spread, and it represents marketmakers' profit on any given transaction, a reward for taking the risk of making the market. The implication of this spread is that investors will only be able to buy at a higher price and sell at a lower price than that printed in the newspaper. Of course, since the share service is, in effect, merely an historical record of prices the previous day, actual prices subsequently may be very different.

Volume is an indication of the liquidity of a stock – how easy it is to buy and sell. High volume is preferable to low volume but note that large companies are traded much more heavily than small ones. And it is normal for volumes to be high when a company makes an announcement.

Dividends depend on profits, which in turn depend on the quality of a company's management and the state of the economy. The dividend yield, though, since it is partly determined by the current share price, is a reflection of the way that the market values a share. If the company is thought to have a high growth rate and a secure business, then its current dividend yield will probably be relatively low, since the scope for increasing dividends in the future ought to be above average. Sales will be expanding, earnings growing, and often investment in new products and new capital goods will be substantial.

If, by contrast, the company is involved in a mature or dying industry or is exposed to high levels of business or political risk, its dividend yield will normally be high. Thus, the yield on a share can be a valuable indicator when an investor is deciding between income and capital growth from an investment. For example, a growth stock, perhaps in high-technology industries, suggests a preference for capital appreciation, while a share in a company in a mature industry like textiles would indicate a desire for income.

$$\text{Dividend yield (per cent)} = \frac{\text{dividend per share} \times 100}{\text{share price}}$$

Of course, as we saw in Chapter 2, the dividend is, to some degree, an arbitrary figure, decided at the whim of the company. Hence the figure for yield is not always a good indicator of the value of a share. Price/earnings ratios are generally better since they are independent of possibly arbitrary corporate decisions.

Price/earnings ratios are the most commonly used tool of stock market analysis. Essentially, they compare a company's share price to its annual earnings, indicating the number of years it would take it, at its current earning power, to earn an amount equal to its market value. Shares are often described as selling at a number times earnings or on a multiple. In general, the higher a company's ratio, the more highly rated it is by the market: investors expect the relative expense of the company's shares to be compensated for by higher than average earnings over the next few years. But high ratios can also mean that the market is expecting a poorly performing company to be on the receiving end of a takeover bid, with the predator being prepared to pay a premium for control.

High price/earnings ratios are usually associated with low yields, and certainly they move in opposite directions. Thus, a high ratio suggests a growth stock, and is, like a low yield, an indicator of an investment where capital growth might be more important than income.

Investors can use price/earnings ratios to gauge whether one company's share price is too high or too low compared with competitors with similar products and earnings performance, compared with the market as a whole, or compared with past ratios. If a p/e ratio is above average, investors expect profits to rise and, hence, their prospective dividends: the higher a p/e ratio, the greater the confidence in the company. But high ratios are often viewed as overpriced, while low ones are viewed as bargains.

Since the methods of calculating the ratios can give significantly different results, the investor's prime concern should be to use ratios that are consistent (that is, from the same source) when making comparisons. It is also important to be aware of the difference between the historic ratios in the newspaper and what the market's expectations are for the future, expressed more through forecasts of prospective price/earnings ratios. Reports on companies might also distinguish historic and prospective yields. In addition, there is a distinction between nil and net ratios: the former ignores the distribution of dividends. Chapter 18 contains some examples of yield and p/e ratios.

$$\text{Price/earnings ratio} = \frac{\text{share price}}{\text{earnings per share}}$$

■ Evaluating weekly performance

Monday's edition of the *Financial Times* brings some important changes to the share information service, concentrating on changes that do not take place daily. Figure 5.2 shows an example. The special weekly columns provide information on the following:

■ **Price change:** the weekly percentage change in the price of the stock.

■ **Dividend:** the dividends paid in the company's last full financial year. A double dagger sign shows that the interim dividend has been cut in the current financial year, while a single dagger indicates an increased interim dividend.

■ **Dividend cover:** the ratio of profits to dividends, calculated by dividing the earnings per share by the dividend per share. This indicates how many times a company's

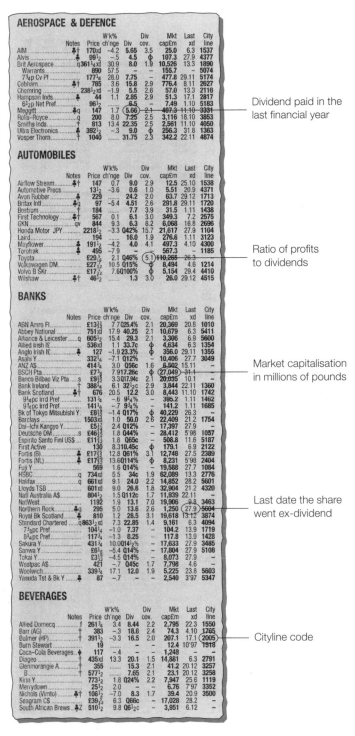

Fig. 5.2 London share service (weekly)

dividend to ordinary shareholders could be paid out of its net profits. Another way of looking at dividend cover is as a percentage of profits: this is the way it is done in the United States where it is known as the payout ratio.

■ **Market capitalisation:** an indication of the stock market valuation of the company in millions of pounds sterling. It is calculated by multiplying the number of shares by their market price. In order to calculate the number of shares in issue from the figures listed here, the market capitalisation figure can be divided by the market price. If there are other classes of share capital in issue, their value would need to be added in order to calculate the company's total market capitalisation.

■ **Ex-dividend date:** the last date on which a share went ex-dividend, expressed as a day and month unless a dividend has not been paid for some time, in which case the date may be a month and year. On and after this date, the rights to the last announced dividend remain with the seller of the stock. What happens is that the share register is frozen on the xd date and the dividend will be paid to the people on the register at that time. Until it is paid, buyers of the share will not receive the next payment. The price is adjusted down a little to account for this.

■ **Cityline:** the FT Cityline code by which real-time share prices are available over the telephone by calling 0906 003 or 0906 843 plus the four-digit code for any given share. This telephone information service is designed primarily for investors wanting to keep track of their own investments or the activity of the UK and world stock markets at any point during the day or night.

The key information from this listing is the figure for dividend cover. This indicates how safe the dividend is from future cuts. The higher the figure, the better able the company will be to maintain its dividend if profits fall. Even at a time of losses, a company may decide to pay dividends out of its reserves, though this clearly could not continue indefinitely.

A relatively high dividend cover might also reflect a commitment to investment and growth, implying a substantial retention of earnings to be ploughed back into the business. Contrariwise, if the dividend cover is too high, the shareholders may complain that the company should increase its payout. Chapter 18 contains some examples of dividend cover.

$$\text{Dividend cover} = \frac{\text{earnings per share}}{\text{dividend per share}}$$

Market capitalisation is a measure of the size of a company. Since the total value of a company's shares will rise and fall according to its financial results, it is a good guide to performance over time. It also has other advantages over alternative yardsticks of size: it gives a proper weighting to banks and commodity groups, which get distorted in lists based on turnover; and it takes account of loss-making companies, which disappear from lists based on profits.

$$\text{Market capitalisation} = \text{number of ordinary shares} \times \text{share price}$$

Other share dealings

On Saturday, the newspaper expands its share price coverage to cover dealings in securities that are not included in the standard FT share information service (see Figure 5.3). It covers many fixed interest securities issued by companies, as well as dealings in some smaller company shares and securities where the principal market is outside the British Isles. The actual selection is variable according to whether a stock has been traded during the five trading days ending each Thursday. If it has not been traded it will generally not be included. Information is provided on:

- **Name and stock type:** Chapter 2 detailed some of the different forms of corporate finance available, and these securities provide a number of examples. Smith and Nephew's 3.85 per cent cumulative preference shares with a par value of £1, for instance, are shares that pay a fixed dividend, 3.85 pence. The payment can be suspended in the event of losses, but when the company returns to profit, all dividends in arrears are guaranteed to be paid ahead of dividends on ordinary shares.

- **Prices:** these are reproduced from Thursday's Stock Exchange official list. They show the prices at which business was done in the 24 hours up to 5.15pm on Thursday. For shares where no business was recorded during that period, the latest recorded business in the previous four days is listed with the relevant date.

Trading volume

The back page of the newspaper's second section includes a useful reference table with the trading volume and basic price information for a selection of the largest capitalised and most active stocks (see Figure 5.4). The information includes:

- **Volume, price and change:** the daily trading volume for these stocks (including all of the constituents of the FTSE 100 index, which are discussed in detail in the next chapter and listed in Appendix 2) plus the day's closing price and change on the previous trading day. Trading volume figures count both the buying and the selling of a particular share, so that the number of shares actually changing hands is really half of the total. A dagger symbol indicates a FTSE 100 index reserve.

Trading volume is an indication of the liquidity of a stock. The higher the figure, the easier it will be to buy or sell significant quantities of a stock without having a major impact on its price.

LONDON STOCK EXCHANGE - DEALINGS

Barclays Bank PLC 12% Uns Cap Ln Stk 2010 - 131 (07Je00) 2 (07Je00) 2 (06Je00)
Barclays Bank PLC 16% Uns Cap Ln Stk 2002/07 - 113 (07Je00)
Bass PLC ADR (1:1) - 11.0073 (07Je00)
Bass PLC 10⅜% Deb Stk 2016 - 144.4 (07Je00)
Bellway PLC 9.5% Cum Red Prf 2014 £1 - 104 (06Je00)
BFS Overseas Inc & Gwth (Jersey) Ld Zero Div Pref Shs 1p - 140 (07Je00)
Blue Circle Industries PLC ADR (1:1) - 6.3125 (01Je00)
BOC Group PLC 12¼% Uns Ln Stk 2012/17 - 149 53 ½ (06Je00)
Boots Co PLC ADR (2:1) - 16.3125 .467 (06Je00)
Bournemouth & West Hampshire Water PLC 8.5% Cum Irrd Pref £1 - 108½ (05Je00)
BP Amoco PLC ADR (6:1) (Each Cnv into 6 Ord $0.50) - 55.1875 .3125 .7625* .95 (07Je00) 6.4375 .5 .625 .875 7
BP Amoco PLC 8% Cum 1st Prf £1 - 128 (07Je00)
BP Amoco PLC 9% Cum 2nd Prf £1 - 144 (05Je00)
Bpt PLC 10½% Cum Prf £1 - 140 (07Je00)
Bradford & Bingley Building Society 11⅝% Perm Int Bearing Shs £10000 - 138 (06Je00)
Bristol & West PLC Prf £1 - 97½ (07Je00) ½
Bristol & West PLC 13⅜% Uns Perp Sub Bds - 164 (07Je00) 9 (07Je00) 70 (07Je00)
Bristol Water Hldgs PLC Non-Vtg Ord £1 - 800 (07Je00)
Bristol Water PLC 8¾% Cum Irrd Prf £1 - 120¼ (02Je00)
Bristol Water PLC 12½% Red Deb Stk 2004 - 112 (07Je00)
Britannia Building Society 13% Perm Int Bearing Shs £1000 - 172 (07Je00)
British Airways PLC ADR (10:1) - 58.5 (07Je00) 9.58 (07Je00)
British Energy PLC 'A'Shs 60p - 50 (0) 50 (07Je00) 4 (1)
British Land Co PLC 10½% Dfd 1st Mtg Deb Stk 2019/24 - 143½ (01Je00)
British Sky Broadcasting Group PLC ADR (6:1) - 112.9 (07Je00) 4.4283 (06Je00) 9.73 (06Je00) .73 (06Je00)
British Sugar 10¾% Red Deb Stk 2013 - 132.08984375 (06Je00)
British Telecommunications PLC ADR (10:1) - 151.52 (06Je00)
Brixton Estate PLC 9.5% 1st Mtg Deb Stk 2026 - 136 (05Je00)
Brunel Holdings PLC 4.6p (Net) Cnv Cum Red Prf 20p - 27 (05Je00)
Budgens PLC 5% Cnv Uns Ln Stk 2003 - 102 (06Je00)
Bulmer (H.P.) Hldgs PLC 8¾% 2nd Cum Prf £1 - 108¼ (06Je00)
Burford Group PLC 9⅝% 1st Mtg Deb Stk 2019 - 130.05859375 (02Je00)
Burmah Castrol PLC ADR (3:5) - 41 (01Je00)
Burndene Investments PLC 15% Uns Ln Stk 2007/12 - 140 (05Je00)
Cadbury Schweppes PLC ADR (4:1) - 26.1875
Caradon PLC 'B'Shs £1 - 92 (06Je00)
Carlton Communications PLC ADR (5:1) - 62.475 (06Je00)
Cgnu PLC 8⅜% Cum Irrd Prf £1 - 115½ (07Je00) ¾ (07Je00) 6 (07Je00) 7½ (07Je00) ½ (07Je00) ½ (07Je00) ½ (07Je00)
Cgnu PLC 8¾% Cum Irrd Prf £1 - 121 (07Je00) 2 (07Je00)
Cheltenham & Gloucester PLC 11¾% Perp Sub Bds £50000 - 146 (07Je00)
Chemex International PLC Ord 1p - 7½ (10, 51, 4, 10)
Cleveland Place Hldgs 3¾% Irrd Deb Stk - 67 (07Je00)
Coats Patons Ld 4½% Uns Ln Stk 2002/07 - 91 (05Je00)
Coats Patons Ld 6¾% Uns Ln Stk 2002/07 - 95 (05Je00)
Coats Viyella PLC 4.9% Cum Prf £1 - 76 80 (05Je00)
Coats Viyella PLC 6¼% Snr Cnv Bds 09/08/03 £1000 (Rg) - 93 (05Je00)
Cohen (A.) & Co PLC Non.V'A'Ord 20p - 65 (02Je00)
Cookson Group PLC 7% Cnv Bds 2/11/2004 (Rg) - 97½ (07Je00)
Co-Operative Bank PLC 9.25% Non-Cum Irrd Prf £1 - 108 (07Je00) 8 (07Je00) 8 (07Je00) 9 (07Je00) ¼ (07Je00) ¼ (07Je00) ¼ (07Je00)
Co-Operative Wholesale Society Ld 7⅝% 1st Mtg Deb Stk 2018 - 110 (02Je00)
Cordiant Communications Group PLC ADR (5:1) - 22.428962 .4375 (06Je00) .452031 (06Je00)
Corus Finance PLC 11½% Gtd Deb Stk 2016 - 143 (06Je00)
Coventry Building Society 12⅛% Perm Int Bearing Shs £1000 (Reg) - 163 (07Je00)
Daily Mail & General Trust PLC Ord 12.5p - 1875 (06Je00)
Danone FF10 - Eur250.4 4.5 (02Je00)
De Beers Centenary Finance PLC 8¼% Ln Stk 2009 - 104 (06Je00)
Debenhams Retail PLC 7¼% Uns Ln Stk 2002/07 - 101 (05Je00)
Dee Valley Group PLC Non Vtg Ord 5p - 375 (02Je00)
De Vere Group PLC 7% Cnv Subord Bds 2003 £1 (Regd) - 96 (07Je00) 6 (07Je00) 6 (07Je00) 6 (07Je00) 7½ (07Je00)
Dewhurst PLC Ord 10p - 113 5
Diageo PLC ADR (4:1) - 34.27 (07Je00) .355 (07Je00) .5625
Ecclesiastical Insurance Office PLC 8.625% Non Cum Irrd Prf £1 - 98 (07Je00) 8 (07Je00)
Elementis PLC Red 'B' Shs 1p - ½ (4, 6, 7, 5) 1¼ (7)
Enterprise Oil PLC 10¾% Uns Ln Stk 2013 - 126 (06Je00)
Eurotunnel PLC/Eurotunnel SA 1991 Wts (1E PLC & 1ESA Wt to Sub Uts) (Reg) - 3 (06Je00)
Fairey Group PLC New Ord 5p (FP/PAL - 16/06/00) - 422 (06Je00)
Falcon Hldgs PLC Ord 5p - 200 (1)
Feedback PLC 10% Cnv Red Prf Shs £1 - 380 (07Je00) 475 (07Je00) 550 (07Je00) 50 (07Je00) 50 (07Je00)
First Debenture Finance PLC 11.125% Severally Gtd Deb Stk 2018 - 149¾ (06Je00)
Fuller, Smith & Turner PLC 8% 2nd Cum Prf £1 - 120 (05Je00)
Gallaher Group PLC ADR (4:1) - 19.7075 (06Je00) 20.625 (07Je00)
General Accident PLC 7⅞% Cum Irrd Prf £1 - 110½ (07Je00)
General Accident PLC 8⅞% Cum Irrd Prf £1 - 126½ (07Je00) 7½ (07Je00) ½ (07Je00)
Genesis Emerging Markets Fund Ld Realisation Shs $0.01 - 17.3
GKN PLC Non-Cum Red 'B' Pref Shs 11.7p - 7 (07Je00) 7 (07Je00) 7 (07Je00) 7 (07Je00) 7 (07Je00) 7 (07Je00) 15 (07Je00) 5 (07Je00)
Glaxo Wellcome PLC ADR (2:1) - 54.3 (07Je00) .5 (07Je00) .5625 (07Je00) .59 (07Je00) .625 (07Je00) .63 (07Je00) .77 (07Je00) .79 (07Je00) .875 (07Je00) .9441 (07Je00) .97 (07Je00)
Grafton Group PLC Uts (Compr 1 Ord Eur0.50 & 1 C Ord Shr) - p1200 (02Je00)
Granada Group PLC 10% 1st Mtg Deb Stk 18/2/18 - 136 (02Je00)
Great Portland Estates PLC 9.5% 1st Mtg Deb Stk 2016 - 127½ (02Je00)
Great Portland Estates PLC 10¾% 1st Mtg Deb Stk 2021 - 150.528 (02Je00)
Haco Ld 10⅝% Several Deb Stk 2017 - 137.30078125 (06Je00)
Halifax PLC Non-Cum Fxd Rte Sterling Prf £1 - 78 (31My00) 9 (31My00) 9 (31My00) 80½
Halifax PLC 9.375% Perp Sub Bds - 115 (07Je00) 27 (07Je00)
Hanson PLC ADR (5:1) - 37.248759
Heart of Midlothian PLC Ord 10p - 93½ (07Je00)
Highbury House Communications PLC Ord 5p (Rfd -01/01/2000) - p60 1 2 (02Je00)
Holt (Joseph) PLC Ord 25p - 2150 (06Je00)
Housing Finance Corp Ld 8⅝% Deb Stk 2023 - 121.544 (01Je00)
HSBC Bank PLC 14% Subord Uns Ln Stk 2002/07 - 105 (07Je00)
HSBC Hldgs PLC 11.69% Subord Bds 2002 £1 (Reg) - 95 (07Je00)
Imperial Chemical Industries PLC ADR (4:1) - 33.875 (07Je00)
Incepta Group PLC Wts to Sub for Ord - 90 (07Je00)
India Fund 'B'Shs - p123 (05Je00)
India I.T. Fund Ld Red Ptg Prf $0.01 - $64.5 (07Je00) 5 (07Je00) .5 (07Je00) 8 (07Je00) 8 (07Je00)
Indocam Himalayan Fund NV Ord NLG0.01 - 18 (02Je00)
Innovation Group PLC Ord 2p - 280 (1) 3 (5, 10) 5 (5, 10, 2) 300 (5, 24) 2 (1) 5 (2, 5) 10 (3, 10, 32, 10, 0) 2 (5, 10) 5 (1, 5) 7 (3) 20 (3, 0, 5) 2 (1) 3# (3) 5 (20) ¼ (20) 7 (5) 30 (5) 2 (1) 3 (3) 40 (0, 2, 5) 5 (5) 52 (0) 5 (5, 0)
Invensys PLC ADR (2:1) - 7.75 8.093 (07Je00)
JWE Telecom PLC Ord 1p (Rfd - 01/04/00) - 123 ½ 7 8 (07Je00)
Knowledge Management Software PLC Ord 1p - 155 (07Je00) 60 (07Je00) 75 (07Je00) 8.85 (07Je00) 80 (07Je00) 80 (07Je00) 1
Land Securities PLC 7% Cnv Bds 30/9/2008 £1000 (Rg) - 124 (07Je00) 5 (07Je00)
Laporte PLC 'B' Ord 1p - ¾ (6)
Laporte PLC New 'B' Ord 1p - ¾ (20, 1, 5, 12)
Leeds & Holbeck Building Society 13⅜% Perm Int Bearing Shs - 168 9 (06Je00)
London Finance & Investment Grp PLC Wts to Sub for Ord - 14½ (07Je00)
Lonmin PLC ADR (1:1) - 9.821 (07Je00)
Luminar PLC Wts to Sub for Ord - 260 75 (05Je00)
Maisha PLC Ord 1p - 11 (2, 5)
Manchester Building Society 8% Perm Interest Bearing Shs - 108 (06Je00)
Marks & Spencer PLC ADR (6:1) - 24.54826
McCarthy & Stone PLC 7% Uns Ln Stk 1999/2004 - 91 (02Je00)
MEPC PLC Non-Cum Red Prf 'B' Shs 96p - 87 (06Je00)
MEPC PLC 10¾% 1st Mtg Deb Stk 2024 - 158.58 (05Je00)
MEPC PLC 8% Uns Ln Stk 2000/05 - 97 (06Je00)
MEPC PLC 10½% Uns Ln Stk 2032 - 143 (07Je00)
Morrison (Wm.) Supermarkets PLC 5¼% Cum Red Cnv Prf £1 - 473 83 (05Je00)
MSW Technology PLC Wts to Sub for Ord - 3 (07Je00)
National Grid Company PLC 4¼% Exch Bds 2008 £1000 (Reg) - 138½ (05Je00)
National Grid Company PLC 4¼% Exch Bds 2008 £1000 (Br) (Reg S) - £1.361736 (02Je00)
National Power PLC ADR (4:1) - $23.73 (07Je00)
National Westminster Bank PLC 9% Ser'A'Non-Cum Prf £1 - 120 (07Je00) 2 (07Je00)
Newcastle Building Society 10¾% Perm Int Bearing Shs £1000 - 140 (07Je00)
Newcastle Building Society 12⅝% Perm Int Bearing Shs £1000 - 151 65 (06Je00)
Northern Foods PLC 6¾% Cnv Sub Bds 08/08/08 £1000 (Rg) - 98 (02Je00) ½ (07Je00)
Northern Rock PLC 12⅝% Perp Sub Nts (Br) - 156# (06Je00)
Oao Gazprom ADS (Repr 10 Ord Rur10) (144A) - $6.36 (07Je00)
Optometrics Corp US$0.01 - 20 (01Je00)
Orb Estates PLC Cnv Ln Nts 2003 - 0.125 (07Je00)
Paramount PLC Cum Sec Cnv Red Prf Shs £1 - 60 (02Je00)
Parthus Technologies PLC Ord IEP0.025 - 205 (1, 3, 4, 2, 3, 2) 6 (36, 100, 15, 25) 7 (5, 1, 0, 25, 50) 8 (4, 5, 3, 0, 6, 2, 0, 10, 2, 1, 0, 50, 1, 3, 5, 1, 10, 1, 2, 5, 50, 30, 2, 5, 10, 5, 110, 250, 300, 5, 1, 8, 3, 1, 2, 4, 1, 0, 2, 0, 5, 10, 4, 1, 5, 0, 8, 0, 5, 2, 50) 9 (5, 50) .96 (07Je00) 10 (1, 2, 1, 3, 7, 1, 2, 1, 2, 0, 1, 0, 2, 1, 0, 1, 3, 1, 0, 2, 0, 1, 0, 3, 0, 1, 0, 1, 5, 7, 10, 50, 25) 1 (2) 2 (10, 5, 2, 0, 1, 3, 1, 2, 1, 0, 3, 1, 2, 1, 0, 10, 50, 40, 15, 50, 40) 3 (25, 3, 1, 2, 0, 1, 0, 1, 0, 1, 2, 0, 1, 3, 2, 1, 0, 1, 25) 4# (2) 4 (25) 5 (07Je00) 5 (07Je00) 5# (1) 5 (1, 5, 2, 5, 1, 3, 1, 5, 1, 5, 25, 100, 35, 50, 5) 6 (50) 7 (02Je00) 8 (2, 50) 20 (3, 2, 1, 0, 3, 1, 4, 5, 1, 12, 6, 15, 25, 15, 100) 1 (1, 2) 2 (1, 0) 3 (12, 1, 0, 1, 2, 0, 1, 0, 2, 1, 3, 1, 8, 1, 6, 2, 1, 0, 5, 1, 0, 1, 2, 1, 0, 1, 2, 0, 5, 1, 70, 0, 1, 2, 10) 4# (5) 4# (25) 5# (1) 5# (10) 5# (3)
Paterson, Zochonis PLC 10% Cum Prf £1 - 116 (06Je00)
Peel Hldgs PLC 9⅞% 1st Mtg Deb Stk 2011 - 116 (02Je00)
Perkins Foods PLC Cnv Red Prf 12.5p - 99 (07Je00) 101 (07Je00) .05 (07Je00) 2 (07Je00) 2 (07Je00)
Premier Farnell PLC ADR (2:1) - 14.0625
Premier Farnell PLC 89.2p Cum Cnv Red Prf (Sterling Coupon) - 14 (07Je00)
Queens Moat Houses PLC 10¼% 1st Mtg Deb Stk 2020 - 111 (05Je00)
Rank Group PLC ADR (2:1) - 4.08735
R.E.A.Hldgs PLC 9% Cum Prf £1 - 60 (02Je00)
Regal Hotel Group PLC Cnv Cum Red Prf 2001 £1 - 70 (7) ½ (0)
Retail Corp PLC 4.55% (fmly 6½%) Cum 3rd Prf £1 - 78 (01Je00)
Reuters Group PLC ADR (6:1) - 102.17 (07Je00) .31 (06Je00) .4 (07Je00) 3.564 (07Je00)
REXAM PLC 'B' Shs £1 - 95
Rio Tinto PLC Ord 10p (Br) - 1020
Rio Tinto PLC ADR (4:1) - 60.997967 (05Je00)
Rolls-Royce PLC ADR (5:1) - 17.78206
Royal & Sun Alliance Ins Group PLC 7⅜% Cum Irrd Prf £1 - 98¾ (07Je00) 100¼ (07Je00) ¼ (07Je00)
Ryanair Holdings PLC Ord IEP0.02 - p528 (07Je00) 8 (18) *33.6287 (23) 7 (1) 43 (1) 4 (35) 5 (1)
Saatchi & Saatchi PLC ADR (5:1) - 25.29848
Sainsbury (J) PLC ADR (4:1) - 19.55 (07Je00) .658 (07Je00)
Sanctuary Group PLC Wts to Sub for Ord - 34¼ 6
Scarborough Building Society 8.5% Perm Int Bearing Shs - 111 (06Je00)
Scottish Asian Investment Co Ld Ptg £0.01 (Glasgow Reg) - 173
Scottish Media Group PLC 6.50% Cnv Uns Ln Stk 2007 - 142 (07Je00)
Severn River Crossing PLC 6% Index-Linked Deb Stk 2012 - 154 (07Je00)
Severn Trent PLC 'B' Shs 38p - 28 37
Shell Transport & Trading Co PLC ADR (6:1) - 51.5 .5625 .645 .6875 2 (07Je00) .03 (07Je00) .1875 (07Je00)
Shoprite Group PLC Ord 5p - 13 (0) 5 (10)
Sidlaw Group Ld 7½% Uns Ln Stk 2003/08 - 90 (06Je00)
Skipton Building Society 12⅞% Perm Int Bearing Shs £1000 (Reg) - 162 5 72 (06Je00)
SkyePharma PLC 'B' Warrants - 6½ (20)
Smith & Nephew PLC 3.85% (Net) Cum Prf £1 - 80 (05Je00)
SmithKline Beecham PLC ADR (5:1) - 61.31 (07Je00) .5 (07Je00) .54 (07Je00) .8525 (07Je00) .95 (07Je00) 2.2 (07Je00) .23 (07Je00)
Smith Wh PLC Non Cum Red Prf Shs 53.75p - 37 (02Je00)
Smith Wh PLC 5⅛% Red Uns Ln Stk - 92 (07Je00)
South East Water PLC 10% Red Deb Stk 2013/17 - 129 (05Je00)
Stanelco PLC Ord 0.1p - 3 (25, 10) .25 (5) .5 (10, 30, 25)
Statpro Group PLC Ord 1p - 66 (06Je00)
Tate & Lyle PLC ADR (4:1) - 15.528
Tate & Lyle PLC 10¾% Uns Ln Stk 2003/2008 - 105 (07Je00)
Tdg PLC 'B' Shs 34.4p - 34 (07Je00)
Telewest Communications PLC ADR (10:1) - 47.856 (06Je00)
Tesco PLC 4% Uns Deep Discount Ln Stk 2006 - 88 (07Je00)
Thistle Hotels PLC 10¾% 1st Mtg Deb Stk 2014 - 132 (05Je00)
Three Valleys Water PLC 4% Irrd Cons Deb Stk (fmly Rickmans Wtr) - 74 (06Je00)
Three Valleys Water PLC 4% Irrd Deb Stk (Colne Stk) - 79 (06Je00)
Tops Estates PLC Wts to Sub for Ord - ¼ (05Je00)
Tops Estates PLC 7½% Cnv Uns Ln Stk 2020 - 100 (07Je00) 3 (07Je00)
Upton & Southern Hldgs PLC 5p (Gross) Cum.Cnv.Red.Pref.Shs.50p - 140 (06Je00)
Vodafone Airtouch PLC ADR (10:1) - 48.375 .725 (07Je00) .75 .875 .966086 9 * 9 (07Je00) .125 .4375 .55 (07Je00)
Walker (Thomas) PLC Ord 5p - 65 (2)
Weston Medical Group PLC Ord 1p - 172 (20) 3 (0, 2)
Whitbread PLC 11⅝% Deb Stk 2011 - 138½ (07Je00)
Williams PLC 10¾% Cum Prf £1 - 140 (06Je00)
Wilson (Connolly) Hldgs PLC 10½% Cum 2nd Prf £1 - 130 (01Je00)
Wireless Group PLC Ord 10p - 240 (50) 2 (0, 2, 1, 15)
Wolverhampton & Dudley Breweries PLC 6.5% Deb Stk 2019 - 101 (07Je00)
Wyevale Garden Centres PLC 8.5% (Net) Cnv Cum Red Prd £1 - 414 (05Je00)

Fig. 5.3 London Stock Exchange: dealings

TRADING VOLUME

■ **Major Stocks Yesterday**

	Vol 000's	Closing price	Day's change		Vol 000's	Closing price	Day's change
3i	1,709	1446	-6	Kingfisher	3,012	498¼	-29½
AMVESCAP	1,582	864½	-10	Kingston Comms.	1,073	1070	-33
Abbey National	10,595	869½	+3½	Land Securities	1,991	773½	+7½
Alliance & Leicester	1,819	660	-½	Legal & General	16,359	158¾	-2½
Allied Domecq†	6,080	313¼		Lloyds TSB	15,335	645½	-17½
Allied Zurich	4,332	642½	+10	Logica	1,536	2267	-52
ARM Holdings	1,374	4152	+52	Marconi	5,859	826	-33½
Anglo American	607	2850	-11	Marks & Spencer	6,257	262¾	-5½
Assoc. Brit. Foods†	444	409	-32	Matalan†	685	582	-8
AstraZeneca	4,052	2551	-130	Misys	2,796	963	+46
BAA	24,639	394¼	-35¼	National Grid	3,378	595	-2
BG Group	6,295	357	-7¾	National Power	5,381	320¼	+1½
BOC	1,573	1269	-3	Norwich Union	7,583	415	+6
BP Amoco	35,401	522½	+8	Nycomed Amersham	4,718	532	-13
BSkyB	7,103	1798	-165	Old Mutual	6,869	156	-¾
BT	21,620	1222	-19	Pearson	1,069	2296	-36
Baltimore Tech	610	9597	-601	P & O	5,300	663½	+10
Bank of Scotland	6,896	710½	+23	Prudential	4,295	922	-26½
Barclays	2,939	1672	+31	Psion	338	4600	-195
Bass	2,310	756½	-6½	Railtrack	1,921	688	-1½
Billiton	4,345	274	+4½	Reckitt Benckiser	1,428	600¾	+¾
Blue Circle	1,337	414¼	-1	Reed Intl.	11,698	466¼	+16
Boots	4,379	519¼	-12	Rentokil Initial	32,080	157¾	+4¼
Bowthorpe†	567	1298	+43	Reuters	11,877	1405	-12
Brit. Aerospace	15,258	356¼	-¾	Rio Tinto	3,141	1015½	+27½
British Airways	5,699	335¾	-7	Rolls Royce	8,930	200	+8
Brit. Amer. Tobacco	56,265	298½	+6½	Royal & Sun Alliance	10,598	378½	-¼
CGU	6,348	869½	+20½	Royal Bank Scotland	8,381	852½	+10
CMG	575	5834	+24	Sage Group	2,852	827	+3
COLT Telecom	2,248	3319	-80	Sainsbury	7,012	280	-5½
Cable & Wireless	7,243	1299	-12	Schroders	364	1298	+40
Cable & Wire Comms	8,331	1128	-24	Schroders N/V	91	1092	-3
Cadbury Schweppes	7,185	418¼	-15½	Scot. & Sthn Energy	1,499	548	-11
Capita	2,034	1705	+92	Scottish Power	5,401	527¼	+9¼
Carlton Comms.	2,825	779½	+11½	Sema	3,154	1344	+12
Celltech	1,735	1230	-40	Shell Transport	24,736	485¾	+9
Centrica	15,976	248¾	-5¾	Shires Pharms†	1,214	1061	+8
Compass	1,559	833	-17	SmithKline Beecham	11,757	811	+19
Corus Group	12,678	102	-2	Sth African Breweries	250	525½	+7
Daily Mail & Gen.	721	1323	+37	Standard Chartered	4,650	914½	-4½
Diageo	7,405	448¼	+½	Sun Life & Provincial	1,134	442½	-7¼
Dixons	6,708	302	-25¼	TeleWest Comms.	19,040	563	+15¼
EMAP	2,697	1234	-19	Tesco	20,410	201¼	-2¼
EMI	1,281	650	-3	Thus	3,728	639½	-32
Electrocomps†	880	657½	+7½	Unilever	10,021	389	-1
Energis	1,462	3396	-73	Utd. News & Media	1,704	892½	+17
Foreign & Col. I T†	1,247	251	-1	Utd. Utilities	967	702½	+7½
Freeserve	3,436	510½	-35	Vodafone AirTouch	191,650	355¾	-8½
GKN	2,119	761½	-64	WPP	7,153	1064	-6
Glaxo Wellcome	7,953	1736	+35	Woolwich	3,667	355¼	-7¾
Granada	5,389	688½	-10				
GUS	2,941	406	+3¾				
HSBC	14,013	752	+1				
Halifax	4,051	672	-13				
Hays	12,367	417½	+38	Based on trading volume for the FTSE 100 constituent companies and reserves yesterday until 4.30pm.			
Hilton	14,296	292	+12	† indicates a FTSE 100 index reserve. All trades are rounded. Source: Financial Times Information			
ICI	3,225	499¼	-5				
Invensys	6,690	286	-½				

Fig. 5.4 Trading volume

■ Rises and falls, highs and lows, main movers

The newspaper also carries three other lists for quick reference on share price movements. First, there is a list of rises and falls for broad share categories as in Figure 5.5, which shows:

■ **Rises and falls:** the daily version of this table shows how many securities rose, fell and stayed at the same price level during the previous trading session. It is broken down into ten different categories of security and shows how movements in the main share price indices were reflected in trading across various broad market subdivisions. Saturday's version also lists rises and falls on the week as a whole.

RISES AND FALLS YESTERDAY			
	Rises	**Falls**	**Same**
British Funds	10	49	8
Other Fixed Interest	0	0	9
Mineral Extraction	41	56	27
General Manufacturers	56	137	137
Consumer Goods	48	100	102
Services	133	278	209
Utilities	6	17	10
Financials	62	108	105
Investment Companies	130	239	305
Others	69	161	186
Totals	555	1,145	1098

Data based on those companies listed on the London Share Service.

Fig. 5.5 Rises and falls yesterday

The second list covers individual stocks that have recorded new highs and lows for the past 12 months (see Figure 5.6):

NEW 52 WEEK HIGHS AND LOWS

Data based on intra-day share trading in those companies listed on the London Share Service.

NEW HIGHS (45).
AUTOMOBILES (1) Toyota Motor, **CONSTRUCTION & BUILDING MATERIALS (1)** Ultraframe, **DISTRIBUTORS (2)** Mitsubishi Corpn, Young (H), **FOOD PRODUCERS & PROCESSORS (1)** Highlands, **GENERAL RETAILERS (1)** Ted Baker, **INFORMATION TECHNOLOGY HARDWARE (3)** Mitsubishi, NEC Corpn, Toshiba Corpn, **INVESTMENT COMPANIES (22)** Baring Emerging European, Baring Emerging European Wrts, Central European Growth, Close FTSE 100 Inc & Gwth, English & Scottish Investors, Fleming Claverhouse, Fleming Continental, Fleming US Discovery IT, Govett Euro Enhanced, Investment Trust of Inv Tsts Wrts, Johnson Fry Utilities Zero Pref, Jupiter European Inv Wrts, M & G Recovery Capital, Martin Currie Portfolio IT, Mercury European Wrts, Murray Extra Return IT Cap, Robeco N/Vtg, Robeco Sub Shares, Rolinco Sub Shares, Tribune, Warrants & Value, Witan Inv, **MEDIA & PHOTOGRAPHY (3)** Cordiant Communications, Flextech, Television Corpn, **OIL & GAS (1)** Victoria Petroleum, **PHARMACEUTICALS (1)** Goldshield, **REAL ESTATE (2)** Dencora, Dencora 6 1/4pc Cum Cnv Red Pref, **SOFTWARE & COMPUTER SERVICES (1)** Easyscreen, **SUPPORT SERVICES (2)** Hawtal Whiting, Penna, **TELECOMMUNICATIONS SERVICES (1)** Estonian Telecom, **AIM (3)** BCO Technologies, New Capital Invest, Raphael Zorn Hemsley.
NEW LOWS (72).
GILTS (3) Treasury 13 3/4pc 2000-03, Treasury 13pc 2000, Treasury 2pc Index-Linked 2006, **AUTOMOBILES (1)** Avon Rubber, **BANKS (1)** Bank of Scotland 9 1/4pc Irrd Pref, **BEVERAGES (1)** Barr (AG), **CHEMICALS (1)** Ellis & Everard, **CONSTRUCTION & BUILDING MATERIALS (5)** Baggeridge Brick, Darby Group, Halstead (J), Morrison Construction, Mowlem (J), **DISTRIBUTORS (2)** Caffyns, Lookers 8pc Cnv Cum Red Pref, **DIVERSIFIED INDUSTRIALS (2)** Barlo Group, Staveley Inds, **ELECTRICITY (1)** Hafslund B, **ELECTRONIC & ELECTRICAL EQUIPMENT (1)** Oxford Instruments, **ENGINEERING & MACHINERY (7)** Bodycote Intl, Firth Rixson, Kvaerner AS B, L Gardner, Metalrax, Stadium Group, Tinsley (E), **FOOD & DRUG RETAILERS (2)** Donatantonio, Thorntons, **FOOD PRODUCERS & PROCESSORS (2)** Crean (J), Devro, **GENERAL RETAILERS (2)** Arnotts, Country Gardens, **HEALTH (2)** Huntleigh Technology, SSL Intl, **HOUSEHOLD GOODS & TEXTILES (1)** Silentnight, **INSURANCE (2)** Atrium Underwriting, Goshawk Insurance, **INVESTMENT COMPANIES (7)** Aberdeen Prfd 5 3/8pc RPI Linked Deb 2007, Cairngorm Bldg Societies Units, Dartmoor Inv 6 1/4pc RPI-Lk Deb '05, First Pacific, Fleming Geared Gwth 13pc Cum Prfd, HSBC China Fund, Investment Trust of Inv Trusts, **LEISURE, ENTERTAINMENT & HOTELS (1)** Friendly Hotels, **MEDIA & PHOTOGRAPHY (1)** Character Group, **MINING (5)** De Beers 40pc Pref, Durban Deep, East Rand Proprietary, Resolute, Zambia Copper Invs, **PACKAGING (1)** Coral Products, **REAL ESTATE (6)** Land Securities 10pc Deb 2025, Land Securities 10pc Deb 2027, Land Securities 10pc Deb 2030, Quintain Estates & Development, Rodamco Utd Kingdom, Smart (J), **RESTAURANTS, PUBS & BREWERIES (1)** Regent Inns, **SOFTWARE & COMPUTER SERVICES (1)** Trace Computers, **SUPPORT SERVICES (4)** Securicor, Semple Cochrane, Shanks, StepStone, **TRANSPORT (2)** Alpha Airports, BWA Group, **AIM (7)** Gartland Whalley & Barker, Internet Indirect, Interregnum, Lady in Leisure, Linton Park, Private & Commercial Fincl, nanoUniverse.

Fig. 5.6 New highs and lows

■ **Highs and lows:** this table shows which shares have on the previous trading day reached new high or low points for the past 12 months. If space is limited, only the number of shares in each sector is listed and not their names.

The highs and lows list helps to highlight companies that are moving against the trend of their sector. Warnings signs would start to flash if a company featured repeatedly in the "new lows" section when the sector as a whole was not moving in this direction. The list can be used in conjunction with the listing of rises and falls to compare individual share price movements with overall market sector moves.

Some technical analysts also use highs and lows as a means of checking the underlying health of the market. They like an index to be "confirmed" by an increase in new highs because that is an indication of a broad market rise. Similarly, if the number of new lows starts to diminish, that may be a sign that the index is close to bottoming.

The third list covers the "main movers": the stocks that had the biggest percentage rises and falls the previous day (see Figure 5.7):

MAIN MOVERS

FTSE 350	Closing price	Day's change	Day's chge %
RISES			
Somerfield	57	+7	+14.0
Torotrak	382½	+46½	+13.8
BPB	335	+24¾	+8.0
Trafficmaster	598	+37	+6.6
Whatman	215	+13	+6.4
Stagecoach	63½	+3½	+5.8
Redstone Telecom	315	+15	+5.0
Kelda Group	345	+15¼	+4.6
FALLS			
Powderject	382½	-60	-13.6
CMG	990	-71	-6.7
Debenhams	205	-12¾	-5.9
Cedar Group	835	-50	-5.6
Airtours	340	-20	-5.6
Celltech Group	1135	-65	-5.4
Johnson Matthey	859	-40	-4.4
Mayflower Corpn	160	-7	-4.2

Fig. 5.7 Main movers

▪ Winners and losers

Saturday's Money section includes a table of the FTSE winners and losers (see Figure 5.8). This lists the top and bottom six performing companies over the previous week in three sectors (the FTSE 100, the FTSE 250 and the FTSE SmallCap sector), including their latest price, percentage price change on the week and change on the start of the year. It also lists the top and bottom six performing market sectors.

FTSE winners and losers

Top 100	Fri price (p)	% change: 5 days	since 30/12/99	FTSE SmallCap	Fri price (p)	% change: 5 days	since 30/12/99
Winners				**Winners**			
Celltech Group	1200	14.8	125.8	Harveys Furnishing	163½	39.7	7.9
Billiton	259	9.3	-29.1	Volex Group	1412½	34.5	19.7
Sainsbury(J)	315	9.0	-9.8	Sportsworld Media Group	552½	32.3	12.4
British American Tobacco	400	8.7	13.7	London Clubs International	125½	30.1	2.4
Rio Tinto (Reg)	1065	8.7	-28.8	IMS Group plc	187½	23.0	-37.5
Reed International	500	8.2	7.9	Acal	465	21.6	-8.4
Losers				**Losers**			
BSkyB	1143	-21.3	14.7	Synstar	93½	-28.1	-59.1
Sage Group	621	-19.5	-17.8	Brown & Jackson	129	-12.5	-31.2
Logica	1640	-18.9	2.7	Ashtead Group	95	-10.8	-44.0
Reuters Group	1060	-10.9	24.8	Clinton Cards	108½	-9.6	-56.7
Colt Telecom Group	2510	-10.7	-20.8	Character Group	62½	-9.4	-76.4
CMG	1061	-9.8	-6.9	JZ Equity Partners	198	-8.8	4.8

FTSE 250				Industry Sectors			
Winners				**Winners**			
NSB Retail Systems	247½	22.2	23.5	Tobacco	5475.92	7.2	18.9
British Energy	170	21.4	-52.1	Food & Drug Retailers	2735.75	6.3	6.0
NXT	1180	17.4	-13.2	Mining	4308.20	6.3	-26.5
Easynet	802½	17.2	-53.9	Personal Care & Hse Prods	2181.46	5.3	24.3
Royalblue Group	1420	15.9	35.6	Beverages	3373.78	4.8	6.5
Torotrak	336	14.9	24.0	Speciality & Other Finance	4714.82	3.6	2.1
Losers				**Losers**			
Whatman	202	-16.4	-22.3	Software & Computer Srvcs	3121.78	-9.5	-16.0
Spirent	402	-15.4	11.4	Media & Photography	7657.71	-7.0	6.3
Filtronic	972½	-14.9	-53.9	Telecommunication Srvcs	7945.65	-6.4	-13.6
Fibernet Group	1625	-13.0	-7.7	Steel & Other Metals	2160.48	-6.0	-44.3
BPB	310¼	-11.4	-13.6	Pharmaceuticls	10521.8	-4.6	4.9
British Land Co	400	-10.8	-2.4	Gas Distribution	4321.74	-2.7	12.2

Based on last week's performance.

Fig. 5.8 FTSE winners and losers

■ Issuing new securities

The *Financial Times* provides detailed information on the secondary market for company securities. But the exchanges also have a vital role as a primary market, providing new long-term capital for investment through the offering of new issues. These might be for companies entering their shares on the market for the first time or for companies already listed but requiring further capital. In each case, the newspaper offers extensive coverage.

There are two daily published tables for new securities: equities (ordinary shares issued by newly floated companies); and rights offers (trading in the rights to issues of new shares in existing companies to which current shareholders are given the first right of refusal).

■ Launching companies

Companies can raise money by selling some of their shares to investors before getting them quoted on the stock market. Shares may be being sold by original owners/existing shareholders or by the company to raise new capital: so sometimes the money goes into the business, sometimes to the existing shareholders.

There are three ways of floating shares on the market:

- **Offers for sale or initial public offerings (IPOs):** these are shares offered to the public through advertising and the issue of prospectuses and application forms. The most notable form in the 1980s and 1990s has been the privatisation issues, especially British Gas and British Telecom. These are the kinds of new issue likely to be of most interest to the small, private investor (see Figure 5.9). Also popular have been the "dot-coms" coming to market.

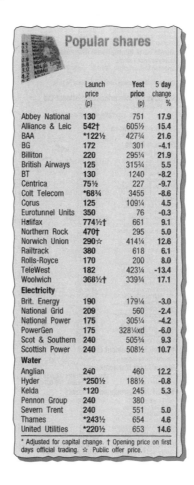

Popular shares			
	Launch price (p)	Yest price (p)	5 day change %
Abbey National	130	751	17.9
Alliance & Leic	542†	605½	15.4
BAA	*122½	427¾	21.6
BG	172	301	-4.1
Billiton	220	295¼	21.9
British Airways	125	315¾	5.5
BT	130	1240	-8.2
Centrica	75½	227	-9.7
Colt Telecom	*68¾	3455	-8.6
Corus	125	109¼	4.5
Eurotunnel Units	350	76	-0.3
Halifax	774½†	661	9.1
Northern Rock	470†	295	5.0
Norwich Union	290☆	414¼	12.6
Railtrack	380	618	6.1
Rolls-Royce	170	200	8.0
TeleWest	182	423¼	-13.4
Woolwich	368½†	339¾	17.1
Electricity			
Brit. Energy	190	179¼	-3.0
National Grid	209	560	-2.4
National Power	175	305¼	-4.2
PowerGen	175	328¼xd	-6.0
Scot & Southern	240	505¾	9.3
Scottish Power	240	508½	10.7
Water			
Anglian	240	460	12.2
Hyder	*250½	188½	-0.8
Kelda	*120	245	5.3
Pennon Group	240	380	
Severn Trent	240	551	5.0
Thames	*243½	654	4.6
United Utilities	*220½	653	14.6

* Adjusted for capital change. † Opening price on first days official trading. ☆ Public offer price.

Fig. 5.9 Popular shares

- **Placings:** these are private sales of shares to a range of investors through a broker. The broker will typically go first to its clients, and subsequently shares may be available to a wider public through the stock market. This is a popular way for smaller companies to come to market, often through the AIM, and companies may combine a placing with an open offer for sale.
- **Introductions:** these take place when there is already a number of shareholders, and the company is simply seeking permission for the shares to trade on the market. Such issues do not raise new capital, but might allow a company to move up from the AIM to the main market, or a foreign company to trade in London as well as in its home market.

Offers for sale are the most prominent form of new issue. They can come in two forms. In the first, the company offers the public a fixed number of shares at a fixed price. The price is set by the sponsors of the issue, usually an investment bank, based on forecasts of likely future profits. The sponsor will have two conflicting objectives in mind: a low enough price to ensure that the shares trade well in the secondary or aftermarket; and a high enough price for the client raising the money.

Since fixed price offers for sale often underprice the issue, they provide a good opportunity for stags. These are investors who buy in anticipation of an immediate price rise and a quick profit right away. Prices often rise well above the sale price when dealings start, and the potential premiums encourage speculators seeking to benefit from the mistakes made by the issuers.

The alternative, and the way to avoid excessive stagging, is the tender offer. In this case, no price is set in advance but, instead, the price is determined by what investors are prepared to pay. Investors arc invited to bid for shares and, if the issue is fully subscribed, the price will generally be set at a little below one at which all available shares can be sold.

With either the fixed price or tender offer, the shares might be oversubscribed, and a decision needs to be made on the appropriate allocation of shares. This might be done by ballot, by scaling down certain over large applications, or by giving preferential treatment to certain investors, usually small, private ones. Alternatively, an issue might be undersubscribed, and this is why new issues are underwritten by big investors who guarantee to buy any unwanted shares. If underwriting is needed, shares will overhang the market as underwriters wait to sell when the price is rising. A result of this is that the share price will tend to stay flat until the majority of the shares are in firm hands, the portfolios of investors who want to hold them.

The timetable for a new issue is usually fairly standard: an early announcement is made without information on the intended share price, prospective yield and price/earnings ratio. This is followed by the publication of the full prospectus, incorporating price and yield details and with a cut-off date for applications and a date on which decisions on the allotment will be made. The Stock Exchange then decides on a date on which official dealings begin.

New issue launches are often affected by the overall state of the market, as in the following example:

The seasonal summer lull in the new issue market is heading for an early start this year after the flotation plans of at least seven companies, worth some £3bn, were demolished by last week's renewed slide in technology shares. The sudden end to the latest IPO boom resulted partly from a return to more traditional valuation models and growing investor scepticism in some of the insubstantial business models being put forward. The collapse of Boo.com, the internet retailer, and Netimperative, the information provider, as well as continued weakness in the value of Lastminute.com also weighed on sentiment. With the exception of Egg, the Prudential's internet financial services arm which cut its flotation price range to £1.1–1.4bn, there was just a handful of small companies that went ahead with their flotation plans last week. The new issue market could be in the doldrums until toward the end of the year and a resurgence might not come until early 2001. By that time, investors are likely to be presented with opportunities that are better worked through and to have had the benefit of an extra round of early stage funding.   (*Financial Times*, 29 May 2000)

Because of the size of the issues and the desire to appeal to first-time investors in the markets, the privatisation issues followed a rather longer schedule. In the case of BT3, the third British Telecom offer in 1993, for example, the government and SG Warburg, the global coordinator of the issue, were keen to ensure that such a significant launch should not have a deleterious effect on the whole market, and that downward pressure on the issue price should be resisted with "stabilising" buying by the underwriters.

The privatisation issues tended to be markedly underpriced, sometimes coming with incentives for the private investor, and positively discriminating against the institutions in terms of allocation and even price. As a consequence, they have been among the most successful new issues of the past 20 years. Saturday's *Financial Times* includes a table of "popular shares", listing all the major UK privatised companies with their launch price, their current price and their percentage increase over the previous week (see Figure 5.9). The table's regular appearance reflects the fact that, for many investors, these are the only shares they own.

Like privatisations, private sector new issues or IPOs are often viewed as a way to quick and easy profits, but for every ten or so successes, there is usually one that goes wrong or seriously fails to perform. As a result, private investors must always show great caution, being careful to study the prospectus, balance sheet, and profit and loss account of any potential investment. As with investing in any company share, it is critical to ask such questions as: Where did the company's profits and growth come from in previous years? What markets does it operate in? Where is its customer base? What is the quality of the management?

Once possible purchases have been highlighted, it should then be asked whether the price is fair. Does it reflect the assets? Is there too much emphasis on potential growth? And are market expectations for this type of business unrealistically high? Paradoxically, a company that has recently reported very good results, or is in fashionable industries such as biotechnology or the internet with its best results at an indeterminate point in the future, may be best avoided.

The *Financial Times* has a special table listing information on shares in newly floated companies (see Figure 5.10):

RECENT ISSUES: EQUITIES

Issue price p	Amt paid up	Mkt. cap (£m.)	1999/00 High	Low	Stock	Close price p	+/-	Div	Div cov	Yld	P/E
-	F.P.	226.6	642½	507	3i Bioscience Inv	507	-5½	-	-	-	-
-	F.P.	143.8	62½	10	†ADVFN.COM	57½	+1	-	-	-	-
250	F.P.	-	317½	250	†bizzbuild.com	287½	+2½	-	-	-	-
2	F.P.	7.22	7	5¾	†Chelford Grp	6¾		-	-	-	-
195	F.P.	245.8	466½	261	Dataflex Hldgs	368	+10	-	-	-	-
§195	F.P.	96.0	230	125	†e-district.net	125	-5	-	-	-	-
40	F.P.	17.4	58	48	†Einstein Channel	48		-	-	-	-
§5	F.P.	93.1	54	40	†Eurovestech	46½	+4	-	-	-	-
195	F.P.	55.8	257	222½	†Focus Solutions	222½	-7½	-	-	-	-
-	F.P.	46.8	39½	38½	†Framlington Net Inc	39		-	-	-	-
-	F.P.	15.6	13½	12½	Do Growth	13		-	-	-	-
3	F.P.	7.58	27¾	6¼	†Fulcrum Pharma	16¼		-	-	-	-
§55	F.P.	108.0	260	196½	†IBNet	196½	-3½	-	-	-	-
25	F.P.	28.5	295	185	†InTechnology	237½	-22½	-	-	-	-
380	F.P.	499.7	550	277½	lastminute.com	332½	+25	-	-	-	-
107	F.P.	207.7	174	156½	Patsystems	165		-	-	-	-
-	F.P.	9.30	52½	32½	†Premier Mngmt	46½		-	-	-	-
-	F.P.	49.0	250	170	†Radio First	205	+7½	-	-	-	-
28	F.P.	19.8	45	37½	†ReGen Therapeutics	38½		-	-	-	-
§20	F.P.	36.3	46	23	†Softtechnet.com	26	+3	-	-	-	-
170	F.P.	32.5	204	198½	†Topnotch Hlth Clbs	199½		-	-	-	-
110	F.P.	21.2	262½	150	†World Careers	262½	+32½	-	-	-	-

New issues within the last six weeks. † Alternative Investment Market. § Placing price. * Introduction. For a full explanation of all other symbols please refer to The London Share Service notes. ‡ When Issued.

Fig. 5.10 Recent issues: equities

- **Issue price:** the price at which the security was issued.
- **Amount paid up:** the amount of the issue price that had to be paid up immediately by the investor. Most issues are fully paid but some, including many government privatisations, have only required the investor to pay in stages. These part-paid shares are highly geared since if, after issue, a premium or discount emerges on the full issue price, it will be a significantly higher percentage of the part-paid investment. A small movement in the full price will be a relatively big movement in the part-paid price.
- **Market capitalisation:** the total value of the new issue.
- **High and low:** figures representing the price highs and lows for the year.
- **Stock:** the name of the security.
- **Price and change:** the closing price the previous night, and the change on the day.
- **Dividend cover, yield and p/e ratio:** for new equity issues, details of the dividend, dividend cover, dividend yield and p/e ratio are provided. In the case of newly floated companies, these figures are based on the figures given in the launch prospectus until the company issues audited financial reports. In many cases, there are no profits as yet, nor is the company paying a dividend, so these columns are blank.

New equity issues remain in the table for around six weeks after the company comes to market depending on the volume of new issues, and most then choose to be transferred to the London share service.

■ Raising extra funds

Rights issues are the way in which companies raise additional equity finance for expansion or refinance if they are overborrowed. They are issues of new shares in a company already on the market to which existing shareholders are given the right of first refusal. Shares are issued in proportion to existing holdings and at a discount to the current share price to give shareholders an incentive to take them up. The discount has the effect of depressing the price of existing shares and so shareholders will naturally want the rights to them. If they do not actually want to buy the shares, they can sell their rights.

The Stock Exchange sets a cut-off date after which the shares go ex-rights ("xr" in the share service tables). After this date the buyer does not get rights, and clearly, at this point, the share price has to adjust. Shares with the rights are known as cum-rights.

Nil paid rights (that is, rights for which the subscription price has not yet been paid) can be bought and sold. Their value is the ex-rights price less the subscription price for the new shares. These too are highly geared investments. The newspaper lists them in a table of rights offers, as in Figure 5.11:

RIGHTS OFFERS

Issue price p	Amount paid up	Latest Renun. date	1999/00 High	Low	Stock	Closing price p	+or-
100	Nil	22/3	190pm	92½pm	I2S	110pm	+17½
300	Nil	20/3	175pm	160pm	Tarsus	172½pm	

pm premium.

Fig. 5.11 Rights offers

- **Issue price and amount paid up:** as for the new issues, these are the price at which new shares are issued and the proportion of price already paid, if any.

- **Latest renunciation date:** the final date by which holders of rights can dispose of their allotments to purchasers who will not have to pay stamp duty. Before this date, all dealings are for cash rather than the account.

- **Closing price (as a premium), change and high and low:** the price quoted for rights to buy new shares, plus the change on the previous day and the highest and lowest points for the year. The price is actually a premium for the right to subscribe. Percentage swings in price can be large because of gearing.

Rights offers normally remain in the table until they are fully paid. The price of rights offers is pitched well below the market price to ensure maximum take-up of the issue although, as with new issues, the shares will be underwritten, usually by an investment bank. A standard issue might aim to raise up to 30 per cent more equity capital with shares at about a 20 per cent discount to market price. Rarely, a company might do a deep discount rights issue that does not need to be underwritten.

The price at which the shares are pitched does not matter since the company already belongs to the shareholders. The only benefit they get is on the yield if the dividend per share remains the same amount. Because the equity is diluted, the price drops: naturally, if the dividend is static, the yield goes up.

Other techniques by which new issues in existing companies can be arranged include vendor placings, placings and bought deals and convertible loan stock sold through the Euromarkets.

There is also the scrip issue or capitalisation issue where a company turns part of its accumulated reserves into new shares. This is essentially an accounting transaction to convert the part of shareholders' funds that is not revealed by stock market capitalisation into stock. It keeps the number of shares in issue in line with the growth of the business, and keeps their prices down. It can also be a tax-efficient way of handing part of the company's added worth back to shareholders.

The Stock Exchange sets a date when shares go "xc" (ex-capitalisation), after which the price will go down. The only real effect is if the dividend remains the same, in which case the yield has gone up. It also makes it difficult to compare share prices over time unless calculations have made the appropriate adjustment. The term "xa" means a share is ex-all, not entitled to scrip issues, rights issues or dividends.

■ Directors' dealings

Saturday's newspaper lists details of the previous week's share transactions by directors in their own companies (see Figure 5.12) showing:

■ **Directors' dealings:** sales or purchases listed by company, sector, number of shares bought or sold, their value in thousands of pounds, and the number of directors involved in the trading activity. The list contains all transactions with a value over £10,000, including the exercise of options if 100 per cent of the stock on which the options were granted is subsequently sold.

The information on directors' share transactions might give an indication of how company "insiders" feel about the prospects for their company's share price both in terms of its relationship to the company's prospective performance and relative to broader market movements. For example, directors frequently buy against the trend of a market fall, perhaps feeling secure in the longer-term prospects for their company's share price. For example:

Hays, a support services company, announced interim results early this month which saw turnover up 17 per cent to £1.03bn and pre-tax profits ahead by 8 per cent to £118.6m. Nevertheless, the share price fell by 46p because the market was unimpressed by the company's lack of a clear e-commerce strategy. Hays retorted that it does use the internet, and Ronnie Frost, chairman, feels the company's current strategies provide the most exciting opportunities since 1983, when he took the chair. John Cole, managing director, appears to agree because he recently bought 14,500 shares at 342p.   (*Financial Times*, 11–12 March 2000)

Sales						Purchases					
Company	Sector	Shares	Value (£'000)	No of directors		Company	Sector	Shares	Value (£'000)	No of directors	
AIT Group	Computer Services	115,000	2116	2		Aegis	Media & Photography	10,000	23	1	
Border TV	Media & Photography	9,500	77	1		Alldays	Food & Drug Retailers	40,000	21	2	
BPP	Support Services	30,000	218	1		Anglian Water	Water	4,000	18	1	
Cadbury Schweppes	Food Producers	15,300	58	1		Associated British Ports	Transport	10,000	23	1	
Cantab Pharmaceuticals	Pharmaceuticals	58,200	414	3		Baronsmead VCT	Investment Companies	72,116	99	1	
Carlton Communications	Media/Photography	3,300,000	27885	1		Bemrose Corporation	Support Services	85,000	425	2	
Deltron Electronics	Distributors	109,210	164	1		British Aerospace	Aerospace & Defence	30,000	95	1	
Electric Data Processing	Computer Services	250,000	935	1		British Vita	Chemicals	10,051	22	1	
Future Integrated Telephony	Telecommunications	50,000	520	1		Cairn Energy	Oil & Gas	450,000	620	5	
Henderson EuroTrust	Investment Companies	4,000	17	1		Caradon	Construction	15,300	21	1	
Hercules Property Services	Support Services	128,849	441	1		Carclo	Engineering	35,000	38	1	
ICM Computer	Computer Services	275,000	2613	3		Cookson	Engineering	19,465	39	2	
Jardine Lloyd Thompson	Insurance	60,000	156	1		Country Gardens	General Retailers	34,019	79	2	
Lambert Howarth	Household Goods	200,000	700	1		Electra Investment Trust	Investment Companies	9,000	100	2	
London Pacific	Other Financial	20,000	251	1		Future Integrated Telephony	Telecommunications	20,000	202	1	
MMT Computing	Computer Services	5,000	43	1		GET Group	Electronic	10,000	22	1	
Nycomed Amersham	Health	65,003	419	1		Hardys & Hansons	Restaurants	6,671	16	4	
Oxford BioMedica	Pharmaceuticals	2,000,000	2216	3		Hays	Support Services	14,500	50	1	
Pifco	Household Goods	27,000	38	1		Helical Bar	Real Estate	50,000	283	2	
Whatman	Engineering	20,000	350	1		Hiscox	Insurance	200,000	172	1	
Sales after exercise of options						Holmes Place	Leisure	90,000	247	2	
Atkins (WS)	Support Services	155,287	1009	1		Independent Insurance	Insurance	795,391	1790	2	
Carlton Communications	Media & Photography	80,750	684	1		Jourdan	Household Goods	400,000	160	1	
Close Brothers	Other Financial	42,955	537	1		Lex Service	Distributors	13,400	50	1	
Galliford	Construction	100,000	27	1		London Securities	Real Estate	20,000	47	1	
Hercules Property Services	Support Services	24,699	84	1		Moorfield Group	Real Estate	1,603,169	449	5	
Jardine Lloyd Thompson	Insurance	100,000	258	2		Murray Emerging Economies	Investment Companies	100,000	71	1	
United News & Media	Media & Photography	109,758	998	1		Northern Rock	Banks	9,200	28	4	
Vodafone AirTouch	Telecommunications	200,000	7205	1		PowerGen	Electricity	15,133	56	1	
						Prowting	Construction	500,000	530	1	
						Reed International	Media & Photography	44,778	198	1	
						Regent Inns	Restaurants	30,000	44	2	
						Royal & Sun Alliance Insurance	Insurance	25,000	85	1	
						Thomson Travel	Leisure	149,412	140	2	

Companies must notify the Stock Exchange within five working days of a share transaction by a director. This list contains all transactions (listed and Aim), including exercise of options (*) if 100% subsequently sold, with a value over £10,000. Information released by the Stock Exchange. Shares traded are ordinary, unless otherwise stated.

Sources: BARRA The Inside Track, Edinburgh, +44 (0) 131-473 7070; Primark Datastream

Fig. 5.12 Directors' dealings

By the same token, sales of stock on which directors have been granted an option as part of their remuneration package might indicate a lack of confidence in market prospects for the stock, at least for the immediate future; of course, it might also indicate that the director simply needs to free up some cash.

The attraction to an investor of following directors' transactions is obvious, but scholarly research in both the United Kingdom and the United States reveals mixed results. On average, it appears that directors are good at deciding when to sell, but not significantly above average at knowing when to buy. The latter result may be because they have too insular a view about their companies' prospects, believing their own propaganda and not taking sufficient account of their competition or the overall economic situation.

"We live in the Age of Performance. Performance means, quite simply,

that your portfolio does better than others."

George J W Goodman
("Adam Smith")

"The past history of the series (of stock price changes) cannot be used to predict the future in

any meaningful way. The future price of the price level or a security is no more predictable than

the path of a series of cumulated random numbers."

Eugene Fama

6

Indices and aggregates

Market indicators

- **FT indices** – the original investment statistics: the FT Ordinary Share index (FT 30); stock market trading data; the FT Gold Mines index
- **FTSE Actuaries share indices** – reading the figures and using the information on the key market indicators: market at a glance; highs, lows and base dates; leaders and laggards; capped indices; monthly averages of stock indices and private investor's indices

The fundamental data of the equities markets are the prices of shares and the various ratios that can be calculated from them. But while this information is highly valuable for understanding both the performance of individual companies and investors' evaluation of their prospects, it does not indicate the state of the market as a whole or a given company's relative performance. This question of share price measurement for the stock market as a whole led to the development of figures for baskets of shares, or indices. An index is purely a number used to compare the value of companies now with their value at the starting date.

All indices are an attempt to create order and direction out of diversity. Stock market indices are designed to pull together the disparate movements of different share prices, each responding to myriad individual pressures, to find out whether the market, or a subsection of it, is moving up or down, in a bullish or bearish direction. There are numerous ways of composing equity indices, each with advantages and disadvantages, and the one selected will depend on just what it is that is being tracked. Indices are important benchmarks for measuring the performance of the fund managers who put money into the stock market on behalf of investors. Most will try to outperform the various benchmarks, though some will passively aim merely to "track" the rise and fall of the indices. In its simplest form, this could be attempted by buying the stocks that constitute the index.

For managers too, such benchmark information is highly valuable for understanding both the performance of their individual companies and investors' evaluation of their prospects. For example, it is important to ensure that the company's share price is not underperforming the overall market, perhaps making the management vulnerable to a hostile bid. Indeed, increasing numbers of companies are making the share price a key management target through programmes of corporate value creation and value-based management.

■ FT indices

Perhaps the *Financial Times'* greatest contribution to investment statistics has been its pioneering of stock market indices. The oldest and most familiar of these is the FT Ordinary Share index, also known as the FT 30 share index, or simply the FT index. It is the longest standing continuous index covering UK equities: started in 1935 with a base 100, it is compiled from the share prices of 30 leading UK companies, chosen to be representative of UK industry and is calculated as a geometric mean. It is biased towards major industrial and retailing companies, the traditional blue chips, but now includes financial and telecoms stocks, which have become more important (see Figure 6.1):

FT 30 INDEX

	Mar 17	Mar 16	Mar 15	Mar 14	Mar 13	Yr ago	*High	*Low
FT 30	3639.5	3677.5	3548.5	3541.0	3517.0	3753.4	**4160.7**	3423.9
Ord. div. yield	2.86	2.84	2.89	2.90	2.92	2.77	**4.22**	2.58
P/E ratio	20.74	20.91	20.51	20.46	20.36	22.88	**25.41**	15.80

FT 30 since compilation: high 4160.7 16/7/99; low 49.4 26/6/40. Base Date: 1/7/35. *For 1999/00.

FT 30 hourly changes

8	9	10	11	12	13	14	15	16	High	Low
3677.5	3748.2	3698.8	3675.9	3652.6	3653.3	3629.0	3638.1	3655.8	3757.5	3624.7

Fig. 6.1 FT 30 index

- **FT 30:** the movements of the FT index over the past five trading days, together with its level a year ago, and the values and dates of its highs and lows for this year. The basis of 100 dates from the index's inception on 1 July 1935.

- **Ordinary dividend yield and price/earnings ratio:** in the same way that the index reflects prices of the component shares, so these reflect the dividends and earnings of the relevant companies.

- **FT 30 hourly changes:** the hourly movements of the FT index through the previous trading day plus the day's high and low point of the index. Originally calculated daily, it is now available as a real-time index like the Footsie (see below).

The FT 30 was for decades the standard barometer of investor sentiment in the City, quoted in the press and on radio and television as regularly as the FTSE 100 index is today. Although in terms of public attention the FT 30 has now been superseded by the Footsie, it still has a role to play. As the oldest surviving stock market index, it represents an important part of financial history and may be used by analysts to compare the impact of great events, such as the outbreak of wars or surprise election results, on the market. Its list of constituents is also used by followers of the O'Higgins method of share selection, which involves finding the ten stocks in the index with the highest dividend yield and selecting the five of those with the lowest price.

The mathematical structure of the index and the fact that all shares count equally regardless of their market capitalisation (the index is unweighted) make it a sensitive short-term indicator of the mood of the market. But it has a downward bias over the long term, and so is not suitable for measuring market levels or the performance of an investment portfolio over time.

In contrast to the Footsie where the components are selected purely on size, judgement has always been important in choosing companies for the FT 30. The aim has been to include a representative cross-section of UK industry. Companies have been removed from the index because they have been taken over, their fortunes have declined, or to make room for more dynamic or market-sensitive shares. For example, British Telecom and British Gas were brought into the index immediately on privatisation. It is a measure of the dynamics of the stock market that only five of the original components remain in the index today (see Appendix 2).

■ Stock market trading data

Listed under "Other London market data" in the newspaper, another table provides information on trading volume across the stock market (see Figure 6.2):

STOCK MARKET TRADING DATA						
	Mar 17	Mar 16	Mar 15	Mar 14	Mar 13	Yr ago
SEAQ bargains	174,710	170,981	145,475	139,851	153,942	105,74
Equity turnover (£m)†	-	7171.2	6804.6	5512.9	5344.0	n/a
Equity bargains†	-	152,142	136.689	134,940	153,555	n/a
Shares traded (m)†	-	1745.7	1677.4	1451.8	1462.7	n/a
Total market bargains‡	-	178,719	163,423	155,733	176,834	-
Total turnover (£m)‡	-	9714.1	9152.8	7519.2	7621.9	-
Total shrs traded (m)‡	2285.4	2234.5	2148.8	1861.5	1921.4	-
Tradepoint turnover (£m)	49.4	74.9	28.5	32.4	25.3	27.0
Tradepoint shrs traded(m)	9.1	15.6	6.8	7.9	5.7	6.8

†Excluding intra-market and overseas turnover but including Crest turnover. *UK only total at 6pm. ‡ UK plus intra-market turnover.

Fig. 6.2 Stock market trading data

■ **SEAQ bargains:** the number of transactions of equities and gilts on the Stock Exchange's SEAQ trading system by 4.30pm on the five most recent trading days, as well as a year earlier. As with trading volume on individual shares, all volume figures should be divided by two since each share is recorded twice as being both bought and sold.

■ **Equity turnover and equity bargains:** the value of the volume of equities traded in millions of pounds; and the number of transactions.

■ **Shares traded:** the actual number of shares to have changed hands. This figure and the equity turnover figure exclude intra-market and overseas turnover but include Crest turnover.

■ **Total market bargains, total turnover and total shares traded:** figures for transactions, value and number of shares traded that include intra-market turnover.

■ **Tradepoint turnover and shares traded:** the value and number of shares traded on Tradepoint, an electronic exchange launched in 1995 to rival the London Stock Exchange.

■ FTSE Gold Mines index

A subsidiary FT equity index tracks the performance of 25 international gold mining companies in Africa (primarily South Africa but also Ashanti in Ghana), Australasia and the Americas (see Figure 6.3). The base value for the Gold Mines index is 1,000 set on the last day of 1992, and the currency basis for the value calculations is US dollars.

■ **Gold mines:** the value of the index at the end of the last two days' trading in London as well as one year ago and the high and low point of the previous 52 weeks. In addition, this index shows the current gross dividend yield and the total return, reflecting both price and dividend performance.

FTSE GOLD MINES INDEX

	Mar 28	% chg on day	Mar 27	Year ago	Gross div yield %	Total return	52 week High	Low
Gold Mines Index (22)	816.34	-0.88	823.61	860.70	2.37	841.63	1231.98	771.32
■ Regional Indices								
Australasia (6)	850.67	-0.32	853.39	1090.95	3.15	886.99	1437.23	819.73
Africa (7)	1066.04	-1.82	1085.77	967.77	4.65	1135.94	1520.93	845.59
Americas (9)	723.96	-0.49	727.50	787.74	1.04	733.40	1135.17	714.95

Fig. 6.3 FTSE Gold Mines index

- **Regional indices:** similar values and yields for the three regional components of the overall Gold Mines index, plus their p/e ratios.

There are three categories of gold mining companies: the "majors" with production of one million ounces of gold per year (around 15 companies); the "independents" with production of over 100,000 ounces a year (around 50 companies); and the "juniors", companies with little or no production but determination to discover some. The two dominant companies, representing more than 40 per cent of the index between them, are Barrick Gold and Anglo Gold. But while the universe of mining stocks worldwide is quite extensive, the total capitalisation of the FTSE Gold Mines index (which includes only companies with production of over 300,000 ounces a year) is small relative to the market capitalisation of leading FTSE 100 companies. Broad criteria for valuing mining companies include the quality, quantity and overall status of a company's production, reserves, management and exploration programme, as well as the political risk of the country in which it is based.

■ FTSE Actuaries share indices

More widely based indices have been developed by the *Financial Times*, the Stock Exchange and the Institute and Faculty of Actuaries. As of November 1995, these have been managed by a joint company, FTSE International. These indices are arithmetically weighted by market capitalisation rather than being based on crude price movements. In other words, the larger a company, the bigger the effect its price movements will have on the index.

The FTSE Actuaries share indices (see Figure 6.4), and notably the All-Share index, are the professional investor's yardstick for the whole UK equity market, for use in analysing investment strategies and as a measure of portfolio performance. There are 39 component indices in the All-Share index relating to different industrial sectors of the market, and nine component indices relating to different levels of capitalisation (including the well-known Footsie). Beyond the All-Share are the new fledgling indices, incorporating companies with a market capitalisation below around £35 million.

FTSE Actuaries Share Indices

Produced in conjunction with the Faculty and Institute of Actuaries

UK series

	£ Stlg Aug 22	Day's chge%	Euro Index	£ Stlg Aug 21	£ Stlg Aug 18	Year ago	Actual yield%	Cover	P/E ratio	Xd adj. ytd	Total Return
FTSE 100	6584.8	+0.7	8483.7	6542.2	6543.7	6322.1	2.03	1.81	27.14	105.61	3033.91
FTSE 250	6886.9	-0.2	8872.9	6903.6	6913.2	6018.1	2.29	1.99	21.91	103.93	3127.51
FTSE 250 ex Inv Co	6919.0	-0.3	8914.3	6942.9	6955.5	6086.0	2.44	2.07	19.80	109.43	3161.77
FTSE 350	3218.5	+0.5	4146.6	3201.7	3202.9	3046.3	2.07	1.84	26.27	51.21	3032.55
FTSE 350 ex Inv Co	3205.7	+0.5	4130.1	3189.1	3190.5	3049.2	2.09	1.85	25.85	51.58	1549.78
FTSE 350 Higher Yield	3117.6	+1.3	4016.6	3077.8	3072.1	3069.7	3.05	1.86	17.60	71.21	2564.29
FTSE 350 Lower Yield	3323.3	-0.3	4281.7	3332.8	3342.1	3016.7	1.01	1.77	55.93	33.74	2500.14
FTSE SmallCap	3456.88	......	4453.74	3455.59	3445.76	2772.51	2.56	1.89	20.65	58.34	3195.16
FTSE SmallCap ex Inv Co	3406.15	-0.1	4388.38	3408.06	3398.07	2753.48	2.72	2.03	18.16	61.47	3192.27
FTSE All-Share	3158.96	+0.5	4069.90	3143.04	3143.84	2965.51	2.09	1.84	25.98	50.37	3021.62
FTSE All-Share ex Inv Co	3145.13	+0.5	4052.09	3129.51	3130.47	2970.87	2.11	1.86	25.47	50.79	1548.47
FTSE All-Share ex Multinational	1079.88	+0.2	1153.12	1077.32	1077.59	-	2.39	1.82	23.06	17.88	1104.40
FTSE Fledgling	2308.60	+0.2	2974.33	2304.59	2296.88	1552.80	2.52	0.48	80.00†	39.99	2718.23
FTSE Fledgling ex Inv Co	2356.72	+0.3	3036.32	2349.24	2339.83	1570.79	2.74	0.44	80.00†	46.32	2796.83
FTSE All-Small	2057.26	+0.1	2650.51	2055.93	2049.88	1579.83	2.55	1.61	24.32	34.83	2426.88
FTSE All-Small ex Inv Co	2074.14	......	2672.26	2073.95	2067.48	1597.59	2.72	1.75	21.03	37.91	2471.57
FTSE AIM	1736.8	+0.3	2237.6	1730.8	1726.1	1108.6	0.42	‡	‡	5.04	1609.88

FTSE Actuaries Industry Sectors

	£ Stlg Aug 22	Day's chge%	Euro Index	£ Stlg Aug 21	£ Stlg Aug 18	Year ago	Actual yield%	Cover	P/E ratio	Xd adj. ytd	Total Return
RESOURCES(14)	6251.83	+1.6	8054.66	6150.87	6145.69	5885.52	2.17	2.23	20.70	114.81	3055.05
Mining(4)	5071.03	+2.7	6533.35	4935.38	4943.95	4831.10	2.65	2.19	17.27	106.01	1732.91
Oil & Gas(10)	7142.88	+1.5	9202.67	7040.55	7031.64	6696.84	2.09	2.24	21.44	127.07	3583.62
BASIC INDUSTRIES(62)	2044.73	-0.4	2634.36	2052.12	2052.11	2458.34	3.73	2.13	12.55	55.34	1303.44
Chemicals(13)	2330.72	-0.4	3002.82	2340.37	2333.36	2718.59	3.96	1.89	13.36	69.05	1307.60
Construction & Bld Matls(47)	1801.60	+0.2	2321.12	1798.56	1801.42	2113.98	3.89	2.60	9.89	49.24	1065.52
Forestry & Paper(1)	8642.11	-1.7	11134.23	8795.53	8539.84	8608.99	5.03	1.64	12.16	480.31	4404.30
Steel & Other Metals(1)	1648.94	-5.8	2124.45	1751.25	1763.29	3302.97	0.00	-	-	‡ 0.00	1147.16
GENERAL INDUSTRIALS(61)	2592.75	-0.6	3340.42	2608.46	2604.26	2315.31	2.98	1.99	16.88	50.19	1633.49
Aerospace & Defence(10)	2414.72	-0.6	3111.05	2430.11	2421.10	2630.63	2.28	2.03	21.53	32.38	1657.68
Diversified Industrials(0)	-	-	-	-	-	-	0.00	-	-	0.00	0.00
Electronic & Elect Equip(20)	8127.59	-0.3	10471.33	8151.33	8169.78	3379.99	2.15	1.98	23.52	107.06	4719.56
Engineering & Machinery(31)	2447.13	-0.9	3152.81	2468.92	2462.21	3015.56	4.84	1.96	10.57	75.09	1723.47
CYCLICAL CONSUMER GOODS(13)	6026.14	-0.8	7763.90	6077.67	6155.12	7064.56	1.80	3.18	17.50	75.44	2499.43
Automobiles(7)	4335.01	-0.9	5585.09	4373.98	4433.06	5111.90	1.40	4.74	15.04	44.55	2479.75
Household Goods & Texts(6)	1992.09	-0.3	2566.55	1998.54	2005.45	2259.11	6.61	‡	‡	71.51	955.89
NON-CYCLICAL CONS GOODS(72)	6158.10	+0.8	7933.90	6106.38	6087.97	5586.10	2.18	1.57	29.23	102.03	2569.20
Beverages(7)	3415.01	-0.2	4399.80	3421.01	3381.32	3567.52	3.55	1.75	16.10	62.81	1436.99
Food Producers & Processors(19)	2834.46	-0.4	3651.83	2844.57	2837.49	3370.72	3.29	1.87	16.23	69.94	1464.46
Health(14)	3172.90	+1.4	4087.86	3129.08	3169.57	2441.78	1.46	2.39	28.65	32.08	2118.39
Packaging(5)	1898.20	-4.0	2445.58	1976.55	2001.93	2235.79	6.31	1.89	8.37	84.68	969.25
Personal Care & Hse Prods(4)	2398.23	+0.2	3089.80	2394.30	2388.84	2398.71	3.28	0.44	69.13	38.49	1093.93
Pharmaceuticals(20)	11980.78	+1.3	15435.66	11830.84	11790.47	9940.77	1.49	1.45	46.43	152.36	4464.77
Tobacco(3)	6031.05	+0.3	7770.22	6012.53	6041.06	6520.90	5.60	1.47	12.10	283.25	1931.17
CYCLICAL SERVICES(224)	4002.88	-1.0	5157.18	4041.51	4046.86	3801.95	1.96	1.61	31.68	57.00	2308.07
Distributors(16)	3035.86	-0.1	3911.31	3031.63	3001.37	2536.76	2.38	1.95	21.59	49.04	1284.12
General Retailers(43)	1633.16	+0.2	2104.12	1630.17	1627.01	2221.94	3.34	1.44	20.86	39.05	1064.29
Leisure Entertmt & Hotels(32)	3504.34	-1.5	4514.88	3558.38	3530.93	3668.74	2.84	1.53	22.92	65.37	2088.67
Media & Photography(46)	7966.68	-1.8	10264.03	8116.62	8153.33	5403.74	1.04	1.46	66.12	60.54	3119.65
Restaurants & Pubs(15)	3202.38	-0.1	4125.84	3199.95	3215.28	3603.21	1.67	1.91	31.42	51.06	1741.18
Support Services(45)	5511.40	-0.9	7100.72	5560.25	5586.60	4713.13	1.67	2.37	25.25	58.07	3755.89
Transport(27)	2961.73	-0.4	3815.80	2974.56	2957.96	3628.38	3.31	1.46	20.74	64.35	1408.11
NON-CYCLICAL SERVICES(23)	4169.99	-1.5	5372.49	4233.40	4257.05	3876.85	1.13	1.39	63.63	31.15	2371.88
Food & Drug Retailers(10)	2870.92	-0.1	3698.80	2873.05	2887.23	2762.36	2.59	1.98	19.49	52.71	2075.65
Telecommunication Services(13)	6600.80	-1.6	8504.27	6711.24	6749.19	6009.22	0.98	1.22	80.00†	41.93	3304.24
UTILITIES(18)	3892.95	-1.2	5015.56	3941.71	3928.34	3794.78	3.58	1.50	18.58	75.14	2014.64
Electricity(8)	3900.78	-1.4	5025.64	3957.42	3943.53	4012.01	3.83	0.97	26.81	80.56	2493.00
Gas Distribution(2)	4466.58	-0.9	5754.61	4506.87	4455.61	3590.16	1.73	2.53	22.84	40.48	2682.52
Water(8)	2550.63	-1.3	3286.15	2585.32	2612.90	2907.38	6.16	1.83	8.88	86.56	1771.05
INFORMATION TECHNOLOGY(69)	3940.92	+1.5	5077.36	3881.11	3898.60	1795.99	0.29	5.99	58.30	8.78	3990.20
Information Tech Hardware(10)	8787.27	+2.2	11321.65	8601.49	8696.50	2225.12	0.34	7.81	37.79	18.18	8882.25
Software & Computer Services(59)	3206.29	+1.0	4130.89	3175.94	3170.60	1747.02	0.24	3.49	80.00†	7.58	3244.67
NON FINANCIALS(556)	3208.62	-0.1	4133.88	3210.29	3213.17	3013.25	1.91	1.80	29.03	45.33	2748.65
FINANCIALS(228)	6266.75	+2.3	8073.89	6123.79	6112.44	5751.41	2.64	1.95	19.44	134.24	3092.51
Banks(11)	9106.96	+3.4	11733.13	8811.37	8750.87	8881.73	2.99	2.13	15.65	242.34	3427.34
Insurance(11)	2564.52	-0.6	3304.04	2579.65	2586.44	2229.80	2.83	0.39	80.00†	54.18	2287.69
Life Assurance(7)	7868.85	+1.8	10137.99	7726.80	7849.65	6952.64	2.64	2.05	17.17	133.63	3711.81
Investment Companies(130)	5681.62	+0.7	7320.02	5639.76	5630.88	4305.13	1.32	1.03	73.18	52.62	2150.04
Real Estate(42)	2104.34	+0.1	2711.16	2102.26	2101.64	2091.20	2.53	1.80	21.90	36.10	1467.91
Speciality & Other Finance(27)	5959.20	+2.3	7677.65	5823.18	5793.74	4247.14	1.55	2.52	25.65	52.83	3806.15

■ Hourly movements	8.03	9.00	10.00	11.00	12.00	13.00	14.00	15.00	16.10	High/day	Low/day
FTSE 100	6533.4	6556.3	6548.9	6553.7	6561.0	6574.2	6579.6	6572.2	6594.2	6605.2	6529.2
FTSE 250	6907.2	6901.6	6903.0	6904.3	6901.3	6905.1	6900.0	6894.9	6897.1	6910.3	6886.9
FTSE SmallCap	3456.37	3456.87	3455.57	3455.24	3455.83	3456.22	3457.05	3456.76	3456.86	3457.58	3454.36
FTSE All-Share	3139.81	3148.55	3145.68	3147.63	3150.37	3155.82	3157.70	3154.43	3163.30	3167.07	3138.70

Time of FTSE 100 Day's high: 15:56:45 Day's low: 8:04:30. FTSE 100 2000 High: 6738.5 (24/03/00) Low: 5994.6 (17/04/00)
Time of FTSE All-Share Day's high: 15:57:00 Day's low: 8:35:00. FTSE All-Share 2000 High: 3195.29 (24/03/00) Low: 2852.60 (17/04/00)

Further information is available on http://www.ftse.com. © FTSE International Limited 2000. All Rights Reserved. 'FTSE', 'FT-SE' and 'Footsie' are trade marks of the London Stock Exchange and The Financial Times and are used by FTSE International under license. † Sector P/E ratios greater than 80 are not shown. ‡ Values are negative. **Deletion:** Blagden (SmallCap).

FTSE

Fig. 6.4 FTSE Actuaries share indices (daily)

Reading the figures

- **FTSE 100:** the Footsie index was started with a base of 1,000 in January 1984 to fill a gap in the market. At that time, the FT 30 index was calculated only hourly, and there was demand for a constantly updated – or real-time – index in view of both the competition from overseas and the needs of the new traded options and financial futures markets. For most purposes, the Footsie has replaced the FT 30. The index, amended quarterly, includes the 100 largest UK companies in terms of market capitalisation – the blue chips – and represents over 78 per cent of total UK market capitalisation.

- **FTSE 250:** an index of the next 250 companies by market capitalisation, those directly beneath the FTSE 100. These are companies capitalised at between £350 million and £3 billion, in total around 14 per cent of overall market capitalisation. It is calculated two ways, one that includes and one that excludes investment companies.

- **FTSE 350:** the combination of the FTSE 100 and the FTSE 250, again calculated both including and excluding investment companies.

- **FTSE 350 Higher and Lower Yield:** these two indices, introduced at the beginning of 1995, are calculated by a quarterly descending ranking of the 350 companies by the size of their annual dividend yield, and then their division into two equal halves as measured by total capitalisation of the 350 companies.

- **FTSE SmallCap:** the 450-plus companies capitalised at up to £350 million, which when added to the 350 make up the All-Share index. Like the 250 and 350, this index is calculated two ways.

- **FTSE All-Share index:** 800-plus companies with a total market capitalisation of about £1,732 billion in 2000, 98 per cent of total UK market capitalisation. Introduced on a daily basis in 1962, it is far more representative than the FT index. Its mathematical structure makes it a reliable yardstick against which to measure portfolio performance, and hence it represents an essential tool for professional investment managers.

- **FTSE Fledgling:** another index launched at the beginning of 1995, this was introduced to indicate the Stock Exchange's concern for smaller companies. It includes the over 700 companies that fail to qualify for the All-Share index (including shares quoted on the AIM), representing 1–2 per cent of total market capitalisation. It is calculated two ways, one that includes and one that excludes investment companies.

- **FTSE All-Small and FTSE AIM:** the former combines the SmallCap and Fledgling indices; the latter is an index of all AIM-listed companies, around 460 in late 2000, with a total market capitalisation of £15 billion.

- **Industry sectors:** aggregate performance measures for key industrial sectors, providing investors with a valuable yardstick for assessing the performance of a stock relative to its sector. The group comprises nine sectors, each of which is further broken down into various sub-sectors. The sub-sectors are broken down into their constituent companies in the London share service.

■ **Non-financials:** formerly known as the FT "500", this includes all companies except financial and property companies and investment companies.

■ **Financials:** financial and property companies broken down into six sub-sectors including investment companies (see Chapter 10).

■ **All indices:** the UK Series lists yesterday's closing value for each index as well as the percentage change on the previous day, the index's value in euros, the two previous days' closing values and the value of the index one year ago. The further performance indicators of actual yield, cover and price/earnings ratio for each index are also provided. Sector values for these ratios can be used as benchmarks for the performance of individual stocks within a sector. No p/e ratios greater than 80 are allowed, since such ratios tend to result from the distortions of loss-making companies, notably in the TMT sectors.

■ **Ex-dividend adjustment year to date:** when a share goes ex-dividend, all else being equal, its price will drop by the amount of the dividend per share. This is the ex-dividend adjustment. The figure in the indices is the cumulative total of the aggregate of the gross ex-dividend adjustments multiplied by the relevant number of shares in issue. It allows the investor to assess the flow of income on a portfolio over the year.

■ **Total return:** calculated at the close of each trading day, total return figures reflect both the price and dividend performance of stocks. The index starts the year at 1,000 and incorporates share price appreciation for the year plus ex-dividend adjustment year to date, assuming that dividends are reinvested.

■ **Hourly movements:** the values of the key indices at hourly intervals throughout the previous day's trading, plus their highs and lows for the day. These are what are known as intra-day values.

Using the information

The Footsie is calculated every 15 seconds from the price movements of the 100 largest UK companies by market capitalisation. Since it incorporates fewer companies than the All-Share index, it can be calculated more rapidly and frequently. The Footsie was the first real-time index in the UK and was introduced mainly as a basis for dealing in equity index options and futures (see Chapter 14). It rapidly became a key indicator of the stock market's mood, not least because it is quoted widely throughout the day. In many respects, the market thinks in terms of the Footsie figures with particular points being seen as psychological watersheds.

The blue chip FTSE 100 constituents (listed in Appendix 2) are mostly multinationals and companies with strong overseas interests, while the FTSE 250 are mainly strongly UK orientated companies. As a result, the former are likely to be more influenced by overseas factors such as exchange rate movements, while the latter may be influenced more by domestic factors such as interest rate movements. Membership of both indices is reviewed every quarter as market caps rise and fall. For the FTSE 100, any share that is 90th or higher automatically joins the index; 111th or lower means automatic relegation.

The FTSE All-Share accurately reflects the whole market. With over 800 constituents, it has a very broad coverage, encompassing 98 per cent of the market's aggregate capitalisation, with each company weighted according to its market value so that a move in the price of a large company has more effect than that of a small one. It can be used as a measure of the market's performance over long periods. It serves as a reliable yardstick against which to assess portfolio performance. As a weighted arithmetic index it is designed to behave as an actual portfolio would behave.

The breakdown into industry groups allows investors to track the performance of particular sectors. This is of great assistance to specialist sector analysts, as well as allowing more general investors to improve their understanding of the structure of the market as a whole. Industrial classification is highly important since it is normally accepted by the stock market and institutional research departments as the basis for the analysis of companies. Correctly classifying all companies traded on the London market is the responsibility of the FTSE Actuaries Industry Classification Committee, made up of market practitioners, investment managers and actuaries.

Over time, as the structure of UK industry has shifted, it has been necessary to amalgamate sectors and create new ones. For example, Radio and TV, Teas and Diamonds have gone, while Health, Media and Photography, and Electricity have been formed. When a new group is created, its initial value is set at the level of its immediate predecessor. In 1999, FTSE International introduced the Global Industry Classification System, allowing comparison across national boundaries as well as across sectors and sub-sectors. There are three levels of classification: economic group, for example, resources; industry sector, for example, oil and gas; and industry sub-sector, for example, oil services or oil integrated.

Institutional investors attempt to beat the index most relevant to their portfolio. Increasingly, investors want a set of indices that covers the entire equity capital structure of the UK market so that they can accurately assess the performance of large, medium and small companies within the framework of the whole market. There has also been a growing interest in the performance of medium-sized companies. The newer indices increase the visibility of many medium and small companies.

The FTSE 350 provides a real-time measure covering around 90 per cent of the UK equity market by value. The SmallCap and Fledgling indices are higher risk but likely to boom in a recovery. They are good for the visibility and marketability of smaller companies. Beyond the markets covered by the All-Share and Fledgling indices is Ofex, an unregulated off-exchange dealing facility for companies not eligible for the AIM or the index. It is offered by the broker JP Jenkins Ltd, with daily share information published in the FT.

The differentiation between Higher Yield and Lower Yield companies in the FT 350 is an interesting reflection of the decreasing importance of dividends as part of the rewards to investors. Indeed, many of the market's hottest stocks pay no dividends at all. Companies normally have relatively high yields because investors expect their share prices to perform relatively badly. There are three main types of high yielding stocks: stodgy companies like utilities that chug along but are unlikely to produce fireworks; companies in decline that are overdistributing their earnings; and recovery shares that may or may not make it back. The Low Yield index comprises the market's darlings, companies that are expected to streak ahead of the pack.

■ Market at a glance

A snapshot of recent price and trading activity in the equities market is provided by the graphs and key indicators published daily on the back page of the newspaper's second section (see Figure 6.5):

■ **FTSE 100 and All-Share indices:** these provide investors with an instant overview of movements in the UK equity market over several months. The FTSE 100 charts also show movements over the past five working days and hourly for the previous day. Graphs featuring the performances of individual share prices relative to the All-Share index or the Footsie also appear frequently in the newspaper, usually linked to a news item or comment in the Lex column. These "price relatives" are very valuable for comparing share performances and for assessing individual price patterns independent of overall market movements.

■ **Equity shares traded:** the volume of shares traded over the same period, excluding intra-market and overseas turnover.

■ **Indices, ratios and sectors:** easy reference for a number of leading market indices and ratios, plus the five best and worst performing sectors and their percentage rises and falls. These include the FTSE non-financials price/earnings ratio, calculated separately from the full index, since banks often trade on a different basis from the rest of the market; the yield ratio, which measures the relationship between the returns on government bonds and equities (see Chapter 11); and two FTSE techMARK indices.

The techMARK is the London Stock Exchange market for innovative technology companies, designed to meet the supposedly unique requirements of technology companies – from those already listed on London's markets to those thinking about a flotation. The market was launched in November 1999 with over 190 companies from across the main market. The intention is: "To create a new dimension to the relationship between companies and investors, bringing innovative companies higher visibility and profile and showing investors exactly where to look for them". It is a part of a growing band of small, highly specialised European stock markets, designed to feed growing investor appetite for technology plays.

■ Highs, lows and base dates

Saturday's edition of the *Financial Times* carries an expanded table of the FTSE Actuaries All-Share index (see Figure 6.6), which shows:

■ **Highs and lows:** the highs and lows for each index both for the current year and for the whole period since it was launched. The latter are loosely termed "all-time" highs and lows.

■ **Equity section or group, base date and value:** details of the launch date and base value for each index.

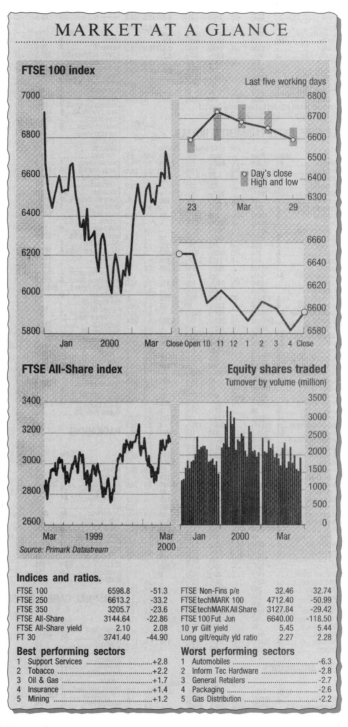

Fig. 6.5 Market at a glance

FTSE Actuaries Share Indices — UK Series

Produced in conjunction with the Faculty and Institute of Actuaries

	£ Stlg Mar 17	Day's chge%	Euro Index	£ Stlg Mar 16	Year ago	Actual yld%	Cover	P/E ratio	Xd adj. ytd	Total Return	1999/00 High		1999/00 Low		Since Compilation High		Since Compilation Low	
FTSE 100	6558.0	......	8273.3	6557.2	6114.3	2.07	1.64	29.45	41.66	2991.53	**6930.2**	30/12/99	**5770.2**	10/2/99	**6930.2**	30/12/99	**986.9**	23/7/84
FTSE 250	6565.8	+0.7	8283.2	6517.4	5463.3	2.39	1.97	21.28	26.32	2946.16	**6838.9**	6/3/00	**4829.1**	22/1/99	**6838.9**	6/3/00	**1379.4**	21/1/86
FTSE 250 ex Inv Co	6580.4	+0.7	8301.7	6534.0	5509.8	2.51	2.03	19.57	26.92	2969.11	**6888.5**	6/3/00	**4834.1**	22/1/99	**6888.5**	6/3/00	**1378.3**	21/1/86
FTSE 350	3185.5	+0.1	4018.7	3181.7	2917.5	2.12	1.69	27.86	19.11	2970.69	**3327.0**	30/12/99	**2749.0**	14/1/99	**3327.0**	30/12/99	**664.5**	14/1/86
FTSE 350 ex Inv Co	3176.2	+0.1	4007.0	3172.8	2923.9	2.14	1.70	27.50	19.30	1519.69	**3324.4**	30/12/99	**2754.9**	14/1/99	**3324.4**	30/12/99	**2211.6**	3/6/97
FTSE 350 Higher Yield	2614.0	-1.3	3297.7	2648.9	2814.0	3.67	1.53	17.82	26.59	2116.78	**3166.5**	6/7/99	**2410.9**	22/2/00	**3166.5**	6/7/99	**674.2**	14/1/86
FTSE 350 Lower Yield	3707.4	+1.0	4677.2	3672.1	3019.6	1.23	1.97	41.14	13.21	2772.36	**3843.1**	6/3/00	**2837.6**	10/8/99	**3843.1**	6/3/00	**669.6**	20/1/86
FTSE SmallCap	3410.33	+1.0	4302.36	3375.77	2373.81	2.20	1.82	25.04	9.27	3105.55	**3565.73**	10/3/00	**2082.76**	4/1/99	**3565.73**	10/3/00	**1363.79**	31/12/92
FTSE SmallCap ex Inv Co	3367.48	+1.0	4248.30	3334.96	2344.62	2.29	1.95	22.46	8.37	3104.93	**3542.40**	10/3/00	**2039.63**	4/1/99	**3542.40**	10/3/00	**1363.79**	31/12/92
FTSE All-Share	3126.18	+0.2	3943.89	3121.09	2825.40	2.12	1.70	27.71	18.26	2959.08	**3242.06**	30/12/99	**2654.62**	14/1/99	**3242.06**	30/12/99	**61.92**	13/12/74
FTSE All-Share ex Inv Co	3116.06	+0.1	3931.12	3111.61	2835.42	2.15	1.71	27.24	18.46	1517.99	**3239.87**	30/12/99	**2664.30**	14/1/99	**3239.87**	30/12/99	**2172.42**	4/6/97
FTSE All-Share ex Multinational	1119.87	......	1170.94	1119.67		2.37	1.82	23.14	5.56	1132.12	**1160.20**	6/3/00	**939.22**	22/9/99	**1160.20**	6/3/00	**939.22**	22/9/99
FTSE Fledgling	2389.96	+0.7	3015.10	2373.40	1293.69	2.52	0.47	80.00†	11.47	2777.82	**2463.91**	10/3/00	**1152.50**	4/1/99	**2463.91**	10/3/00	**31.14**	12/12/94
FTSE Fledgling ex Inv Co	2478.13	+0.7	3126.33	2460.05	1306.40	2.79	0.42	80.00†	13.29	2898.29	**2554.54**	10/3/00	**1157.28**	4/1/99	**2554.54**	10/3/00	**26.13**	12/12/94
FTSE All-Small	2048.67	+1.0	2584.53	2029.15	1344.67	2.26	1.53	28.88	6.36	2381.94	**2136.34**	10/3/00	**1183.45**	4/1/99	**2136.34**	10/3/00	**991.35**	23/11/98
FTSE All-Small ex Inv Co	2072.86	+0.9	2615.06	2053.66	1353.75	2.37	1.65	25.61	6.14	2430.79	**2173.23**	10/3/00	**1181.76**	4/1/99	**2173.23**	10/3/00	**986.74**	23/11/98
FTSE AIM	2537.1	+1.3	3200.7	2503.4	847.1	0.32	‡	‡	1.35	2347.14	**2924.9**	3/3/00	**801.5**	4/1/99	**2924.9**	3/3/00	**761.3**	14/10/98
FTSE Actuaries Industry Sectors																		
RESOURCES(15)	5355.78	-2.0	6756.68	5465.64	4703.19	2.45	1.21	33.70	26.38	2576.58	**6230.56**	17/12/99	**3703.17**	29/1/99	**6230.56**	17/12/99	**980.20**	19/2/86
Mining(4)	4281.64	-3.2	5401.58	4424.33	3220.98	2.81	2.04	17.40	45.19	1443.17	**6009.35**	7/1/00	**2608.07**	8/1/99	**6009.35**	7/1/00	**1000.00**	31/12/85
Oil & Gas(11)	6124.36	-1.8	7726.30	6235.40	5490.63	2.38	1.03	40.80	23.76	3024.01	**6992.50**	15/7/99	**4294.14**	29/1/99	**6992.50**	15/7/99	**982.30**	20/2/86
BASIC INDUSTRIES(68)	2012.32	+0.1	2538.68	2011.26	1983.79	4.11	1.74	14.01	19.32	1260.62	**2489.49**	13/8/99	**1678.48**	22/1/99	**2489.49**	13/8/99	**986.10**	14/1/86
Chemicals(16)	2342.51	-0.7	2955.23	2358.75	2072.54	3.70	1.49	18.17	29.44	1292.16	**2804.37**	13/8/99	**1717.62**	19/1/99	**3165.53**	15/5/98	**979.50**	14/1/86
Construction & Bld Matls(49)	1712.37	+1.5	2160.27	1687.83	1781.66	3.96	2.40	10.50	12.63	992.06	**2138.81**	6/9/99	**1416.03**	22/1/99	**2393.22**	24/1/94	**954.80**	9/9/92
Forestry & Paper(2)	5776.07	+4.3	7286.91	5539.02	4703.19	5.70	0.91	19.20	183.71	2849.09	**8802.72**	20/8/99	**3703.17**	29/1/99	**8802.72**	20/8/99	**980.20**	19/2/86
Steel & Other Metals(1)	2629.88	-8.4	3317.78	2870.61	2410.82	6.41	‡	‡	0.00	1829.60	**4194.57**	7/1/00	**2092.78**	25/1/99	**4194.57**	7/1/00	**962.80**	10/11/87
GENERAL INDUSTRIALS(68)	2385.86	-0.4	3009.92	2396.58	1983.79	2.99	2.04	16.37	16.88	1483.08	**2640.57**	10/1/00	**1678.48**	22/1/99	**2640.57**	10/1/00	**986.10**	14/1/86
Aerospace & Defence(9)	2043.43	+2.8	2577.93	1988.58	2410.82	2.60	2.07	18.53	16.50	1392.30	**2697.04**	4/5/99	**1716.37**	10/3/00	**3336.87**	11/5/98	**962.80**	10/11/87
Diversified Industrials(2)	1547.62	+0.4	1952.42	1541.16	1038.86	1.75	2.31	24.73	0.00	1005.67	**1547.62**	17/3/00	**988.96**	10/3/99	**2231.57**	2/2/94	**950.29**	10/9/98
Electronic & Elect Equip(22)	8117.67	+0.7	10240.99	8061.56	3053.88	1.05	2.10	45.49	12.62	4656.78	**8744.33**	10/3/00	**2687.60**	4/1/99	**8744.33**	10/3/00	**986.80**	29/9/86
Engineering & Machinery(35)	2217.16	-3.3	2797.09	2292.52	2410.82	4.29	2.02	11.57	20.53	1525.91	**3087.26**	16/8/99	**2065.77**	13/3/00	**3336.87**	11/5/98	**962.80**	10/11/87
CYCLICAL CONSUMER GOODS(15)	5870.58	+0.5	7406.14	5842.64	5800.56	1.82	2.88	19.04	3.94	2406.32	**7281.89**	4/8/99	**5061.80**	15/2/00	**7281.89**	4/8/99	**967.50**	14/1/86
Automobiles(7)	4247.27	+0.5	5358.22	4225.71	4436.24	1.26	4.96	15.96	0.81	2405.35	**5324.61**	4/8/99	**3360.84**	4/1/99	**5324.61**	4/8/99	**995.60**	14/1/86
Household Goods & Texts(8)	1854.03	+0.2	2338.98	1850.92	2016.09	7.23	‡	‡	9.92	863.84	**2378.38**	9/9/99	**1639.24**	11/2/00	**3704.44**	24/4/98	**927.10**	21/1/86
NON-CYCLICAL CONS GOODS(72)	5338.67	-1.5	6735.10	5418.10	5800.56	2.36	1.56	27.07	55.19	2209.55	**6538.52**	8/1/99	**4599.68**	14/2/00	**6535.52**	8/1/99	**967.50**	14/1/86
Beverages(7)	2744.19	-1.8	3461.98	2794.00	3647.68	3.55	1.99	14.17	34.35	1145.11	**4019.24**	16/6/99	**2486.92**	10/3/00	**4249.01**	20/7/98	**967.50**	14/1/86
Food Producers & Processors(21)	2576.76	-2.7	3250.76	2648.62	3341.54	3.52	1.98	14.39	20.10	1308.00	**3891.73**	6/1/99	**2232.61**	11/2/00	**4423.56**	8/6/98	**946.10**	14/1/86
Health(13)	2676.49	-0.3	3376.57	2683.52	2501.16	1.83	1.93	28.39	0.44	1765.26	**3074.35**	7/3/00	**2229.46**	10/2/00	**3074.35**	7/3/00	**972.60**	21/1/86
Packaging(6)	1924.84	+0.5	2428.32	1915.70	1750.72	6.88	1.83	7.92	9.82	946.12	**2308.89**	12/1/00	**1459.44**	5/1/99	**3142.02**	11/7/95	**973.30**	14/1/86
Personal Care & Hse Prods(4)	1823.52	+5.9	2300.50	1721.71	2016.09	4.27	0.23	80.00†	1.23	814.45	**2536.55**	30/7/99	**1356.23**	8/3/00	**3704.44**	24/4/98	**927.10**	21/1/86
Pharmaceuticals(18)	10600.36	-1.6	13373.07	10776.98	10484.73	1.66	1.38	43.90	96.90	3931.34	**12075.49**	8/1/99	**8587.25**	24/2/00	**12075.49**	8/1/99	**953.70**	13/1/86
Tobacco(3)	4347.01	+1.0	5484.05	4301.99	6676.98	6.81	1.46	10.06	187.17	1368.80	**8051.85**	18/1/99	**3470.43**	13/3/00	**8051.85**	18/1/99	**992.00**	9/1/86
CYCLICAL SERVICES(230)	4159.82	+0.5	5247.89	4137.13	3775.08	2.11	1.70	27.89	13.16	2372.39	**4465.91**	6/3/00	**3320.27**	18/10/99	**4465.91**	6/3/00	**944.90**	23/1/86
Distributors(19)	2915.73	+0.6	3678.40	2899.33	1950.73	2.59	1.77	21.80	7.40	1214.93	**3030.30**	9/3/00	**1740.69**	21/1/99	**3319.33**	2/2/94	**988.50**	21/1/86
General Retailers(42)	1669.31	-1.8	2105.95	1700.72	2316.83	4.11	1.19	20.49	4.40	1066.22	**2566.47**	14/4/99	**1603.72**	10/2/00	**2566.47**	14/4/99	**870.10**	9/12/88
Leisure Entertmt & Hotels(35)	3782.98	+1.5	4772.48	3728.70	3862.62	2.08	2.23	21.53	33.15	2234.83	**4175.93**	19/4/99	**2988.96**	8/2/00	**4195.54**	9/6/98	**975.40**	21/1/86
Media & Photography(48)	9241.57	+1.8	11658.86	9074.94	5161.31	0.87	1.51	75.83	21.12	3601.53	**10524.02**	6/3/00	**4254.83**	4/1/99	**10524.02**	6/3/00	**976.20**	9/1/86
Rests, Pubs & Breweries(16)	2917.07	-1.6	3680.08	2965.11	3785.82	3.64	1.99	13.82	13.59	1568.03	**4075.84**	5/5/99	**2665.10**	15/2/00	**4441.58**	9/6/98	**962.00**	14/1/86
Support Services(42)	5071.70	-0.3	6398.29	5088.99	5116.66	1.76	2.73	20.83	2.86	3419.79	**5837.38**	18/1/00	**4399.66**	28/5/99	**5837.38**	18/1/00	**939.00**	1/2/91
Transport(28)	2527.21	+0.2	3188.25	2523.06	3562.31	3.79	1.68	15.70	9.56	1177.58	**3807.97**	16/6/99	**2408.73**	16/2/00	**4127.07**	17/7/98	**960.00**	14/1/86
NON-CYCLICAL SERVICES(22)	5905.65	+3.2	7450.38	5724.55	3775.08	0.81	1.45	80.00†	2.30	3338.40	**6335.49**	6/3/00	**3495.09**	4/1/99	**6335.49**	6/3/00	**944.90**	23/1/86
Food & Drug Retailers(10)	2341.33	-3.2	2953.75	2419.07	2365.71	3.47	1.74	16.62	0.99	1660.88	**2999.16**	6/9/99	**2159.34**	28/2/00	**3251.85**	6/7/98	**917.40**	21/1/86
Telecommunication Services(12)	9760.10	+3.6	12313.02	9423.32	5790.26	0.65	1.36	80.00†	3.84	4860.46	**10538.08**	6/3/00	**5599.48**	4/1/99	**10538.08**	6/3/00	**802.50**	3/10/86
UTILITIES(17)	3253.96	-2.5	4105.09	3336.61	3711.89	4.52	1.85	11.98	13.85	1656.10	**4365.30**	18/1/99	**2863.58**	14/2/00	**4497.64**	23/11/98	**802.50**	3/10/86
Electricity(7)	3433.31	-1.5	4331.35	3483.92	4136.34	4.78	1.62	12.93	23.97	2160.17	**5062.92**	18/1/99	**2935.16**	7/2/00	**5062.92**	18/1/99	**995.30**	7/1/91
Gas Distribution(2)	3591.62	-5.1	4531.08	3783.88	3105.10	2.15	2.45	18.95	0.00	2135.44	**3861.52**	9/3/00	**2925.78**	14/2/00	**3861.52**	9/3/00	**994.90**	9/12/86
Water(8)	1990.83	-0.4	2511.57	1998.42	2969.97	8.07	1.92	6.46	8.98	1338.43	**3444.30**	4/1/99	**1803.00**	8/2/00	**3814.45**	1/10/98	**924.70**	1/5/90
INFORMATION TECHNOLOGY(56)	4570.04	+0.3	5765.41	4554.84	1813.11	0.17	5.43	80.00†	2.46	4618.87	**5435.04**	6/3/00	**1476.04**	4/1/99	**5435.04**	6/3/00	**990.67**	8/10/98
Information Tech Hardware(6)	7581.26	......	9564.27	7582.81	1813.11	0.15	6.85	80.00†	0.50	7644.65	**9004.14**	6/3/00	**1476.04**	4/1/99	**9004.14**	6/3/00	**990.67**	8/10/98
Software & Computer Services(50)	4566.94	+0.5	5761.51	4542.83	1813.11	0.18	4.78	80.00†	3.67	4616.01	**5435.32**	6/3/00	**1476.04**	4/1/99	**5435.32**	6/3/00	**990.67**	8/10/98
NON FINANCIALS(563)	3345.88	+0.4	4221.06	3333.92	2852.22	1.89	1.62	32.65	13.80	2838.03	**3421.63**	10/3/00	**2722.86**	22/1/99	**3421.63**	10/3/00	**63.49**	13/12/74
FINANCIALS(230)	5146.20	-0.6	6492.28	5177.04	5576.93	3.05	1.89	17.40	63.86	2507.75	**6233.96**	31/3/99	**4708.69**	22/2/00	**6233.96**	31/3/99	**972.20**	23/1/86
Banks(11)	7349.06	-1.5	9271.33	7459.30	8701.69	3.48	1.92	14.99	132.92	2729.12	**9862.10**	30/4/99	**6567.57**	22/2/00	**9862.10**	30/4/99	**950.60**	23/1/86
Insurance(12)	1757.63	-0.1	2217.36	1760.08	2300.98	4.17	1.59	15.04	34.60	1551.40	**2447.72**	6/1/99	**1538.38**	13/3/00	**2859.97**	9/4/98	**870.90**	25/8/92
Life Assurance(9)	6725.68	-0.4	8484.90	6751.58	6636.68	3.01	2.29	14.54	24.25	3124.19	**8089.08**	2/2/99	**6121.47**	15/2/00	**8089.08**	2/2/99	**967.70**	23/1/86
Investment Companies(126)	5410.51	+0.8	6825.72	5365.36	3834.36	1.39	1.09	65.80	16.09	2033.37	**5481.15**	14/3/00	**3588.08**	13/1/99	**5481.15**	14/3/00	**977.20**	14/1/86
Real Estate(43)	1708.06	+0.8	2154.84	1693.84	1874.21	3.07	1.70	19.21	5.03	1172.27	**2130.88**	9/7/99	**1577.88**	16/2/00	**2431.05**	19/3/98	**718.40**	16/9/92
Speciality & Other Finance(29)	4750.92	+1.5	5993.61	4680.53	4357.93	1.79	2.46	22.65	13.06	3009.13	**4880.14**	7/3/00	**3552.27**	5/1/99	**5215.06**	15/4/98	**856.30**	1/10/90

Year ago figure is based on the most appropriate sector from the pre-April 1999 classification system. For details please see the FTSE website, address below.

■ **Hourly movements**	**8.03**	**9.00**	**10.00**	**11.00**	**12.00**	**13.00**	**14.00**	**15.00**	**16.10**	**High/day**	**Low/day**
FTSE 100	6655.3	6676.7	6629.9	6571.0	6548.9	6555.6	6510.8	6531.3	6588.3	6713.1	6504.1
FTSE 250	6576.5	6618.4	6613.4	6606.9	6594.2	6582.7	6573.4	6551.7	6569.4	6623.4	6547.2
FTSE SmallCap	3401.35	3407.21	3411.07	3412.43	3411.54	3411.40	3409.88	3405.65	3407.90	3413.53	3401.35
FTSE All-Share	3164.07	3175.40	3157.19	3134.06	3124.61	3126.44	3108.46	3114.71	3138.01	3187.73	3105.50

Time of FTSE 100 High: 8:22:30 Low: 14:10:15
Time of FTSE All-Share High: 8:23:00 Low: 14:10:00

Equity section or group	Base date	Base value	Equity section or group	Base date	Base value	Equity section or group	Base date	Base value	Equity section or group	Base date	Base value
FTSE 100	31/12/83	1000.00	FTSE 350 Lower Yield	31/12/85	682.94	FTSE Fledgling	30/12/94	1000.00	FTSE Fledg ex Inv Tr Total Ret	30/12/94	1000.00
FTSE 250 & ex Inv Tr	31/12/85	1412.60	FTSE All-Share	10/4/62	100.00	FTSE Fledgling ex Inv Tr	30/12/94	1000.00	FTSE AIM Total Return	12/5/97	1000.00
FTSE 350	31/12/85	682.94	FTSE All-Share ex Inv Tr	12/5/97	2208.01	FTSE AIM	30/12/94	1000.00	FTSE 350 ex Inv Tr Total Return	12/5/97	1000.00
FTSE 350 ex Inv Tr	12/5/97	2247.50	All Other Headline	31/12/85	1000.00	FTSE Total Return Indices	31/12/92	1000.00	FTSE All-Share ex Inv Tr Ttl Retn	12/5/97	1000.00
FTSE 350 Higher Yield	31/12/85	682.94	FTSE SmallCap & ex Inv Tr	31/12/92	1363.79	FTSE Fledgling Total Ret	30/12/94	1000.00			

Further information is available on http://www.ftse.com. © FTSE International Limited 2000. All Rights reserved. 'FTSE', 'FT-SE' and 'Footsie' are trade marks of the London Stock Exchange and The Financial Times and are used by FTSE International under license. † Sector P/E ratios greater than 80 and net covers greater than 30 are not shown. ‡ Values are negative. **Deletions:** Druid Group (FTSE 250); Gerrad Group (FTSE 250); Meristen (Fledgling); **Promotion:** Brewin Dolphin Holding from FTSE SmallCap to FTSE 250; IMS Group from FTSE SmallCap to FTSE 250.

FTSE INTERNATIONAL

Fig. 6.6 FTSE Actuaries share indices (weekly)

Leaders and laggards

Saturday's newspaper also includes leaders and laggards, a table of notable performances, either good or bad, listing percentage changes in value in the current year for various indices and sectors (see Figure 6.7):

FTSE – LEADERS & LAGGARDS

Percentage changes since December 30 1999 based on Friday March 17 2000

Electronic & Elect .... +35.79	Non-Cyc Cons Goods .... +1.15	Automobiles .... -10.13
Media & Photography ...... +28.26	Electricity .... -0.78	Aerospace & Defence .... -10.81
Software & Comp Serv .... +22.83	Non Financials .... -0.78	Basic Industries .... -11.10
Diversified Indstrls .... +14.97	FTSE All-Share .... -3.57	Resources .... -11.94
FTSE SmallCap .... +10.09	Utilities .... -5.10	Financials .... -12.24
Leisure Ent & Hotels .... +6.64	Chemicals .... -5.22	Res Pubs & Breweries ...... -12.69
Information Tech .... +6.19	FTSE 100 .... -5.37	Water .... -12.71
Telecoms Services .... +6.14	Tobacco .... -5.65	Beverages .... -13.37
Pharmaceuticals .... +5.68	Gas Distribution .... -6.71	General Retailers .... -14.05
Distributors .... +5.29	Food Prods & Process .... -8.06	Inform Tec Hardware .... -14.43
Health .... +5.03	Oil & Gas .... -8.43	Banks .... -15.51
Investment Companies ...... +5.00	General Industries .... -8.45	Life Assurance .... -16.12
Non-Cyclical Service .... +4.83	Packaging .... -8.69	Insurance .... -18.62
Personal Care .... +3.90	Cyclical Cons Goods .... -9.14	Eng & Machinery .... -20.15
Cyclical Services .... +3.21	Food & Drug Retailer .... -9.31	Transport .... -20.89
Speciality & Oth Fin .... +2.85	Support Services .... -9.51	Mining .... -27.00
FTSE 250 .... +1.88	Real Estate .... -9.59	Forestry & Paper .... -27.63
Household Gds & Text ...... +1.80	Const & Building Mat .... -9.93	Steel & Other Metals .... -32.14

Fig. 6.7 FTSE leaders and laggards

- **Index:** the percentage changes in the year in various detailed markets and subsections of the FTSE Actuaries indices. Based on the preceding Friday's closing prices, FT and sector indices are ranked in order of percentage increase in value in the current year to date.

Capped indices

Institutional investors use indices for two reasons: benchmarking and derivative trading. The benchmark index is used for performance measurement, analysing and structuring asset allocation decisions, analysing and managing portfolio risks, as well as being used for a range of stock, sector and market analysis. It often determines the universe within which the fund manager may invest, and holdings in stocks comparative to their weightings within the index determines the level of risk being taken in order to outperform the index. An indexed fund that holds all stock in the index at their index weightings offers the least risk; while an active manager investing in stocks outside the index or concentrated in a small number of stocks heavily overweighted relative to the index offers a much higher risk.

Indexing has become a popular investment strategy. But following Vodafone's takeover of Mannesmann in 2000, its weighting became more than 10 per cent of the FTSE 100 index. And since UK and European Union legislation forbids managers of unit trusts from holding more than 10 per cent in any one stock, it became clear that it was unfair to ask index trackers to measure up against an index that they were not actually allowed to replicate.

The Vodafone deal, combined with other recent and imminent cross-border "mega-mergers", has resulted in a declining number of large companies accounting for an increasingly large proportion of the indices. Investors with funds focused on a single market have become increasingly concerned about the higher levels of risk that such market concentration causes and have been examining the options available to reduce that risk. The long-term solution is to move away from highly concentrated domestic indices to more diversified international indices, and this is beginning to happen (see Chapter 9). In the meantime, the alternative is to cap the weighting of the largest companies in an index and that is what FTSE International has done by introducing capped versions of the FTSE 100 and All-Share indices. These cap indices limit any single stock to an index weighting of 10 per cent.

Monthly averages and private investor's indices

A monthly FT table shows monthly averages for a range of indices over the past four months plus the highest and lowest closing values for the FTSE 100, FTSE 250, FTSE 350, FTSE All-Share and FT 30 in the previous month (see Figure 6.8).

MONTHLY AVERAGES OF STOCK INDICES

	June	May	April	March
FTSE Actuaries Indices				
FTSE 100	6455.1	6210.2	6312.7	6541.5
FTSE 250	6514.7	6227.5	6236	6639.7
FTSE 350	3138.7	3017.1	3060.2	3183.9
FTSE Non-Financial	3218.62	3093.98	3156.97	3351.59
FTSE Financial Group	5532.84	5319.48	5267.23	5109.08
FTSE All-Share	3078.46	2959.31	3000.1	3126.1
FTSE Eurotop 100	3776.47	3732.90	3751.61	3811.93
FTSE Eurotop 300	1613.90	1607.47	1598.89	1624.77
FTSE World	371.04	358.52	371.79	374.23
FTSE Indices				
FTSE Govt Securities	105.49	104.55	105.1	104.66
FT Fixed Interest	142.37	142.08	143.3	144.63
FT 30	3705.1	3635.4	3638.8	3667.7
FTSE Gold Mines	815.95	797.67	780.45	834.2
SEAQ Bargains (5.00pm)	94,184	98,628	115,036	142,635

	Highest close June	Lowest close June
FTSE 100	6626.4 2nd	6239.0 22nd
FTSE 250	6601.0 16th	6307.7 24th
FTSE 350	3203.8 2nd	3050.2 22nd
FTSE All-Share	3136.42 2nd	2996.80 22nd
FT 30	3771.0 16th	3658.0 9th

Fig. 6.8 Monthly averages of stock indices

A further table, which appears in Saturday's FT, contains an alternative series of indices intended for use by private investors (see Figure 6.9).

These indices, produced by FTSE International, in conjunction with the Association of Private Client Investment Managers and Stockbrokers, are designed to give private investors a benchmark against which to measure the performance of their own portfolios. The indices show the investment performance in terms of capital (that is, excluding income) of three model portfolios over four time periods, ranging from one month to five years. The portfolios are: an income one, which contains many UK shares and bonds; a growth one, which is more heavily weighted towards shares; and a balanced one, which is a mix of UK and overseas shares, bonds and cash. These weightings are based on portfolios run by 24 firms of stockbrokers:

- **Growth:** this portfolio contains 60 per cent UK equities, 25 per cent international equities, 40 per cent bonds and 5 per cent cash.

- **Balanced:** this portfolio contains 55 per cent UK equities, 20 per cent international equities, 20 per cent bonds and 5 per cent cash.

- **Income:** this portfolio contains 50 per cent UK equities, 5 per cent international equities, 40 per cent bonds and 5 per cent cash.

- **Other indices:** the table also shows the performance of the three indices that are used to calculate the performance of the portfolios themselves, plus a measure of inflation. The indices are the FTSE All-Share, which reflects the overall performance of the UK stock market, the FTSE World Ex UK, which reflects the performance of world stock markets other than the UK; and the FTSE UK Gilts index (see Chapter 11).

Private investor's indices

Capital performance		% change			
	24/08/2000	1 month	3 months	One year	Five years
Growth	3430.62	2.43	6.52	8.90	79.65
Balanced	2973.81	2.05	5.72	7.46	67.85
Income	2272.8	1.23	4.20	3.92	47.53
FTSE All-Share index	3151.57	2.57	8.20	6.36	81.85
FTSE World Ex UK (Loc)	373.72	3.71	6.53	20.44	108.51
FTSE UK Gilts (All Stocks)	155.86	-0.64	-0.52	-1.42	11.27
RPI	170.5	-0.35	0.24	3.27	13.74

Fig. 6.9 Private investor's indices

The private investor's indices are meant to be indicative rather than precise. They are not meant to be an absolute measure to which brokers aspire. For one thing, the indices take no account of the effects of charges and tax. What is more, they will not reflect exactly the asset mix of an investor's individual portfolio, which can have a dramatic effect on performance. Brokers are all too aware of the danger of private investors using the benchmarks as a stick to beat them with for perceived poor performance. Some refuse to use them, arguing that the whole point of getting a broker to manage a portfolio is a bespoke service. The investor can dictate the precise investment objectives and influence both the asset mix and the stock selection.

Both these last two FT tables include indices on equity markets outside the UK, the subject of the next three chapters.

"A random walk down Wall Street."

Burton Malkiel

"Wall Street: A thoroughfare that begins in a graveyard and ends in a river."

Anon

7

NYSE and Nasdaq

The US equity markets

- **US markets** – the dominant world exchanges: the New York Stock Exchange; the Nasdaq
- **US indices** – the Dow, the S&P and the Nasdaq

■ US markets

The *Financial Times* provides extensive coverage of the US stock markets, particularly in its international editions. These feature a complete listing of all shares (or common stocks as they are known in the United States), including prices, price changes, highs and lows, volumes traded, yields and price/earnings ratios quoted on the New York Stock Exchange, together with extensive coverage of the American Stock Exchange (Amex) and the market for over-the-counter stocks, the National Association of Securities Dealers Automated Quotation service (Nasdaq). The UK edition also lists details on a significant number of leading US stocks (see Figure 7.1), and all editions carry the main composite indices, ratios and trading activity on the US markets.

With many major stocks traded in both London and New York, and increasing interaction between the two markets, the performance of equity prices on Wall Street can have a significant impact on prices in London, and vice versa. This internationalisation of major equity markets was graphically illustrated during the October 1987 crash, the impact of which spread rapidly from Wall Street to the London Stock Exchange.

■ The New York Stock Exchange

The New York Stock Exchange (NYSE) is the main US exchange (see Figure 7.2). It lists the largest US corporations and is known colloquially as the Big Board. As of 2000, the NYSE listed 3,025 companies with a total market capitalisation of $16,500 billion. It is the world's largest equities market, tracing its trading origins in lower Manhattan to 1792. An auction-based marketplace with a central trading floor, the NYSE is a members-owned non-profit organisation. Since 1953, the number of companies or "seats" on the exchange has been constant at 1,366. The NYSE table shows:

- **NYSE stocks:** each stock listing begins with information on the price highs and lows for the year to date, and the abbreviated name by which the stock is known. For example, UAL is United Airlines.

- **Dividend, yield, p/e and sales:** the last declared dividend worked out at an annual rate in dollars (dividends are usually paid quarterly); the current dividend yield, a percentage calculated as the dividend divided by the current price multiplied by 100; the price/earnings ratio, calculated as the current price divided by the current annual earnings per share; and "Volume 100s", the volume of round lots (100 shares each) of the stock traded on the previous day.

- **Prices:** the price high and low for the day, the closing quote and the change on the previous day's closing price.

The second stock exchange in New York, and the second largest traditional market is the Amex (American Stock Exchange), now owned by the Nasdaq (see below). Elsewhere in the country, there are five more of these traditional exchanges: the Pacific

Highs & Lows shown on a 52 week basis

AMERICAS

UNITED STATES (Aug 16 / US$)
(4 pm close)

		+/-	High	Low	Yld	P/E
AMR	32 3/4	-1/2	*39	20 3/4	....	10.9
ACE Ltd♣	35 1/8	-1/16	*37 1/4	14 1/16	1.5	16.3
ADCTel♣	41 9/16	+1/16	49	8 5/8	....	....
AESCrp	56 1/16	-13/16	*59 11/16	34 1/4	....	51.4
AK Ste	11 5/16xd	....	*20 1/8	7 7/8	4.4	18.9
AMFM	77 15/16	-3/8	*85 5/8	53	....	....
AT&T	32 1/8	+15/16	*60 3/4	29 11/16	2.7	16.5
ATTLMd	23 15/16	+1 3/8	*30 3/4	19 3/16	....	15.3
ATTLMB	27 7/8	-1/8	*36 9/16	22 1/2	....	17.8
AT&TWr	25 15/16	+5/16	*33 7/8	23 9/16	....	....
AXAFin	45 1/4	-7/8	*47 15/16	25 15/16	0.2	18.1
AbbttL	40 11/16xd	+1/2	*45 3/16	29 3/8	1.9	25.1
AdobeS	115 15/16	-4 3/16	143 5/16	44 7/8	0.1	48.5
AdvMic	64 3/16	+11/16	*97	28	....	....
Aetna	58 5/16xd	+11/16	*73 11/16	38 1/2	1.4	12.5
AFLAC	55 1/16xd	-2 5/8	*58 15/16	33 9/16	0.6	24.3
AgIntT	41 3/4	-1	*161	38 1/4	....	29.6
AirPrC	36 3/16	+1/2	*39 1/16	23	2.1	....
Albtsn	30 1/8	-1/4	*39 1/4	23 1/16	2.5	34.6
AlcnAl	33 3/8	+3/8	*45 15/16	29 1/16	1.8	10.9
Alcoa	34 7/16xd	+1/8	*43 5/8	27 1/4	1.5	19.7
AlxBld	26 15/16xd	-1/16	27 1/2	17 15/16	3.3	17.0
AllegE	35 1/2	+1/16	*35 11/16	23 5/8	4.8	18.8
AllegT	21 13/16	+1/16	*26 13/16	16 1/8	3.7	15.9
Allerg	70 1/8	-1 3/16	*81 1/2	44 1/2	0.5	45.8
AllWst	10 5/8	+1/4	*12 1/16	5 5/16	....	....
Allste	28 13/16	-1/16	*30 7/16	17 3/16	2.4	11.5
Alltel	56 11/16	-5 7/8	*82 15/16	55 9/16	2.3	11.1
Altera	59 3/4	+1 13/16	62 9/16	19 3/16	....	79.7
Amz.co	38 5/8	+1 1/16	113	27 7/8	....	....
Ambac	63 15/16xd	-2 13/16	*68 11/16	38 7/8	0.8	13.1
Amdocs	69 3/4	+4 3/4	*96	32 7/16	....	....
AmdaHs	66 15/16	+1 7/16	*70 1/8	47 13/16	0.9	8.5
AEP	35 3/8xd	+1/16	*38 1/2	25 15/16	6.8	18.6
AmExpr	57 5/16	-1 7/8	*60 7/16	39 13/16	0.6	28.8
AmGenl♣	71 15/16xd	-1 3/16	*76 1/4	45 5/8	2.4	19.7
AmGrtA	19 3/8	+1/16	*24 1/16	15 5/16	4.1	10.7
AmHome	57 11/16xd	+7/16	*61 9/16	39 3/8	1.6	21.7
AmIntl	86 3/16	-1/2	*89 15/16	52 5/8	0.2	37.5
AmNtln	62 1/8	-1 1/8	73 3/8	49	4.6	7.5
AmPwCv♣	23 1/16	-1 7/8	48 13/16	16	....	21.8
Ameren	39 5/8	+3/8	*39 5/8	27 9/16	6.4	12.9
AmOnLn	54 11/16	....	*82 7/8	48 1/4	....	....
AmStnd♣	48 5/16	-1/2	*49 3/4	34 5/16	....	11.8
Amgen	67 11/16	-1/16	80 7/16	37	....	62.1
Amsth	18 1/4	-1/2	*20 1/16	12 3/4	4.4	22.8
Anadrko♣	59 7/8	+1 3/8	*60	27 5/8	0.3	47.5
Analog	94 7/16	+17 5/8	*100	41 5/16	....	....
Andrew	25 1/8	-1 1/8	42 1/16	11 3/16	....	29.9
AngId	20 7/8xd	+5/8	*28 11/16	18	6.6	....
AnBsch	83 1/16xd	-1 7/16	*87 1/2	54 5/8	1.6	25.7
Aon Cp	37 1/16	-5/8	*42 3/4	20 11/16	2.4	23.9
Apache	59 3/16	+1/2	*61 1/2	32 1/8	0.5	16.1
AppMat	80 15/16	+3 1/8	115	31 1/8	....	38.2
AppleC	48 1/2	+1 13/16	75 3/16	28 3/4	....	11.2
ArchDn	9 1/2xd	+1/8	*13 7/16	8 13/16	2.1	19.0
ArchCm	26 3/16xd	+1/4	*26 7/16	19 1/4	5.9	15.5
ArmstH	16 3/8xd	+1/4	*36 13/16	15 5/16	11.7	....
ArrwEl♣	34 5/16	+1 3/16	*46	20 1/2	....	24.9
AshInd	36	+1/8	*37 3/16	28 5/8	3.1	8.4
AsFstC	27 9/16xd	....	*29 11/16	15 3/4	0.9	12.8
AtHome	13 9/16	-5/16	59 3/4	12 7/8	....	....
Atmel	33 13/16	+1 3/16	61 3/8	15 1/16	....	39.3
AuData	58 1/4	+1/8	*58 11/16	40	0.6	44.8
AutoZn	22 1/16	-5/16	*32 1/2	21	....	11.9
Autdsk	24 15/16	+3/16	56 1/16	17	1.0	28.3

		+/-	High	Low	Yld	P/E
Englhd	18 13/16	-3/16	*19 5/8	12 9/16	2.1	10.9
Enron	84	+1 7/8	*84 1/2	41 3/8	0.6	60.4
Ensco	40 1/4	+1 5/16	*40 1/2	20 1/4	0.2	....
Entrgy♣	31 15/16xd	+11/16	*31 15/16	15 15/16	3.8	12.1
Equifx	25 7/16	-1/8	*29 11/16	19 7/8	1.5	16.2
EqInFd	149 15/16	-1 5/16	219 1/8	143 1/4	1.9	....
EqOffP	30 3/8	-1/16	*31 7/16	22 7/8	5.5	17.8
ELaudA	43 11/16	-1 3/8	*55 7/8	38 1/8	0.5	36.7
ExnMob	82 3/4xd	+1 7/16	*86 5/16	69 7/8	2.1	23.1
FDX HI	40 3/4	-5/16	*47 15/16	30 9/16	....	17.3
FMC Cp	66 1/16	+7/16	*67 1/16	46 1/8	....	10.8
FPL	54 5/8	+1 1/16	*54 7/8	36 3/8	4.0	12.7
FanMae♣	57 1/8xd	-7/16	*65 5/8	47 7/8	2.0	15.0
FedMgl	11 7/16	-3/16	*20 11/16	8 15/16	0.1	4.1
FdDpSt	25 1/16	-1/2	*53 7/8	21	....	7.3
FifThd	44 5/8	-1/2	50 5/16	29 5/16	1.6	29.6
FstDta	49 3/8	-9/16	*57 11/16	39	0.2	17.0
FstSec	15 7/16xd	+1/16	31	10 3/4	3.6	18.0
FstTenn♣	21	-1/4	*29 1/16	15 15/16	4.2	11.8
Fst Un	28 7/8	-5/8	*38 7/8	24 1/2	6.6	....
FVirBk	42 3/4	+3/16	*43 3/8	29	3.5	14.8
Firstr	23 3/4	-7/8	*28	16 3/8	2.7	25.0
Fstegy♣	25 3/16xd	-3/8	*27 3/16	18	6.0	9.8
FltBst	39 1/16	-11/16	*42 1/2	25 1/8	3.1	14.9
Fluor	32	+1/8	*48 1/2	23 15/16	3.1	10.5
Ford	28 1/8xa	-5/16	*31 7/16	22 1/16	7.1	4.9
FrtJam♣	32 11/16	+3/16	*33 15/16	16 7/16	1.8	22.2
ForBrd	25 13/16xd	+3/16	*33 1/4	19 1/4	3.6	14.0
FrnkRs	34 5/8	-1/4	*39 3/16	24 5/8	0.7	15.5
FredMc	44 1/16	-1/4	*51 5/8	36 7/8	1.5	13.9
FrMCGB	9 1/4	+1/8	*21 7/16	8 3/16	....	14.7
GPU	31 3/8xd	-1/8	*31 7/8	23 7/16	6.9	28.0
Ganntt♣	56 1/16	-1	*81 11/16	52 1/4	1.5	16.2
Gap	25 9/16	-7/8	*53 3/4	25 1/16	0.3	19.1
Gatewy	62	+1/16	*75	43 5/8	....	39.7
GenDyn	61 1/8	-1/8	*62 15/16	36 1/4	1.7	15.9
GenEle	56 3/4	-1/2	*57 3/8	41 11/16	1.0	48.1
GnMill	33 7/8	-5/8	*41 3/4	29 3/8	3.2	16.5
GenMtr	64 11/16xd	+1 1/8	*94 5/8	56 15/16	3.1	7.1
GnMtrH	28 1/16	+1/16	*57 7/8	24 5/8	....	....
GenuPt	21 3/8	....	*26 11/16	19 15/16	5.1	9.8
GrgiaP	28 1/16xd	-1/2	*51 15/16	24 1/2	1.8	6.0
Gillte	29 15/16xd	....	*42 7/8	28 3/16	2.2	25.2
GlaxoW	58 13/16xd	+15/16	*64 7/16	45 1/4	2.0	29.6
Global	29 13/16	-11/16	61 13/16	20 1/4	....	....
GloMar	32 1/2	+13/16	*32 9/16	14 7/8	....	....
GWstFn	47 13/16xd	-13/16	*49 15/16	26 7/8	0.4	15.5
GldmnS	112 1/2xd	-5 11/16	*128	69 3/8	0.4	18.0
Gdrich	37 7/8	+7/16	*38 15/16	21 9/16	2.9	25.2
Gdyear	23 3/16xd	-7/16	*31 5/8	19 9/16	5.2	13.2
GraceW	9 7/8	....	*15 1/8	9	....	4.9
GrngrW	32 1/8xd	+1/8	*56 7/8	28 1/2	2.1	17.5
GLksCh	32 1/16	+5/8	*40 7/16	26 1/2	1.0	13.2
GrnptF	26 1/8xd	+1/16	*26 3/8	15	3.8	10.0
Guidan	58	-3/4	*75 3/8	44	....	39.2
HCAHlt	33 1/2xd	-1 3/8	*35 13/16	18 3/4	0.2	74.4
HCRMn	12 9/16	+1/16	*17 3/8	6 1/2	....	....
Halbtn	54	+2 9/16	*54	33 7/16	0.9	....
Hanna♣	7 15/16	+1/8	*13 15/16	7 11/16	6.3	....
HarcGn	61 7/16	+7/16	*62 1/2	32 3/4	1.4	37.2
HarlyD	45 3/16	+9/16	*46 5/8	29 1/2	0.2	44.3
Harrah	26 5/8	-9/16	*28 1/8	17	....	15.5
Harris	29 7/8	-1/16	*39 3/8	23 3/4	0.7	....
HtfFnS	64 3/8	-1/4	*69 3/8	29 3/8	1.5	16.4
Hasbro	10 3/4xd	+1/8	*19 1/8	10 3/16	2.2	12.6
Hlthsh	5 5/8	-1/8	*8 9/16	4 3/4	....	....
Heinz	39 7/16	-3/4	*45 7/8	30 13/16	3.7	15.7
Hrcule	14 3/8	-1/16	*28	11 3/4	7.5	12.1
Hrshey	45 7/16	-3/4	*55 13/16	37 3/4	2.5	21.1
HewPac	111 7/16	+1 7/16	*155 1/2	101 1/16	0.6	36.3
Hlhmrd	32 13/16xd	+7/8	*38 3/8	28 3/4	2.4	18.1
Hilton	10 1/16	-1/16	*11 1/16	6 3/8	0.8	15.5
Hitach	113 1/2	+1 5/16	*163 7/8	109 1/2	0.6	55.1
HmeDep	51 1/16	-2 7/16	*70	44 1/8	0.3	47.3
HmstkM	5 11/16	+1/4	*8	5 1/4	0.9	....
Hnywel	34 7/16xd	-11/16	67 3/16	32 1/8	2.2	16.2

		+/-	High	Low	Yld	P/E
PnzQkr	12 1/2	+1/8	*13 1/8	8 3/8	6.0	....
PeplSf	24 1/4	-11/16	27 3/4	12	....	....
PepBot	28 1/2	-3 9/16	*33 5/8	16 1/4	0.3	19.0
Pepsic	44	-1 15/16	*47 1/16	29 11/16	1.3	32.6
Pknelm	78 7/16	+2 7/16	*84	38	0.7	53.4
Pfizer	43 5/16	+11/16	*49 1/4	30	0.8	71.0
PhmcCp	57 3/4	+15/16	*59 7/16	33 3/4	0.8	....
PhelpD	43 9/16xd	-1/2	*73	36 1/16	4.6	....
PhMorr	33 3/16	+3/4	*33 7/16	18 11/16	5.8	9.6
PhillP	57 3/4xd	+1	*58 1/8	36	2.4	12.6
PinWCp♣	41 11/16xd	....	*42 1/4	25 11/16	3.4	11.2
Pitney	36	+11/16	*54 1/8	33 3/4	3.2	13.9
Polrd	17 9/16	-3/16	*28 7/16	16 1/4	3.4	15.7
PotElP	25 11/16	+1/8	*27 7/8	19 1/16	6.5	14.8
Prxair	44 1/2	+9/16	*54 15/16	31 3/8	1.4	15.3
ProctG	62 1/2xd	+7/16	*118 3/8	53	2.2	20.0
ProgOh	74	-5/8	*100	45	0.4	....
Provdn	109 3/4	-3/8	*115 3/8	58 1/8	0.2	28.4
PrudAD	28 3/4	+1/4	*30 15/16	26 1/2	2.4	....
PbSvEG	35 7/8	-5/16	*38 3/16	25 11/16	6.0	10.2
QuakrO♣	73 13/16	-1 1/16	*80 11/16	45 13/16	1.5	28.4
Qualcm♣	60 1/2	-7/8	200	39 5/16	....	30.4
QwestC	48 9/16	-7/8	*65	37 5/8	....	77.1
Rdshck	63 11/16	-2 3/8	*69 3/4	35 1/16	0.3	40.1
RlstnP	22 1/8	-1/16	*22 15/16	16 3/4	1.3	11.7
Rank	4.87	....	9.13	4	7.7	25.7
RythnB	28 3/8	....	*29 9/16	17 1/2	2.8	....
RDgstA	39 7/8	-1 1/2	*41 7/8	28 3/8	0.5	26.4
Reebok	19 1/4	-1/8	*20 5/16	6 15/16	1.6	9.8
RegFin	21 1/2	-3/8	37 1/8	18 5/16	5.0	8.9
RelEgy	37 3/16xd	....	*37 7/16	19 3/4	4.0	5.3
Relstr	53 9/16	....	*53 11/16	23 3/4	1.6	18.9
RiteAi	4.50	-.19	*12.25	4.12	....	....
Rckwll	39xd	+5/8	*54 1/2	31	2.6	11.6
RohmH	29 3/8xd	+1/2	*49 7/16	25 11/16	2.7	18.2
Rouse	26 3/16	+1/16	*27 1/8	20 1/8	5.0	14.2
Rowan	30	+5/8	*33	19 1/16	....	....
RDutch	60 5/8xd	-5/16	*65 5/8	50 7/16	2.1	19.5
RyderS	22 3/16	+1 3/16	*25 1/8	17 7/16	2.7	15.3
SAFECO	25 3/8	-1/8	*27 3/8	18	5.8	26.7
SBC Cm	41 5/16	-3/4	*50	34 13/16	2.5	21.4
SPX	179 3/4	+10 1/4	*186	74	....	....
Staple	16 3/4	-11/16	*28 3/4	13 3/16	....	33.5
Safewy	50 5/8	+1 3/16	*51 3/8	30 3/4	....	24.7
St Joe	29 3/4	-1/8	*31 3/8	23 1/16	0.3	22.5
StJude	37 1/4	-1 7/8	*46 1/8	23 5/8	....	37.6
StPaul	46 5/16	-11/16	*49 9/16	21 5/16	2.3	10.9
SaraLe	18 3/4	+1/8	*22 1/4	13 3/8	2.9	13.6
SchrPl	41 13/16xd	+1 5/16	*51 3/8	30 1/2	1.3	27.2
Schlmb	86 1/4	+4 1/8	*86 1/4	53	0.9	....
Schwab	37 3/8xd	-7/16	*44 3/4	22 7/16	0.1	65.6
SciAtl♣	71 5/8	-5 9/16	*94	24 7/16	0.1	74.6
Scripp	51 1/4	+11/16	*51 13/16	42 3/8	1.1	27.0
Seagte	54 3/4	+3 1/16	*75 7/16	35 3/4	....	39.1
Seagrm	56 1/4	-1 1/16	*65 3/16	43 1/16	1.2	....
SldAir	53 9/16	+9/16	*61 7/8	43 3/8	....	28.5
SearsR	31 1/4	+15/16	*43 1/2	25 1/4	2.9	7.2
Sempra♣	19 9/16	+5/16	*19 5/8	16 3/16	5.1	10.1
ServCp	2.12	....	*7.44	2.12	16.9	....
SvMstr	9 1/4	-1/16	*14 15/16	8 3/8	4.3	12.5
Shawln	13xd	....	*17 5/16	10 15/16	1.5	8.6
ShellT	51 5/8xd	-5/16	*54 1/16	39 5/8	2.5	20.8
SherWil♣	23 1/2xd	-7/16	*27 5/8	17 1/8	2.3	11.9
SigmAl	29 3/4	+1 1/16	*36 1/4	20 3/16	1.0	18.6
SlcnGr	4.50xc	+.13	*4.87	2.01	....	....
SimPrp♣	24 5/16xd	-1/16	*27 1/16	21 7/8	8.3	24.8
SKBchm	66 1/4xd	+15/16	*71 15/16	52 1/2	1.4	39.4
SmftSt	12 1/4	+1/2	25 5/8	10 7/8	....	7.7
SnpOnT	31 3/8	+1/2	*31 3/4	20 7/8	3.1	12.4
Solotn	41 7/16	+1 1/8	*49 1/2	20 1/4	....	50.4
Sonoco♣	19 3/8xd	-1/8	*23 1/2	17 1/2	4.1	10.5
SthnCo	27 5/16xd	-1/4	*27 7/8	20 3/8	4.9	13.7
Sthtst♣	28 5/16	1/8	*37 7/8	20 7/8	3.5	10.2
SWAir	24 3/8	+3/8	*25	15	0.1	24.1
SprFON♣	34 1/16	-1 1/2	*67 13/16	33 5/16	1.5	13.2

Fig. 7.1 American equities

Stock Exchange (with trading floors in both Los Angeles and San Francisco), the Midwest Stock Exchange in Chicago, the Boston Stock Exchange, the Philadelphia Stock Exchange and the Cincinnati Stock Exchange. Each of these smaller exchanges has some exclusive stocks, usually small or locally owned companies, but they also trade stocks that are listed on the NYSE or the Amex, "dual listed" stocks; no stocks trade on both the NYSE and the Amex.

NEW YORK STOCK EXCHANGE PRICES

2000 High	2000 Low	Stock	Div	Yld. %	P/ E	Vol 100s	High	Low	Close Quote	Ch'ge Prev. Close
17	8 5/8	EnhncFin	0.24	1.5	28	156	16	15 13/16	15 15/16	+1/16
61 1/2	46 1/8	ENI	1.23	2.1	17	345	60 1/16	58 7/8	59 3/16	-2 1/8
90 9/16	41 3/8	Enron	0.50	0.6	61	23408	89 15/16	85	85 1/2	-4 1/2
38 1/16	13 11/16	Enron OilG	0.14	0.4	7	12100	u38 1/16	37	37 15/16	+3/16
41 1/4	20 1/4	Ensco	0.10	0.2		5168	41	40 1/16	40 5/8	-7/16
68 11/16	35 13/16	EntercmCom			61	1160	44 3/8	41 5/8	42 15/16	-1 1/16
32 3/16	15 15/16	Entrgy♠ x	1.20	3.8	11	6784	u32 3/16	31 1/2	31 1/2	-11/16
25 1/2	18	EntPrdPrt	2.10	8.7	9	274	24 9/16	24 1/4	24 1/4	-1/8
20 9/16	15 1/4	EntrvsnCm				929	19 3/4	19 3/8	19 7/16	
138	31 5/8	EnzBio				1515	53	48 3/8	53	+4 9/16
132	33 5/16	Equant				1233	39 15/16	38 7/16	39 15/16	-5/16
29 11/16	19 7/8	Equifx x	0.37	1.5	15	3759	25 1/2	24 11/16	25	-1/16
59 3/4	32 1/4	EqtbRs x	1.18	2.1	21	1072	57 3/4	57	57 7/16	+5/8
31 7/16	22 7/8	EqOffP	1.80	6.2	17	4011	29 1/2	29 1/8	29 1/8	-5/16
51 3/16	38 11/16	EqResPrp	3.26	6.7	17	1862	49 1/2	48 1/4	48 3/8	-3/4
55 7/8	38 1/8	ELaudA	0.20	0.5	34	5683	42 7/16	41 1/2	42	-1/4
32 7/8	20 1/2	EthanAlln	0.16	0.6	12	1008	28 5/8	27 7/8	27 7/8	-5/16
4	1 7/8	Ethyl	0.25	11.8	2	731	2 1/8	2 1/16	2 1/8	+1/16
44	20 11/16	EverRein	0.24	0.6	12	1104	40 15/16	40	40 3/8	+3/8
14 1/8	6	ExtStayAm			23	2280	u14 5/16	13 5/8	14 1/4	+3/4
86 5/16	69 7/8	ExnMob x	1.76	2.1	23	47297	83 3/8	82 9/16	82 15/16	-1 5/8

- F -

2000 High	2000 Low	Stock	Div	Yld. %	P/ E	Vol 100s	High	Low	Close Quote	Ch'ge Prev. Close
39 15/16	18	FactsetRsc	0.12	0.4	47	240	34 3/8	33 7/16	33 7/8	-9/16
49 1/2	25 3/4	FchldSemi				2784	42 1/4	41 5/16	41 5/16	-3/16
22 1/2	14 1/4	FamDlrStr	0.22	1.3	17	5693	17 3/4	17 1/2	17 9/16	
65 5/8	47 7/8	FanMae♠ x	1.12	2.0	14	32742	58 1/4	55 1/8	55 1/4	-2 15/16
20	12 1/4	FBL Fin	0.36	2.8	7	32	13	12 3/4	13	+1/8
47 15/16	30 9/16	FDX Hl			16	4582	40 1/8	39 5/16	39 13/16	+3/8
22 5/16	17 3/4	FedRlty	1.80	8.8	15	367	20 13/16	20 1/2	20 9/16	-3/16
20 11/16	8 15/16	FedMgl	0.01	0.1	3	2513	11 3/16	10 3/4	11	-1/4
22 1/16	14 3/4	Federal Sg x	0.76	3.5	16	2436	u22 1/8	21 15/16	22	+1/16
53 7/8	21	FdDpSt			7	10044	27 1/2	26 13/16	27 5/16	+7/16
23 1/4	16 1/2	FelcorLdg	2.20	9.6		376	23 1/16	22 3/4	22 7/8	-1/16
25 1/8	17 5/16	Ferro Corp x	0.58	2.8	10	507	20 7/8	20 7/16	20 13/16	+1/8
36 1/2	6 1/2	Finova	0.72	10.2	2	14719	7 1/4	d6 5/16	7 1/16	+1/16
17 3/4	10 1/4	FstAmFin	0.24	1.5	20	310	16 3/16	15 7/8	16 1/8	+1/8
21	16 1/4	FstBncpHld	0.44	2.3	10	77	18 3/4	18 3/4	18 3/4	-1/16
57 11/16	39	FstDta	0.08	0.2	16	11912	48 1/4	47 1/2	47 3/4	+3/8
32 1/8	25 5/8	FstIndRlty	2.48	8.5	11	531	29 9/16	29 1/4	29 5/16	-1/16
29 1/16	15 15/16	FstTenn♠	0.88	4.2	11	713	21 1/8	20 11/16	21 1/16	+1/8
38 7/8	24 1/2	Fst Union	1.92	6.5		15481	29 3/4	29 7/16	29 5/8	+1/16
43 3/8	29	FVirBk	1.48	3.5	14	341	42 13/16	42 3/16	42 3/4	+5/16
28	16 3/8	Firstr	0.65	2.7	25	9461	24 7/16	24 3/16	24 1/4	
27 3/16	18	Fstegy♠ x	1.50	6.4	9	3932	23 13/16	23 7/16	23 7/16	-7/16
51	19 7/8	FshrScient			27	1165	22 1/4	22	22 1/8	+1/16
42 1/2	25 1/8	FltBstF	1.20	2.9	15	10541	41 13/16	40 3/4	41 1/16	-3/8
21	12 1/8	FleetwEnt	0.76	5.4	5	493	14 3/16	13 15/16	14 1/16	+5/16
17 5/8	8 11/16	FlemOk x	0.08	0.5		1887	16 3/8	16	16 5/16	-3/8
51	37 1/8	FlorEastCs	0.10	0.2	42	23	44 1/2	44 1/8	44 1/2	+1/8
43 1/4	28	FlorRock	0.50	1.3	11	44	39 1/8	38 3/16	38 15/16	+11/16
23 1/4	11 11/16	Flowersind	0.53	2.5	65	2959	21 5/16	21	21 1/16	-1/4
17 7/8	10 9/16	Flowserve	0.56	3.2	37	462	17 5/8	17 3/8	17 5/8	+1/4
48 1/2	23 15/16	Fluor	1.00	3.4	9	11261	29 5/8	28 1/8	29	-5/8
67 1/4	46 1/8	FMC Cp			11	1891	u68 13/16	66 11/16	68	+1 5/16
54 5/8	31	FormEconAD	0.50	1.2		485	42 7/8	42 3/4	42 3/4	+1/8
27 5/8	18 3/8	Foodmkr			11	838	23 1/8	22 13/16	23	
39 3/8	20 3/4	Ftstar			11	631	31 3/8	30 3/4	31 1/8	+5/8
31 7/16	22 1/16	Ford x	2.00	7.2	4	30583	28 1/4	27 5/16	27 15/16	+1/2
119 3/8	57 3/8	Forest La			71	5996	100 15/16	97 1/4	98	-2
33 15/16	16 7/16	FrtJam♠	0.60	1.9	21	3621	32 3/8	32	32 5/16	+5/16
33 1/4	19 1/4	ForBrd x	0.92	3.6	14	3874	25 15/16	25 5/8	25 7/8	+1/4
9 1/2	5 3/16	FostWh x	0.24	3.5		680	6 15/16	6 7/8	6 7/8	-1/8
17 9/16	7 5/8	FndHlthSys			15	2265	17 1/4	16 3/4	17 1/16	-1/8
34 3/4	21 5/8	FoxEnt				1139	28 7/16	28 3/16	28 5/16	-1/8
55 3/16	36 3/8	FPL x	2.16	4.0	12	6540	54 5/8	53 11/16	54 1/16	-5/8
25 1/4	21 11/16	FrchseFin	2.12	9.2	8	534	23 1/16	22 3/4	23	
39 3/16	24 5/8	FrnkRs	0.24	0.7	16	4035	36 11/16	36 1/4	36 1/4	-1/8
51 5/8	36 7/8	FredMc	0.68	1.6	13	30770	43 5/8	41 5/8	41 7/8	-1 15/16
18 3/4	8 1/16	FrMcGA			26	1441	9 3/16	8 7/16	9 1/8	+11/16
21 7/16	8 3/16	FrMCGB			14	5903	9 9/16	8 7/8	9 3/8	+1/2
9 5/8	3 11/16	FremGn	0.16	4.5		1424	3 11/16	d3 9/16	3 9/16	-1/8
9 15/16	5 3/4	FrshDelMnt			7	734	6	5 7/8	5 15/16	
22 7/16	13 15/16	FurnBrnds			8	2562	16 13/16	16 3/8	16 1/2	-1/8

2000 High	2000 Low	Stock	Div	Yld. %	P/ E	Vol 100s	High	Low	Close Quote	Ch'ge Prev. Close
44	16	Kemet			18	13609	31 7/8	31	31 11/16	+11/16
11 13/16	9 11/16	Kemper Mun x	0.82	7.0		125	u11 13/16	11 5/8	11 11/16	-1/16
33 13/16	19 1/8	Kennmt x	0.68	2.8	14	4806	24 1/2	23 7/8	24 1/16	-7/16
67 15/16	39 7/8	KerrMc	1.80	3.0	10	3725	62 3/4	60 7/8	60 7/8	-1 3/4
23	15 9/16	KeyCp	1.12	5.7	7	3000	20 1/16	19 3/4	19 3/4	-1/8
36 15/16	20 3/16	KeyspE	1.78	5.3	15	4144	34 3/8	33 5/8	33 13/16	-1/2
68 1/8	42 1/4	KimbCl	1.08	1.9	17	8919	58 7/16	57 3/8	57 1/2	-5/8
42 13/16	32 3/4	KimcoRlty	2.72	6.8	14	416	40 11/16	40 1/16	40 1/16	-11/16
45 1/16	36 3/8	KndrMrgnE	3.10	7.3	15	805	43 3/16	42 1/16	42 11/16	-9/16
39 1/8	19 7/8	KndrMrgn	0.20	0.5	18	3772	38 1/8	36 3/4	36 3/4	-1 3/8
47 1/4	19 3/4	KingPhm				2929	36	35 1/16	35 11/16	+5/8
30 3/16	16 3/4	KLM	0.82	3.2		230	26 1/8	25 11/16	25 15/16	+9/16
10 3/8	6 9/16	Kmart			12	11553	7 5/16	7 1/8	7 1/8	-3/16
44 1/8	35	KmartPfT	3.88	10.6		z0	36 7/16	36 7/16	36 7/16	+3/16
59 3/4	44 3/16	KnRidd	0.92	1.7	9	7967	55 7/8	53 1/2	53 3/4	-2 1/4
66 1/2	33 1/2	Kohls			65	4650	58 15/16	57 3/4	58 1/2	+1/2
17 13/16	11 1/8	Korea Fd	0.06	0.5		575	13	12 11/16	13	+1/4
23 7/16	14 1/16	Kroger			24	27275	22	21 9/16	21 13/16	-3/8
268	130 1/2	Kyocera CP	0.37	0.2		486	166 3/8	163 9/16	166 3/16	+7 1/8

- L -

2000 High	2000 Low	Stock	Div	Yld. %	P/ E	Vol 100s	High	Low	Close Quote	Ch'ge Prev. Close
90 1/4	28 7/8	LSI Lg♠			38	17189	39 3/4	38 3/8	38 7/8	-1/2
65 1/16	35 11/16	L3 Comms			29	507	62 1/2	60 13/16	62	+11/16
17 11/16	13 1/2	LaZBoy x	0.32	1.9	10	270	16 5/8	16 3/8	16 9/16	-1/16
12 1/8	3 15/16	LaborRdy			14	556	4 1/16	d3 7/8	3 15/16	-1/16
21 7/8	17 1/2	Laclede Gs	1.34	6.4	16	129	21	20 3/8	21	+1/2
28 1/4	18 13/16	Lafarge x	0.60	2.5	6	2336	24 1/2	23 7/8	24 1/8	-5/16
5 5/8	5/16	Laidlaw				1304	3/8	d5/16	5/16	-1/32
42 11/16	32	LkehdPipe	3.50	8.6	19	84	41	40 7/16	40 5/8	-3/8
61 1/2	26 7/16	LndEnd♠	0.20	0.8	22	1829	26 15/16	d26 3/8	26 1/2	-1/16
19 3/8	11 3/8	LasIRe				96	18 7/16	17 13/16	18 5/16	+3/8
36 1/4	19 1/4	Lear Corp			5	4329	24 9/16	24 1/8	24 5/16	-1/4
32 1/4	19 11/16	Lee Enterp	0.64	2.3	15	204	28 5/16	27 3/4	28 5/16	+1/4
57 5/16	30 11/16	Legg Mason	0.36	0.7	18	2131	49 1/16	48 1/16	48 1/4	-1/4
22 9/16	15 1/16	LeggPl x	0.44	2.4	12	2533	18 15/16	18 5/8	18 5/8	-3/16
138 1/4	60 5/8	Lehman x	0.44	0.3	11	9463	135 7/16	131 3/16	135 3/8	+3 15/16
29 7/16	15 1/4	Lennar Crp	0.05	0.2	8	2369	25 15/16	25	25 3/4	+3/4
15 1/8	7 7/8	Lenxintl	0.38	2.8	8	600	13 11/16	13 7/16	13 11/16	+1/8
28 1/8	20 5/8	LeucNt	1.58	6.1	21	271	25 7/8	25 3/16	25 7/8	
135 7/8	43 3/16	Lexmrk			22	6666	59	57 1/16	58	+5/16
24 9/16	15 1/4	LG&E Engy	1.27	5.2	18	1356	u24 9/16	24 7/16	24 1/2	+1/16
13 1/8	9 3/4	LibASEq♠	1.48	11.3		670	13 1/16	12 15/16	13 1/16	+1/16
43 7/8	30 3/4	Liberty Cp	0.88	2.3	12	115	39 9/16	38 5/8	38 13/16	-5/8
25 1/4	17 7/8	LibFincl x	0.40	1.7	10	477	23 3/8	23	23 3/16	-1/8
29 1/8	22	LibProp	2.08	7.6	13	689	27 1/2	27 1/8	27 1/4	-5/16
108 15/16	54	Lilly x	1.04	1.4	27	19455	77 3/16	75 1/2	75 5/8	-1 9/16
25 7/8	14 7/16	Limitd	0.30	1.5	18	9362	20 3/16	19 5/8	19 13/16	-7/16
49 7/16	22 5/8	LincnN♠	1.16	2.4	18	4249	49	47 3/4	47 15/16	-1 1/8
36 3/8	17 15/16	LinNThng			20	2692	29 15/16	28 9/16	28 7/8	-1
56 11/16	26 13/16	Litton			17	1555	u58 1/2	56 1/4	58 1/2	+1 13/16
48 5/16	31	LizClb x	0.45	1.0	13	2912	44 1/4	43 3/4	43 13/16	-9/16
21 13/16	17 9/16	LNR Prp	0.05	0.2	7	109	21 3/16	21 1/8	21 1/8	
30 9/16	16 1/2	LockhM	0.44	1.5	17	5222	28 11/16	27 7/8	28 7/16	+1/16
6 1/8	2 1/4	LoewCnplx				54	3 1/16	2 15/16	2 15/16	-1/16
88 3/4	38 1/4	Loews x	1.00	1.2	13	1605	82 7/8	80 1/2	82 1/8	-7/8
26	15 15/16	LongsDrug	0.56	2.9	11	394	19 1/4	18 3/4	19 1/16	-1/16
17 3/4	10 5/8	Longview F	0.48	4.3	14	1275	11 1/8	10 15/16	11 1/16	+1/16
25 3/4	5	LoralSpc				6840	7 1/4	6 13/16	6 15/16	-1/8
35	15 3/4	LsDryfsG			30	949	33 9/16	32 5/8	33 3/8	-1/8
15 13/16	9 1/4	LouisP x	0.56	5.3	6	2165	10 5/8	10 5/16	10 1/2	+1/8
67 1/4	40 3/8	Lowes	0.14	0.3	23	17830	49 1/8	47 11/16	49 1/8	+5/8
4 5/16	2	LTV ♠ x	0.12	6.0		3022	2 1/16	d1 15/16	2	
33 7/8	20 5/8	Lubrzl x	1.04	4.7	10	1428	22 1/4	21 7/16	22	+3/8
77 1/2	39 5/8	LucentTch x	0.08	0.2	43	146401	41 1/8	40	40 7/16	-3/8
17	7 7/8	Luxottica	0.03	0.2	32	6227	15 1/2	14 7/8	15 1/2	+3/16
19 1/2	8 7/16	Lyondell P x	0.90	7.1	5	8399	12 5/8	12 1/16	12 5/8	+3/4

Fig. 7.2 New York Stock Exchange prices

The smaller regional exchanges offer some distinct features. For example, as it is three hours behind New York, the Pacific market offers continued trading in dual listed NYSE shares after the NYSE has closed. The Midwest market makes no extra charge for odd-lot transactions, deals of less than a round lot of 100 shares, and odd-lot orders on the NYSE for dual listed stocks are often transferred there. The Philadelphia market carries a number of options, including an option on the sterling/dollar exchange rate, prices for which are carried on the FT Currencies and Money page (see Chapter 13). Like the London market, the Cincinnati has no trading floor, with all transactions conducted by computer and telephone.

The Nasdaq

The NYSE has been around for over two centuries. But in recent years, the NYSE's position as the dominant US stock exchange has been challenged by the Nasdaq, which likes to describe itself as "the stock market for the next century". Run by the National Association of Securities Dealers (NASD), this automated quotation (hence Nasdaq) system was the first screen-based, non-centralised market and now ranks as the world's second largest marketplace by value of all companies listed. As of 2000, 4,796 companies were listed on the Nasdaq with a total market capitalisation of $5,048 billion.

The Nasdaq's origins lie in the mid-1960s, when the Securities and Exchange Commission (the US equivalent of the FSA) decided that the market for small stocks not listed on the major exchanges was suffering because there was no reliable mechanism for sharing prices. The NASD opened such a centralised market in 1971 to provide a high-tech method of setting stock prices and trading securities "over the counter". In contrast with the physical trading floor of the NYSE, trading on the Nasdaq is dispersed among more than half a million computer terminals on which "market traders" (independent dealers) post prices at which they are prepared to buy and sell shares.

With less onerous listing requirements than the NYSE, the Nasdaq has always welcomed small, young companies with no earnings, few shares and low share prices, but which are operating in fast-growing industries like information technology and biotechnology. Indeed, the exchange has become synonymous with the technology stocks that are its highest fliers. Such major players as Microsoft, Apple Computers, Intel and Cisco Systems all started here. And while computer companies constitute 15 per cent of the companies on the Nasdaq, they represent 50 per cent of its market value. The FT has a daily half-page of information on the Nasdaq (see Figure 7.3), which shows:

■ **Nasdaq 100:** these are the largest and most active 100 non-financial US stocks on the Nasdaq, based on market capitalisation. Eligibility criteria for the Nasdaq 100 include a minimum average daily trading volume of 100,000 shares. Generally, companies also must have "seasoned" on the Nasdaq or another major exchange, which means they have been listed for a minimum of two years. If a security would otherwise qualify to be in the top 25 per cent of the companies included in the 100 by market capitalisation, then a one-year seasoning criterion applies. If the security is a foreign security, the company must have a worldwide market value of at least $10 billion, a US market value of at least $4 billion, and average trading volume of at least 200,000 shares per day. In addition, foreign securities must be eligible for listed options trading (see Chapter 13).

■ **Nasdaq LargeCap:** this is the second tier of Nasdaq companies.

Nasdaq - 100

Stock	Div.	P/E	Vol 100s	High	Low	Last	Chng
Adaptc		14	35517	24	23 5/16	23 3/4	+3/4
ADCTel♣		125	82839	43 3/8	41 7/16	41 9/16	+1/16
AdlphCm			7418	32	30 3/8	31	-1/2
AdobeS	0.10	48	9517	123 7/16	113	115 15/16	-4 3/16
Altera		79	81380	61 13/16	58 5/8	59 3/4	+1 13/16
Amz.com			95954	39 7/8	37 1/2	38 5/8	+1 1/16
AmPwCv♣		21	18691	25 3/8	22 5/16	23 1/16	-1 7/8
Amgen Inc		62	41907	69 5/8	67 1/2	67 11/16	-1/16
ApolGp		42	2169	39	36 1/4	36 15/16	-1 1/16
AppMat		38	194601	81 13/16	79	80 15/16	+3 1/8
AppleC		11	25301	49	46 13/16	48 1/2	+1 13/16
ApMcrCct		401	44942	168	159 3/4	164 5/8	+3 1/2
AtHome			34334	14 5/8	13 1/2	13 9/16	-5/16
Atmel		39	89048	34 15/16	33 7/16	33 13/16	+1 3/16
BdBth&B		36	16599	18 15/16	17 13/16	18 1/8	-7/16
Biogn♣		32	61766	71 1/4	70	70 1/4	+2 11/16
Biomet	0.11	49	11470	33 3/16	31 1/4	32 7/8	+1 5/8
BMCSft		22	55622	20 15/16	19 1/2	20 9/16	+1 7/16
Brdvsn			142161	30 3/8	27 3/4	28	-2
Chiron		49	8016	47 7/16	45 1/8	45 11/16	-1 1/16
CIENA		859	61557	173 1/2	163 1/8	163 1/4	-6 3/4
Cintas Cp	0.19	35	5380	45	41 3/8	41 11/16	-2 5/8
CiscoSys		161	350663	64 1/4	62 5/16	63 1/16	-1/8
Citrix		33	42656	20 5/8	19 1/8	19 5/8	-1/2
CMG Info			27918	38 3/4	36 9/16	37 7/16	-3/8
CNET		5	12353	28	26 1/8	27 1/2	-3/8
CmcstA		36	79383	37 5/8	35 11/16	36 9/16	+15/16
Cmpwre		11	75228	8 5/16	7 7/8	8 1/8	+3/16
CmvTch		61	21631	84 1/8	77 1/4	78 5/16	-3 1/8
ConEFS		38	6884	29 7/16	28 1/2	28 13/16	-5/16
CnxSys♣		489	75376	35 1/2	33 1/2	34 1/4	+9/16
Costco		25	65107	33 7/8	32 7/16	33 1/16	-1 11/16
DellCmp		52	290999	38 13/16	37 5/16	38 7/16	+3/8
DlrTreeSt		37	10001	41 1/16	40	41 1/16	+1
EBay		575	90123	61	52 5/16	57 1/2	+5 5/8
EchostrCm			25660	39 9/16	37 13/16	38 1/16	-11/16
ElctArt♣		74	7834	93	88 1/2	90 3/8	-1 1/8
EricsnB	0.03	164	80457	19 1/2	19	19 3/8	+3/8
Fiserv		41	9707	54 1/4	52 5/8	53 3/8	+3/8
GemstrTV		164	15947	66 3/8	65 1/16	65 5/8	+1/2
Gnzyme		43	5033	71 1/2	68 9/16	70 1/16	+1 7/16
GlobalC			38017	31 1/4	29 5/8	29 13/16	-11/16
Immunx		191	199535	48 1/8	39 1/2	40 5/16	-6 3/4
Intel x	0.08	48	245098	69 1/2	67 9/16	68 1/16	+3/16
Intuit		16	32573	47 11/16	43	47 5/8	+4 7/8
ITwoTech		1046	20664	151 5/16	144 1/2	146 9/16	-1 3/16
JDSUph			77036	120 3/16	118 5/8	119 7/16	+1 1/4
KLA-Tn		38	42490	54 5/8	52 5/8	53 1/4	+1/2
LegtSys			12283	8 15/16	d8 3/16	8 5/16	-5/8
LvlThrC♣			19267	62 7/8	59	59 5/8	-2 3/16
LinearTec x	0.12	69	33978	68 1/8	64 3/8	64 5/8	-1
Lycos		185	34556	62 7/8	60 1/8	61 1/16	+3 1/8
Maximl		77	42126	u79 1/4	76 1/16	78 1/2	+2 1/2
MclUSA			82403	17 1/8	16 1/8	16 15/16	+1
MedImm		169	24547	75	69	69 9/16	-4 7/16
MetmdFib			21936	37 5/16	35 3/8	36 1/4	+3/16
McroTch		43	10023	69 5/16	66 3/8	67 1/8	-2 1/16
Micsft		39	224028	72 1/4	70 9/16	71	-5/8
Miller H	0.14	18	2282	32 3/4	32	32 1/2	+9/16
Molex♣	0.10	43	7476	49 5/8	46 3/4	48 13/16	+1 11/16
NtwkAp		353	66754	89 3/4	84 13/16	88 5/16	+3 3/8
NtwkAs		53	18532	19 1/8	18 1/2	18 7/8	
NextlA			39169	57 1/4	53 11/16	54	-3/4
NEXTLINK			42639	35	33	34 11/16	[illegible]

Stock	Div.	P/E	Vol 100s	High	Low	Last	Chng
VeritasSfw			53054	111 5/8	103 5/16	109 13/16	+7 9/16
VISX		20	6032	25 7/16	23 3/4	24 1/4	+3/16
VitesSm		278	51239	78 3/4	74 1/16	77 15/16	+4
VceStrmW			26755	130 15/16	124 3/4	126 7/8	-4 9/16
WrldCm		34	185416	35 13/16	34 1/2	34 7/8	-1/4
Xilinx♣		38	35746	86 1/2	83 3/16	85 1/16	+9/16
Yahoo		558	55741	138	133 1/2	134	+1 11/16

Nasdaq LargeCap

Stock	Div.	P/E	Vol 100s	High	Low	Last	Chng
24/7 Media			5697	12 11/16	11 3/4	12 1/8	+5/16
724 Soltns			2706	36 3/4	30	35 5/8	+5 11/16
Abgenix♣			2966	57	55	56 9/16	+13/16
Abt.com			1822	31 1/4	29 1/2	30 3/4	+5/8
AccrSfwre			2213	23 1/8	21	21 7/16	-11/16
Actuate		419	3611	27 3/8	24 3/4	27 1/4	+2 1/16
ACTV♣			3160	14 1/4	13 5/8	13 7/8	-1/8
Acxiom Cp		21	4736	25 1/4	24 1/2	24 7/8	-1/16
AdptBr			5267	24 13/16	21 5/8	24 1/16	+1/8
AdlphBus			24909	13 1/16	10 1/16	12 1/2	+15/16
ADTRAN		32	4460	59 7/16	56 3/8	56 1/2	-1 9/16
AdvDigInfo		10	7504	15	14 1/4	14 15/16	+3/8
AdvEngyInd		39	3130	49 15/16	46 9/16	49 13/16	+4 1/4
AdvFCm		10	26418	40 15/16	39	40	+1 11/16
AdvRadio			1538	10 7/8	9 11/16	10 3/16	-7/16
AdventSftw		77	1618	60 5/16	56 1/4	58	-1 3/4
Aerfix			19562	35 13/16	28 9/16	32 5/16	+5 3/16
AetherSys			14663	138 5/8	124 1/8	129 1/2	-7 1/2
Afymtx			4970	132 7/16	125 3/4	127 5/16	-1/16
AGNCY.CM			1499	24 13/16	22 3/4	22 15/16	-15/16
AgileSftw			2836	59 5/8	56 1/2	57	-5/16
AirGtePCS			519	63 1/4	62	63	+5/8
AirnetCom		1	749	24 11/16	22	22 3/4	+1/2
AkamaiTch			12609	78 1/2	75	75 3/16	+1/8
Akzo ADR	0.53	29	530	41 13/16	41	41 11/16	-1 13/16
Almosa♣			2644	24 1/2	23 3/8	23 3/4	-1
AlxBld x	0.90	17	186	27	26 3/4	26 15/16	-1/16
AlexionPh			1332	74	70 1/4	70 7/8	-1 3/16
Alkrms			33262	37 3/8	33 3/8	35 3/8	+2
Allaire		265	5423	33 3/4	31 1/8	31 7/8	+7/8
AllgTel			27118	45 1/4	42 1/2	44 9/16	+2 5/16
AlSmcnd		1	3005	24 3/4	23 9/16	23 15/16	-1/8
AllCapCp	1.84	10	1886	20 1/16	19 15/16	20	+1/16
AlldRiser			2365	9 3/4	9 1/4	9 7/16	
Allscr♣			495	24 1/2	23 5/16	24 1/2	+2
Alpha Ind		50	10977	39 1/4	35 5/16	36 11/16	-1 1/16
AlteonWbSy			4626	146 9/16	142 3/4	143 11/16	+1/8
Amcor	0.87		17	13 1/8	13 1/16	13 1/16	-1/8
AmMgmtSy		14	8694	24 1/4	23 9/16	24 1/8	+1/8
AmNtln	2.84	7	119	63 7/16	61	62 1/8	-1 1/8
AmEglOutf		10	10369	21 5/8	19 5/8	21 1/2	+1 7/8
AmSprCp			1698	43 1/4	40 3/8	42 1/8	+1 3/8
AmeriTrade			12604	15 1/8	14 3/8	14 9/16	-9/16
AmkorTch		31	11838	27 3/4	25 3/4	27 1/16	+9/16
Anadigics		43	17482	31 7/8	29 5/8	31 1/2	+2 7/16
Andrew Cp		29	5711	26 7/16	24 7/8	25 1/8	-1 1/8
AndrxCp♣		76	6848	85 5/8	83 1/8	84 15/16	+1/4
answrthnk		46	2095	17 1/4	15 3/4	17 1/4	+1 1/2
ANTEC Cp		35	4883	45	42 1/2	44 1/4	+1 13/16
Antigncs			165	16 1/4	15 3/8	15 5/8	-5/8
Applebees	0.10	10	1031	24	23 1/8	23 3/8	-1/8
AppNet			9496	40 5/16	38	38 5/8	-1 3/8
Ariba			36752	145	136 13/16	137 7/16	-5 1/4
ARMHld		900	2671	31 1/4	29 7/8	30 5/8	-3/8
Arrwin	0.24	19	112	35 1/2	34 15/16	34 15/16	-9/16
ArtTchGrp			20052	98	92 1/8	97	+5 7/8
ArthCare		38	5501	34 3/4	33 1/16	34 1/4	+7/8
ASE Test			4728	25 3/4	24 3/8	25 1/2	+1 1/4
AskJeevs			4761	18 7/8	17 7/8	18 3/16	+3/16
ASM Intl		88	1235	26 1/4	25 1/2	25 3/4	+1/4

Fig. 7.3 Nasdaq prices

US indices

The United States provides the largest range of stock price indices (see Figure 7.4):

US INDICES

Dow Jones	Mar 17	Mar 16	Mar 15	1999/00 High	1999/00 Low	Since compilation High	Since compilation Low
Industrials	10595.23	10630.60	10131.41	**11722.98** (14/1/00)	9120.67 (22/1/99)	**11722.98** (14/1/00)	41.22 (8/7/32)
Home Bonds	95.39	95.05	94.65	**106.88** (13/1/99)	94.65 (15/3/00)	**107.17** (9/12/98)	54.99 (1/10/81)
Transport	2623.83	2678.88	2521.71	**3783.50** (12/5/99)	2263.59 (7/3/00)	**3783.50** (12/5/99)	13.23 (8/7/32)
Utilities	289.93	295.77	284.02	**333.45** (16/6/99)	269.20 (14/12/99)	**333.45** (16/6/99)	16.53 (8/7/32)

DJ Ind. Day's high (u) (u) Low (u) (u) (Theoretical♠)
Day's high 10763.38(10632.46) Low 10567.31 (10138.34) (Actual♠)

Standard and Poors	Mar 17	Mar 16	Mar 15	1999/00 High	1999/00 Low	Since compilation High	Since compilation Low
Composite‡	1464.47	1458.47	1392.14	**1469.25** (31/12/99)	1212.19 (14/1/99)	**1469.25** (31/12/99)	4.40 (1/6/32)
Industrials♥	1841.29	1831.68	1757.62	**1841.93** (31/12/99)	1461.72 (14/1/99)	**1841.93** (31/12/99)	3.52 (30/6/32)
Financial♥	129.31	129.16	118.84	**151.42** (22/4/99)	110.12 (25/2/00)	**151.42** (22/4/99)	7.13 (4/9/74)
Others							
NYSE Comp.	632.98	634.44	605.02	**663.12** (16/7/99)	576.17 (15/10/99)	**663.12** (16/7/99)	4.64 (25/4/42)
Amex Comp	1011.00	1017.65	996.12	**1033.33** (10/3/00)	683.61 (4/1/99)	**1033.33** (10/3/00)	524.20 (16/7/96)
NASDAQ Cmp	4798.13	4717.39	4582.62	**5048.62** (10/3/00)	2208.05 (4/1/99)	**5048.62** (10/3/00)	54.87 (3/10/74)
Russell 2000	574.77	574.24	558.87	**606.05** (9/3/00)	383.37 (23/3/99)	**606.05** (9/3/00)	123.36 (7/12/93)

RATIOS

	Mar 17	Mar 10	Mar 3	Year ago
Dow Jones Ind. Div. Yield	1.46	1.56	1.49	1.60
	Mar 15	Mar 8	Mar 1	Year ago
S & P Ind. Div. yield	0.98	0.99	0.99	1.12
S & P Ind. P/E ratio	34.89	34.53	38.67	40.63

US DATA

MARKET ACTIVITY

Volume (million)	Mar 17	Mar 16	Mar 15
NYSE	1313.85	1482.30	1302.81
Amex	52.146	76.025	65.303
NASDAQ	1691.90	2048.11	1945.08

NYSE	Mar 17	Mar 16	Mar 15
Issues Traded	3,464	3,482	3,455
Rises	1,407	2,431	1,914
Falls	1,575	646	1,122
Unchanged	482	405	419
New Highs	47	54	29
New Lows	51	52	143

NYSE TRADING ACTIVITY

Volume : 1,313,846,000

ACTIVE STOCKS

Friday	Stocks traded	Close price	Day's change
AmOnLne	20,571,800	64⅞	+3⅜
Compaq	19,335,500	30	+9/16
NtlNtw	17,572,900	128 15/16	+9 3/16
CrnvlA	16,682,800	21 7/16	-4 3/16
LucentTch	16,360,100	70½	+1½
PhMorr	13,705,900	20 1/16	-3/16
Boeing	12,533,800	37 3/16	+1 9/16
Citgrp	12,455,700	57	+1/16
WalMrt	12,283,100	55 11/16	+¾
Pfizer	11,946,300	35 13/16	-11/16

BIGGEST MOVERS

Friday	Close price	Day's change	Day's chge %
Ups			
WallaceCS	12⅝	+2½	+24.7
FchldSemi	36⅝	+4¾	+14.9
Wolverine	12¾	+1⅝	+14.6
CSK Auto	14	+1¾	+14.3
Downs			
IntrmSrv	19¼	-8 3/16	-29.8
Hnywell	47¼	-13½	-22.2
CrnvlA	21 7/16	-4 3/16	-16.3
UnBnCl	26½	-4 7/16	-14.3

NASDAQ TRADING ACTIVITY

Volume :1,691,903,000

ACTIVE STOCKS

Friday	Stocks traded	Close price	Day's change
Micsft	40,436,000	99⅜	+4
Oracle	32,889,000	79 13/16	-2⅛
Intel	30,360,600	129⅞	+4 13/16
DellCmp	29,813,500	56 7/16	+1 7/16
MCIWcm	28,370,700	43 11/16	-1 3/16
CiscoSys	26,189,100	135	+3 5/16
AVT Crp	19,610,600	11 15/16	-15 11/16
ETrade	19,429,800	29¼	+3 1/16
SunMic	16,202,000	96⅛	+5⅜
Qualcm	15,356,600	136¼	+3⅜

BIGGEST MOVERS

Friday	Close price	Day's change	Day's chge %
Ups			
CaliperTch	102	+25	+32.5
Lanoptics	26¾	+5⅝	+26.6
AvenueA	58	+11	+23.4
MTI Tch	38 3/16	+7⅛	+22.9
Downs			
AVT Crp	11 15/16	-15 11/16	-56.8
CumulusOne	13 1/16	-3⅞	-22.9
HispBrCp	106 7/16	-21 15/16	-17.1
VentanaMd	43¾	-8¾	-16.7

Fig. 7.4 US indices and US data

- **Dow Jones Industrials:** or the Dow Jones Industrial Average (DJIA), the main US index, takes the stock prices of 30 blue chip companies (see Appendix 2) and measures their movements. It is calculated by adding the New York closing prices and adjusting them by a "current average divisor", an adjustable figure formulated to preserve the continuity of the Dow over time amid changes in its component parts. Specialist indices are also provided for three other groups of stocks: Home Bonds, Transport (20 airlines, railroads and trucking companies) and Utilities (15 gas and power companies). For all four indices, the information provided comprises: the closing figures for the day alongside the closing for the previous two trading days; the highest and lowest trading level for the year with dates; and the highest and lowest trading level since compilation began, also with dates.

- **Standard & Poor's (S&P):** the Composite index consists of 500 companies listed on the New York Stock Exchange; the other two indices cover the Composite's Industrials (400 companies) and Financial stock (40 companies) sub-groups. The remaining companies are 20 transport companies and 40 utilities. While neither as comprehensive as the NYSE Composite nor as famous as the DJIA, the S&P 500 is generally regarded as a more comprehensive guide to the US market, accounting for nearly 80 per cent of the total NYSE capitalisation. Like the FTSE Actuaries series, individual companies are weighted according to their market capitalisation, allowing for the fact that some stocks exhibit a greater influence over the market than others.

- **NYSE Composite index:** the most broadly based of the US indices, covering all common stocks on the exchange.

- **Amex Composite index:** an index of over 800 companies listed on the American Stock Exchange.

- **Nasdaq Composite:** an index of the electronic stock market. This index is often used as an indicator of the market for stocks in technology and the industries of the future.

- **Russell 2000:** this is one of a family of 21 US equity indices produced by the Frank Russell Company. The indices are weighted by market capitalisation and include only common stocks domiciled in the United States and its territories. All are subsets of the Russell 3000 Index, which represents approximately 98 per cent of the US equity market. The Russell 1000 measures the performance of the largest 1,000 companies in the Russell 3000, making up 92 per cent of that index. This index, the Russell 2000 measures the performance of the remaining 2,000 companies in the Russell 3000, and hence is an indicator of how the stocks of smaller companies are doing. As of 2000, the average market capitalisation of the stocks in this index was $580 million, and the largest company in the index had a market capitalisation of $1.5 billion.

- **Dividend yields and price/earnings ratios:** yields for the Dow and S&P are calculated on the basis of the last declared dividend worked out at an annual rate. The S&P Industrials' p/e ratio is measured by dividing the last four quarterly earnings figures into the latest share price.

- **Market activity:** the volume of stocks traded on the NYSE, the Amex and the Nasdaq on the last three trading days, together with information on the number of issues traded, aggregate rises and falls, and new highs and lows on the NYSE. These are broad indicators of the recent pattern of the market's movements and the level of activity.

- **Active stocks:** figures on the previous day's ten most actively traded stocks on both the NYSE and the Nasdaq, including the number of shares traded and the stocks' closing prices and changes on the previous day.

- **Biggest movers:** prices and price changes on the stocks with the biggest percentage rise and falls on both the NYSE and the Nasdaq.

The Dow is one of the oldest stock market indicators, and has been published daily in *The Wall Street Journal* since 1896. Periodic additions and subtractions keep the index as a reflection of the broader economy. Only one of its original 12 members still remains in the current 30 – General Electric. The index often reaches new "highs" but since it is not adjusted for inflation, it can only reliably indicate direction of movement. For example, at the end of the 1800s, the Dow stood at 65.73. A century later, on the last trading day of 1999, it closed at 11,497.12, almost three times the closing price five years before.

The Dow – not strictly an index but rather an "average" – has traditionally been the most widely followed indicator in the United States, providing a guide to the daily mood of industrial stock markets in the same way as the FT 30 share index did for the United Kingdom. But it is now challenged by myriad other market indicators such as the S&P 500 and the Nasdaq Composite. Most market operators agree the S&P is a far better market gauge, not only because with 500 stocks it is more representative but also because the S&P is weighted by capitalisation rather than price. It is preferred by professional money managers and widely used as a benchmark for tracking instruments.

With the rise to prominence of the Nasdaq, its primary indicator, the Nasdaq Composite has increased in importance. Typically, nowadays, the Dow and the Nasdaq are quoted alongside each other as guides to the market's latest progress, with the former loosely taken to represent "old economy" stocks and the latter the "new economy".

Typical FT coverage of what is happening on Wall Street (the collective noun for American financial markets, analogous to "the City" for London's markets) looks like this:

> Technology and pharmaceutical issues weighed on Wall Street as the Nasdaq tumbled, while retail stocks and Coca-Cola helped the Dow to eke out a modest gain. The Dow Jones Industrial Average edged 21.83 higher at 11,260.61 and the Standard & Poor's 500 index shed 13.69 at 1,507.08. The tech-weighted Nasdaq Composite plunged 91.15 to 4,143.18.

"The best is good enough."

German proverb

"The trouble with our times is that the future isn't what it used to be."

Paul Valery

8

European equities

Stock markets in the euro-zone and beyond

- **European equities** – share price movements on leading European markets
- **FTSE Eurotop indices** – the new performance measures of Europe's stock markets; the FTSE Eurotop 300; FTSE € Stars; other European indices
- **The changing world of European stock markets**

■ European equities

Since the launch of the single European currency in 1999 and as the euro-zone becomes more integrated, much of the currency risk associated with cross-border European investing in equities and other assets has disappeared. As a result, investors are increasingly taking a pan-European view: the industry sector in which companies operate, rather than their nationality or the location of their headquarters, is becoming more important.

The *Financial Times* has responded to these developments by greatly expanding its coverage of continental European markets. Its World Stock Markets pages carry share price information on a substantial number of companies listed in the EMU (economic and monetary union) countries (see Figure 8.1) plus extra tables on the stock markets in Germany and France with their key indices, most active stocks and biggest movers. And the new Euro Markets page adds data on a range of indices for the overall European equity markets, many recently developed by FTSE International, as well as information on a variety of currencies, money, bonds and derivatives.

■ FTSE Eurotop indices

The FTSE Actuaries share indices European series, launched in 1997, cover in detail the daily movements of the FTSE Eurotop group of indices created by FTSE International in collaboration with Amsterdam Exchanges (see Figure 8.2). These have been created to give investors a wide-ranging family of "real-time" equity indices covering the European market, against which to measure performance and to encourage the development of derivatives for speculative purposes and for investors to hedge exposures. The table shows the performance of the regional and sectoral indices in euro terms. Investors can also see indices that exclude those countries, such as the UK, which did not join the single currency in the first wave:

- **Index information:** the columns across indicate the name of the index; its closing value in euros; the previous day's percentage change in the index; the day's change expressed in points; the untaxed dividend yield produced by the constituent companies; ex-dividend adjustment; and the total return delivered by the index constituents – the combination of capital gains through changes in share prices and income from dividends reinvested.

- **FTSE Eurotop 300:** this index measures the performance of the 300 largest companies in Europe in terms of market capitalisation, whether they are in the euro-zone or not. The index represents about 70 per cent of the region's total market capitalisation and has become an accepted European benchmark. The index is broken down into three regional sub-indices: one for Eurotop 300 companies located in the euro-zone, one for those outside the euro-zone and one excluding companies located in the UK.

- **FTSE Eurotop 100:** this index consists of the 100 largest companies in Europe according to market capitalisation. It has been designed specifically for the creation of derivatives (stock index futures and options), which need to be based on baskets of very liquid, easily tradeable stocks.

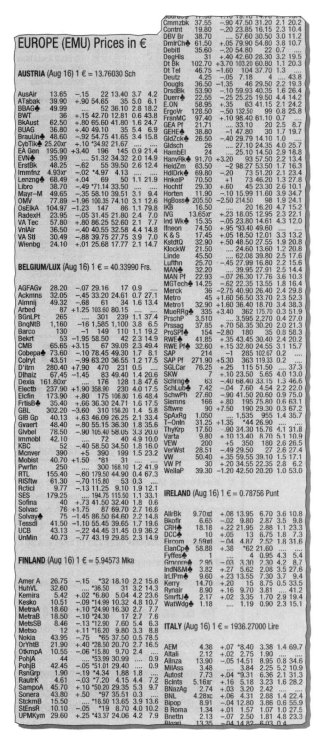

Fig. 8.1 European stock markets

FTSE Actuaries Share Indices — European series
Produced in conjunction with the Faculty and Institute of Actuaries

Jun 27	Euro Index	Day's %	change points	Yield gross %	xd adj ytd	Total retn (Euro) €
FTSE Eurotop 300	1596.32	-0.49	-7.78	1.70	19.73	1696.86
FTSE E300 Eurobloc	1792.43	-0.29	-5.27	1.54	22.25	1887.69
FTSE E300 Ex-Eurobloc	1417.59	-0.70	-10.01	1.88	17.37	1517.82
FTSE E300 Ex-UK	1750.70	-0.37	-6.52	1.51	21.92	1837.62
FTSE Eurotop 100	3722.04	-0.47	-17.65	1.54	41.03	1375.37
FTSE Eurobloc 100	1464.63	-0.34	-4.96	1.55	18.26	1533.24
FTSE EuroMid	1437.03	+0.02	+0.30	2.58	28.74	1558.06
FTSE EuroMid Eurobloc	1352.10	-0.40	-5.39	2.78	29.27	1445.75
FTSE EuroMid Ex-UK	1418.34	+0.10	+1.40	2.40	27.40	1505.04
FTSE Eurotop 300 Industry Sectors						
RESOURCES	1364.60	-1.00	-13.79	2.27	21.06	1488.19
Mining	1338.15	+1.63	+21.42	3.05	27.64	1443.02
Oil & Gas	1315.96	-1.19	-15.79	2.22	19.76	1404.56
BASIC INDUSTRIES	1252.10	+0.43	+5.38	2.76	28.03	1340.27
Chemicals	910.70	+0.57	+5.13	3.06	23.92	973.33
Construction & Bld Matls	1308.18	+0.42	+5.45	2.13	16.01	1363.46
Forestry & Paper	1026.72	-0.90	-9.32	4.48	44.26	1160.31
Steel & Other Metals	1397.90	+1.29	+17.79	0.00	0.00	1484.43
GENERAL INDUSTRIALS	1686.43	-1.42	-24.26	1.70	23.59	1781.29
Aerospace & Defence	868.89	-0.47	-4.12	2.18	9.29	911.90
Diversified Industrials	1051.70	-2.39	-25.79	2.17	18.90	1117.18
Electronic & Elect Equip	2452.10	-0.98	-24.35	1.07	20.73	2527.24
Engineering & Machinery	947.64	-1.41	-13.50	3.20	31.90	1014.16
CYCLICAL CONS GOODS	1353.44	+0.16	+2.18	2.23	25.87	1447.69
Automobiles	800.57	+0.41	+3.24	2.85	19.84	845.75
Household Goods & Texts	2589.11	-0.25	-6.61	1.18	25.31	2684.39
NON-CYC CONS GOODS	1345.12	+0.61	+8.15	1.55	14.83	1420.82
Beverages	992.50	-0.47	-4.69	2.72	8.76	1049.63
Food Producers & Procesrs	942.84	-0.50	-4.74	1.88	14.58	986.08
Health	1546.29	+5.84	+85.32	0.89	17.31	1610.73
Packaging	747.01	-0.06	-0.42	2.38	0.00	758.27
Personal Care & Hse Prods	1509.21	+1.28	+19.04	0.90	11.01	1550.30
Pharmaceuticals	1231.58	+0.97	+11.86	1.27	12.34	1268.68
Tobacco	1580.55	-0.26	-4.18	4.53	27.27	1712.53
CYCLICAL SERVICES	1453.37	-0.85	-12.40	1.66	14.50	1540.78
Distributors	1112.27	-3.47	-40.00	1.90	14.69	1180.61
General Retailers	938.88	-0.39	-3.72	2.22	9.67	987.33
Leisure Entertmt & Hotels	984.34	-2.81	-28.46	2.27	20.26	1040.31
Media & Photography	1934.21	-1.31	-25.70	1.02	11.71	2001.47
Restaurants & Pubs	792.52	-0.84	-6.75	3.22	12.47	855.39
Support Services	1092.23	+0.99	+10.72	1.08	9.93	1128.87
Transport	833.79	-0.34	-2.83	3.01	16.59	890.95
NON-CYCLICAL SERVS	1985.15	-0.46	-9.08	1.06	10.59	2077.94
Food & Drug Retailers	1223.83	+0.46	+5.61	1.68	16.64	1281.36
Telecommunication Servs	2034.07	-0.56	-11.40	0.99	8.87	2095.09
UTILITIES	1412.51	-0.65	-9.28	3.24	26.28	1578.15
Electricity	1027.84	-0.59	-6.15	3.53	21.88	1122.97
Gas Distribution	1403.37	-0.76	-10.69	1.68	13.04	1585.44
Water	791.19	-0.95	-7.55	6.41	20.43	906.31
FINANCIALS	1467.54	-0.07	-1.08	2.22	25.14	1567.33
Banks	988.14	-0.22	-2.22	2.65	21.08	1048.89
Insurance	1193.53	+0.78	+9.19	1.40	12.84	1241.24
Life Assurance	1261.49	-0.73	-9.23	1.98	14.47	1316.75
Investment Companies	1674.27	-1.53	-26.01	1.67	24.35	1773.33
Real Estate	680.81	-3.18	-22.33	4.07	22.28	742.35
Speciality & Other Fin	1472.18	-0.53	-7.84	0.97	8.48	1543.65
INFORMATION TECH	2834.24	-1.84	-53.06	0.36	10.00	2875.39
Information Tech Hardware	3570.08	-2.31	-84.32	0.36	12.71	3625.14
Software & Computer Serv	1174.61	+0.55	+6.42	0.36	3.96	1187.99

Fig. 8.2 FTSE Actuaries share indices European series

- **FTSE EuroMid:** this index consists of European stocks that are included in the FTSE World Index (see Chapter 9) but which are too small to qualify for the FTSE Eurotop 300 – an index of European mid-cap stocks.

- **Industry sectors:** indices for economic groupings (broad areas of industrial activity) and individual industrial sectors, categorised under the FTSE Global Industry Classification System.

The FTSE Eurotop 300

The FT's Euro Markets page also carries share price and other financial data for all the constituents of the Eurotop 300 (see Figure 8.3).

These companies' share prices are already listed on the world stock markets and London share service pages of the newspaper (expressed in local currencies). So why this table? For one thing, it brings together all the companies in the index in one place. They are likely to emerge as members of a new "super-league" of leading European businesses, as fund managers focus more on investing across the continent.

In addition, the table expresses companies' share prices in euros so as to allow easier comparisons. Companies are also grouped by sector rather than by country since investors are increasingly focusing on comparisons between European companies in the same sector when making investment decisions. The table also indicates which companies have their headquarters in euro-zone countries by marking them out in bold.

The table includes, furthermore, additional financial data not always shown in other listings. These are market capitalisation, the company's share price multiplied by the number of shares in issue; and the volume of trading in the shares on the latest trading day. The final column shows the share's yield, its annual dividend payment expressed as a percentage of the share price. These figures are gathered from local stock exchange data and, currently, given difference statistical methods are not necessarily comparable across national boundaries.

FT coverage of the share performance of the leading European companies as reflected in the Eurotop 300 and other leading indices is illustrated in the following extract, which focuses on the "TMT" stocks:

> European stock markets surged to new highs on Friday as investor enthusiasm for technology, media and telecommunications (TMT) shares returned with a vengeance. In London, the FTSE 100 index, which had been stuck in a 6,000–6,600 range for much of the year, surged 122.3 to 6,795. The Paris and Copenhagen markets recorded all-time highs, as did the pan-European FTSE Eurotop 300 index, while the Amsterdam bourse finished just short of a new peak, and in Helsinki the HEX index rose 5.1 per cent with the help of a surge in mobile telecoms group Nokia. The TMT sectors had been behind the so-called "new economy" surge in stock markets in the last quarter of 1999 and the first quarter of this year. But TMT stocks sold off sharply in the spring on worries about excessive valuations. On Friday, however, it seemed as if investors had resumed their love affair with the three sectors. At 5pm London time, the FTSE Eurotop telecoms sector was up 5 per cent on the day, computer software had gained 4.8 per cent and the media sector 3.1 per cent.
>
> (*Financial Times*, 1 September 2000)

FTSE EUROTOP 300

Jun 27

Name	Price (Euro)	Chge + or -	Mkt cap Euro(bn)	Vol (m)	Yld
AEROSPACE & DEFENCE					
BAE Systems	6.85	+.03	20.5	6.5	1.9
Rolls R	3.97	−.04	6.2	3.6	2.9
Smiths Ind	13.88	+.09	4.4	0.8	2.6
Thomson CSF♣	40.60	-1.40	6.8	0.3	1.5
AUTOMOBILES					
BMW	31.09	−.42	19.3	-	1.3
DaimlerChrys♣	56.77	+.73	57.6	-	4.1
Fiat	27.23	−.17	10.0	0.9	2.3
GKN	13.80	−.37	9.9	3.0	0.7
Michelin B	34.50	+.94	4.6	0.7	2.1
Peugeot♣	216.50	+.10	9.8	0.1	1.2
Pirelli Spa	2.76	−.01	5.2	4.0	3.0
Renault	45.20	+1.05	10.8	0.4	1.7
Valeo	58.35	+1.20	4.8	0.1	2.6
Volkswagen	39.41	−.12	12.3	-	1.9
BANKS					
ABN Amro	25.30	-	37.2	9.1	3.2
Allied Irish	9.05	−.31	7.8	1.6	3.7
Almanij	42	+.60	8.2	0.1	1.9
Alpha Credit Ba	42.20	+.88	6.8	0.1	2.1
Abbey Natl	12.25	+.08	17.4	2.3	5.2
Alliance & L	8.92	−.09	4.7	1.0	5.2
Banca di Roma	1.25	−.02	6.7	7.9	1.0
Banca Intesa	4.49	+.06	21.6	16.0	1.8
Monte Paschi	4.04	+.01	8.7	7.2	20.2
Bca Naz de L	3.61	−.04	5.7	4.9	1.6
BBV Argentaria	15.37	−.13	48.5	4.8	1.5
Banco Popular	32.49	+.24	7.2	0.4	2.1
Banco Santander	10.90	+.03	44.8	5.4	1.7
Bank Austria	51.25	+.08	4.5	0.1	2.0
Bank of Ireland	6.63	−.02	6.6	2.3	3.5
Bay Hypo Ver♣	66.29	+.88	27.9	-	1.3
Banco Comercial	5.24	−.14	5.2	109.5	1.8
Bca Populare	8.44	−.68	10.4	43.3	0.6
BNP	95.10	-2.40	42.1	1.1	1.8
Bank Scot♣	9.69	+.07	12.2	3.0	2.2
Barclays	25.97	+.32	38.4	3.4	3.1
Commerzbank	38.40	−.35	19.1	-	2.1
Commercial Bank	47.01	+.52	4.0	0.1	1.9
CCF	149	−.50	11.0	-	1.5
Credit Lyona	47.89	−.01	11.7	0.6	1.0
Cr Suis(Rg)♣	206.01	-1.73	56.4	0.4	2.2
Danske Bank	122.99	-2.22	6.5	-	2.7
Deutsche Bank	85.10	+.59	52.3	-	1.4
Dexia	157	-1	15.1	0.1	1.9
Dresdner Bank	42.25	+.05	21.9	-	2.0
ForeningsSparba	15.54	−.11	8.2	0.3	3.8
Fortis (B)♣	28.81	−.02	21.1	0.5	2.0
Fortis (NL)♣	29	−.22	14.3	2.2	2.6
HSBC (75p)	11.93	+.06	101.8	22.5	3.0
Halifax	9.57	−.01	21.5	1.3	4.0
KBC Holdings	45.20	+1.02	13.5	0.1	2.0
LloydsTSB	9.93	−.12	54.6	17.2	4.3
National Bank o	42.50	+.85	9.7	2.2	2.0
Nordic Baltic [	7.17	−.32	20.6	5.4	2.9
Rolo Banca	19.14	−.09	8.4	0.3	4.6
Ryl Bk Scot♣	16.41	+.17	43.6	3.8	2.8
SanPaolo-IMI	17.08	+.22	23.9	5.5	3.0
S-E-Banken A	11.54	−.04	7.8	1.2	3.6
Societe General	61.20	−.30	25.9	2.0	2.5
Sv Handelsb A	14.88	.23	0.7	0.0	2.4
Stand Chrtd	13.16	−.13	14.1	2.4	2.8
UBS AG (Reg)♣	152.41	−.73	65.5	0.6	2.3
Uni Credito Ita	4.88	+.04	24.4	17.2	2.7
Woolwich	4.35	−.11	6.6	4.1	4.4
BEVERAGES					
Allied-Dom	5.61	+.05	6.0	5.9	2.9
Diageo	9.18	−.19	31.4	8.2	3.5
Heineken	61.90	+.50	19.4	1.2	0.6
Scot & New	8.43	+.17	5.3	2.3	4.9
Sth Africa B♣	7.93	+.02	6.1	1.3	3.4
CHEMICALS					
Air Liquide	132	+.20	12.0	0.1	1.8
Akzo	43.15	+1.23	12.3	1.9	2.3
BASF	41.01	+.56	25.6	-	2.7
Bayer♣	38.89	+.13	28.4	-	3.3
BOC♣	15.17	+.03	7.5	2.5	3.8
Burmah Castrol	26.41	−.13	4.7	0.5	2.8
Ciba Spec Ch (R	66.19	+.29	4.4	0.1	2.0
Clariant (Reg)	386.83	-4.10	5.6	-	1.7
Degussa-Huels	30.50	−.60	4.8	-	3.3
ICI	8.15	−.08	5.9	1.8	6.3
Solvay♣	69.45	+.55	5.8	-	2.4
CONSTRUCTION & BUILDING					
Bouygues	738	+1	23.9	-	0.4
Blue Circle♣	6.78	+.02	4.9	0.7	3.8
CRH♣	18.85	+.35	7.4	0.3	1.1
Holderbank B	1,260.59	-16.22	6.9	-	1.1
Hanson♣	7.57	−.01	5.6	1.2	2.8
Lafarge	82.90	+1.20	9.0	0.4	2.5
Skanska B	37.54	−.12	3.9	0.1	3.8
Saint Gobain♣	143.20	+1.20	12.5	0.2	2.5
DISTRIBUTORS					
Elec Comps♣	10.04	−.36	4.4	0.4	1.9
DIVERSIFIED INDUSTRIALS					
E.ON♣	50.65	-2.85	38.1	-	2.5
RWE♣	35.31	−.78	16.7	-	2.8
Suez-Lyon des E	186.60	-2.70	37.0	0.3	1.6
Vivendi	93.05	−.95	55.6	2.3	1.1
ELECTRICITY					
Edison	9.99	−.25	6.3	1.2	1.3
Elect de Port	18.35	+.06	5.4	0.2	3.5
Electrabel	261.40	+1.80	14.2	-	3.6
Endesa	20.85	−.40	22.1	3.9	2.3
Enel	4.52	+.04	18.9	12.0	2.7
Iberdrola	13.60	−.20	12.3	3.0	2.6
Natl Grid♣	8.22	−.11	12.2	6.7	2.7
Nat Power♣	6.58	−.10	7.4	1.7	3.6
PowerGen♣	9	−.02	5.9	1.9	6.2
Scot & Sthn♣	8.92	+.06	7.6	0.6	5.1
Scot Power♣	8.76	−.02	16.2	1.4	4.5
Union Fenosa	19.82	−.18	6.0	5.7	1.6
ELECTRONIC & ELECTRICAL EQUPT					
ABB Ltd	129	-1.20	38.7	0.5	1.5
Alstom	29	-	6.2	0.3	1.9
Invensys♣	3.94	+.02	13.8	31.7	3.2
Philips Electro	52.90	-1.45	71.8	14.7	0.6
Lagardere♣	84.75	+3.40	10.4	0.2	0.9
Legrand	237.30	+8.30	5.1	-	0.7
Schneider El♣	70.75	−.25	11.4	0.3	1.9
Siemens	158.65	-1.35	94.4	-	0.6
ENGINEERING & MACHINERY					
ASSA ABLOY	20.20	−.36	4.7	0.2	0.4
Atls Copco A	20.74	−.36	2.9	0.5	2.7
Atls Copco B	19.91	−.54	1.4	0.3	2.9
Linde	41.50	−.50	4.7	-	2.7
MAN♣	33.63	+.64	3.7	-	2.5
Sandvik ♣	21.82	−.73	5.6	0.5	-
Scania A	26.30	−.08	2.6	-	3.2
Scania B	26.78	−.20	2.7	-	3.1
Thyssen-Krupp	16.85	+.05	8.7	-	4.3
Volvo A	22.30	−.85	3.1	0.5	3.8
Volvo B	23.31	−.67	7.1	2.0	3.6
FOOD & DRUG RETAILERS					
Ahold	30.94	+.25	23.3	5.3	1.6
Carrefour	74	+1	51.6	0.8	0.6
Casino	95.05	−.45	7.7	0.1	1.3
Sainsbury♣	4.75	−.01	9.1	3.8	4.8
Tesco	3.28	−.04	22.5	14.9	2.2
FOOD PRODUCERS & PROCESSORS					
A B Foods	7.14	−.03	5.7	0.8	2.4
Cadbury Schw♣	6.62	−.06	13.5	5.6	2.4
Danone	136.40	−.40	20.2	0.5	1.3
Nestle R♣	2,095.60	-10.87	82.6	0.1	1.3
Numico	49.80	-	7.1	2.1	1.2
Unilever NV CVA	50.80	−.10	29.0	3.7	2.5
Unilever♣	6.61	−.06	19.2	7.0	3.0
FORESTRY & PAPER					
Stora Enso A	9.80	+.39	2.0	-	4.1
Stora Enso R	9.15	−.12	5.0	2.1	4.4
UPM-Kymmene	26.75	−.55	6.9	0.7	4.7
GAS DISTRIBUTION					
BG	6.73	+.17	23.6	13.5	2.2
Centrica	3.35	−.22	13.4	17.0	1.2
Gas Natural SDG	19.35	−.15	8.7	0.5	1.0
GENERAL RETAILERS					
Boots	7.69	−.28	6.9	4.1	5.2
Castorama Du	275.50	+11.50	10.7	0.1	0.8
Dixons	4.29	+.08	8.2	8.1	1.5
GUS♣	6.46	−.07	6.5	2.9	5.3
H & M B	20.68	−.78	15.1	2.8	0.8
Kingfisher♣	9.19	−.15	12.7	3.4	2.5
Metro AG	35.60	+.40	10.8	-	2.9
Marks & S	3.78	+.01	10.9	8.5	3.8
Pinault Printem	235	−.60	27.9	0.2	0.8
HEALTH					
Nycomed Amer♣	10.51	+.58	6.7	2.0	0.9
HOUSEHOLD & TEXTILES					
Christian Dior	249.90	+.90	11.3	0.1	1.1
Electrolux B♣	16.38	+.13	5.8	0.9	2.6
LVMH	451.80	-3	44.3	0.1	0.8
Richemont A (Br	2,718.79	+4.93	14.2	-	0.3
Swatch Br	1,358.75	+1.82	4.9	-	0.5
Swatch Reg	274.46	-2.74	4.1	-	0.6
I.T. HARDWARE					
Alcatel SA	69.90	-1.10	79.1	4.9	0.6
ARM Holdings	11.95	−.51	11.7	4.6	-
ASM Lithography	47.60	+1.15	19.9	7.3	-
Ericsson B	20.80	−.60	149.2	28.6	0.3
INFINEON TECHNO	92.50	+5.08	28.5	-	-
Marconi	14.78	−.36	40.6	5.5	0.6
Nokia	56.10	-1.85	262.4	14.4	0.4
Sagem	1,255	-54.50	10.0	-	0.2
ST Microelctron	70.35	-1.75	60.9	2.2	-
INSURANCE					
Allianz	376	-	92.2	-	0.3
AGF	56.40	−.20	10.4	0.2	2.9
Axa	170.10	+4.70	66.5	1.1	1.2
Allied Zuric♣	12.43	+.13	19.6	9.1	1.9
Baloise (Reg)	1,038.43	-8.99	6.1	-	1.5
Ergo Versich	116	-1.50	8.8	-	0.9
Generali	34.91	+.21	43.7	4.2	0.6
ING Group♣	67.94	+.09	64.6	3.9	2.4
Munich Re ♣	324.30	+8	58.3	-	0.3
Ras	11.42	−.13	8.2	1.8	1.9
Royal Sun Al	6.49	+.19	9.3	13.3	6.1
Swiss Re R	2,111.74	-19.28	30.2	-	1.5
Zurich Allie♣	526.32	-2.24	25.6	0.1	2.1
INVESTMENT COMPANIES					
3i Group♣	21.67	−.57	13.1	6.0	0.9
Foreign & C♣	4.18	−.02	4.1	0.4	1.1
GBL	253.10	+1.60	6.2	-	1.6
Investor B	14.29	−.34	6.5	0.4	2.5
Investor A♣	14.05	−.16	4.4	0.2	2.6
LEISURE ENTERTAINMENT & HOTELS					
Accor	43.76	+.36	8.1	0.3	2.1
Granada	9.88	−.51	18.5	15.4	1.6
Hilton Grp♣	3.98	−.13	6.0	1.8	3.2
Preussag	35.23	−.22	6.1	-	2.2
LIFE ASSURANCE					
Aegon♣	38.29	−.09	51.2	4.7	1.6
Alleanza Assic	13.11	−.15	9.4	1.2	0.9
CGNU	16.14	+.04	36.2	5.8	3.8
Legal & Gen	2.55	−.13	13.1	26.8	2.6
Mediolanum	17.47	−.28	6.3	1.0	0.4
Prudential	14.86	−.31	29.1	5.0	2.5
Swiss Life (Reg	629	-1	7.4	-	1.1
Skandia♣	26.30	+.16	26.9	2.9	0.2
Sun Life & P♣	8	−.03	8.2	0.3	3.0
MEDIA & PHOTOGRAPHY					
B Sky B♣	20.69	−.15	37.8	2.1	-
Canal +	185.20	+.20	23.3	0.3	0.4
Carlton C	13.40	−.05	9.0	4.6	1.9
Daily Mail A	17.95	−.33	6.8	0.1	0.7
Elsevier-NDU CV	12.55	−.01	8.4	3.8	2.2
Emap♣	16.65	−.12	4.2	0.5	1.8
EMI♣	10.04	−.47	7.9	1.0	2.6
L'Espresso	12.62	−.58	5.4	2.9	0.6
Mediaset	16.42	−.05	19.4	2.5	1.1
Pearson♣	33.69	-1.06	21.1	0.6	1.1
Reed Int	8.87	+.19	10.2	8.6	1.8
Reuters	19.39	−.61	27.6	2.8	1.2
Seat Pagine	3.75	−.09	7.6	16.8	2.8
SES	172.12	+.25	4.0	-	1.1
Utd News♣	14.78	+.02	7.4	2.5	2.4
VNU NV	56.95	-1	12.8	0.8	0.8
Wolters Kluwer	20.44	+.43	0.2	1.0	1.0
WPP♣	14.98	−.50	11.6	7.6	0.3
MINING					
Ang Am	49.55	−.13	20.2	0.3	3.0
Billiton♣	4.21	+.15	9.0	9.8	2.7
Rio Tinto	16.54	+.44	18.4	4.2	3.3
OIL & GAS					
BP Amoco♣	10.08	−.29	227.7	41.5	2.0
ENI	6	+.01	48.0	32.4	2.6
Norsk Hydro♣	42.51	−.46	5.6	0.2	2.3
Repsol-YPF	20.65	−.37	24.5	3.0	1.6
Royal Dutch	66.50	−.45	142.6	6.2	2.3
Shell Trans♣	9.07	−.03	90.2	12.9	2.5
Total Fina Elf	163.50	+.50	118.4	2.2	1.4
PACKAGING					
Alusuisse Reg	678.08	−.38	4.3	-	-
PERSONAL & HOUSEHOLD PRODUCTS					
Beiersdorf	90.10	−.90	7.6	-	0.8
l'Oreal	865	+16	58.5	0.1	0.4
Reckitt & C♣	11.93	−.13	7.5	1.0	3.4
PHARMACEUTICALS					
Aventis SA	75.40	+1.40	58.8	2.1	0.6
AstraZeneca♣	46.15	−.53	81.5	2.3	1.5
Elan Corp♣	46.25	+.45	12.4	-	-
Glaxo Wlcme♣	29.92	+.45	109.1	9.5	2.0
Novartis R	1,635.79	+39.14	118.0	0.4	1.3
Novo Nordisk	174.36	+1.78	11.3	0.4	0.8
Roche Hold GS	10,090.51	-122	70.9	-	0.6
ROCHE HLDS (BR)	11,043.05	-264.69	8.8	-	0.6
Sanofi-Synthlbo	49.85	+1.35	36.4	0.9	0.6
Schering♣	56.32	+.19	11.5	-	1.5
SmKl Bchm	13.61	+.16	76.6	15.6	1.5
UCB	37.76	+.61	5.5	0.1	1.0
REAL ESTATE					
Land Sec	12.14	−.40	6.3	2.2	4.1
RESTAURANTS & PUBS					
Bass	11.57	−.01	10.2	2.5	4.5
Compass♣	12.94	−.42	8.8	8.1	0.8
Whitbread	9.48	+.20	4.7	2.2	5.0
SOFTWARE & COMPUTER SERVICES					
Cap Gemini	192.50	+4.50	23.3	0.5	0.5
CMG PLC	14.82	−.07	8.8	1.7	0.2
Freeserve PLC	5.09	−.74	1.3	6.7	-
Intracom	40	+1.45	3.9	0.1	0.6
Logica PLC	26.60	+.09	10.7	1.1	0.2
Misys♣	9.25	−.11	5.3	2.4	0.6
SAP (Pref)	214.20	+1.20	28.4	-	0.2
SAP	174.48	+.63	31.9	-	0.3
Sage Group PLC	8.32	+.02	10.5	4.6	0.1
Sema Gp♣	14.75	−.07	6.9	1.5	0.3
Terra Networ	42	+.50	2.9	0.8	-
SPECIALITY & OTHER FINANCE					
Amvescap♣	16.50	+.29	11.2	1.4	0.9
Bnc Fideuram	16.42	−.48	14.9	1.6	0.6
Electrafina	139	+.90	1.4	-	1.9
Mediobanca	10.40	+.34	6.2	6.3	1.1
Schroders N	14.58	−.27	1.0	0.3	2.0
Schroders♣	17.32	−.67	3.9	1.9	1.7
STEEL & OTHER METALS					
Corus	1.57	+.02	4.9	10.1	-
SUPPORT SERVICES					
Adecco (Reg)	888.61	+27.93	15.7	-	0.6
Capita Group PL	25.01	+.10	5.4	0.3	0.2
Hays♣	5.93	+.10	10.2	6.5	0.9
Randstad Hld	37.80	+1.50	4.4	1.1	1.8
Rentokil Ini	2.39	−.02	5.7	57.4	2.7
Securitas B	24.81	-1.22	8.4	1.3	0.5
Sodexho	180	+2.40	6.0	0.1	1.0
TNT Post Groep	26.60	+.40	12.7	2.6	1.4
TELECOMMUNICATION SERVICES					
BT♣	14.42	−.20	94.3	28.7	2.5
Cable & W	18.70	+.32	51.9	9.5	1.3
Colt Telecom Gr	37.61	-1.20	26.3	0.9	-
Deutsche Teleko	63.50	−.04	80.8	-	1.0
Eircom	2.70	−.08	6.0	6.0	1.7
Equant	45.75	+.42	9.2	0.5	-
Europolitan	13.63	+.56	5.6	0.8	0.8
Energis	42.62	-2.02	13.3	1.4	-
France Telecom	157.90	-5.60	51.0	2.3	0.6
Hellenic Teleco	26.33	+.54	6.4	0.3	2.5
Netcom Sys B	77.47	+.72	6.6	0.4	-
Olivetti	3.89	−.03	18.7	32.8	0.8
Panafon	12.30	+.35	1.5	0.4	0.9
Portugal Teleco	11.42	+.33	10.7	4.4	1.8
KPN	47.50	-1.36	45.4	4.0	1.1
Sonera	51.70	-3.25	16.1	3.3	0.2
Swisscom (Reg.)	377.14	−.21	9.6	0.1	2.6
Tecnost Spa	4.06	−.04	12.0	11.6	-
Tele Danmark	73.77	-1.25	16.0	0.3	1.8
Telecel Comm	16.47	−.09	3.5	0.4	1.4
TIM	10.80	−.11	71.7	12.3	1.6
Telecom Italia	14.38	−.11	75.7	7.0	2.2
Telefonica	21.50	+.95	71.0	33.5	-
TeleWest♣	4.25	−.52	12.3	8.7	-
Utd Pan Euro Co	32.40	+.40	7.1	6.3	-
Vodafone	4.74	-	291.7	155.8	0.4
TOBACCO					
Altadis	16.20	−.10	5.2	1.3	1.6
BAT Inds♣	7.13	+.02	15.5	8.3	5.0
Imperial Tob	9.82	−.16	5.1	0.8	4.8
TRANSPORT					
BAA	7.97	−.02	8.5	3.3	3.3
B Airways	6.07	-	6.6	3.2	4.7
D/S 1912 B	11,011.61	-59.79	5.9	-	-
Lufthansa	24.22	+.20	9.2	-	2.3
Ocean Group PLC	17.54	−.40	5.2	0.9	1.8
P & O	9.24	−.13	6.3	1.8	5.7
Railtrack♣	14.75	+.03	7.6	0.8	2.9
WATER					
Thames Water♣	13.02	−.26	4.6	0.3	6.1
Utd Utils♣	10.55	−.01	5.8	4.9	6.8

Notes

Price data and market capitalisations supplied by FTSE International.

Market capitalisation figures are based on shares used in index calculations. Shares are not counted where foreign ownership restrictions apply. Market caps may include secondary lines not eligible as constituents.

Stocks in bold type are domiciled in Emu countries.

Trading Volumes and yields derived from local domestic markets and supplied by Financial Times Information.

Company classifications are based on those used for the FTSE Eurotop share indices.

Annual/Interim reports can be obtained for companies with a ♣ marked by the name. Annual Reports Service telephone +44 20 8391 6000. For further details see Share Price pages.

Fig. 8.3 FTSE Eurotop 300

■ FTSE €Stars

The Euro Markets page also carries a picture of the latest movements of another new index called the FTSE €Stars (see Figure 8.4). This index, launched in June 1999, is made up of 28 highly liquid, blue chip constituents from five different euro-zone stock markets and is designed to be the easiest cross-border index to trade in Europe. The constituents are simply those stocks that are common to all major cross-border pan-European and euro-zone derivative indices – what its designers hope will come to be known as the "Magic 28". They account for almost 40 per cent of the market capitalisation of the FTSE World Index Eurobloc benchmark.

The constituents of the index will be reviewed annually and there is no set limit to the number of companies included. As of late 2000, the companies in the index were ABN Amro, Aegon, Ahold, Alcatel, Allianz, Axa-UAP, Banco Bilbao Vizcaya Argentaria, Banco Santander Central Hispano, Bayer, Carrefour, DaimlerChrysler, Deutsche Bank, Deutsche Telekom, Eon, Ente Nazionale Indrocarburi (ENI), France Telecom, Generali Assicurazioni, International Nederlanden Group, Koninklijke Philips Electronic, L'Oréal, Royal Dutch Petroleum, Siemens, Telecom Italia, Telefonica de Espana, TotalFina Elf, Unilever and Vivendi.

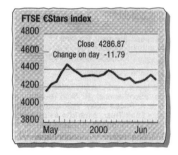

Fig. 8.4 FTSE €Stars index

■ Other European indices

The Euro Markets page also gives the latest values of five other leading indices that focus on continental Europe (see Figure 8.5). These are rivals to the FTSE Eurotop indices and are managed by Dow Jones and Morgan Stanley Capital International.

The newspaper also gives details on shares traded on two other markets: the Easdaq and the Euro.NM. These two are battling it out to become Europe's answer to the Nasdaq market in the United States, which specialises in innovative companies, many from the technology field, and many quite large companies. Both are aimed at professional investors.

The Euro.NM is a pan-European grouping of regulated stock markets dedicated to high growth companies. Its members are Le Nouveau Marché (of the Paris Stock Exchange), the Neuer Markt, Germany's exchange for technology and internet stocks (part of the Deutsche Börse), Euro.NM Amsterdam (Amsterdam Exchanges), Euro.NM Brussels (Brussels Exchanges) and Nuovo Mercato (Italian Exchange).

OTHER INDICES

	Jun 27	Jun 26	Jun 23
DJ Stoxx 50	4915.83	4951.33	4964.58
DJ Euro Stx 50	5209.53	5235.39	5240.58
MSCI Europe	1539.36*	1546.63	1545.63
MSCI Euro	1487.37	1494.15	1492.09
MSCI Pan-Euro	1379.98	1389.77	1389.62

Source: Financial Times Information. *Subject to revision next day. (u) unavailable.

Fig. 8.5 Other European indices

The Easdaq describes itself as the only pan-European stock market, offering international growth companies and investors seamless cross-border trading, clearing and settlement within a unified market structure.

In the autumn of 2000, FTSE International launched a new series of European technology indices in collaboration with Deutsche Bank and Nomura International. The FTSE eTX indices cover all European technology companies with a market value greater than €110 million, including stocks traded on junior markets like the Euro.NM as well as the main bourses. The overall index is called the FTSE eTX All-Share and it comprises seven sectors: e-commerce, internet, software, computer hardware, semiconductors, computer services and telecoms equipment. There is also a group of medium and small-cap indices called the FTSE eTX Innovation, which consists of all qualifying technology companies outside the Eurotop 300.

The changing world of European stock exchanges

Driven in large part by the knowledge that investors want a single trading platform for the largest blue chip European stocks but also by the impact of new technology and the internet, the world of national stock exchanges is changing fast. The multitude of national exchanges is being rationalised and it is not yet clear how it will play out. On the one hand, trading might turn out to be most efficient if it is concentrated in several large traditional exchanges (perhaps eventually only one) that can deliver economies of scale and liquid markets. On the other hand, it might be better to have nimble competition between exchanges with an emphasis on cost-cutting and improved trading technologies – with perhaps a common settlement system.

At the time of writing, much is up in the air. There is the planned formation of Euronext, a merger of the Paris, Brussels and Amsterdam exchanges, as well as the proposed merger of the London Stock Exchange and the Deutsche Börse to form iX (international exchanges). In addition, two broad exchange alliances were emerging: the Global Equity Market (GEM) – Euronext plus New York, Tokyo, Australia, Hong Kong, Toronto, Mexico and São Paulo – and iX – London and Frankfurt linked to the Nasdaq. But in the early autumn of 2000, the iX plans were thrown into disarray by the bid for the London Stock Exchange by OM Gruppen, owner of the Swedish stock market. The outcome remains unclear but the ultimate aim is to create a pan-European capital market that can match the United States for liquidity, offers round-the-clock trading and is efficient enough to compete with new electronic exchanges.

"In London and New York share prices get out of line in value, but in other places they get even further out of line. You get better bargains in addition to more bargains by looking worldwide."

Sir John Templeton

"The time to buy is when blood is running in the streets."

Baron Nathan Rothschild

9

Other international equities

Emerging stock markets and world indices

- **World stock markets** – share price movements on leading global markets
- **International equity indices** – the standard performance measures of the world's stock markets
- **The FTSE All-World index series** – reading the figures and using the information for these global market indicators
- **International equity investing** – emerging markets

The abolition of exchange control restrictions and the widespread deregulation of financial markets have made possible the globalisation of trading in equities. This has led to an upsurge in the buying and selling of shares across national boundaries. In the United Kingdom, the removal of exchange controls in 1979 led to a massive upsurge in foreign investment. During the 1980s, an increasing proportion of Japan's enormous capital surplus was for the first time being directed towards the world's equity markets. In the United States, fund managers had long taken an excessively parochial view but had made cautious moves towards greater foreign equity investment. This pace has quickened in recent years.

London remains a pivotal point in the global equity market, but it is just one market, albeit in a favourable time zone. For many years, New York has been attracting more equity business, and for a while Japan outstripped the United States in terms of market capitalisation before Tokyo's major shakeout in 1990.

■ World stock markets

The International Companies and Finance pages of the *Financial Times* contain the bulk of global corporate news: financial results, whether quarterly, half-yearly or annual; essential developments in bids and deals; new or revised funding arrangements; changes to shareholding structures; joint ventures; or new products or production processes. In fact they contain anything that is valuable for an accurate and timely assessment of trends and prospects for shareholders and potential investors alike.

The reports attempt to cover all markets in the FTSE world indices, plus many more that are heavily traded and might have an historical relationship with the United Kingdom or with UK companies, such as those in the old Commonwealth or the Americas.

World stock price listings in the UK edition of the newspaper cover nearly 3,000 shares, a little over a third being US shares from the two New York exchanges (the NYSE and the Amex) and the national screen-based trading market (Nasdaq), and just under a quarter from Japan. The other world markets covered are Austria, Belgium and Luxembourg, Denmark, Finland, France, Germany, Greece, Ireland, Italy, the Netherlands, Norway, Portugal, Spain, Sweden, Switzerland, Australia, Hong Kong, Malaysia, Singapore, Canada, Mexico, Brazil and South Africa.

International editions of the newspaper expand on the coverage for these countries (notably the United States), and add listings for the Czech Republic, Poland, Turkey, Indonesia, New Zealand, South Korea, Taiwan and Thailand. The prices for all national markets are as quoted on the individual exchanges and are mostly last traded prices.

Nowadays it is much easier to deal in foreign shares, and, because of market interactions, it is important to understand these markets. One problem for international investors is the unreliability of indicators such as price/earnings ratios for the purposes of international comparison. Different countries employ different accounting conventions, and therefore often differ in their treatment of the earnings component of such ratios.

■ International equity indices

The international equity indices are a useful tool in the world of international investment, acting as valuable barometers of local market performance for investors faced with limited background knowledge of foreign stocks. In such circumstances the active management of an international portfolio may be too costly and risky an exercise, and many fund managers may aim merely to match the performance of equity indices. The more passive management of indexed funds relies largely on the computerised tracking of price movements, and international equity indices have become the key benchmarks for performance measurement.

Figure 9.1 shows indices for the main international markets:

■ **Indices:** for most markets, a single national index is recorded daily with the base date indicated. The base figure for almost all indices is 100. The table shows the last three trading days' values for each index, plus recent highs and lows, yield and p/e ratio. There is also usually a comment on what is driving overall market movements.

All these indices are benchmarks commonly used by local investors. They are designed to provide an accurate reflection of the daily movement of individual markets. More than one national index is published in the case where a single index does not give the full picture or where two or more are commonly used. For example, one national index may comprise the market's major companies while a second may reflect a wider market. In Australia, the Metals and Minerals index is given alongside the All-Share Ordinary index because of the heavy weighting of resource stocks in the Australian market.

For France there are two indices: the broadly based SBF 250 and the CAC 40, a real-time index of the largest stocks. In Germany, two indices are commonly used: the Frankfurter Allgemeine Zeitung (FAZ) Aktien and the XETRA Dax real-time index introduced at the end of 1987.

The Nikkei is the most widely quoted measure of stock price movements on the Tokyo Stock Exchange, the world's third biggest in terms of market capitalisation. Not strictly an index but an average of 225 shares, it is not weighted according to market capitalisation, so smaller firms can move the index as much as bigger ones. The index is run by the *Nihon Keizai Shimbun*, Japan's main financial daily newspaper. Nikkei is an abbreviation of the newspaper's name. The Nikkei is a benchmark similar to the Dow or the FT 30 but is more widely followed than the comprehensive Tokyo Stock Exchange index (Topix). The latter provides a more accurate guide to the state of the overall market.

In South Africa, the heavy preponderance of gold shares makes publication of the Gold index indispensable. Since the index moves very closely in line with the gold price, the Johannesburg Stock Exchange (JSE) Industrial index is used to monitor the rest of the market.

Local indices carry great credibility in their local markets, but do not provide the whole picture for the global investor. For example, they may include equities not freely available to international fund managers or some national issues may be illiquid from the viewpoint of committing funds globally.

WORLD MARKETS AT A GLANCE

Country	Index	Mar 20	Mar 17	Mar 16	1999/00 High	1999/00 Low	✾ Yield	✾ P/E
Argentina	General	21156.82	21156.68	21506.16	**23162.96** 6/5/99	**14484.90** 14/1/99	3.14	20.8
♣ Shares slightly higher in thin early trade with Telefonica de Argentina spearheading gains.								
Australia	All Ordinaries	3228.1	3203.4	3180.2	**3251.00** 7/3/00	**2779.70** 19/10/99	2.81	23.4
	All Mining	639.3	640.3	644.9	**785.20** 10/1/00	**552.10** 12/4/99		
News Corp and AMP made strong gains while resources sector, banks and telecoms fell and falls were in line with rises.								
Austria	ATX Index	1108.24	1093.36	1112.33	**1326.28** 4/5/99	**1011.25** 22/1/99	2.08	12
Underlying sentiment upbeat, but trading volumes low, as shares took lead from strong performance in neighbouring centres								
Belgium	BEL20	2852.02	2835.08	2906.66	**3691.92** 6/1/99	**2532.24** 13/3/00	1.85	13.2
	Brussels Cash	16851.43	16824.58	17083.75	**21753.78** 6/1/99	**15270.60** 13/3/00		
Stocks ended slightly higher after remaining within narrow band as market consolidated after Friday's profit-taking.								
Brazil	Bovespa	17719.81	17511.24	17642.22	**18685.58** 8/2/00	**5057.00** 14/1/99	3.95	21.1
♣ Market buoyed by rumours British Telecom was considering a bid for Spain's Telefonica which is major player in Brazil.								
Canada	Metals Minis✦	3696.80	3594.57	3741.91	**4792.15** 7/1/00	**2853.44** 18/2/99	1.25	26.5
	TSE 100✦	598.14	587.63	586.09	**589.21** 6/3/00	**376.30** 3/3/99		
	TSE300Comp✦	9669.40	9528.81†	9488.04	**9580.90** 6/3/00	**6180.30** 3/3/99		
♣ Market put aside rate worries and was sharply higher in morning trade, with tech stocks powering the gains.								
Chile	IGPA Gen♥	5231.08	5253.07	5240.93	**5659.34** 9/2/00	**3297.63** 14/1/99	3.55	24.1
♣ Market edged ahead in morning trade in thin trade as investors await today's decision on US interest rates.								
China	Shanghai A	1809.04	1765.29	1711.17	**1850.53** 3/3/00	**1126.21** 18/5/99	1.19	38.8
	Shenzhen A	568.35	552.07	533.84	**573.18** 3/3/00	**333.77** 18/5/99		
	Shanghai B	37.10	37.51	35.69	**61.18** 29/6/99	**21.38** 9/3/99		
	Shenzhen B	81.01	80.75	75.92	**125.42** 29/6/99	**41.56** 10/3/99		
Hard-currency B shares were mixed on thin volumes in wake of Taiwan's elections.								
Colombia	IBB	(u)	967.81	975.65	**1237.28** 14/5/99	**850.79** 4/2/99	2.33	5.5
Czech Republic	PX 50	660.3	666.6	671.0	**673.50** 14/3/00	**333.40** 1/3/99	na	na
Stocks lost ground, pushed down by domestic selling with investors concerned about possiblility of higher US rates today.								
Denmark	KFX	299.64	298.77	289.70	**299.64** 20/3/00	**187.77** 15/3/99	1.25	22.2
Shares edged up in thin trade with late rallies in Tele Danmark and Novo Nordisk pulling benchmark index into black.								
Egypt	Cairo SE Gen	667.27	(c)	(c)	**695.41** 14/2/00	**396.42** 11/1/99	na	na
Estonia	Tallinn General	168.04	170.32	169.07	**171.99** 14/3/00	**91.34** 15/1/99	na	na
Shares broadly lower, hit by profit-taking and absence of market moving news.								
Finland	Hex General	16820.44	16312.65	15834.77	**18277.35** 6/3/00	**5679.65** 10/2/99	0.8	55.8
Market sharply higher as technology, media and telecoms issues renewed rally that began last week.								
France	SBF 250	4070.51	4033.90	3989.61	**4217.91** 6/3/00	**2507.84** 13/1/99	1.64	26
	CAC 40	6352.51	6304.28	6258.53	**6545.98** 6/3/00	**3958.72** 13/1/99		
Bourse scored gains as investors piled once more into telecoms and technology stocks.								
Germany	FAZ Aktien	2447.30	2431.55	2340.71	**2502.47** 6/3/00	**1489.80** 4/3/99	1.31	22
	XETRA Dax	7872.38	7710.92†	7583.96	**8064.97** 7/3/00	**4668.52** 3/3/00		
Market lifted by gains in heavyweights Siemens and SAP as investors flocked back to tech sector.								
Greece	Athens Gen	4849.07	4845.08	4759.89	**6355.04** 17/9/99	**2798.21** 13/1/99	1.39	31.7
	FTSE/ASE 20	2699.00	2706.26	2676.60	**3301.69** 20/9/99	**1758.87** 13/1/99		
Equities marginally higher, with gains capped by weakness in banks and state controlled stocks.								
Hong Kong	Hang Seng	17234.46	17082.99	16359.00	**17951.43** 8/3/00	**9076.33** 10/2/99	2.35	23.9
	HSCC Red Chip	1579.5	1542.10	1494.04	**1682.82** 6/3/00	**659.52** 8/2/99		
China Telecom and Pacific Century made solid gains while HSBC and Hutchison eased and fallers were double the risers.								

Fig. 9.1 World markets at a glance

Country	Index	Mar 20	Mar 17	Mar 16	1999/00 High		1999/00 Low		✠ Yield	✠ P/E
Portugal	BVL 30	6144.84	6169.62	6147.73	6511.49	3/3/00	4221.78	11/8/99	1.89	17.3
	PSI 20	13918.5	13974.91	13940.76	14822.59	3/3/00	9475.79	16/9/99		
Stocks lower in quiet session with PT Multimedia and Sonae weighing on bourse.										
Romania	BET Index	549.20	564.93	571.35	644.36	1/2/00	325.78	21/4/99	na	na
Russia	RTS	215.85	218.88	222.48	224.82	10/3/00	54.48	28/1/99	na	na
Shares weak and traders said they expected further falls after weekend's presidential election.										
Singapore	SES All-S'pore	583.73	586.63	(c)	695.59	3/1/00	351.45	10/2/99	2.43	23.3
	Straits Times	2077.10	2094.47	(c)	2582.94	3/1/00	1286.56	10/2/99		
Banks were clipped back as falling issues nearly trebled the rises. Electronics stocks lifted against the flow.										
Slovakia	Sax	74.65	74.16	73.11	96.88	14/1/99	70.19	10/3/00	na	na
South Africa	JSE All Share	8014.8	7997.6	7939.1	9226.50	17/1/00	5404.90	4/1/99	2.21	14.8
	Gold (IX14)	1160.5	1147.5	1163.7	1423.60	5/10/99	795.00	15/7/99		
	JSE Indl.	9483.7	9539.7	9559.7	10196.00	17/1/00	6261.50	4/1/99		
Market closed largely firmer on fresh appetite for resource stocks after recent sharp losses.										
South Korea	KoreaCmpEx**	850.51	855.57	841.22	1059.04	4/1/00	498.42	24/2/99	0.75	29.3
Hyundai Electronics and Samsung Electronics made good gains while Kasdaq OTC shares slid and falls beat rises 11 to 10.										
Spain	Madrid SE	1114.8	1114.76	1104.70	1146.21	6/3/00	823.57	6/8/99	1.56	22.8
	IBEX 35	12362.4	12369.8	12260.9	12816.80	6/3/00	9140.70	6/8/99		
Broad market flat in spite of sharp gains in some high tech stocks, including heavyweight Telefonica.										
Sri Lanka	CSE All Share	518.89	519.75	519.79	602.63	14/12/99	512.20	23/6/99	na	na
DFCC Bank hardened while National Development Bank and John Keells slipped. Turnover was very thin.										
Sweden	AffarsvardnGen	(u)	6540.6	6382.9	6960.60	6/3/00	3268.40	13/1/99	1.21	32.1
	Stockholm Gen	6596.72	6412.79	6249.55	6812.74	6/3/00	3183.18	13/1/99		
Ericsson provided lead that took broad market sharply higher.										
Switzerland	SMI Index	7166.9	7100.6	7131.5	7668.80	6/1/99	6616.70	10/8/99	1.33	19.9
	SPI General	4922.66	4866.28	4871.47	5047.21	17/1/00	4362.03	10/2/99		
Bourse closed higher as old economy shares continued to rise.										
Taiwan	WeightedPr.**	8536.05	8763.27	8682.76	10202.20	17/2/00	5474.79	5/2/99	1.07	32.9
Nervously lower in wake of Democratic Progressive Party's election victory. Turnover was very thin at T$80bn.										
Thailand	Bangkok SET	400.99	399.74	395.83	545.91	22/6/99	313.65	11/2/99	0.74	12.7
Banking sector made modest gains while other financials rose 3.7 per cent and rises nearly doubled the fallers.										
Turkey	IMKB Nat 100	17443.92	(c)	(c)	19577.27	18/1/00	2408.87	25/1/99	1	22.7
Market lower as profit-taking eroded early gains, which reflected optimism on economic outlook.										
Venezuela	IBC	5980.79	5891.30	5771.94	6531.35	13/5/99	3705.91	5/3/99	na	na
Zimbabwe	ZSE Industrial	14640.13	14609.75	14661.27	17607.48	19/1/00	6465.64	5/1/99	na	na
Shares edged up but brokers forecast losses for rest of week with confidence shaken by farm invasions.										
WORLD	FTSE World($)	(u)	376.45	374.62	381.23	31/12/99	299.56	3/3/99	na	na
	MS Capital Int$	(u)	1401.6^	1392.8	1411.30	29/12/99	1121.90	10/2/99	na	na
CROSS-BORDER	DJ Stoxx 50	5052.07	4989.04	4933.87	5156.72	6/3/00	3260.29	10/2/99	na	na
	DJ Euro Stx 50	5286.71	5231.35	5175.23	5464.43	6/3/00	3325.56	10/2/99	na	na
	FTSE Multinatls	(u)	1166.79	1163.57	1186.92	17/1/00	984.29	18/10/99	na	na
	FTSE Global 100	(u)	1190.52	1185.22	1201.59	17/1/00	988.20	18/10/99	na	na
	FTSE E300	(u)	1608.66	1600.73	1646.66	6/3/00	1164.86	10/2/99	na	na
	FTSE E100	(u)	3779.47	3746.33	3849.08	6/3/00	2663.70	10/2/99	na	na
	HSBC Drgn	(u)	369.18	357.69	392.29	4/1/00	204.59	9/2/99	na	na
	ING Brngs Emrg	(u)	185.61	183.86	199.61	9/2/00	108.82	15/1/99	na	na

A table in Saturday's newspaper lists the key world market indices, their latest values, and their percentage changes on a week previously and on the beginning of the year (see Figure 9.2).

Market week

		Friday value	% change: since 5day	31/12/98
UK	FTSE All-Share	3126.18	-0.9	16.9
UK	FTSE 100	6558.0	-0.2	11.5
UK	FTSE 250	6565.8	-3.8	35.2
UK	FTSE SmallCap	3410.33	-4.4	64.7
UK	FTSE Fledgling	2389.96	-3.0	108.5
UK	Hoare Govett Sm Co	3025.14	-3.6	55.5
UK	Gilts: FTSE All Stks	158.39	1.0	-5.7
Global	FTSE World ($)	†374.62	1.6	22.0
Global	FTSE World(local)	†343.42	1.5	25.9
Global	Barings Em Mkts($)	185.61	-3.0	60.9
US	Dow Jones Indl	*10643.32	7.2	15.9
US	S&P Composite	*1467.31	5.2	19.4
Japan	Nikkei 225	19566.32	-0.9	41.4
Europe	FTSE Eurotop 300	†1600.73	-2.1	35.3
Germany	Dax	7684.74	-3.7	53.6
France	CAC40	6304.28	-3.2	59.9
Italy	Comit 30	493.47	-2.2	40.4
HK	Hang Seng	17082.99	-4.2	70.0

†Previous close. *Latest available. Sources: Hoare Govett, FTSE Intl, Reuters

Fig. 9.2 Market week

■ The FTSE All-World index series

The FTSE All-World index series covers global equity markets (see Figure 9.3). Owned by FTSE International, launched in March 1987, and based on over 2,600 equity securities from 49 countries, these indices represent at least 90 per cent of the total market capitalisation of the world's main stock exchanges.

FTSE All-World Index Series

Aug 16

	US Dollar index	Day %	Mth %	YTD %	Gross Div Yield
FTSE All-World Index (2401)	206.88	0.0	-2.1	0.0	1.3
FTSE World Index (2072)	370.99	0.0	-2.0	-2.7	1.3
FTSE World Europe (613)	391.82	0.3	-1.7	-4.7	1.7
All-World Developed (1833)	207.19	0.0	-2.0	0.0	1.3
All-World All Emerging (568)	197.59	0.8	-4.4	0.0	1.8
All-World Adv Emerging (260)	202.24	0.9	-4.9	0.0	1.8
All-World Emerging (308)	183.82	0.5	-2.5	0.0	2.0
All-World ex US (1838)	205.15	0.4	-2.3	0.0	1.5
All-World ex UK (2250)	206.88	0.0	-2.4	0.0	1.2
All-World ex Japan (1992)	208.69	0.0	-1.6	0.0	1.4
All-World Dev ex US (1270)	207.43	0.3	-2.2	0.0	1.5
All-World ex Eurobloc (2123)	207.34	0.0	-1.9	0.0	1.2
All-World Nordic (122)	180.68	0.0	-14.6	0.0	1.2
All-World Euro-Pacific (1503)	202.86	0.4	-2.6	0.0	1.5
Americas (786)	210.09	-0.3	-1.6	0.0	1.1
Argentina (13)	321.80	-2.2	-19.2	0.0	3.4
Brazil (29)	219.91	-2.0	3.5	2.1	1.5
Chile (22)	349.17	-0.2	1.7	0.0	2.4
Colombia (10)	321.52	-2.5	-4.7	0.0	6.9
Mexico (27)	2065.71	0.4	-10.8	-4.4	0.9
Peru (9)	331.34	0.2	3.0	0.0	3.0
Venezuela (6)	325.11	-1.5	-9.3	0.0	3.5
North America (670)	209.92	-0.2	-1.6	0.0	1.1
Canada (107)	369.89	0.7	2.8	30.9	1.1
USA (563)	609.66	-0.3	-1.8	1.0	1.1

FTSE Industry Sectors

	US Dollar index	Day %	Mth %	YTD %	Gross Div Yield
Resources (114)	387.73	1.4	4.3	3.2	2.1
Mining (42)	227.83	1.5	3.1	-16.4	2.5
Oil & Gas (72)	391.61	1.4	4.5	6.3	2.1
Basic Industries (251)	168.33	0.2	-1.9	-13.0	2.2
Chemicals (78)	235.93	0.1	-1.9	-10.1	2.2
Construction & Bldg Matls (83)	110.42	0.2	-3.0	-8.5	2.1
Forestry & Paper (37)	181.03	0.2	-1.4	-22.1	2.8
Steel & Other Metals (53)	187.42	0.4	-0.6	-19.3	1.9
General Industrials (216)	465.84	-0.1	1.6	4.5	1.2
Aerospace & Defence (18)	286.72	-1.0	4.1	-4.1	1.8
Diversified Industrials (53)	319.26	0.3	1.4	7.8	1.6
Electronic & Elect Equip (62)	720.54	-0.1	2.2	8.6	0.9
Engineering & Machinery (83)	229.67	0.1	-1.9	-11.1	1.8
Cyclical Cons Goods (100)	471.44	-0.3	-1.8	-11.2	1.6
Automobiles (48)	236.12	-0.8	-2.1	-8.6	1.9
Household Goods & Text (52)	195.09	-0.2	-1.2	-16.2	1.1

	US Dollar index	Day %	Mth %	YTD %	Gross Div Yield
Europe (686)	205.84	0.3	-1.6	0.0	1.7
United Kingdom (151)	386.09	0.4	0.9	-10.0	2.1
Europe ex UK (535)	203.42	0.3	-2.8	0.0	1.5
Czech Republic (8)	97.45	-0.6	2.1	0.0	0.4
Denmark (28)	560.26	0.7	4.0	12.8	1.0
Greece (57)	311.03	-1.6	-9.0	-41.4	2.2
Hungary (14)	91.80	3.2	1.7	0.0	1.3
Norway (38)	306.77	1.0	4.1	0.9	1.7
Poland (24)	93.30	0.7	-6.7	0.0	1.1
Russia (8)	115.26	-0.8	21.7	0.0	1.3
Sweden (34)	886.74	0.9	-11.6	1.2	1.2
Switzerland (27)	394.27	0.6	1.1	2.4	1.3
Turkey (19)	76.31	-0.2	-4.2	0.0	1.7
Eurobloc (278)	204.32	0.2	-2.8	0.0	1.6
Austria (20)	151.00	-0.3	3.4	-13.0	2.4
Belgium / Luxembourg (23)	305.95	-0.2	3.7	-11.7	2.5
Finland (22)	1185.54	-1.5	-25.2	-16.3	1.2
France (58)	431.57	0.5	0.2	2.2	1.5
Germany (41)	303.44	-0.1	-1.2	-2.9	1.4
Ireland (15)	390.06	0.5	-0.3	-14.8	1.7
Italy (45)	182.16	0.3	-1.6	11.6	1.1
Netherlands (20)	539.58	0.2	-1.8	-4.3	1.8
Portugal (13)	207.73	-1.2	-4.6	-8.4	2.3
Spain (21)	387.17	1.0	1.1	-6.2	1.4

	US Dollar index	Day %	Mth %	YTD %	Gross Div Yield
Non-Cyc Cons Goods (247)	409.48	0.2	1.2	6.5	1.4
Beverages (32)	506.98	-1.9	3.4	8.3	1.5
Food Producers & Proc (79)	342.49	0.1	1.0	1.2	2.1
Health (34)	781.12	0.2	1.9	22.9	0.8
Packaging (18)	364.83	0.4	1.9	-20.3	2.0
Personal Care & Hse Prds (16)	553.27	0.4	0.4	-22.2	1.6
Pharmaceuticals (54)	657.40	0.6	-0.3	11.6	1.1
Tobacco (14)	414.89	1.1	22.5	26.7	5.3
Cyclical Services (368)	461.32	-0.7	-5.5	-10.8	0.9
Distributors (38)	144.94	0.2	-3.1	0.3	0.9
General Retailers (78)	414.61	-2.3	-12.3	-25.1	0.9
Leisure Ent & Hotels (36)	348.36	-1.1	-2.4	7.5	0.6
Media & Photography (82)	478.02	0.9	-2.3	-4.8	0.8
Restaurants & Pubs (12)	219.91	-0.2	-1.0	-14.6	1.3
Support Services (28)	846.72	-0.2	-3.2	-14.8	1.2
Transport (94)	170.83	-0.2	-0.6	-2.2	1.4

	US Dollar index	Day %	Mth %	YTD %	Gross Div Yield
Asia Pacific (817)	199.71	0.5	-4.5	0.0	1.1
Japan (409)	144.47	0.1	-5.7	-15.9	0.7
Asia Pacific ex Japan (408)	218.77	1.6	-0.5	0.0	2.3
Australia (70)	225.45	1.0	2.0	-4.0	3.4
China (11)	413.05	1.8	15.0	0.0	1.8
Hong Kong - China (68)	476.46	1.1	1.9	1.7	2.6
India (29)	342.42	2.9	-13.5	0.0	1.7
Indonesia (19)	50.51	-1.0	10.4	-44.6	2.9
Korea South (28)	371.16	4.3	-10.4	0.0	1.2
Malaysia (24)	311.38	0.6	-6.0	0.0	1.3
New Zealand (15)	53.35	0.6	-2.6	-18.0	4.6
Pakistan (10)	349.27	1.0	-0.3	0.0	5.7
Philippines (21)	50.79	-0.3	-6.2	-41.9	1.9
Singapore (45)	291.62	1.9	7.4	-14.2	1.2
Taiwan (38)	311.45	2.2	-7.3	0.0	1.0
Thailand (30)	20.27	1.9	1.6	-39.3	1.3
Middle East & Africa (112)	220.82	0.6	3.3	0.0	3.7
Egypt (23)	83.67	2.7	-7.1	0.0	6.6
Israel (25)	112.22	-0.2	6.7	0.0	8.5
Morocco (8)	93.39	-0.3	-3.3	0.0	2.5
South Africa (56)	299.99	0.8	3.3	-11.2	2.6
Europe ex Eurobloc (408)	204.83	0.4	-0.4	0.0	1.9
Europe ex Ebloc ex UK (257)	200.53	0.6	-3.0	0.0	1.3

	US Dollar index	Day %	Mth %	YTD %	Gross Div Yield
Non-Cyclical Services (112)	477.79	-0.8	-12.1	-22.7	1.2
Food & Drug Retailers (31)	391.80	-0.1	-2.6	-22.4	1.2
Telecom Services (81)	335.75	-0.9	-13.4	-22.7	1.3
Utilities (109)	283.17	-0.1	6.5	15.5	3.2
Electricity (79)	255.25	-0.3	5.8	8.6	3.8
Gas Distribution (25)	316.58	0.6	8.4	38.1	1.6
Water (5)	208.10	-1.9	5.3	3.1	5.9
Financials (408)	279.41	-0.3	4.5	3.6	1.9
Banks (162)	275.08	-0.2	5.8	-0.3	2.4
Insurance (60)	347.72	-0.1	4.9	11.6	1.1
Life Assurance (28)	455.26	-0.1	1.9	-4.2	1.9
Investment Companies (23)	345.44	0.1	0.6	10.5	1.6
Real Estate (19)	143.58	0.4	3.8	-0.6	2.8
Speciality & Other Fin (77)	282.46	-1.0	1.7	11.0	1.0
Info Technology (147)	275.27	0.5	-6.5	-0.7	0.2
Info Tech Hardware (91)	315.12	0.6	-7.5	12.8	0.2
Software & Comp Servs (56)	194.18	0.0	-3.4	-28.9	0.1

FTSE

Fig. 9.3 FTSE All-World index series

Reading the figures

- **Regional indices:** the complete world series has 24 regional indices. Figures are shown for these and for each country index, including the value of the index in dollars, the change on the previous day and month and since the start of the year, plus the gross dividend yield.

- **Market classifications and cross-border indices:** the index classifies markets as "developed" (23 countries, representing nearly 97 per cent of the total market capitalisation), "advanced emerging" (Brazil, Greece, Israel, Mexico, South Africa, South Korea and Taiwan) or "emerging" (19 countries). The All-World index comprises all countries; the World index comprises all developed and advanced emerging countries; and the All-Emerging index comprises all advanced emerging and emerging countries.

- **FTSE industry sectors:** stocks are also allocated to sectors under the FTSE Global Industry Classification System, which in turn generate indices of sectoral or subsectoral performance. The classification system features ten economic groups,

39 industry sectors and 101 industry subsectors. This revised system was introduced in 1999 to reflect the changing economic realities of the business world and to harmonise the sectoral breakdowns of the whole family of FTSE indices – UK, European and world – to allow global comparisons across sectors.

Using the information

The standard equity indices of Figure 9.1 act as barometers of local market performance for investors faced with limited background knowledge of foreign stocks. Designed to give an accurate reflection of the daily movement of individual markets, they carry great credibility in their local markets. But they may not provide the whole picture for the global investor, particularly if they include equities not freely available to overseas investors or in closely held local companies. That is the advantage of the FTSE All-World series, a set of high quality indices of the international equity market for use as a benchmark by the global investment community.

Markets, companies and securities are only included under the following criteria: the local exchange must permit direct equity investment by non-nationals; accurate and timely data must be available; there should be no significant exchange controls that would prevent the timely repatriation of capital or dividends; significant international investor interest in the local equity market must have been demonstrated; and there must be adequate liquidity. Also excluded are companies where 75 per cent or more of the issued capital is controlled by dominant shareholders, or where less than 25 per cent of the shares are available to investors through the local market. Each subset aims to capture at least 70 per cent of the total market value of all shares listed on the domestic exchange or 85 per cent of the eligible universe of stocks. In some countries, this is not possible because of restrictions on foreign shareholdings.

The indices aim to cover a significant proportion of the stocks listed in each market rather than concentrating merely on the largest companies, and encompass around 15 per cent of an estimated universe of more than 15,000 listed companies. Companies and markets are only included where a timely and reliable source of daily price movements is available, but the number of US companies (by far the most broadly based of the world's equity markets) is limited to under 600 under the rules of the indices. To ensure that they reflect a reasonable marketability of shares, companies with a market capitalisation of less than $100 million are generally excluded. This cut-off level is lowered, however, in the case of countries whose average market capitalisation is less than $100 million.

The All-World index is designed to represent global equity markets and to reflect the increases in cross-border equity investment, particularly from the United States and Japan. As the shift continues towards global and sector-based investment strategies, it responds to a growing need for global and cross-border sectoral benchmarks. It also allows international investors to manage both their developed and emerging market portfolios within a single structure and coordinate their exposures across all types of risk. It is intended mainly for such end-users as pension fund managers, consultants and money managers. Its primary function is global equity performance measurement, hence it is essential that shares that make up the index can be purchased and sold. But it is also being used for the creation of derivative products, such as stock index funds (see Chapter 13). An increasing number of companies are running funds designed to track the world indices or one or more of their sub-series.

International equity investing

Direct investing in international equities is an increasingly attractive proposition. The widespread deregulation of financial markets has made dealing shares across national boundaries much easier. Nowadays, it is quite possible to get a stake in industries that do not exist at home and in economies with more favourable growth prospects or at different stages of the business cycle. International investments are also likely to afford superior returns to those available in a single market, especially if they encompass some of the emerging markets of the newly industrialising world. There are greater risks associated with such returns, but the range of choice in the global equity market offers strong potential for diversification.

At the level of the individual company, there are frequently problems in comparing the relative merits of companies across markets. It is important to remember that financial reporting and accounting standards vary, and that indicators such as price/earnings ratios are often unreliable for international comparisons. Countries employ a variety of accounting conventions in their treatment of corporate profits. There are also differences in dealing and settlement arrangements, in rules on the size of investments, and in provisions for the custody and transfer of share certificates.

There is also the danger of adverse currency fluctuations: foreign exchange risk is likely to be the biggest threat to overseas transactions. Linkages between world equity markets can also affect the performance of an international portfolio. For example, with many major stocks traded in both London and New York, the two markets have become highly interdependent. Others might have a lower degree of correlation, if they respond in different ways to prevailing global economic conditions.

Another attractive area for the international equity investor is that of new issues. Buying shares the first time they are offered to the public, whether in privatisations of state-owned corporations or previously private companies coming to market, can be very profitable, perhaps especially for investors with relatively short investment horizons. In Europe, the new issue boom has partly arisen from the UK government's programme of privatisation, encouraging investors and issuers to enter the market, and other countries to launch their own selling agendas. Worldwide, it has been influenced by the weight of demand from investing institutions and the stress they place on quality control in new issues.

The success of the UK privatisation programme has inspired numerous other governments to turn their public sector companies into publicly quoted ones. For the global investor, there may be opportunities in the Far East, Latin America, and the formerly planned economies of central and eastern Europe. Many of the companies on the block are large, stable businesses with leading positions in their market sectors. After privatisation, they will become answerable to shareholders, presumably focusing far more on profitability, growth and cash flow. This could lead to some major gains in their value over the longer term, in addition to first-day appreciation. Potentially dramatic increases in profitability also offer the prospect of fast growth in dividends.

Important considerations with global issues include international differences in accounting practices and settlement arrangements; the identity and reputation of the sponsor; the language in which the prospectus is written; whether some issues are not available to non-residents; and the procedures for scaling down an application in the event of oversubscription.

■ Emerging markets

Both for multinational businesses and for private and institutional investors, the markets of the developing world are becoming more and more appealing. This is partly a response to such political developments as the collapse of communism and the increasingly global embrace of liberal democratic values, which may have reduced the sovereign or country risk of overseas investments. But naturally enough, economic forces also play a critical role: relatively lower labour costs are an attraction to multinationals to shift production to the developing world, as are the vast markets those workers represent for global brands like Coca-Cola, Marlboro and McDonald's.

Despite a series of spectacular financial crises, the 1990s were a decade of dramatic growth for emerging markets. At the end of 1990, there were 8,920 companies listed on emerging markets. At the end of 1999, that figure was 26,314 firms, with combined market capitalisation of $3.07 trillion, 8.5 per cent of total world stock market capitalisation. The value of trading in 1999 was $2.8 trillion (9 per cent of the world total) compared to $31 trillion across all world markets.

In emerging markets, currency risks are likely to be compounded by political risks, the greater sensitivity of investors to the signs of impending devaluation or depreciation, and the impact of fundamental economic events elsewhere in the world. The "flight to quality" following the Mexican devaluation of early 1995 showed all of these in action: the arrival of a new government with untested macroeconomic policies, the dangers of current account deficits and limited reserves, and the increases in US interest rates making dollars relatively more appealing than pesos. The Asian and Russian crises of 1997/8 followed similar patterns.

The *Financial Times* carries regular data on the emerging stock markets of Latin America, east and south Asia, Europe and the Middle East, which are attracting increasing investor attention. The tables are prepared by Standard & Poor's and the International Finance Corporation, a subsidiary of the World Bank, as a complement to the much more comprehensive daily coverage of the FTSE All-World series (see Figure 9.4).

Emerging markets:
S&P/IFCI indices
Dollar terms

May 18 Market		Day's chg %	% Chg since 31/12/99
Latin America			
Argentina	890.73	-1.4	-16.3
Brazil	392.72	-1.0	-14.5
Chile	610.10	-0.5	-0.5
Colombia[1]	282.40	-0.2	-19.9
Mexico	732.87	-1.7	-14.7
Peru[2]	153.15	-0.8	-4.7
Venezuela[3]	434.47	+0.5	+9.4
East Asia			
China[4]	53.64	-4.9	+1.3
India[7]	90.75	+0.2	-21.9
Indonesia[8]	27.08	-2.0	-42.7
Korea[5]	81.54	-2.1	-25.5
Malaysia	146.41		+14.5
Pakistan[9]	143.57	+1.3	+10.4
Philippines	83.55	-0.9	-32.7
Sri Lanka[10]	53.34		-31.1
Taiwan, China[6]	189.96	+0.1	+7.2
Thailand	59.66	-2.3	-33.6
Europe			
Czech Rep	57.21	+1.9	+8.2
Greece	771.51	+1.7	-24.2
Hungary[11]	290.52	+0.5	-10.1
Poland[12]	629.27	-0.9	-1.7
Russia	95.82	-2.6	+6.4
Slovakia	27.98	-4.3	-15.4
Turkey[14]	483.32	-3.6	-6.8
Mideast/Africa			
Egypt	71.02	-3.6	-11.3
Israel	174.87	+0.7	+10.5
Jordan	182.37	+1.3	-12.7
Morocco	136.73	-0.2	-11.5
S Africa[13]	145.23	-1.4	-25.7
Zimbabwe[15]	244.49	+6.1	-3.5
Regions			
Composite	267.79	-1.0	-12.3
Latin America	577.67	-1.1	-12.3
Asia	163.88	-1.1	-10.2
EMEA	159.35	-0.9	-15.1
Europe	234.58	-0.8	-13.1
Eastn Europe	94.87	-1.1	-0.1
ME & Africa	65.79	-1.0	-17.7
Comp - Malay	264.80	-1.1	-13.9
Asia - Malay	158.72	-1.3	-14.2

Base date: Dec 1988=100 except those noted which
are: (1)Feb 1 1991; (2)Dec 31 1992; (3)Jan 5 1990;
(4)Dec 31 1992; (5)Jan 3 1992; (6)Jan 4 1991;
(7)Nov 6 1992; (8)Sep 28 1990; (9)Mar 1 1991; (10)
Dec 31 1992; (11)Dec 31 1993; (12)Dec 31 1992;
(13)Dec 31 1992; (14)Dec 31 1992; (15)Aug 2 1993;
(16) July 2 1993.
Latest indices were unavailable for this edition.

Fig. 9.4 S&P/IFCI emerging markets indices

"The management of stock exchange investments of any kind is a low pursuit from which it is a good thing for most members of our society to be free."

John Maynard Keynes

"Put not your trust in money, but put your money in trust."

Oliver Wendell Holmes

10

Trusts and funds

The managed money markets

- **The managed funds service** – reading the figures and using the information on authorised investment funds – unit trusts and OEICs (open-ended investment companies); other UK unit trusts

- **Investment companies**

- **Insurances;** management services

- **Offshore and overseas** – opportunities for non-UK investors: FSA recognised funds; regulated funds; offshore insurances; other offshore funds

- **US mutual funds**

- **Exchange traded funds** (ETFs)

Managed funds are collective investment vehicles that are run by investment companies to provide professional management of investors' money. These funds in turn may be linked to other financial products. Managed funds are an easy way for small, private investors to get into share buying.

The managed funds service

The *Financial Times* managed funds service provides investors with information relating to a substantial number of managed funds. The information is provided by the individual management groups to a specific formula laid down for UK authorised bodies by the regulator. The address and telephone number of the group are normally given under its name, except in the case of those offshore funds that have not been authorised by the Financial Services Authority (FSA) to be promoted for general sale in the United Kingdom. This does not mean that they are in some way suspect; it merely signifies that the country in which they are based has not applied for designated territory status. This status is only given if the country's regulatory system is deemed to be at least equal to that ruling in the United Kingdom.

Authorised investment funds

Unit trusts and OEICs (open-ended investment companies) offer professional management of funds pooled together and divided into units whose value is based on the market valuation of the securities acquired by the fund. Hence the value of the units varies in accordance with the movement of the market prices of the securities owned by the fund. Authorised unit trusts are unit trusts that have been approved as being suitable for general promotion and sale in the United Kingdom.

The attraction of unit trusts is that they enable small investors to achieve the advantages available to large investors of cheaper dealing costs and a spread of investments to reduce risk. They can also be tailored to meet the particular needs of investors looking for capital growth or income, or to go into specific sectors and overseas markets. They are therefore also widely used by stockbrokers and fund management groups. Since capital gains tax on sales and purchases made within the fund does not have to be paid, unit trusts have the additional advantage of favourable tax treatment.

A unit trust is divided into equal portions called units. Their prices are calculated daily to reflect the actual market value of the assets of the trust. Under the deed creating the trust, unit trust management groups have an obligation to keep investors properly informed about movements in the value of these units. Instead of having to circulate information to each unit holder individually, it is accepted by the authorities that this obligation can be discharged by regular publication of the unit prices in certain national newspapers, in particular the *Financial Times* (see Figure 10.1):

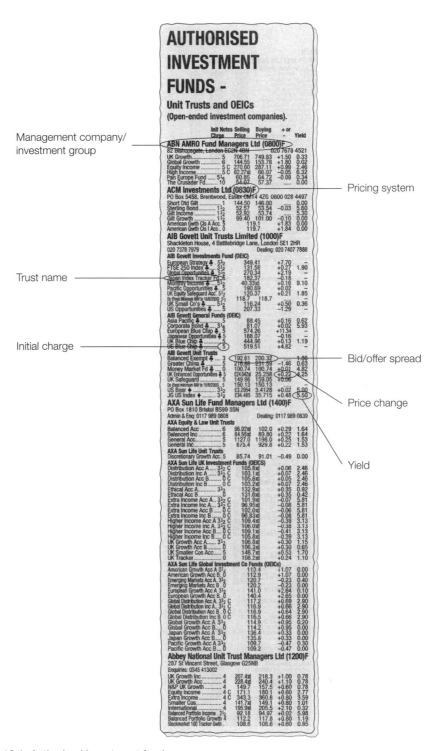

Fig. 10.1 Authorised investment funds

Reading the figures

- **Name of the investment group, its pricing system and trust name:** each investment group is listed together with its component trusts, and the basis of its pricing system. The price regime for each group is measured at a certain cut-off point, the figure in brackets representing a time, and calculated on a forward (F) or historical (H) basis. The trust name will indicate what kind of assets the trust invests in.

- **Initial charge:** the second column indicates the percentage charge imposed on buyers of the fund by the manager to cover the "front load" costs of administration and marketing plus commission paid to intermediaries. The initial charge is included in the buying price of units. If the initial charge is 5 per cent, out of every £100 invested, £5 is retained by the management group to cover its costs, leaving the remaining £95 to be actually invested in the fund.

- **Notes:** the third column notes any special features of the trust. For example, the letter E denotes that there may be exit charges when units are sold, and the letter C indicates that there will be a periodic management charge, typically 1–1.5 per cent annually.

- **Selling price/buying price:** the fourth and fifth columns show the gap between the selling or bid price, at which units can be sold, and the buying or offer price, at which they can be bought. These are calculated by the group assessing the value of the underlying securities held at the most recent lowest market dealing price (plus other assets like uninvested income and undistributed income), adding the various costs involved such as dealing charges, and dividing the total by the number of units issued. The selling and buying prices for shares of an OEIC and units of a single-price unit trust are the same.

- **Price change:** the sixth column compares the mid-point between the selling and buying prices with the previous quotation. It may be unchanged, or show an upward or downward trend, according to changes in the value of the underlying securities or an alteration in the bid/offer spread. Since Saturday's newspaper carries the price change for the last day's trading of the week, the Monday paper replaces this column with the trust's Cityline number. Real-time unit trust prices can be obtained by dialling 0906 843 0010 plus the relevant five-digit code.

- **Yield:** the last column indicates income paid by the unit trust as a percentage of the offer price. The quoted yield reflects income earned by the fund during the previous 12 months, and therefore only relates to past performance.

Using the information

The information provided means that investors can calculate how much their unit trust holdings are worth, and how they are performing on a day-to-day basis. Details of charges made by individual fund groups are also provided.

The spread is used by unit trust groups to collect the initial charge imposed to cover the expense of setting up and promoting the fund as well as recouping other costs.

Under the formula laid down by the FSA, the spread for unit trusts can only be moved up and down within a limited scale. If there is a surplus of sellers, the spread tends to be based at the bottom end of the scale. Conversely, if there is an excess of buyers, the spread is raised to the upper end of the scale, enhancing the value of the fund. The spread also reflects the fact that there are spreads in the prices of the shares in which trusts invest: like all investors, they buy at offer prices and sell at bid prices.

It is important to be aware of a unit trust's pricing policy, whether "historic", based on the price set at the most recent valuation of its portfolio of assets, or "forward", based on the price to be set at the next valuation. In the latter case, investors can never be sure of the price of a purchase or sale in advance of it being carried out.

Unit trusts are open-ended in that within reason there is no limit to the number of units a given trust can issue. An investor who wants to sell his or her units back to the trust will cause the trust either to find other willing owners or to sell some of its assets to pay for the buyback.

The income received by unit trusts on their investments must be paid out to unit holders, but there is often a distinction between income and accumulation units. With the former, the investor receives the appropriate share of dividends earned by the trust as cash; with the latter, income is added to the value of each unit, that is, the income is reinvested. There are often separate listings for the prices of income and accumulation units, the latter being higher because of the reinvested income. Unit trusts with low or even nil yields are those concentrating on capital growth rather than providing income.

Unit trusts were originally conceived to offer a spread of investments across the market, but they are now often much more focused, specialising by asset type (mainly equities but also bonds and currencies) and by the countries and regions in which they are invested, by the size of companies and the kind of industries, and by whether they are primarily pursuing income, capital appreciation or a combination of the two. The relationship between risk and return in the chosen market is important to selection, as are the investor's own investment goals: income, capital growth or total return. Unit trusts should generally be seen as a long-term investment: they need time to recoup the dealing charges.

The performance of unit trusts is assessed in more detail in Saturday's *Financial Times*. A half-page presents information on the overall winners and losers (the top and bottom five funds in terms of returns over one, three, five and ten years), and the top five and sector average performances for these four periods for over 20 different fund types, ranging from those investing in UK smaller companies' equities to those trading international bonds. Figure 10.2 shows a couple of examples, as well as a table for various indices.

The tables show the result of investing £1,000 in a trust over the four different time periods. It is important to remember that these are merely an historical record and cannot be a guide to future performance. The volatility figure shows the absolute variability of the trust's performance, measured by standard deviation of monthly price movements over three years. As a rule of thumb, the more volatile a fund's progress (the higher the figure), the higher the return investors demand from it to compensate for the additional risk, and the more wary potential new investors should be. The yield is the

Indices	1 year (£)	3	5	10	Volatility	Yld%
Average Unit Trust	1163	1427	1921	3208	5.3	2.3
Average Investment Trust	1233	1551	2053	3319	7.6	4.1
Bank	1030	1116	1196	1599	0.1	4.0
Building Society	1019	1086	1150	1536	0.1	2.2
Stockmarket: FTSE All-Share	1046	1426	2121	3628	4.3	2.2
Inflation	1030	1088	1142	1401	0.3	-

UK All Companies	1 year (£)	3	5	10	Volatility	Yld%
Solus UK Special Situations	2278	2949	3576	4881	8.6	1.2
ABN AMRO UK Growth	1715	2557	3490	7589	6.8	0.3
Dresdner RCM UK Mid-Cap	1483	2188	3190	4725	8.1	-
HL UK Performance Acc	1572	2154	-	-	5.7	1.5
Norwich UK Growth	1603	2092	2794	4501	6.6	1.1
SECTOR AVERAGE	1051	1372	1963	3104	4.7	1.2

UK Smaller Companies	1 year (£)	3	5	10	Volatility	Yld%
Close Beacon Investment	3159	3434	4675	-	15.1	-
Duncan Lawrie Smaller Cos	2177	3321	4175	-	11.7	-
Edinburgh UK Smaller Cos A	2164	2728	3170	6613	10.5	0.4
Marlborough HH Special Sits	2087	2543	-	-	8.9	0.6
Murray Smaller Companies	2513	2454	3233	5590	9.9	-
SECTOR AVERAGE	1395	1638	2284	3542	6.6	1.0

Fig. 10.2 Unit trusts

annual income paid to unit holders as a percentage of the units' value. For some funds, there is no yield shown since income is reinvested rather than distributed to unit holders.

The indices show performance, volatility and yield figures for an average unit trust, an average investment trust, representative bank and building society accounts, the FTSE All-Share index and inflation.

Volatility is a measure of the riskiness of a security that shows how much its price bounces around. The volatility figures in this table are based on a statistical measure known as "standard deviation". The higher the figure, the more the price will fluctuate. Bank and building society deposits, for example, have virtually zero volatility since capital values do not fluctuate. But the average unit and investment trusts are both more volatile than the FTSE All-Share, the proxy for the UK market as a whole. In this table, the market's volatility is 4.3 while the average unit and investment trusts show 5.3 and 7.6 respectively. Yet over the longer periods assessed, the returns provided by the trusts are lower – partly because of costs – than those theoretically available from the index. The theory that high risks are balanced by high rewards clearly has some limitations.

Saturday's newspaper also generally includes a table of new unit trust launches with details of their target yields, charges, minimum investment levels, availabilities to participate in tax-free savings schemes and any special offer discounts. Unit trusts are generally offered at a fixed price for a limited period.

Other UK unit trusts

These are trusts that are not authorised by the FSA and which are therefore not open to investment by members of the general public. They are available only to specific buyers such as pension funds, charities and local authorities.

Investment companies

Investment companies or investment trusts exist to invest in the equity of other companies, and their business consists entirely of buying, selling and holding shares. Like unit trusts, they provide an accessible vehicle for small investors to achieve a wide spread of investments. Investment trusts differ from unit trusts, however, in the sense that they issue equity themselves, and hence their shareholders hold a direct stake in the profits of the trust rather than merely the profits of a unit of shareholdings. They are also closed ended; there is a finite number of shares in issue. Their performance is listed in the FT London share service (see Figure 10.3), which shows:

- **Prices and yields:** latest prices, price changes, highs and lows for the year and yield as in the standard share coverage.
- **Net asset value (NAV), discount and premium:** the NAV figure is the market value per share of the various securities in which the trust has invested, and therefore what, in theory, the trust might be worth if it were liquidated immediately. The discount (rarely is it a premium) is where the share price typically stands in relation to the NAV per share. The amount of the discount is calculated as a percentage of the NAV per share. These figures are of key importance to investors in making their buying and selling decisions.

The figures are supplied by a leading broker, BT Alex Brown, and are the result of a daily simulation of changes in portfolio values. Calculations of the discount are generally reliable but, in some cases, such as recent new issues with substantial uninvested cash or funds that have radically restructured their portfolios, the estimates may need to be treated with caution.

Investment trust shares traditionally sell at a discount to their underlying asset value. In the 1974 bear market, discounts were as wide as 45 per cent and although they have mainly narrowed, they add an additional uncertainty to investment trust share price prospects. In general, the more significant the discount from net asset values per share to share prices, the more tempting an investment trust will be as a takeover target.

Discounts are important but need to be interpreted with a fair degree of caution. For one thing, the basis on which NAVs are calculated is as "fully diluted". This means that they assume that if the company has warrants in issue with an exercise price that is lower than the NAV, those warrants will be exercised rather than expire worthless. This would dilute the assets available for the ordinary shares. Where an investment company has warrants in issue, the share price information gives details immediately following the information on the ordinary shares.

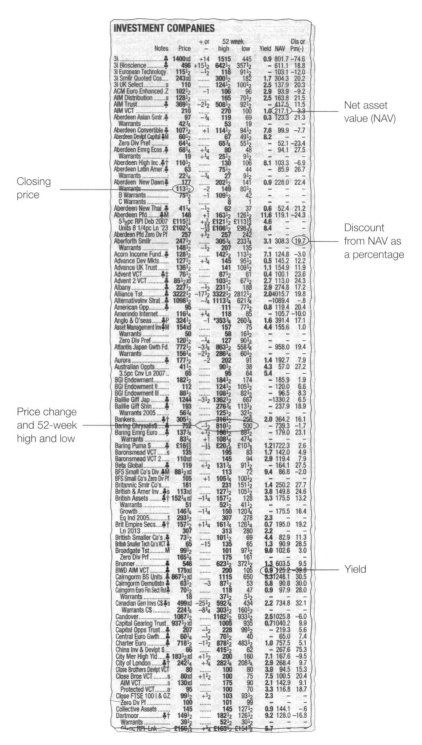

Fig. 10.3 London share service: investment companies

Net asset value (NAV)

Closing price

Discount from NAV as a percentage

Price change and 52-week high and low

Yield

Investors should resist the temptation to assume that the discount represents the amount of value that would be released if the company were wound up. In practice, investors tend to get back less than this for two main reasons. First, the NAV quoted assumes any debt issued by the company that ranks ahead of the shares would be deducted at its par (nominal) value. In practice, the debt would have to be repaid at its market value, which for many companies represents a significantly higher cost. Second, any winding up involves added charges, such as fees to advisers, the costs of cancelling the management contract and the costs of liquidating the portfolio. These are not reflected in the discount.

These two factors can have a substantial impact on the quoted discount. For the sector as a whole, it is estimated that debt accounts for 3 per cent of the assets while the winding-up costs could amount to another 3 per cent.

Compared to unit trusts, the commission charged on investment trusts is usually cheaper and the bid/offer spread narrower. But it is not possible to make minute comparisons of unit and investment trusts: the unit trust figures take account of the spread between buying and selling prices, while the investment trust figures take mid-prices in both cases. Comparisons thus flatter investment trusts. In addition, the narrowing of investment trust discounts makes them look better than unit trusts on longer-term comparisons.

Below the unit trust analysis in Saturday's *Financial Times* is a half-page of figures for investment trusts. As with unit trusts, this includes the overall winners and losers (the top and bottom five funds in terms of returns over one, three, five and ten years), and the top five and sector average performances for these four periods for over 20 different fund types. These fall into six broad categories: general trusts with an international portfolio of shares; trusts investing in specific geographical areas; trusts investing in specific market sectors; trusts aiming to generate high income; trusts aiming for capital growth; and trusts with a split capital structure.

Ten per cent of funds under investment trust management are in split capital trusts. These are companies with more than one class of share capital. The traditional variety is relatively simple: income shares get all the income, and capital shares get any capital growth over the life of the trust. Nowadays splits are highly complex, with several different types of security with differing rights and risks, and aiming to satisfy different investment needs. For example, at one extreme, zero dividend preference shares offer a low risk investment with a predetermined return; at the other, capital shares offer the potential for a high capital return at winding up but also the possibility that the shares will be valueless at the end of the trust's life. For zero dividend preference shares, discounts are meaningless because the shares have a predetermined return. The prices of "zeros" are primarily influenced by interest rates, which dictate how attractive that return is to capital-seeking investors, rather than the change in the company's net assets.

Some but not all unit and investment trusts can be put into an individual savings account (ISA), which shields investors against both income and capital gains tax. ISAs are personal investment vehicles launched in the United Kingdom in 1999.

Saturday's newspaper typically lists new investment trust launches with details of their target sizes and yields, charges, issue prices, minimum NAVs, relationships with tax-free savings schemes and ISAs, and offer periods. Since investment trusts typically trade at a discount to their NAV, investments in new issues may initially fall in value.

■ Insurances

These are funds that are managed by insurance companies and are linked to other savings products such as investment bonds, regular premium policies or pension contracts. The FT listings follow the same pattern as for unit trusts, except there is rarely a yield figure since income is automatically reinvested (see Figure 10.4):

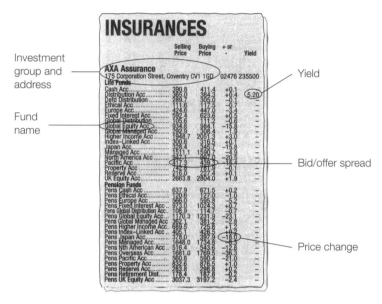

Fig. 10.4 Insurances

■ Management services

These are unit-linked insurance funds that are managed mainly by intermediaries. They are often known as "broker bonds". Many of them are underwritten by insurance companies.

Offshore and overseas

These are funds that operate like unit trusts or investment companies but are based in small, independent jurisdictions, often with a more liberal tax regime and lighter supervision than the United Kingdom. Nevertheless, the funds are still effectively operating under the advice or management of groups offering authorised unit trusts in the United Kingdom (see Figure 10.5). They are often located in the Channel Islands, Bermuda and the Cayman Islands, which offer low rates of tax and a high degree of privacy to companies and wealthy individuals. For the UK-based investor, there is virtually no tax advantage in investing in these funds, but there may well be for the expatriate or other overseas investor.

Offshore funds have various potential drawbacks. The charges are generally higher than their unit trust or investment company equivalents, but are often not clearly disclosed. The total annual cost of investing in an offshore fund can be up to four times higher than the quoted management fee. On average, the total cost of an offshore equities fund is almost one percentage point higher than the quoted fee. Investors also need to keep a careful eye on the safety of their assets when buying offshore. The level of investor protection may not match that of the United Kingdom. Investors should check whether the manager and the custodian firm (which has responsibility for looking after the assets) are regulated and whether they are covered by any compensation scheme.

FSA recognised funds

These are offshore funds that are based in designated territory-status countries and the European Union and for which authorisation for promotion in the United Kingdom has been secured from the FSA. These funds can be sold freely without any restrictions and their full names, addresses and telephone numbers are therefore included in the listing.

Regulated funds

These funds are based in designated territory-status countries that comply with local regulations but have not applied for official FSA recognition for sale in the United Kingdom. They cannot be promoted in the United Kingdom and therefore only the names are listed.

Offshore insurances

These are funds that are run by insurance companies that are based in countries with designated territory status for insurance products. The funds listed are linked to products that the companies are authorised to promote in the United Kingdom. Such authorisation must be sought from the FSA.

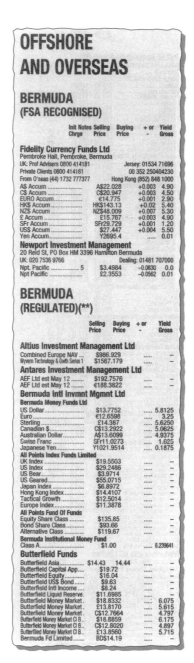

Fig. 10.5 Offshore and overseas

■ Other offshore funds

These are funds based in countries throughout the world but predominantly in tax havens. They cannot be advertised in the United Kingdom and again only the names are listed.

US mutual funds

The US equivalent of the UK managed money market is the mutual fund industry. As with unit trusts and investment trusts, the money invested in a mutual fund is pooled to buy a range of stocks, bonds and/or other assets.

The *Financial Times* does not carry information on US mutual funds but they are well covered in *The Wall Street Journal*. The US newspaper covers both open-end funds for which the fund will sell as many shares as investors want (the equivalent of unit trusts) and closed-end funds for which there are only a limited number of shares (the equivalent of investment trusts). There is also a distinction between load funds, which charge a commission when bought and sold, and no-load funds, which only charge a management fee. The typical fund charges 0.75 per cent of an investor's assets.

The US mutual fund market has grown dramatically in the last 20 years. Some funds are simply cash substitutes known as money market funds (the UK equivalents are discussed in Chapter 1), which invest in very short-term interest-bearing securities. Next are bond funds, which own securities with average maturities exceeding 90 days. Lastly, there are equity funds, which invest across a range of different US and international stocks and shares.

Equity mutual funds have been one of the great success stories of the bull market that started in the early 1980s. Their professional management of large pools of capital appears to offer small individual investors some of the key advantages enjoyed by large institutional investors: a spread of investments to reduce risk, and reduced dealing costs. Certainly, small investors who buy stocks directly have historically faced much higher trading costs because they could not match pooled funds' ability to negotiate lower commissions from brokers. Nor do such investors typically have the size of assets to achieve effective diversification.

The wide selection of mutual funds now available allows individual investors to get exposure to many more asset classes, geographical markets and investment styles than was possible in the past. But at the same time, because there are so many funds, it has become very difficult to choose between them. An entire industry has grown up to support the mutual fund business, providing information and apparently helping investors evaluate funds. Fund consumers in the United States – and increasingly elsewhere – now have access to enormous amounts of data about their investments.

Fund rating is usually done on the basis of past performance, past volatility and expenses (though some rating agencies try to be more forward-looking and offer explicit recommendations). Morningstar, for example, which rates all mutual funds, awards between one and five stars based on a mechanical formula. These stars are not recommendations, but they are naturally used as marketing tools, and floods of money go into funds that have five stars on the assumption that those that have done well in the past will continue to do so in the future.

■ Exchange traded funds

April 2000 saw the first UK appearance of a new investment product that bears many similarities to index tracking investment funds. The exchange traded fund (ETF) and its cousin, the traded index security, are now covered in the London share service (see Figure 10.6).

ETFs are a concept first introduced in 1993 in the United States, where there is now over $30 billion invested in them and where they seem to be very attractive to private investors. While tracking an index clearly helps investors of all kinds to spread risk and gain exposure to a wide variety of companies, it can be both difficult and expensive for private investors to do on their own. ETFs make the whole process simpler and cheaper. Well-known US ETFs include "spiders" (Standard & Poor's Depositary Receipts), which represent the S&P 500 index, "diamonds", which represent the Dow Jones Industrial Average (ticker symbol "DIA") and "qubes", which represent the Nasdaq 100 ("QQQ").

What makes ETFs appealing is that they are neither unit trusts (mutual funds) nor investment trusts and they eliminate the main drawbacks of the two most common vehicles for passive index investing. Open-ended funds have two drawbacks: a fund's net asset value is quoted and so investors can buy or sell only once a day; and investors who do not sell may incur capital gains tax if redemptions force the fund manager to sell some shares. Closed-end funds are priced continuously but temporary mismatches of demand and supply can lead to hefty discounts to the trust's net asset value.

ETFs are the first product to be listed on the London Stock Exchange's extraMARK, a new "attribute" market for innovative new investment products. Shares in each ETF can be bought and sold via a broker like any other equity. Once issued, the price moves up and down in line with the target index. The key benefits are that they offer diversification by allowing an investor to get exposure to a basket of securities in a single trade; ease of access; and efficiency of pricing because they are open-ended.

ETFs are traded continuously. They can be bought on margin or sold short, which allows more sophisticated trading strategies. Trades can also be settled using the underlying shares rather than cash, which should prevent discounts to the fund's net asset value and cuts down on taxable capital gains:

Fig. 10.6 Traded index securities and exchange traded funds

- **Traded index securities:** FTSE 100 TRAINS (TRAded INdex Securities) are individual securities that are designed to replicate the FTSE 100 index plus any dividends received from index shares. All the underlying shares in the FTSE 100 are purchased and then rebalanced as the composition of the index changes. So investing in TRAINS is equivalent to investing in a fully replicated basket of FTSE 100 stocks. The securities are issued and managed by HSBC James Capel (launched in 1997) and listed on the London Stock Exchange. The value of one TRAINS is equivalent to the value of ten times the FTSE 100.

- **iShares:** the first ETF product to be listed and traded on extraMARK is from Barclays Global Investors, the world's biggest index fund manager. The iFTSE 100 tracks the FTSE 100 and was first listed on extraMARK at the end of April 2000.

- **Price information:** as with regular shares, the daily table gives details of a fund's price, price change, 12-month high and low, volume, yield and p/e ratio, plus on Mondays, weekly price change, dividend, cover, market capitalisation, last ex-dividend date and Cityline code.

"I used to think that if there was reincarnation, I wanted to come back as the president or the

pope. But now I want to be the bond market: you can intimidate everybody."

James Carville, Adviser to Bill Cinton

"Driving a car involves a foot on the gas, hands on the wheel, and eyes on the road.

Navigating on the bond market requires a foot on interest rates, a handle on the prospects of

being repaid, and an eye on inflation."

Steven Mintz

11

Bonds and gilts

The international capital markets

- **Government bonds** – the UK gilt market: UK gilts prices; fixed interest indices; benchmark government bonds
- **Corporate bonds** – fixed income securities from non-sovereign debtors: new international bond issues; international and US corporate bonds; euro-zone bonds; bond and equity market volatility

Bonds are debt instruments, securities sold by governments, companies and banks in order to raise capital. They normally carry a fixed rate of interest, known as the coupon, have a fixed redemption value, the par value, and are repaid after a fixed period, the maturity. Some carry little or no interest (deep discount and zero coupon bonds), rewarding the buyer instead with a substantial discount from their redemption value and, hence, the prospect of a sizeable capital gain.

As seen in Chapter 1, the prices of bonds fluctuate in relation to the interest rate. The secondary market for bonds provides the liquidity necessary for a thriving primary market. This now exists not only for government bonds, but also on an international scale for all kinds of debt instruments.

National boundaries are no longer an obstruction to lenders and borrowers meeting in a market to buy and sell securities. It is possible for borrowers in one country to issue securities denominated in the currency of another, and for these to be sold to investors in a third country. Often, such transactions will be organised by financial institutions located in yet another country, usually one of the three primary centres of these international capital markets – London, New York and Tokyo.

The International Capital Markets pages of the *Financial Times* attempt to keep track of developments in these markets and other areas that involve the raising of capital across borders. These include the growing markets in derivative products (such as futures, options, and interest rate and currency swaps) and in cross-border new equity issues. The newspaper also tracks developments in important government bond markets such as the US Treasury bond market and, of course, the market in UK government bonds, known as gilt-edged stock or gilts.

From Tuesday to Friday, daily reports cover the market in international bonds, including government and corporate bonds. On Monday, the Markets Week page examines the prospects for the week ahead, particularly focusing on the markets in New York, London, Frankfurt and Tokyo. These markets, like the international equity markets, are not compartmentalised. In the interdependent world of international finance, developments in one market will often influence many others. For example, a sharp rally in gilts is likely to prompt a similar rally in corporate bonds denominated in sterling, which may in turn encourage borrowers to launch new issues.

■ Government bonds

As discussed in Chapter 4, the government of a country finances many of its activities through borrowing from lenders by issuing bonds. In the United Kingdom, government bonds are known as gilt-edged securities and they trade in a secondary market run by leading marketmakers.

UK gilts prices

Detailed price information on the UK government bond market is published daily under the heading UK gilts – cash market. These are classified under four headings based on their time to redemption: "shorts" with lives up to five years, "medium dated" with lives from five to 15 years, "longs" with lives of over 15 years, and undated, irredeemable stocks like Consols and War Loan. The classifications reflect the current life of the stock rather than the life when it was issued, and so stocks get reclassified as their date of maturity draws closer. There is also a fifth category, index-linked gilts, the yields of which are tied to the rate of inflation.

The gilt market is moved by economic and financial news, notably the movements of interest rates and inflation. The key to understanding it is that as interest rates go up, bond prices go down, making the coupon an effective rate of interest. Since high rates may be used to support a weak currency, a weakness in the currency may signal future increases in the interest rate, and a damaging effect on gilt prices. Similarly, prospects of inflation may lead to rate increases and bond price falls. Inflation also erodes the value of bonds since their prices and yields, unless index-linked, do not keep pace with rising prices generally. Hence, it is important for investors in bonds to look for changes in expectations about the future rates of interest and inflation. Other price determinants include the degree of risk (credit risk in the case of companies), the opportunity cost of other potential investments, the exchange rate and the time value of the bonds.

The market for gilts is run by primary dealers, the gilt-edged marketmakers (GEMMs) who have an obligation to maintain a market and a right to deal directly with the Bank of England. Transactions are for immediate or cash settlement, hence cash market as opposed to futures market. Institutional investors generally deal directly with the primary dealers. Figure 11.1 shows FT listings of UK gilts prices:

Stock name and coupon

Redemption date

Interest yield

Redemption yield

Closing price

Price change

Price high and low for the past 12 months

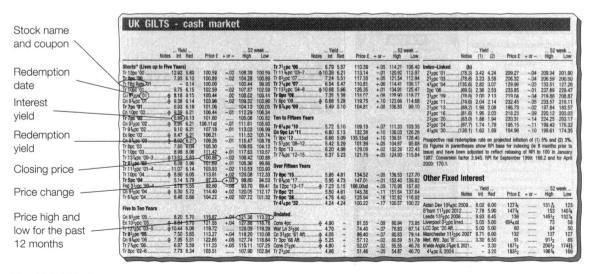

Fig. 11.1 UK gilts

- **Stock name and coupon:** the name given to a gilt is not important except as a means of differentiating it from others. The coupon, however, indicates how much nominal yield the owner is entitled to receive annually. Most gilts are issued in units of £100 (their par value), and so the percentage is equivalent to the number of pounds the owner receives. The coupon is a good indication of the interest rates the government was obliged to pay at the time of issue, and of the broad movements in the rate over the years.

- **Redemption date:** the year of redemption by the government, the specific date on which repayment of the loan will take place. If there are two dates, there is no specific date for repayment, but the stock will not be redeemed before the first one, and must be by the second one.

- **Interest yield:** this yield (also known as the income, earnings or flat yield) depends on the current price of the stock. It is calculated by dividing the coupon by the current price. This explains mathematically why bond prices always fall when interest rates rise and vice versa: since the coupon is, by definition, fixed, the price and yield are in an inverse relationship. To maintain a competitive yield when interest rates rise, the price has to fall.

- **Redemption yield:** this figure indicates the total return to be secured by holding on to a stock until it is finally redeemed by the government. It thus includes the capital gains or losses made at redemption as well as the income from the coupon. If the current price is below £100, the redemption yield will be bigger than the interest yield since, assuming the bond is held to redemption, there will also be a capital gain. More usually, gilts trade at a price greater than their repayment value and thus the redemption yield is lower than the interest yield. A new investor who intends to hang on to the bond until redemption would thus be locking in a capital loss.

- **Price, price change and the year's high and low points:** the price is the middle price between the buying and selling price quoted by marketmakers for a nominal £100 of stock. Each gilt has this par value, and moves of a point mean that it has risen or fallen by £1 in price. Like a share, gilts can be "ex-dividend" (xd), which means a buyer is not entitled to receive the latest coupon.

- **Index-linked gilts:** with these bonds, the interest and redemption value are adjusted to account for movement in the retail prices index with a time lag of eight months. In this way, they maintain their real value, and hedge their owners against inflation. The price of the hedge is the lower nominal coupon rate compared to that earned by non-index-linked gilts. The yield columns of the table give two possible redemption yields, one based on the assumption of 5 per cent inflation, the other on the assumption of 3 per cent inflation. The table also indicates the base date for the indexation calculation.

- **Other fixed interest:** these are other sterling bonds, many of which have been issued by local authorities such as Birmingham and Leeds.

Monday's newspaper has a variation on the listing for UK gilts, indicating the percentage price change on the previous week, the total amount of the stock in issue in millions of pounds (a fixed sum since the stock is guaranteed by the government to be redeemed at that amount, the bond equivalent of market capitalisation), the dates on which the interest is paid (twice yearly), the last ex-dividend payment of interest and the Cityline telephone number for real-time updates on the gilt price. The amount in issue is a good indication of the liquidity of the market: the bigger the amount, the easier the gilt will be to buy and sell.

The market price of a gilt reflects its redemption value, coupon and other rates. It is not directly determined by its redemption value until the redemption date gets closer. As a gilt approaches redemption, its price will get closer and closer to £100, the amount for which it will be redeemed.

Long-dated gilt prices move most in response to expectations of interest rate changes. Since their maturity value is fixed, they are a good indicator of expected trends in the rate of interest and the rate of inflation. As explained in Chapter 1, investors expect higher rates of return for longer-term investments. If short-term rates become higher than long-term rates, investors will move out of long-term assets. Thus, short- and long-term rates tend to move together. The yield curve is a means of comparing rates on bonds of different maturities, as well as giving an indication of the tightness of monetary conditions. Longer-term yields are usually higher because of the greater degree of risk (time and inflation risk). When short-term rates are higher, there is a negative or inverted yield curve, conventionally a sign of impending recession.

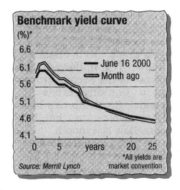

Fig. 11.2 UK benchmark yield curve

Monday's newspaper includes a picture of the current yield curve for benchmark UK government bonds (see Figure 11.2) as well as of the yield curves for national government bonds in New York, Frankfurt and Tokyo. These indicate the yields on typical bonds for each possible time to maturity. In this example, the yield curve is inverted. This is in part because the Bank of England has raised short rates substantially to counter a potential inflationary threat: the market evidently expects the Bank to succeed in fighting inflation and for rates eventually to be brought down again. But the inversion mainly results from strong demand for longer-dated gilts from investing institutions and a relative shortage of supply as the public finances are in such good shape with a budget surplus rather than the usual deficit. High demand and scarce supply drive prices up and yields down.

Interest and redemption yields quoted only apply to a new buyer. The yields for investors already in possession will depend on the price they paid. But, in both cases, the yields can be calculated exactly, in contrast with equities where both the dividend and capital gain or loss are uncertain. This reflects the greater degree of risk associated with investment in equities.

$$\text{Interest yield} = \frac{\text{coupon} \times 100}{\text{gilt price}}$$

The difference between interest yield and redemption yield is important to the investor because of the tax implications. Income from gilts is taxed but capital gains are not. Hence, the net return is determined by the composition of the total return.

The investor will also want to compare bond and equity yields. The yield gap (long-term bond yields minus the dividend yield on shares) is a good indicator of the relative rates, although at times, due to fears of inflation and the opportunities for capital gains on shares, there is a reverse yield gap. An alternative indicator (carried in Saturday's Money Watch table, Figure 1.3 in Chapter 1) is the yield ratio, the long gilt yield divided by the equity dividend yield. This ratio usually exceeds 2.

Index-linked bonds pay investors a known rate of interest independent of the inflation rate: both the coupon and the redemption payment are revalued in line with inflation. Along with Australia, Canada and Sweden, the UK is one of the few countries to issue such bonds, which now account for about 17 per cent of the government's outstanding stock of debt.

Index-linked stocks are valuable when inflation is feared; they are not so good when the real rates of return on gilts are high, that is, when nominal yields are above the rate of inflation. The difference between the long bond yield and the real yield on index-linked stocks is an indicator of expected inflation.

Private investors are becoming increasingly interested in bonds and gilts as investments. Banks recognise this and are actively promoting this group; Saturday's newspaper now regularly features advertisements and brochures for bond issues clearly directed at the private investor. It also includes a table examining gilt issues in terms of the best value for investors in different tax brackets (see Figure 11.3). The table takes three different levels of tax status and lists the best yielding gilts in each of five categories, providing the stock names and their current prices, yields and volatility. The basic principle behind the table is that since interest on gilts is taxed but capital gains are not, the higher the proportion of total return that is capital gains, the better for higher rate taxpayers.

In 1997, the UK government began issuing a new type of gilt-edged security called a strip. These are created when a conventional bond is broken down into its constituent parts, which can then be held or traded separately. A normal ten-year bond, for example, pays a coupon twice a year for ten years and a final large principal repayment at the

Gilt issues – best value v tax status

Your capital gain on a gilt – a UK government bond – is tax free. However, you pay tax on the interest. Therefore, gilts which deliver a higher proportion of their total return as capital gain are more tax efficient, and – other things being equal – more attractive to higher rate taxpayers. Yield is redemption yield and takes account of any change in the capital value over period to maturity. Volatility is a measure of the sensitivity of the stock price to changes in yield. Ex=Exchange; Con=Conversion; Tr=Treasury.

NON-TAXPAYERS	Stock	Price	% Yield		Volatility
CONVENTIONAL <5yr	Treas 9.75%, 2002	107.30	6.10		1.90%
5-10yr	Treas 8.50%, 2005	113.15	5.66		4.40%
10-15yr	Conv 9.00%, 2011	131.16	5.25		7.32%
>15yr	Treas 8.00%, 2015	132.62	4.95		9.73%
INDEX-LINKED	Index 2.50%, 2001	209.85	7.33‡‡	4.21♦	1.18%
	Index 2.50%, 2003	206.85	6.67‡‡	3.56♦	2.72%
20% TAXPAYERS					
CONVENTIONAL <5yr	Treas 5.00%, 2004	97.33	4.75		3.59%
5-10yr	Treas 7.50%, 2006	110.02	4.21		5.37%
10-15yr	Treas 6.25%, 2010	108.17	4.03		8.14%
>15yr	Treas 8.00%, 2015	132.62	3.62		10.59%
INDEX-LINKED	Index 2.50%, 2001	209.85	6.82‡‡	3.70♦	1.19%
	Index 2.50%, 2003	206.85	6.16‡‡	3.05♦	2.74%
40% TAXPAYERS					
CONVENTIONAL <5yr	Treas 5.00%, 2004	97.33	3.73		3.67%
5-10yr	Treas 5.75%, 2009	103.95	2.97		8.04%
10-15yr	Treas 6.25%, 2010	108.17	2.84		8.65%
>15yr	Treas 4.25%, 2032	97.46	2.67		21.56
INDEX-LINKED	Index 2.50%, 2001	209.85	6.30‡‡	3.20♦	1.20%
	Index 2.50%, 2003	206.85	5.64‡‡	2.54♦	2.77%

‡‡=Money yield (current inflation assumed). ♦=Real yield (adjusted for inflation). Source: Barclays Capital

Fig. 11.3 Gilt issues: best value versus tax status

end of the ten years. Under the new arrangements, a bond can be stripped to make 21 separate instruments: 20 strips based on the coupons, which mature after six months, a year, 18 months, two years and so on; and one strip based on the principal, which matures after ten years.

The strips pay no interest but since they are zero coupon instruments, they are sold at a discount, offering the investor a capital gain when they mature at their face value. The idea is that because these offer investing institutions exactly the kind of maturity profile that they want, they might be willing to pay more for them. Other countries' experience is that strips tend to trade at a small premium compared to conventional bonds.

A typical report on the market for gilts looks like this:

> UK gilt prices fell yesterday with the focus in the market on the Bank of England's Monetary Policy Committee meeting. Today, the committee will announce whether UK interest rates are to remain on hold or whether they will rise. The pound's recent fall against the dollar has increased some worries about inflation. December gilt futures were down 0.15 at 112.45. US Treasury prices also fell yesterday as concern continued to mount over rising oil prices and a wave of corporate and agency debt expected to flood on to the market in the weeks ahead.
>
> (*Financial Times*, 7 September 2000)

This demonstrates some of the major influences on the gilt market. For example, the threat of higher US inflation (driven by the prospect of higher oil prices feeding through to producer and retail prices) implies returns, in terms of both interest and capital appreciation, that are eroded in value. The threat of higher inflation in the UK also suggests the possibility of higher interest rates, which, though promising for income, implies the prospect of falling bond prices.

Exchange rates also play an important role in the bond market, as the report indicates. The weakness of the pound suggests that the Bank of England may be obliged to raise interest rates, leading to falling bond prices. What is more, given the extensive interconnections of global bond markets, the movements of interest rates and bond prices in the United States are likely to affect UK rates and prices in the same direction. For example, lower bond prices and higher yields in the United States than in the United Kingdom might tempt international bond investors to move out of UK gilts and into US bonds, pushing down the prices of the former.

In fact, the two economies (and indeed the rest of the world) are linked even more fundamentally in the patterns of their economic growth and business cycles. For example, indications of resurgent economic growth suggest that there will be the future threat of inflationary pressures from a boom. Furthermore, since the rate of interest typically goes up in a time of economic buoyancy, bond prices tend to fall on the upswing of the business cycle.

■ Fixed interest indices

As well as individual bond prices, the *Financial Times* provides indices for a broad range of UK fixed interest instruments. The FTSE Actuaries government securities UK indices (see Figure 11.4) are designed to perform roughly the same service for professional investors in gilt-edged stocks as the corresponding FTSE equity indices have provided for investors in ordinary shares. They are produced at the close of business each day that the Stock Exchange is open and published in the following day's newspaper, normally Tuesday to Saturday. The indices cover UK gilts and index-linked government securities, with the number of stocks in each sector on each day shown after the name of that sector. The information displayed falls into two sections: price indices and yield indices:

■ **Price indices:** there are 12 indices, seven covering the market for all conventional UK government stocks (shorts, three categories of medium-dated, longs, irredeemable, and all stocks) and five for index-linked securities (one each for under and over five years, five to 15 years, and over 15 years to redemption, plus all stocks).

■ **Yield indices:** there are 15 indices of yields, five based on maturity for regular gilts, one for irredeemables and ten for index-linked securities, based on different maturities and inflation assumptions. The number of yield indices is a compromise between the need for an easily comprehensible snapshot of the market, and the need to represent some of its complexities.

FTSE Actuaries Government Securities   **UK Indices**

Price Indices UK Gilts	Thu Jun 15	Day's chge %	Accrued interest	xd adj ytd	Total Return	Duration Yield	Years	% Weight
1 Up to 5 years (15)	114.69	+0.06	1.17	4.35	1263.34	5.89	2.16	35.25
2 5-10 years (8)	157.37	-0.09	1.22	5.68	1353.18	5.48	5.70	26.43
3 10-15 years (5)	173.89	-0.33	3.20	4.06	1473.89	5.15	8.14	11.15
4 5-15 years (13)	162.38	-0.16	1.77	5.22	1388.51	5.36	6.41	37.58
5 Over 15 years (5)	221.80	-0.60	0.92	5.99	1637.70	4.70	12.15	26.53
6 Irredeemables (2)	308.07	-0.97	0.98	7.61	1926.36	4.82	21.17	0.64
7 All stocks (35)	156.08	-0.21	1.38	5.14	1396.32	5.09	6.38	100.00

Index-linked	Thu Jun 15	Day's chge %	Accrued interest	xd adj ytd	Total Return	% Weight
1 Up to 5 years (3)	228.02	+0.02	0.92	3.14	1230.49	16.26
2 Over 5 years (8)	266.63	-0.03	1.93	3.03	1488.07	83.74
3 5-15 years (4)	245.37	-0.01	1.62	2.82	1365.48	38.66
4 Over 15 years (4)	286.62	-0.04	2.22	3.26	1603.46	45.08
5 All stocks (11)	259.38	-0.02	1.74	3.05	1450.42	100.00

Yield indices	Jun 15	Jun 14	Yr ago
5 yrs	5.72	5.72	5.23
10 yrs	5.25	5.22	5.10
15 yrs	4.93	4.88	4.99
20 yrs	4.73	4.68	4.92

† Flat yield to date.

Yield indices	Jun 15	Jun 14	Yr ago
Irred †	4.82	4.77	5.04

Real yield	····· Inflation 0% ·····				····· Inflation 5% ·····			
	Jun 15	Dur yrs	Jun 14	Yr ago	Jun 15	Dur yrs	Jun 14	Yr ago
Up to 5 yrs	4.40	2.38	4.40	3.38	3.16	2.39	3.16	2.42
Over 5 yrs	2.14	12.80	2.14	2.08	1.91	12.90	1.91	1.86
5-15 yrs	2.40	8.97	2.40	2.14	2.08	9.00	2.07	1.84
Over 15 yrs	2.01	16.27	2.01	2.04	1.84	16.36	1.83	1.87
All Stocks	2.22	10.99	2.22	2.13	1.96	11.13	1.95	1.88

FT Fixed Interest Indices

	Jun 15	Jun 14	Jun 13	Jun 12	Jun 9	Yr ago	High*	Low*
Govt. Secs. (UK)	105.29	105.62	105.75	105.91	105.93	109.14	101.66	106.56

	Jun 15	Jun 14	Jun 13	Jun 12	Jun 9	Yr ago	High*	Low*
Fixed Interest	142.21	142.78	143.16	143.44	143.84	149.71	146.76	141.91

Fig. 11.4 FTSE Actuaries government securities UK indices

The tables provide the following information:

- **Value:** the first two columns of the price indices list current value and the percentage change on the previous trading day's value.

- **Accrued interest:** interest on gilt-edged stocks is paid in twice-yearly instalments. Accrued interest simply records the amount of interest included in each day's price index that has accumulated on the stock since the last dividend payment.

- **Ex-dividend adjustment to date:** the amount of income that a holder of a portfolio of stocks proportionate to the index would have received in the year to date, credited on the ex-dividend date for each stock.

- **Total return:** this figure indicates the returns on the index, including both interest payments and the capital gain (or loss).

- **Duration yield and years:** the yield figure indicates the average yield on stocks included in each index. The duration years measure is a weighted average time to maturity of the components of the index. Both indicators can be used by investors to compare the returns and price volatility of different maturity stocks.

- **Percentage weighting:** this indicates the proportion of the total index taken up by a specific category of stocks.

- **Highs and lows:** Saturday's newspaper adds information on the highs and lows for the year, with dates, for the 15 yield indices.

- **Government securities (UK):** the movements of a representative cross-section of gilt-edged stocks, the Government Securities index, over the past five trading days, the value of the index a year ago and its high and low points for the year to date. This index began from a base of 100 in 1926, and the notes to the table detail its high and low since compilation.

■ **Fixed interest:** the movements of a broader range of fixed interest stocks, including those issued by the UK government, local government, public boards and by UK industrial companies. As with the gilts index, this charts the index values over the past five trading days, one year ago and at its zenith and nadir both for the year and since compilation.

The price indices and the ex-dividend adjustment can be used to work out an appropriate market rate of return, using whatever tax rate is appropriate on income. The indices can provide a basis for performance measurement.

The FT yield indices can be used to monitor the difference in yield between gilt-edged stocks and equities (the yield gap), as a guide to market rates in making valuations and in setting the terms for new issues.

■ Benchmark government bonds

Coverage of government bond markets outside the United Kingdom picks out items of importance or interest from internationally tradeable government bond markets throughout the world and, where relevant, related futures and options activity. Figure 11.5 shows the daily FT table of benchmark bonds in key markets, which includes:

■ **National markets:** a summary of daily movements in important benchmark bonds in a number of major markets.

■ **Benchmarks:** bonds are described by redemption date and coupon, the bid price, the yield according to the local market standard (as standards vary, yields are not necessarily comparable) and the change in the yield from the previous day, week, month and year

A related table shows the spreads on ten-year benchmark government bonds (see Figure 11.6). For each country, there is a figure for bid yield on a ten-year bond (the yield an investor would receive for buying a ten-year bond) and figures for spreads against ten-year bunds (German government bonds) and US Treasury bonds. The spread indicates the additional yield an investor would receive for buying, say Australian debt as opposed to comparable US debt. It is the premium for yield compared to the benchmark, a reward for the additional risk. If the figure is negative, it indicates that the bond in question is viewed as less risky than a bund or Treasury bond.

The FT also carries a table of prices, yields and spreads for a variety of government bonds in emerging markets (see Figure 11.7). As these bonds are typically thought to be more risky than the ones in developed countries (that is, there is a stronger possibility that the governments will default on the debt), the spreads over Treasuries are correspondingly higher. In other words, to compensate for the additional risk, additional returns are on offer.

In addition to the standard price, yield and spread information, this table provides measures of the riskiness of the different securities. Standard & Poor's and Moody's are credit-rating agencies, which evaluate the risk of default on both government and

BENCHMARK GOVERNMENT BONDS

Jun 15	Red Date	Coupon	Bid Price	Bid Yield	Day chg yield	Wk chg yield	Month chg yld	Year chg yld
Australia	03/02	9.750	106.1982	5.92	+0.03	-0.04	-0.36	+0.78
	09/09	7.500	109.2444	6.17	+0.03	-0.02	-0.27	-0.10
Austria	02/02	4.375	98.9000	5.06	-0.05	-0.13	+0.05	+2.01
	01/10	5.500	99.8181	5.52	+0.02	-0.02	-0.12	+1.15
Belgium	06/02	8.750	107.0600	4.97	-0.06	-0.16	-	+1.94
	09/10	5.750	101.6587	5.53	+0.03	-0.04	-0.14	+0.90
Canada	12/01	5.250	98.8800	6.07	+0.06	-0.10	-0.37	+0.77
	06/09	5.500	97.2500	5.90	+0.01	-0.08	-0.35	+0.23
Denmark	11/01	8.000	102.9090	5.73	-0.06	-0.10	+0.12	+2.45
	11/09	6.000	102.6200	5.63	-0.02	-0.07	-0.14	+0.84
Finland	09/01	10.000	105.9700	4.86	-0.03	-0.13	+0.01	+2.11
	02/11	5.750	102.8317	5.39	+0.03	-0.01	-0.19	+0.85
France	01/02	4.000	98.7300	4.85	-0.06	-0.19	-0.06	+1.77
	04/07	5.500	101.8433	5.17	+0.01	-0.05	-0.19	+1.24
	04/10	5.500	101.2194	5.34	+0.03	-0.03	-0.15	+0.90
	04/29	5.500	98.7195	5.59	+0.06	-0.01	-0.08	+0.26
Germany	12/01	4.000	98.8100	4.84	-0.06	-0.13	-0.02	+1.85
	01/07	6.000	104.5243	5.16	+0.02	-0.07	-0.20	+1.10
	01/10	5.375	101.4050	5.18	+0.02	-0.01	-0.17	+0.88
	01/30	6.250	111.5757	5.45	+0.02	+0.02	-0.11	+0.17
Greece	01/02	7.600	101.6300	6.45	-	-0.04	+0.08	-0.52
	01/09	6.300	101.3700	6.08	-0.01	-0.06	-0.16	+0.09
Ireland	10/01	6.500	102.0600	4.85	-0.04	-0.19	-0.14	+1.65
	04/10	4.000	89.2426	5.44	+0.03	-0.01	-0.18	+0.89
Italy	02/02	3.000	96.9500	4.95	-0.03	-0.15	-0.04	+1.81
	07/05	4.750	97.7900	5.26	-0.01	-0.08	-0.17	+1.57
	11/09	4.250	90.9800	5.49	+0.01	-0.03	-0.14	+0.95
	11/29	5.250	91.5800	5.85	+0.01	+0.02	-0.03	+0.34
Japan	12/01	6.000	108.5050	0.29	-0.01	-0.10	+0.04	+0.09
	06/05	3.400	111.4960	1.03	-0.02	-0.07	-0.07	+0.31
	12/09	1.900	102.2210	1.65	+0.02	-0.01	-0.05	+0.10
	03/20	2.500	107.0470	2.06	-0.02	-0.06	-0.10	-0.46
Netherlands	02/02	3.000	97.1100	4.85	-0.06	-0.17	-0.11	+1.86
	04/10	7.500	116.1434	5.34	+0.03	-	-0.18	+0.85
New Zealand	03/02	10.000	104.7951	7.00	+0.03	-	-	+1.69
	07/09	7.000	100.6587	6.90	+0.01	+0.02	-0.19	+0.29
Norway	05/01	7.000	100.0800	6.88	+0.02	+0.07	+0.10	+1.62
	05/09	5.500	96.0000	6.09	+0.01	-	-0.17	+0.65
Portugal	03/02	5.750	101.1800	5.01	-0.06	-0.20	-0.04	+2.10
	05/10	5.850	102.0929	5.57	+0.02	-0.02	-0.12	+0.92
Spain	07/02	4.250	98.6100	4.96	-0.05	-0.13	-0.11	+2.00
	01/10	4.000	89.2785	5.46	-	-0.01	-0.17	+0.86
Sweden	04/02	5.500	101.0390	4.87	+0.01	-0.09	-0.06	+1.21
	04/09	9.000	127.1190	5.10	+0.02	+0.03	+0.03	+0.25
Switzerland	07/02	4.500	101.2000	3.88	+0.03	+0.10	+0.08	+2.11
	08/10	3.500	95.7800	4.01	-	-	-0.05	+1.30
UK	11/01	7.000	101.1600	6.11	+0.01	-0.11	-0.29	+0.91
	11/04	6.750	104.2900	5.64	-0.02	-0.06	-0.26	+0.48
	12/09	5.750	104.3700	5.16	+0.03	-	-0.16	+0.19
	12/28	6.000	124.1200	4.49	+0.05	+0.07	-	-0.32
US	02/02	6.500	99.9688	6.51	-	-0.10	-0.40	+0.87
	11/04	5.875	98.2188	6.34	-	-0.09	-0.43	+0.48
	02/10	6.500	103.2500	6.05	-	-0.07	-0.37	+0.08
	05/30	6.250	104.5625	5.92	+0.01	+0.04	-0.20	-0.18

Fig. 11.5 Benchmark government bonds

10 YEAR BENCHMARK SPREADS

Aug 30	Bid Yield	Spread vs Bund	Spread vs T-Bonds		Bid Yield	Spread vs Bund	Spread vs T-Bonds
Australia	6.41	+1.11	+0.50	Netherlands	5.46	+0.16	-0.44
Austria	5.66	+0.36	-0.24	New Zealand	6.91	+1.61	+1.00
Belgium	5.66	+0.36	-0.24	Norway	6.29	+0.99	+0.39
Canada	5.89	+0.59	-0.01	Portugal	5.69	+0.39	-0.21
Denmark	5.69	+0.39	-0.21	Spain	5.60	+0.30	-0.30
Finland	5.53	+0.23	-0.37	Sweden	5.34	+0.04	-0.56
France	5.47	+0.17	-0.43	Switzerland	3.81	-1.49	-2.09
Germany	5.30	-	-0.60	UK	5.40	+0.10	-0.50
Greece	6.01	+0.71	+0.11	US	5.90	+0.60	-
Ireland	5.57	+0.27	-0.33				
Italy	5.67	+0.37	-0.23				
Japan	1.87	-3.43	-4.04				

Source: Interactive Data/FT Information
London closing. * New York closing.
Annualised yield basis.

Fig. 11.6 Ten-year benchmark spreads

corporate bonds. The rating system used by Standard & Poor's, for example, varies from AAA (triple-A) for a bond with minimal default risk through AA, A, BBB, BB, B, CCC, CC, C and D in increasing order of riskiness. A plus or minus sign indicates whether a bond has been recently up or downgraded. An upgrade means it has been rated as being at less risk of default.

EMERGING MARKET BONDS

Jun 15	Red date	Coupon	S&P* Rating	Moody's Rating	Bid price	Bid yield	Day's chge yield	Mth's chge yield	Spread vs US
■ EUROPE €									
Croatia	03/06	7.375	BBB-	Baa3	99.3368	7.51	+0.05	-0.29	+1.30
Slovenia	03/09	4.875	A	A3	92.5523	5.99	+0.05	-0.29	-0.09
Hungary	02/09	4.375	BBB+	Baa1	88.2628	6.16	-0.04	-0.12	+0.08
■ LATIN AMERICA $									
Argentina	02/20	12.000	BB	B1	94.0000	12.84	-	-0.73	+6.85
Brazil	01/20	12.750	B+	B2	96.0000	13.33	+0.13	-0.84	+7.34
Mexico	02/10	9.875	BB+	Baa3	102.6000	9.45	+0.14	-0.67	+3.40
■ ASIA $									
China	12/08	7.300	BBB	A3	97.2373	7.75	-0.03	-0.55	+1.63
Philippines	01/19	9.875	BB+	Ba1	84.6979	11.94	-0.01	-0.46	+5.94
South Korea	04/08	8.875	BBB	Baa2	103.9367	8.18	-0.03	-0.62	+2.06
■ AFRICA/MIDDLE EAST $									
Lebanon	10/09	10.250	BB-	B1	98.7500	10.46	+0.09	+0.23	+4.38
South Africa	10/06	8.375	BBB-	Baa3	94.2724	9.60	+0.05	-0.56	+3.39
Turkey	09/07	10.000	B+	B1	94.5000	11.12	+0.11	+0.46	+4.96
■ BRADY BONDS $									
Argentina	03/23	6.000	BB	B1	67.2500	9.55	-0.02	-0.40	+3.58
Brazil	04/14	8.000	B+	B2	73.5000	11.96	+0.11	-0.98	+5.93
Mexico	12/19	6.250	BB+	Baa3	81.7500	8.13	-	-0.41	+2.13
Venezuela	03/20	6.750	B	B2	69.5000	10.42	+0.04	-0.64	+4.43

Fig. 11.7 Emerging market bonds

Corporate bonds

Bonds issued by institutions other than governments make up a substantial part of the world's largest bond markets. Because the bulk of bonds issued by non-sovereign debtors are issued by corporations, these fixed income securities are called corporate bonds.

The yields on corporate bonds are generally higher and the prices lower, reflecting the more variable creditworthiness of their issuers and a greater risk of default. These bonds too are classified by rating agencies such as Standard & Poor's and Moody's, which rate bonds according to the risk they carry (ranging from high quality AAA to below grade D).

Low-grade corporate bonds rated as being below investment quality may be issued offering very high yields. Known colloquially as junk bonds, these essentially unsecured, high-yield debt securities peaked in popularity in the late 1980s, and financed a significant portion of the merger and acquisition boom in the United States.

When new corporate bonds are issued, their yields are generally set with reference to benchmark government bonds, offering a spread over the gilt yield in order to make up for the greater risk of default that they bear. Companies unlike governments can always go under, they have a finite lifespan and the market for their bonds is less liquid than the gilt market.

The International Capital Markets pages in Tuesday to Friday's newspaper carry reports on new international bond issues, together with tables of the previous day's prices and issues. These markets have emerged with the growth of what have come to be known as Eurocurrencies. A Eurocurrency is a currency deposited outside its country of origin. For example, a UK exporter might receive dollars but not convert them into pounds. Since the United States, in running persistent trade deficits, exports dollars, banks accumulate these deposits, which are then put to work. This stateless money is free of local regulations and London is its centre. Eurocurrencies are borrowed by loans or the issue of various kinds of debt instrument that "securitise" the money: Euronotes, Eurocommercial paper and Eurobonds.

Eurobonds are the most common. They tap the large stateless pool of cash and are traded in a secondary market of screens and telephones. These are volatile and unregulated markets and they can become illiquid since there is no obligation for anyone to take part.

In many aspects trading activity in these markets is similar to trading in domestic stock markets, particularly in the case of sterling bond issues, industrial debentures and corporate bonds.

New international bond issues

Monday's newspaper rounds up the issues of the previous week with a table of new international bond issues, broken down according to the issuing currency. On Tuesday to Friday, the previous day's issues are listed (see Figure 11.8):

Total amount to be
raised in millions of
units of the relevant
currency

Price of an
individual bond

Yield spread
compared to a
government bond

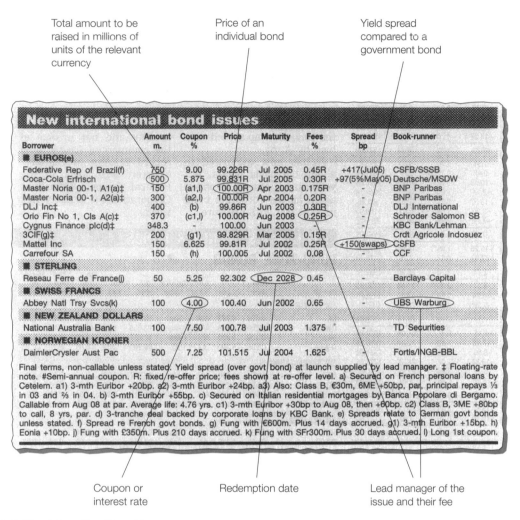

New international bond issues

Borrower	Amount m.	Coupon %	Price	Maturity	Fees %	Spread bp	Book-runner
■ EUROS(e)							
Federative Rep of Brazil(f)	750	9.00	99.226R	Jul 2005	0.45R	+417(Jul05)	CSFB/SSSB
Coca-Cola Erfrisch	500	5.875	99.831R	Jul 2005	0.30R	+97(5%May05)	Deutsche/MSDW
Master Noria 00-1, A1(a)‡	150	(a1,l)	100.00R	Apr 2003	0.175R	-	BNP Paribas
Master Noria 00-1, A2(a)‡	300	(a2,l)	100.00R	Apr 2004	0.20R	-	BNP Paribas
DLJ Inc‡	400	(b)	99.86R	Jun 2003	0.30R	-	DLJ International
Orio Fin No 1, Cls A(c)‡	370	(c1,l)	100.00R	Aug 2008	0.25R	-	Schroder Salomon SB
Cygnus Finance plc(d)‡	348.3	-	100.00	Jun 2003	-	-	KBC Bank/Lehman
3CIF(g)‡	200	(g1)	99.829R	Mar 2005	0.15R	-	Crdt Agricole Indosuez
Mattel Inc	150	6.625	99.81R	Jul 2002	0.25R	+150(swaps)	CSFB
Carrefour SA	150	(h)	100.005	Jul 2002	0.08	-	CCF
■ STERLING							
Reseau Ferre de France(j)	50	5.25	92.302	Dec 2028	0.45	-	Barclays Capital
■ SWISS FRANCS							
Abbey Natl Trsy Svcs(k)	100	4.00	100.40	Jun 2002	0.65	-	UBS Warburg
■ NEW ZEALAND DOLLARS							
National Australia Bank	100	7.50	100.78	Jul 2003	1.375	-	TD Securities
■ NORWEGIAN KRONER							
DaimlerCrysler Aust Pac	500	7.25	101.515	Jul 2004	1.625	-	Fortis/INGB-BBL

Final terms, non-callable unless stated. Yield spread (over govt bond) at launch supplied by lead manager. ‡ Floating-rate note. #Semi-annual coupon. R: fixed/re-offer price; fees shown at re-offer level. a) Secured on French personal loans by Cetelem. a1) 3-mth Euribor +20bp. a2) 3-mth Euribor +24bp. a3) Also: Class B, €30m, 6ME +50bp, par, principal repays ⅓ in 03 and ⅔ in 04. b) 3-mth Euribor +55bp. c) Secured on Italian residential mortgages by Banca Popolare di Bergamo. Callable from Aug 08 at par. Average life: 4.76 yrs. c1) 3-mth Euribor +30bp to Aug 08, then +60bp, par. c2) Class B, 3ME +80bp to call, 8 yrs, par. d) 3-tranche deal backed by corporate loans by KBC Bank. e) Spreads relate to German govt bonds unless stated. f) Spread re French govt bonds. g) Fung with €600m. Plus 14 days accrued. g1) 3-mth Euribor +15bp. h) Eonia +10bp. j) Fung with £350m. Plus 210 days accrued. k) Fung with SFr300m. Plus 30 days accrued. l) Long 1st coupon.

Coupon or
interest rate

Redemption date

Lead manager of the
issue and their fee

Fig. 11.8 New international bond issues

■ **All new issues launched the previous day:** the table gives details of the borrower, currency, amount, coupon, price, maturity, the fees payable to the underwriters, the yield spread over a comparable government bond, and the issue's arranger. The table also carries details of bonds on which terms have been altered or finalised subsequent to launch.

■ **Book runner:** the issuer gives a mandate to one or more lead banks to manage the issue. The fee is paid in the form of a discount on the issue price.

■ International bonds and US corporate bonds

From Tuesday to Friday, the newspaper carries information on the secondary market prices for a range of actively traded corporate bonds (see Figure 11.9). The price, yield, spread (against a comparable government bond) and rating information provided are intended to give a representation of current market conditions in various countries, currencies, sectors, and bond riskiness and time to maturity. For example, the US corporate bond table covers utilities like the telecoms firm Pacific Bell, financial corporations like Banc One, industrial companies like Lucent Technologies and government agencies like Fannie Mae, as well as high-yield bonds. The international bonds table provides details on industrial, financial, local authority and utility bonds issued in a range of currencies. Any of the bonds shown may be used as benchmarks by investors evaluating potential fixed income investments or by companies or governments planning new issues.

US CORPORATE BONDS

Sep 5	Red date	Coupon	S&P* Rating	Moody's Rating	Bid price	Bid yield	Day's chge yield	Mth's chge yield	Spread vs Govts
■ UTILITIES									
Pac Bell	07/02	7.25	AA-	Aa3	100.4128	6.99	-0.02	-0.08	+0.90
NY Tel	08/25	7.00	A+	A1	89.5175	7.97	-	-0.06	+2.31
CWE	05/08	8.00	BBB+	Baa1	102.6038	7.54	-	-0.11	+1.86
■ FINANCIALS									
GECC	05/07	8.75	AAA	Aaa	109.4005	6.96	-0.01	-0.15	+1.28
Banc One	08/02	7.25	A-	A1	100.3078	7.06	-0.01	-0.09	+0.97
CNA Fin	01/18	6.95	BBB	Baa1	82.0824	9.00	-0.16	-0.28	+3.34
■ INDUSTRIALS									
Lucent	03/29	6.45	A	A2	86.3354	7.63	-	+0.15	+1.97
News Corp	10/08	7.38	BBB-	Baa3	97.7886	7.74	-0.01	-0.10	+2.06
TCI Comm	05/03	6.38	AA-	A2	98.0146	7.20	-0.02	-0.10	+1.11
■ AGENCIES									
FHLMC	04/09	5.86	N/A	Aaa	93.6230	6.85	-0.01	-0.18	+1.17
SLMA	05/04	7.01	N/A	Aaa	101.0338	6.68	-0.01	-0.17	+0.78
FNMA	08/28	6.16	N/A	Aaa	91.6082	6.83	-0.04	-0.12	+1.17
FFCB	05/02	5.25	N/A	Aaa	97.9369	6.58	-0.01	-0.17	+0.49
■ HIGH YIELD									
Charter Comm	04/09	8.63	B+	B2	92.0000	-	-	-	-
HMH Prop	08/08	7.88	BB	Baa2	94.0000	-	-	-	-
AMC Ent	02/11	9.50	CCC+	Caa3	36.0000	-	-	-	-

NY latest. *Standard & Poor's. Yields: semi-annual basis.   Source: Interactive Data/FT Information

INTERNATIONAL BONDS

Sep 5	Red date	Coupon	S&P* Rating	Moody's Rating	Bid price	Bid yield	Day's chge yield	Mth's chge yield	Spread vs Govts
■ $									
IBRD	06/10	7.125	AAA	Aaa	102.0512	6.83	+0.01	-0.15	+1.13
Wal-Mart	08/09	6.875	AA	Aa2	99.8370	6.90	-	-0.19	+1.19
Ford	06/10	7.875	A	A2	102.1646	7.55	-	-0.16	+1.85
Viacom	07/10	7.700	BBB+	Baa1	101.6650	7.46	+0.01	-0.09	+1.76
■ C$									
Bayer Landsbank	08/04	9.500	AAA	Aaa	110.8901	6.28	-0.04	-0.12	+0.27
JP Morgan	03/04	6.875	A+	A2	99.8365	6.91	-0.04	-0.06	+0.90
Province of BC	06/03	7.750	AA-	Aa2	104.4180	5.99	-0.04	+0.03	-
Deutsche B FRN	09/02	5.875	AA	Aa3	99.2316	6.29	-0.01	-0.13	+0.33
■ £									
EIB	12/09	5.500	AAA	Aaa	94.1400	6.35	-	-0.01	+1.03
GUS	07/09	6.375	A-	A2	91.0000	7.82	+0.05	-0.10	+2.50
Gallaher	05/09	6.625	BBB+	Baa2	93.1500	7.73	+0.02	-0.15	+2.41
Halifax	04/08	6.375	AA	Aa1	98.2200	6.67	-	-0.08	+1.15
■ SFR									
EIB	01/08	3.750	AAA	Aaa	97.9802	4.07	-	-0.18	+0.30
Italy (REP)	07/10	3.125	AA	Aa3	92.0731	4.12	-	-0.12	+0.29
Hydro-Quebec	05/01	6.750	A+	A2	101.3308	4.70	+0.02	-0.26	+1.08
Gen Elect.	09/01	3.418	AAA	Aaa	99.8134	3.77	+0.01	-0.23	+0.15
■ YEN									
IBRD (World Bk)	03/02	5.250	AAA	Aaa	107.3708	0.42	+0.08	+0.28	-0.26
Spain (Kingdom)	03/02	5.750	AA+	Aa2	108.0900	0.47	+0.02	+0.29	-0.21
KFW Int	03/10	1.750	AAA	Aaa	99.0420	1.86	+0.04	+0.14	-0.07
Procter & Gamble	06/10	2.000	AA	Aa2	99.3815	2.07	-	+0.26	+0.14
■ A$									
IBRD (World Bk)	02/08	6.000	AAA	Aaa	95.7487	6.73	+0.07	-0.16	+0.69
Queenoland Troy	06/06	6.500	AAA	Aaa	100.3299	6.42	+0.05	-0.12	+0.31
S. Aus Gov Fin	06/03	7.750	AA+	Aa2	102.5058	6.73	+0.05	-0.10	+0.56
Quebec, Provn of	10/02	9.500	A+	A2	103.8295	7.42	+0.04	-0.05	+1.19

London closing.   Source: Interactive Data/FT Information
*Standard & Poor's. Yields: Local market standard/Annualised basis.

Fig. 11.9 International bonds and US corporate bonds

This market for corporate bonds offers an alternative method of raising money for companies that do not want to issue stock or accept the conditions of a bank loan. It originally grew up because of the restraints of government regulations in traditional equity and money markets.

It also offers opportunities for interest rate and currency swaps. When a company which can, for instance, easily raise money in sterling because of local reputation needs dollars to fund an acquisition or expansion, it may find an American company in the opposite position and swap debt.

For investors, the markets are international and anonymous – there is no register of creditors – and tax efficient. They offer the chance to play the markets for currencies, debt, equity and interest rates simultaneously, but because of their complexity they are generally restricted to large investment banks.

■ Euro-zone bonds

Similar information is carried in a table of euro-zone bonds (see Figure 11.10). The table shows the prices, yields and spreads of broadly representative bonds in seven categories, including high yield issues and German "Pfandbriefe", and for a variety of credit ratings. It is designed to track the expected development of a large, liquid euro-zone bond market following the launch of the single currency. The "sovereigns" are government bonds from the four European Union countries that are currently outside the euro-zone.

The replacement of ten currencies by a single currency has automatically removed currency risk for a large and liquid pool of funds currently restricted to domestic markets. The effects are manifold. First, and most important, the removal of currency risk for cross-border investments within the euro-zone creates a market to rival the size of the US bond market. German pension fund managers and French insurance companies are no longer restricted to a diet of mostly domestic government bonds and related securities. They can now buy Italian or Finnish government bonds without worrying about currency volatility. As a result, governments are forced to be much more investor friendly than in the past. This includes the introduction of much more transparent auction programmes, the advent of fully fledged strip trading on government paper and a further opening of the auction process to foreign participation.

This will also push investors into non-government bonds. Tight fiscal policy and the convergence of euro-zone government bond yields around those of German government bonds have meant a collapse of yields in Italy and Spain and declining yields across continental Europe, driving a switch from government bonds to equities and corporate bonds. Since good returns in the past came from favourable currency fluctuations, investors are increasingly forced to look at paper with lower credit rating if they want to outperform the indices. So the second effect of the single currency is the creation of a fully fledged corporate bond market, including high-yield bonds, as investors move down the credit curve in search of higher returns.

Since there is now no possibility of currency depreciation with euro-zone government bonds, prices no longer reflect that risk. Instead, they have adjusted to price the risk of default, something that was an impossibility as long as governments could always print enough of their own currency to meet their obligations as they fell due. Another key indicator is the yield curve on the benchmark euro government bond (see Figure 11.11). That curve and the level of euro interest rates are influenced by the actions of the European Central Bank in Frankfurt.

EURO-ZONE BONDS

Aug 30	Red date	Coupon	S&P* Rating	Moody's Rating	Bid price	Bid yield	Day's chge yield	Mth's chge yield	Spread vs Govts
■ SOVEREIGNS									
UK	01/03	4.750	AAA	Aaa	98.445	5.45	-0.01	+0.09	+0.24
Denmark	09/08	4.625	AA+	Aaa	92.802	5.77	-0.02	+0.09	+0.48
Sweden	01/09	5.000	AA+	Aaa	95.747	5.64	-0.02	+0.09	+0.34
Greece	05/10	6.000	A-	A2	100.460	5.93	-0.01	+0.03	+0.63
■ SUPRANATIONALS									
ADB	10/07	5.500	AAA	Aaa	97.826	5.88	-0.01	+0.09	+0.60
EIB	04/09	4.000	AAA	Aaa	88.142	5.78	-0.02	+0.09	+0.48
Eurofima	12/09	5.625	AAA	Aaa	97.576	5.97	-0.01	+0.09	+0.67
World Bank	04/05	7.125	AAA	Aaa	105.445	5.73	-0.01	+0.08	+0.48
■ UTILITIES									
EDF	01/09	5.000	AA+	Aaa	94.099	5.91	-0.01	+0.13	+0.61
TEPCO	05/09	4.375	AA	Aa2	88.005	6.20	-0.01	+0.09	+0.90
Iberdrola	05/09	4.500	AA-	A1	87.943	6.34	-0.01	+0.08	+1.04
Powergen (UK)	07/09	5.000	A	A2	88.763	6.72	-0.01	+0.08	+1.42
■ FINANCIALS									
BNG	10/10	5.625	AAA	Aaa	98.264	5.85	-0.01	+0.08	+0.55
Dexia CLF	04/09	4.750	n/a	Aa1	91.846	5.98	-0.01	+0.07	+0.68
Deutsche Finan	07/09	4.250	AA	Aa3	87.836	6.06	-0.01	+0.07	+0.76
Bayer Hypo	01/10	5.625	A+	Aa3	96.692	6.09	-0.01	+0.09	+0.79
■ INDUSTRIALS									
Reseau Ferred	04/10	5.250	AAA	Aaa	95.272	5.90	-0.01	+0.07	+0.60
Statoil	06/11	5.125	AA-	Aa2	91.583	6.21	-0.01	+0.09	+0.91
Alcatel	02/09	4.375	A	A1	87.491	6.33	-0.01	+0.06	+1.03
Marconi	03/10	6.375	BBB+	A3	97.911	6.67	-0.01	+0.09	+1.37
■ PFANDBRIEFE									
Rhein Hypo	12/01	5.500	AAA	Aaa	100.073	5.42	+0.00	+0.13	+0.24
Depfa	02/05	5.000	AAA	Aaa	97.388	5.68	-0.01	+0.11	+0.43
Euro Hypo	02/07	4.000	AAA	Aaa	90.500	5.81	-0.02	+0.09	+0.53
Depfa	01/10	5.500	AAA	Aaa	97.402	5.86	-0.02	+0.05	+0.56
■ HIGH YIELD									
Jazztel	12/09	13.250	CCC+	Caa1	85.500	16.32	+0.00	+1.13	+11.02
GTS	12/09	11.000	B	B3	58.000	21.69	+0.20	+4.73	+16.39
Kappa Beheer	07/09	10.625	B	B2	102.250	10.23	-0.03	-0.01	+4.93
Colt Telecom	12/09	7.625	B+	B1	89.500	9.36	-0.45	-0.11	+4.06

Fig. 11.10 Euro-zone bonds

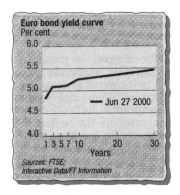

Fig. 11.11 Eurobond yield curve

■ Market volatility

A final table on the International Capital Markets page gives an indication of the volatility or riskiness of global bond and equity markets (see Figure 11.12). The first column provides the latest reading for the volatility index, followed by the change on the previous reading, the reading for a month ago and the 52-week high and low. A "RiskGrade" of 100 corresponds to the average volatility of the international equity markets during "normal market conditions". So anything less than 100 is less volatile than global stock markets in normal times. In this example, the bond markets are clearly less volatile than the equity markets, and the European bond markets are currently less volatile than the American bond markets and less volatile than they have been over the past year.

RISKGRADE VOLATILITY

Bond markets	Aug 1	Day change	Month ago	52 wk high	52 wk low
Europe	29	0	32	52	29
Americas	41	-1	44	52	35
Asia	21	-1	22	47	21
Global	34	-1	43	65	34
Equity markets	**Aug 1**				
Europe	98	-2	116	135	82
UK	79	-2	94	115	69
Americas	95	-2	108	146	72
Asia	109	3	116	139	72
Global	111	-1	125	156	83

RiskGrades are calculated daily by RiskMetrics. They are designed to measure the riskiness of today's global market returns. A RiskGrade of 100 corresponds to the average volatility of the international equity markets during normal market conditions. Data shown is one day in arrears. More information is available at www.riskgrades.com

Fig. 11.12 RiskGrade volatility

"The prevailing wisdom is that markets are always right. I take the opposite position.

I assume that markets are always wrong. Even if my assumption is occasionally wrong,

I use it as a working hypothesis."

George Soros

"Money is a good servant, but a bad master. Money made it easier for earlier societies to

escape from slavery or serfdom. But money, though essential, is only a means, not an end.

You cannot eat it, drink it, wear it, or live in it."

Douglas Jay

12

Cash and currency

The foreign exchange and money markets

- **The currency markets** – determining the rates of exchange for sterling, the dollar, the euro and other leading currencies: reading the figures and using the information on exchange rates for the pound spot and forward; the dollar spot and forward; the euro spot and forward; other currencies of the world

- **The money markets** – determining the price of money and short-term financial instruments: UK interest rates; world interest rates; US interest rates

The currency markets are global markets for foreign exchange (forex). Their primary purposes are to allow companies and other organisations to purchase goods from abroad, and for foreign investment or speculation. Hence they are markets largely of concern to companies and financial institutions or investors in stocks that are particularly sensitive to currency or interest rate movements.

The money markets include the foreign exchange markets but also cover the domestic UK market for short-term loans essentially between the major institutions of the City: banks, accepting houses, discount houses and the Bank of England.

One page of the *Financial Times*, the Currencies and Money page, is given over largely to recording dealing rates and brief reports of trading in the foreign exchange and money markets. It is headed by a brief report describing the major events in the foreign exchange markets during the previous day's trading. In addition, there are more detailed descriptions of the experiences of individual major currencies, both on the previous day and over a rather longer timespan. These items generally discuss the main factors affecting exchange rates.

With the exception of the domestic money market in its various forms, these are international markets in which business is conducted 24 hours a day by telephone and computer screen. As the London markets close in the evening, business is handed over to New York, which overlaps with Tokyo for a couple of hours each afternoon. Thus, there are no official closing rates in these international markets. The newspaper takes a representative sample of rates from major participants in the London markets at around 5pm local time each trading day.

■ The currency markets

Foreign exchange markets exist to facilitate international trade, and allow companies involved in international trade to hedge transactions through the forward purchase or sale of relevant currencies at a fixed rate, designed to counteract any potential losses through future rises or falls in their values. In practice however, the bulk of turnover in these markets is attributable to speculation, and while speculation provides the markets with necessary liquidity, it can also destabilise those markets, hence creating a further need for hedging.

As in all markets the value of currencies in the international market is determined by supply and demand. The main players are the foreign exchange dealers of commercial banks, hedge funds and foreign exchange brokers. However, the market is often significantly affected by the intervention of central banks on behalf of governments. So, in this marketplace there is considerable interaction between the authorities and market professionals.

According to the Bank for International Settlements, the central bank for central banks, average daily turnover on the world's foreign exchange markets reached almost $1,500 billion in April 1998, 26 per cent higher than when it last measured forex flows in 43 different countries three years earlier. Transactions involving dollars on one side of the trade accounted for 87 per cent of that forex business. Almost a third of all forex trading takes place in London, by far the world's largest centre, with New York and Tokyo second and third. Although London forex trading grew more slowly than New York over the three years to 1998, its average daily turnover remains greater than New York and Tokyo combined, having risen from $464 billion to $637 billion.

To put these figures into perspective, daily trading volume on the New York Stock Exchange (NYSE) is only about $20 billion; activity in short-term US government securities is around ten times that at $200 billion; and so at $1,500 billion, foreign exchange trading is seven and a half times the volume of trading in short-term US government securities and 75 times NYSE trading. This volume is far greater than the size of foreign currency reserves held by any single country. The forex markets cannot be ignored: for their size and forecasting ability; and for the potential that developments in these markets have for the future of the dollar as the world's dominant currency.

In the past, trading in the real economy controlled relative currency relationships. Since most currency flows were to settle trading patterns, there was a balance as goods and capital moved at about the same speed. But now the leads and lags are the other way around. Because financial flows are many times the size of trade flows and because financial flows are nearly instantaneous, currency market levels now tend to set trade: if a country's currency becomes low relative to others, domestic producers find it easier to export. The market sets the economy.

Speculation provides liquidity but makes the markets volatile and prediction difficult. Currency swings can be vast and often not very attached to fundamentals. They are particularly damaging for companies that rely heavily on exports or imported raw materials.

The core determining factor of a currency's value is the health of the real national economy, especially the balance of payments current account. If there is a surplus on the current account, that is, a country sells more goods than it buys, then buyers have to acquire that currency to purchase goods. This adds to foreign reserves and bids up the price of that currency. As it rises, exports rise in price, fall in quantity and the currency falls again. Conversely, a current account deficit implies the need to sell the local currency in order to acquire foreign goods. Persistent current account deficits, particularly if allied with relatively low foreign reserves, indicate a problem.

A currency's value is also affected by the level of inflation and the domestic rate of interest. High rates of interest and low inflation make a currency attractive for those holding assets denominated in it or lending it to borrowers. So typically one country raising interest rates while others remain the same will raise the value of that currency as money flows into the country. This will have a limited effect if the fundamentals are wrong, that is, if there is a persistent deficit on the current account.

A significant factor determining short-term currency values is market sentiment. There can be a self-fuelling process in which enthusiasm for a currency, or the lack of it, drives the rate. Speculators might decide, as they did with the pound sterling on Black Wednesday in September 1992 and during the Asian and Russian crises of 1997/8, that a currency is overvalued or simply that there are speculative gains to be made. Short selling will then cause it to fall, often in spite of government intervention.

Currency attacks are triggered when a small shock to the fundamentals of the economy is combined with systemic weaknesses in the corporate and banking sectors. One facet of such systemic weaknesses is the effect of belated hedging activity by some economic actors in the economy whose currency is under attack. The more these actors try to hedge, the greater is the incentive for others to follow suit. This unleashes a whiplash effect, which turns a potentially orderly depreciation into a collapse of the currency. In other words, if speculators believe a currency will come under attack, their actions will precipitate the crisis; while if they believe the currency is not in danger, their inaction will spare it from attack – attacks are self-fulfilling.

The magnitude of the shock necessary to trigger an attack need not be large, which makes predictions very difficult. Nevertheless, it is possible to draw some broad conclusions on the vulnerability of currencies to attack. In particular, there must be a pre-existing weakness, which will prevent the authorities from conducting a fully fledged defence of the currency by raising interest rates. The weakness may not be lethal in itself (though it can become lethal once the situation deteriorates) so it is a necessary condition but not a sufficient condition for a speculative attack.

Self-fulfilling attacks may affect any country – with a fixed exchange rate and high capital mobility – that is in the grey area between "fully safe" and "sure to be attacked". Recent research suggests that countries with strong trade links with a country that has recently experienced a currency crisis is highly likely to face an attack itself – the growing phenomenon of contagion in foreign exchange markets.

■ The pound spot and forward

Currencies are measured in terms of one another or a trade-weighted index, a basket of currencies. The value of a currency in a trade-weighted index is assessed on a basis that gives a value appropriate to the volume of trade conducted in that currency. The *Financial Times* provides detailed information on three currencies in the world: the pound, the dollar and the euro. A large number of international contracts are struck in these currencies and the dollar particularly is used globally as a reserve currency.

Figure 12.1a lists spot and forward prices for the pound against the currencies of the other major industrialised countries.

Reading the figures

■ **Closing mid-point, change on day and day's mid-point high and low:** yesterday's closing price for immediate delivery of pounds, the mid-point between the prices at which they can be bought and sold; the change on the previous day's price; and the day's high and low for mid-point prices, the highest and lowest prices at which dealings have taken place during the European trading day. Since sterling is the largest currency unit, all prices are given in so many euros, dollars, etc. to the pound.

POUND SPOT FORWARD AGAINST THE POUND

Jun 21		Closing mid-point	Change on day	Bid/offer spread	Day's Mid high	Day's Mid low	One month Rate	One month %PA	Three months Rate	Three months %PA	One year Rate	One year %PA	Bank of Eng. Index
Europe													
Austria*	(Sch)	21.8014	+0.0879	920 - 108	21.9138	21.7872	21.7724	1.6	21.7148	1.6	21.5001	1.4	100.1
Belgium*	(BFr)	63.9133	+0.2578	857 - 408	64.2420	63.8720	63.8282	1.6	63.6593	1.6	63.0299	1.4	99.0
Denmark	(DKr)	11.8118	+0.0461	075 - 161	11.8744	11.8059	11.8003	1.2	11.7839	0.9	11.7502	0.5	100.8
Finland*	(FM)	9.4203	+0.0380	162 - 243	9.4690	9.4140	9.4078	1.6	9.3828	1.6	9.2901	1.4	77.0
France*	(FFr)	10.3928	+0.0419	883 - 973	10.4463	10.3861	10.379	1.6	10.3515	1.6	10.2492	1.4	101.8
Germany*	(DM)	3.0988	+0.0125	974 - 001	3.1157	3.0962	3.0947	1.6	3.0865	1.6	3.056	1.4	98.5
Greece*	(Dr)	533.062	+2.0550	749 - 376	535.810	530.891	534.151	-2.5	535.587	-1.9	533.287	0.0	58.1
Ireland*	(I£)	1.2478	+0.0050	473 - 483	1.2542	1.2470	1.2461	1.6	1.2428	1.6	1.2306	1.4	87.8
Italy*	(L)	3067.77	+12.3800	644 - 909	3083.58	3065.78	3063.68	1.6	3055.58	1.6	3025.37	1.4	72.6
Luxembourg*	(LFr)	63.9133	+0.2578	857 - 408	64.2420	63.8720	63.8282	1.6	63.6593	1.6	63.0299	1.4	99.0
Netherlands*	(Fl)	3.4915	+0.0140	900 - 930	3.5096	3.4893	3.4869	1.6	3.4776	1.6	3.4432	1.4	97.9
Norway	(NKr)	13.0320	+0.0318	261 - 379	13.1243	13.0256	13.0387	-0.6	13.0537	-0.7	13.1264	-0.7	91.5
Portugal*	(Es)	317.637	+1.2810	500 - 774	319.272	317.426	317.214	1.6	316.375	1.6	313.247	1.4	89.3
Spain*	(Pta)	263.617	+1.0630	503 - 730	264.980	263.450	263.266	1.6	262.57	1.6	259.974	1.4	74.2
Sweden	(SKr)	13.0618	+0.0316	521 - 715	13.1450	13.0521	13.0393	2.1	12.9961	2.0	12.8676	1.5	85.2
Switzerland	(SFr)	2.4568	+0.0026	559 - 577	2.4781	2.4559	2.4512	2.7	2.4402	2.7	2.3986	2.4	106.2
UK	(£)	-	-	-	-	-	-	-	-	-	-	-	104.2
Euro	(€)	1.5844	+0.0064	837 - 851	1.5931	1.5832	1.5823	1.6	1.5781	1.6	1.5625	1.4	79.75
SDR	-	1.126900	-	-	-	-	-	-	-	-	-	-	-
Americas													
Argentina	(Peso)	1.4988	-0.0085	985 - 990	1.5182	1.4977	-	-	-	-	-	-	-
Brazil	(R$)	2.7185	+0.0071	173 - 197	2.7333	2.7067	-	-	-	-	-	-	-
Canada	(C$)	2.2086	-0.0087	074 - 097	2.2331	2.2074	2.2083	0.2	2.2077	0.2	2.2046	0.2	80.3
Mexico	(New Peso)	14.8009	-0.0648	932 - 086	14.9546	14.7898	14.964	-13.2	15.2912	-13.3	16.5809	-12.0	-
USA	($)	1.4991	-0.0085	988 - 993	1.5185	1.4980	1.5	-0.7	1.5018	-0.7	1.5104	-0.8	109.2
Pacific/Middle East/Africa													
Australia	(A$)	2.4897	-0.0142	872 - 922	2.5300	2.4847	2.4899	-0.1	2.4901	-0.1	2.4912	-0.1	78.0
Hong Kong	(HK$)	11.6816	-0.0671	789 - 843	11.8329	11.6742	11.6853	-0.4	11.6985	-0.6	11.766	-0.7	-
India	(Rs)	66.9213	-0.3930	064 - 362	67.7250	66.9064	67.1888	-4.8	67.6297	-4.2	69.5417	-3.9	-
Indonesia	(Rupiah)	12996.77	-6.29	961 - 392	13084.90	12896.80	13053.04	-5.2	13230.12	-7.2	13868.36	-6.7	-
Israel	(Shk)	6.1551	-0.0297	466 - 636	6.1636	6.1466	-	-	-	-	-	-	-
Japan	(Y)	158.135	-0.9240	063 - 206	160.170	158.010	157.335	6.1	155.725	6.1	148.87	5.9	155.4
Malaysia‡	(M$)	5.6964	-0.0325	954 - 973	5.7695	5.6931	-	-	-	-	-	-	-
New Zealand	(NZ$)	3.1632	-0.0094	600 - 664	3.2010	3.1571	3.1647	-0.6	3.1685	-0.7	3.1906	-0.9	82.5
Philippines	(Peso)	64.1594	-0.2152	988 - 200	64.3200	63.9988	64.3451	-3.5	64.748	-3.7	66.8762	-4.2	-
Saudi Arabia	(SR)	5.6223	-0.0319	211 - 234	5.6948	5.6184	5.6272	-1.0	5.6359	-1.0	5.6689	-0.8	-
Singapore	(S$)	2.5988	-0.0147	976 - 999	2.6316	2.5976	2.5917	3.3	2.5772	3.3	2.5195	3.1	-
South Africa	(R)	10.3895	+0.0021	802 - 987	10.4777	10.3754	10.4259	-4.2	10.506	-4.5	10.9202	-5.1	-
South Korea	(Won)	1677.81	-9.3500	746 - 817	1699.20	1676.71	-	-	-	-	-	-	-
Taiwan	(T$)	46.2008	-0.2785	181 - 834	46.8199	46.1181	46.1638	1.0	46.1027	0.8	45.8717	0.7	-
Thailand	(Bt)	58.7253	-0.2445	780 - 726	59.4040	57.7830	58.6918	0.7	58.6945	0.2	58.7356	0.0	-

Bid/offer spreads in the Pound Spot table show only the last three decimal places. Sterling Index calculated by the Bank of England. Base average 1990 = 100. Index rebased 1/2/95. * EMU member. The exchange rates printed in this table are also available on the internet at **http://www.FT.com.**

Fig. 12.1a Pound spot and forward against the pound

- **Bid/offer spread:** a representative spread on the price at the close. Different banks may quote slightly different rates at the same time, particularly if the market is moving in a very volatile fashion. As with shares, marketmakers buy currencies at a lower price than they sell them in order to make a profit. The spreads are shown only to the last three decimal places.

- **Forward rates:** prices on contracts struck for settlement one month, three months or one year ahead, or prices implied by current interest rates; and the annualised interest rate differential between the two countries that implies. Forward currency rates and interest rates are intimately connected. A bank given an order to supply dollars against pounds in three months' time will in theory (out of simple prudence) purchase the dollars at once and leave them on deposit for three months. If dollars are yielding less than pounds, it will lose interest by switching from pounds to dollars. It naturally passes this cost on to the customer by charging more for three months dollars than it would for spot dollars. The forward dollars are sold at a premium: the buyer receives fewer dollars per pound. The curve of forward rates, at a premium (the currency units cost more forward, that is, the buyer receives fewer per pound the longer forward they are purchased) or a discount, is essentially determined by the interest rates available for deposit of these currencies relative to sterling. The lower the interest rate available, the higher the effective cost of buying that currency in advance, and this is reflected in the forward rates.

■ **Bank of England index:** the relative trade-weighted position of currencies against the pound compared to a base value of 1990=100. So a figure of 79.95 for the euro would indicate that it has weakened by over 20 per cent against the pound, weighted by volume of trade since 1990. Calculated by the Bank of England, the index is not a monetary value, but a measure of the strength or weakness of the pound against other currencies.

■ **SDRs:** the Special Drawing Rights (SDR) of the International Monetary Fund (IMF), the units in which the IMF accounts are dominated. This is a currency basket made up of a predetermined amount of different currencies. Its composite character means that this currency substitute is less volatile than the individual units, and it is being used to an increasing extent for commercial purposes.

■ **Pound in New York:** Figure 12.1b details the rates for the pound in the New York market on a spot basis and one, three and 12 months ahead, plus the close on the previous trading day. The sterling/dollar rate is known in the markets as "cable".

■ POUND IN NEW YORK		
Jun 20	····Close ····	··· Prev. close ···
£ spot	1.5180	1.5130
1 mth	1.5189	1.5138
3 mth	1.5206	1.5155
1 yr	1.5292	1.5245

Fig. 12.1b Pound in New York

Using the information

The global foreign exchange market, the huge size of which dwarfs every other international financial market, has always presented technical difficulties for institutions seeking end-of-day rates that are authoritative and consistent. The market functions around the clock in virtually every country and knows no limitations such as fixed trading hours or any obligation to report "closing" rates. Until 1992, no single, consistent, set of forex rates had gained universal acceptance, with the result that the various reference sources used by the investment industry and the wider business community sometimes varied substantially. This problem was compounded when market conditions were volatile.

The rates shown in this and other FT currency tables use data drawn from the WM/Reuters Closing Spot Rates. Developed by the two companies in consultation with leading London financial market practitioners, these now set a daily global standard for the rates required for index calculation, investment management and portfolio valuation. A single suite of rates allows accurate comparisons between competing indices and competing funds. Users of rates for commercial contracts and transactions also benefit from access to a consistent set of data, drawn from the market at a precisely fixed time and rigorously screened to exclude anomalous quotes.

The WM Company calculates and publishes a daily fixing based on market rates derived from Reuters' forex reporting system, and covering around 70 currencies. At short intervals before and after 4pm London time, representative bid, offer and mid-rates against the US dollar are selected from a wide range of contributing banks and forex dealers. Spot rates for all currencies against sterling are then calculated as cross-rates from the dollar parities, reflecting forex market practice. The choice of 4pm as the reference point results from research that suggests that this time not only captures a far larger selection of timely quotes from continental European contributors, but also reflects more accurately the peak trading period for the London and New York markets.

It is possible that by the time the rates are consulted, the markets may have moved quite sharply. The rates in the newspaper cannot guarantee to be up to the minute; what they do provide is a daily record of the market's activities for reference purposes. The rates are frequently used by exporters and importers striking contracts in more than one currency at an agreed published rate.

Businesses frequently need to hedge against currency risk. Typically, a UK business with significant dollar income might sell dollars forward at a particular rate. This protects it against the pound weakening (though it also means gains from it strengthening would be missed), but more importantly makes the exchange rate predictable for that company to aid planning.

International investors too are exposed to currency risk. While investing in foreign equities naturally exposes an investor to the currencies in which they are denominated, exposure can also be achieved by investing in those currencies as assets in their own right. The markets for exchanging sterling, dollars, euros and yen need not only be a means of switching between different national equity markets. They can also be a way to enhance total portfolio returns, to speculate on future shifts in exchange rates or, for the more risk-averse investor, to hedge bets through interest rate and currency diversification.

For the global investor balancing an overall portfolio of equities, bonds and cash, it may be wise to explore the opportunities for holding the cash portion in alternatives to savings accounts or money market funds denominated in the base currency. Interest rate differentials between countries mean that banks and fund managers elsewhere might be offering better returns. And if differentials get wider, there may be currency appreciation benefits as well: on the whole, higher rates in one place will attract more buyers of the currency driving up its value.

An alternative way to get currency exposure is through managed currency funds. These are generally run by international fund management companies, are often located in the Channel Islands for obvious tax advantages, and operate in a similar way to unit and investment trusts: investors buy units in the fund and its managers pursue the best returns they can by investing in the appropriate cash and currency markets. Currency fund data form part of the FT managed funds service discussed in Chapter 10.

Just like trusts, the precise markets in which the funds invest vary considerably and most companies have a good selection from which to choose. Some might be focused on a single currency, investing in short-term money market deposits in its country of origin. Others are multi-currency accounts, perhaps using sterling or the dollar as the point of reference, and moving in and out of other currencies in anticipation of advantageous exchange rate movements. Typically, decisions will be made on the basis of assessing the relevant fundamental economic data; sometimes, they might be based on technical analysis of the past patterns of currency fluctuations.

■ The dollar spot and forward

The dollar has long been the dominant currency in world trade and the United States has often been able to pay for its imports with dollars. Given that fact and the persistent US

DOLLAR SPOT FORWARD AGAINST THE DOLLAR

Aug 17		Closing mid-point	Change on day	Bid/offer spread	Day's mid high	Day's mid low	One month Rate	One month %PA	Three months Rate	Three months %PA	One year Rate	One year %PA	J.P Morgan index
Europe													
Austria*	(Sch)	15.0452	-0.0478	435 - 468	15.0930	15.0140	15.0201	2.0	14.9757	1.8	14.8026	1.6	99.0
Belgium*	(BFr)	44.1066	-0.1403	018 - 114	44.2470	44.0150	44.0329	2.0	43.9031	1.8	43.3954	1.6	98.6
Denmark	(DKr)	8.1550	-0.0271	535 - 565	8.1813	8.1393	8.1436	1.7	8.134	1.0	8.081	0.9	99.1
Finland*	(FM)	6.5009	-0.0207	002 - 016	6.5216	6.4874	6.4901	2.0	6.4709	1.8	6.396	1.6	75.6
France*	(FFr)	7.1721	-0.0228	713 - 728	7.1949	7.1572	7.1601	2.0	7.1391	1.8	7.0565	1.6	99.9
Germany*	(DM)	2.1385	-0.0068	382 - 387	2.1453	2.1340	2.1349	2.0	2.1286	1.8	2.104	1.6	97.2
Greece	(Dr)	368.690	-1.0400	510 - 870	369.750	367.810	369.185	-1.6	369.84	-1.2	366.525	0.6	57.1
Ireland*	(I£)	1.1613	+0.0036	612 - 614	1.1637	1.1576	1.1632	-2.0	1.1667	-1.9	1.1804	-1.6	-
Italy*	(L)	2117.07	-6.7300	684 - 841	2123.80	2112.68	2113.54	2.0	2107.3	1.8	2082.93	1.6	71.8
Luxembourg*	(LFr)	44.1066	-0.1403	018 - 114	44.2470	44.0150	44.0329	2.0	43.9031	1.8	43.3954	1.6	98.6
Netherlands*	(Fl)	2.4095	-0.0077	092 - 097	2.4171	2.4045	2.4055	2.0	2.3984	1.8	2.3707	1.6	97.3
Norway	(NKr)	8.8350	-0.0505	325 - 375	8.8880	8.8309	8.8372	-0.3	8.8445	-0.4	8.8733	-0.4	91.5
Portugal*	(Es)	219.202	-0.6970	178 - 226	219.900	218.750	218.836	2.0	218.19	1.8	215.667	1.6	89.3
Spain*	(Pta)	181.922	-0.5790	902 - 942	182.500	181.550	181.618	2.0	181.083	1.8	178.988	1.6	72.8
Sweden	(SKr)	9.2220	+0.0025	170 - 270	9.2513	9.1755	9.2011	2.7	9.1613	2.6	9.0279	2.1	82.2
Switzerland	(SFr)	1.7081	-0.0048	077 - 084	1.7146	1.7063	1.7032	3.4	1.6944	3.2	1.6589	2.9	104.3
UK	(£)	1.4988	-0.0009	983 - 992	1.5015	1.4967	1.4996	-0.7	1.501	-0.6	1.5071	-0.6	106.4
Euro	(€)	0.9146	+0.0029	145 - 147	0.9165	0.9115	0.9162	-2.0	0.9188	-1.9	0.9296	-1.6	-
SDR	-	0.76230											
Americas													
Argentina	(Peso)	0.9998	-	998 - 998	0.9998	0.9998	-	-	-	-	-	-	-
Brazil	(R$)	1.8045	-0.0025	030 - 060	1.8140	1.8030	-	-	-	-	-	-	-
Canada	(C$)	1.4755	-0.0018	750 - 760	1.4776	1.4750	1.4745	0.9	1.4724	0.8	1.4628	0.9	80.6
Mexico	(New Peso)	9.1900	-0.0130	870 - 930	9.1950	9.1870	9.2675	-10.1	9.4245	-10.2	10.085	-9.7	-
USA	($)	-	-	-	-	-	-	-	-	-	-	-	112.7
Pacific/Middle East/Africa													
Australia	(A$)	1.6849	-0.0129	835 - 863	1.6966	1.6835	1.6845	0.2	1.6841	0.2	1.6834	0.1	77.7
Hong Kong	(HK$)	7.7988	-0.0007	986 - 989	7.7995	7.7986	7.7947	0.6	7.7875	0.6	7.7763	0.3	-
India	(Rs)	45.9000	+0.2100	900 - 100	45.9100	45.6700	46.1525	-6.6	46.49	-5.1	47.91	-4.4	-
Indonesia	(Rupiah)	8335.00	+15.00	000 - 000	8350.00	8310.00	8378.5	-6.3	8462.5	-6.1	8840	-6.1	-
Israel	(Shk)	4.0380	-0.0039	360 - 400	4.0400	4.0350	-	-	-	-	-	-	-
Japan	(Y)	108.540	-0.0300	500 - 580	108.650	108.250	107.955	6.5	106.815	6.4	101.805	6.2	155.4
Malaysia‡	(M$)	3.8000	-	000 - 000	3.8000	3.8000	-	-	-	-	-	-	-
New Zealand	(NZ$)	2.2109	-0.0081	090 - 129	2.2188	2.2085	2.2091	1.0	2.2073	0.6	2.2078	0.1	-
Philippines	(Peso)	44.9000	-0.0700	000 - 000	45.0000	44.8000	45.016	-3.1	45.248	-3.1	46.49	-3.5	-
Saudi Arabia	(SR)	3.7509	+0.0002	507 - 510	3.7510	3.7507	3.7525	-0.5	3.755	-0.4	3.7591	-0.2	-
Singapore	(S$)	1.7165	-0.0007	162 - 167	1.7190	1.7145	1.7106	4.1	1.6989	4.1	1.6507	3.8	-
South Africa	(R)	6.9265	-0.0185	215 - 315	6.9475	6.9075	6.9486	-3.8	6.9904	-3.7	7.1688	-3.5	-
South Korea	(Won)	1114.50	-0.6500	400 - 500	1115.00	1114.00	-	-	-	-	-	-	-
Taiwan	(T$)	31.0500	-0.0475	000 - 000	31.1000	31.0000	31.017	1.3	30.9475	1.3	30.6695	1.2	-
Thailand	(Bt)	40.8350	+0.0500	200 - 500	40.8500	40.6200	40.76	2.2	40.67	1.6	40.37	1.1	-

‡ Official rate set by Malaysian government. The WM/Reuters rate for the valuation of capital assets is 3.80 MYR/USD. Bid/offer spreads in the Dollar Spot table show only the last three decimal places. UK, Ireland & Euro are quoted in US currency. J.P. Morgan nominal indices Aug 16: Base average 1990 Bid, offer, mid spot rates and forward rates in both this and the pound table are derived from THE WM/REUTERS 4pm (London time) CLOSING SPOT and FORWARD RATE services. Some values are rounded by the F.T. * EMU member. The exchange rates printed in this table are also available on the internet at **http://www.FT.com**

Fig. 12.2 Dollar spot and forward against the dollar

current account deficit, the country is consistently exporting dollars, which then move around world markets and economies. Hence the importance of the dollar spot and forward rates published in the *Financial Times* (see Figure 12.2). The table shows:

- **Prices for the dollar spot and forward:** the equivalent range of information as the pound spot and forward.

- **Pounds and euros:** all prices, except for sterling, the Irish pound and the euro, are quoted in terms of francs, guilders, etc. to the dollar. Sterling, the Irish pound and the euro are quoted in dollars rather than in so many units to the dollar. It is important to bear this in mind when comparing forward rates and the direction of movement of the dollar against these currencies.

- **JP Morgan index:** like the Bank of England index, these figures show the relative trade-weighted position of currencies, in this case against the dollar. The base is 1990=100.

EURO SPOT FORWARD AGAINST THE EURO

Aug 15		Closing mid-point	Change on day	Bid/offer spread	Day's mid high	low	One month Rate	%PA	Three months Rate	%PA	One year Rate	%PA
Europe												
Czech Rep.	(Koruna)	35.3966	+0.1106	742 - 189	35.4189	35.2520	35.4179	-0.7	35.4399	-0.5	35.5393	-0.4
Denmark	(DKr)	7.4623	+0.0025	597 - 648	7.4934	7.4498	7.4644	-0.3	7.4769	-0.8	7.5176	-0.7
Greece	(Dr)	337.071	-0.0810	861 - 282	337.470	336.581	338.1431	-3.8	339.6877	-3.1	340.6685	-1.1
Hungary	(Forint)	260.938	+0.1420	799 - 077	261.077	260.390	262.3517	-6.5	264.6878	-5.7	273.5159	-4.8
Norway	(NKr)	8.1162	+0.0426	121 - 202	8.1261	8.0657	8.1324	-2.4	8.1622	-2.3	8.2818	-2.0
Poland	(Zloty)	3.9578	+0.0197	524 - 632	3.9737	3.9493	-	-	-	-	-	-
Romania	(Leu)	20405.46	+232.0400	642 - 449	20414.49	20396.42	-	-	-	-	-	-
Russia	(Rouble)	25.3943	+0.3367	796 - 090	25.4090	25.1151	-	-	-	-	-	-
Slovakia	(Koruna)	42.5310	-0.0565	792 - 827	43.2933	41.4487	-	-	-	-	-	-
Sweden	(SKr)	8.3608	+0.0508	544 - 672	8.3685	8.3177	8.3557	0.7	8.3445	0.8	8.3218	0.5
Switzerland	(SFr)	1.5608	+0.0066	601 - 614	1.5619	1.5552	1.5588	1.5	1.5551	1.5	1.5398	1.3
UK	(£)	0.6062	+0.0060	059 - 064	0.6070	0.6001	0.6069	-1.4	0.6081	-1.3	0.6125	-1.0
Americas												
Argentina	(Peso)	0.9130	+0.0094	128 - 132	0.9132	0.9056	-	-	-	-	-	-
Brazil	(R$)	1.6474	+0.0187	461 - 487	1.6505	1.6341	-	-	-	-	-	-
Canada	(C$)	1.3584	+0.0171	576 - 591	1.3591	1.3452	1.3598	-1.2	1.3618	-1.0	1.3683	-0.7
Mexico	(New Peso)	8.4380	+0.0701	316 - 444	8.4471	8.3678	8.5273	-12.7	8.6885	-11.9	9.4109	-11.5
USA	($)	0.9132	+0.0091	130 - 134	0.9134	0.9058	0.9148	-2.1	0.9174	-1.8	0.9281	-1.6
Pacific/Middle East/Africa												
Australia	(A$)	1.5669	+0.0079	652 - 686	1.5686	1.5537	1.5692	-1.8	1.5731	-1.6	1.5891	-1.4
Hong Kong	(HK$)	7.1227	+0.0712	209 - 245	7.1245	7.0652	7.1302	-1.3	7.1443	-1.2	7.2181	-1.3
India	(Rs)	41.7652	+0.4275	469 - 835	41.7835	41.3951	42.0192	-7.3	42.4174	-6.2	44.1451	-5.7
Indonesia	(Rupiah)	7616.09	+171.24	073 - 146	7631.46	7455.10	7665.59	-7.8	7763.76	-7.8	8209.06	-7.0
Israel	(Shk)	3.6884	+0.0259	830 - 938	3.6965	3.6603	-	-	-	-	-	-
Japan	(Y)	99.5754	+0.6813	170 - 337	99.9000	99.1000	99.1943	4.6	98.4435	4.5	94.9075	4.7
Malaysia	(M$)	3.4702	+0.0348	694 - 709	3.4709	3.4421	-	-	-	-	-	-
New Zealand	(NZ$)	2.0353	+0.0272	330 - 375	2.0375	2.0124	2.0389	-2.1	2.0448	-1.9	2.0724	-1.8
Philippines	(Peso)	41.0301	+0.4834	298 - 304	41.1304	40.6070	41.2183	-5.5	41.5523	-5.1	43.1989	-5.3
Saudi Arabia	(SR)	3.4251	+0.0344	242 - 260	3.4260	3.3974	3.4326	-2.6	3.4450	-2.3	3.4889	-1.9
Singapore	(S$)	1.5702	+0.0185	696 - 708	1.5715	1.5544	1.5675	2.1	1.5616	2.2	1.5349	2.2
South Africa	(R)	6.3354	+0.0866	294 - 413	6.3413	6.2650	6.3678	-6.1	6.4237	-5.6	6.6635	-5.2
South Korea	(Won)	1019.27	+9.9000	891 - 963	1019.63	1018.91	-	-	-	-	-	-
Taiwan	(T$)	28.3549	+0.2841	030 - 067	28.4067	28.1600	28.3772	-0.9	28.4059	-0.7	28.4857	-0.5
Thailand	(Bt)	37.2905	+0.4821	595 - 215	37.3275	36.8651	37.2645	0.8	37.2523	0.4	37.3421	-0.1
UAE	(Dirham)	3.3542	+0.0336	534 - 550	3.9985	3.2713	3.3604	-2.2	3.3705	-1.9	3.4106	-1.7

Euro Locking Rates: Austrian Schilling 13.7603, Belgium/Luxembourg Franc 40.3399, Finnish Markka 5.94573, French Franc 6.55957, German Mark 1.95583, Irish Punt 0.787564, Italian Lira 1936.27, Netherlands Guilder 2.20371, Portuguese Escudo 200.482, Spanish Peseta 166.386. Bid/offer spreads in the Euro Spot table show only the last three decimal places. Bid, offer, mid spot rates and forward rates are derived from THE WM/REUTERS CLOSING SPOT and FORWARD RATE services. Some values are rounded by the F.T.

Fig. 12.3 Euro spot and forward against the euro

The euro, spot and forward against the euro

Since the launch of the single European currency in January 1999, the FT has carried a similar table to those for the pound and the dollar for the euro (see Figure 12.3). In addition to providing comparable information on the euro spot and forward, the table gives the "locking rates" at which the 11 original members of the euro-zone set their currencies. There is further discussion of the single currency and the European economy more generally in Chapter 16.

Other currencies of the world

Monday's newspaper carries a table of virtually every currency of the world, showing its value in terms of four key currencies: sterling, the dollar, the euro and the yen (see Figure 12.4). The rates given are usually the average of the latest buying and selling

FT GUIDE TO WORLD CURRENCIES

The table below gives the latest available rates of exchange (rounded) against four key currencies on Friday, June 23, 2000 . In some cases the rate is nominal. Market rates are the average of buying and selling rates except where they are shown to be otherwise. In some cases market rates have been calculated from those of foreign currencies to which they are tied.

		£ STG	US $	EURO €	YEN (X 100)
Afghanistan	(Afghani)	7099.30	4726.25	4425.90	4532.05
Albania	(Lek)	211.045	140.500	131.571	134.727
Algeria	(Dinar)	111.847	74.4600	69.7284	71.4005
Andorra	(French Fr)	10.5218	7.0047	6.5596	6.7169
	(Sp Peseta)	266.889	177.677	166.386	170.377
Angola	(Readj Kwanza)(5)	11.0833	7.3785	6.9096	7.0753
Antigua	(E Carib $)	4.0557	2.7000	2.5284	2.5891
Argentina	(Peso)	1.5012	0.9994	0.9359	0.9583
Armenia	(Dram)	797.765o	531.100	497.349	509.278
Aruba	(Florin)	2.6888	1.7900	1.6762	1.7165
Australia	(Aus $)	2.5184	1.6766	1.5701	1.6077
Austria	(Schilling)	22.0721	14.6942	13.7603	14.0904
Azerbaijan	(Manat)	6576.19o	4378.00	4099.78	4198.11
Azores	(Port Escudo)	321.581	214.087	200.482	205.291
Bahamas	(Bahama $)	1.5021	1	0.9365	0.9589
Bahrain	(Dinar)	0.5663	0.3770	0.3531	0.3615
Balearic Is	(Sp Peseta)	266.889	177.677	166.386	170.377
Bangladesh	(Taka)	76.6072	51.0000	47.7590	48.9044
Barbados	(Barb $)	2.9892	1.9900	1.8635	1.9082
Belarus	(Rouble)(4)	1462.29m	973.500	913.039	934.938
Belgium	(Belg Fr)	64.7067	43.0775	40.3399	41.3075
Belize	(B $)	2.9592	1.9700	1.8448	1.8891
Benin	(CFA Fr)	1052.18	700.470	655.957	671.688
Bermuda	(Bermudian $)	1.5021	1	0.9365	0.9589
Bhutan	(Ngultrum)	67.1026	44.6725	41.8336	42.8369
Bolivia	(Boliviano)	9.1929	6.1200	5.7311	5.8685
Bosnia Herzegovina	(Marka)	3.1373	2.0886	1.9558	2.0027
Botswana	(Pula)	7.7368	5.1507	4.8234	4.9390
Brazil	(Real)	2.7361v	1.8215	1.7058	1.7467
Brunei	(Brunei $)	2.6017	1.7321	1.6220	1.6609
Bulgaria	(Lev)	3.1212	2.0779	1.9459	1.9925
Burkina Faso	(CFA Fr)	1052.18	700.470	655.957	671.688
Burma	(Kyat)	9.3881	6.2500	5.8528	5.9932
Burundi	(Burundi Fr)	990.494	659.404	617.501	632.309
Cambodia	(Riel)	5762.05	3836.00	3558.51	3643.86
Cameroon	(CFA Fr)	1052.18	700.470	655.957	671.688
Canada	(Canadian $)	2.2225	1.4796	1.3856	1.4188
Canary Is	(Sp Peseta)	266.889	177.677	166.386	170.377
Cp. Verde	(CV Escudo)	175.102	116.572	108.916	111.528
Cayman Is	(CI $)	1.2317	0.8200	0.7679	0.7863
Cent. Afr. Rep	(CFA Fr)	1052.18	700.470	655.957	671.688
Chad	(CFA Fr)	1052.18	700.470	655.957	671.688
Chile	(Chilean Peso)	807.679	537.700	503.529	515.606
China	(Renminbi)	12.4327	8.2769	7.7509	7.9368
Colombia	(Col Peso)	3190.09	2123.75	1988.79	2036.49
Comoros	(Fr)	766.221	510.100	477.683	489.140
Congo	(CFA Fr)	1052.18	700.470	655.957	671.688
Congo (DemRep)	(Congo Fr)	6.7595	4.5000	4.2140	4.3151
Costa Rica	(Colon)	461.445	307.200	287.677	294.577
Cote d'Ivoire	(CFA Fr)	1052.18	700.470	655.957	671.688
Croatia	(Kuna)	12.2431	8.1507	7.6327	7.8157
Cuba	(Cuban Peso)	31.5441	21.0000	19.6655	20.1371
Cyprus	(Cyprus £)	0.9207	0.6129	0.5740	0.5877
Czech Rep.	(Koruna)	57.7197	38.4260	35.9840	36.8471
Denmark	(Danish Krone)	11.9601	7.9623	7.4563	7.6351
Djibouti Rep	(Djib Fr)	255.357	170.000	159.197	163.015
Dominica	(E Carib $)	4.0557	2.7000	2.5284	2.5891
Dominican Rep	(D Peso)	23.6881	15.7700	14.8427	15.1987
Ecuador	(Sucre)	37552.5o	25000.0	23411.3	23972.8
	(Sucre)	37552.5a	25000.0	23411.3	23972.8
Egypt	(Egyptian £)	5.2142	3.4713	3.2507	3.3286
El Salvador	(Colon)	13.1584	8.7600	8.2033	8.4001
Equat'l Guinea	(CFA Fr)	1052.18	700.470	655.957	671.688
Estonia	(Kroon)	25.1084	16.7155	15.6533	16.0287
Ethiopia	(Ethiopian Birr)	12.1700	8.1020	7.5871	7.7691
Falkland Is	(Falk £)	1	0.6657	0.6235	0.6384
Faroe Is	(Danish Krone)	11.9601	7.9623	7.4563	7.6351
Fiji Is	(Fiji $)	3.1036	2.0662	1.9349	1.9813
Finland	(Markka)	9.5372	6.3492	5.9457	6.0883
France	(Fr)	10.5218	7.0047	6.5596	6.7169
Fr. Cty/Africa	(CFA Fr)	1052.18	700.470	655.957	671.688
Fr. Guiana	(Local Fr)	10.5218	7.0047	6.5596	6.7169
Fr. Pacific Is	(CFP Fr)	191.443	127.450	122.001	124.927
Gabon	(CFA Fr)	1052.18	700.470	655.957	671.688
Gambia	(Dalasi)	19.2119	12.7900	11.9773	12.2645
Georgia	(Lari)	2.9817	1.9850	1.8589	1.9034
Germany	(D-Mark)	3.1373	2.0886	1.9558	2.0027

		£ STG	US $	EURO €	YEN (X 100)
Ghana	(Cedi)	7660.73	5100.00	4775.90	4890.44
Gibraltar	(Gib £)	1	0.6657	0.6235	0.6384
Greece	(Drachma)	539.660	359.270	336.439	344.508
Greenland	(Danish Krone)	11.9601	7.9623	7.4563	7.6351
Grenada	(E Carib $)	4.0557	2.7000	2.5284	2.5891
Guadeloupe	(French Fr)	10.5218	7.0047	6.5596	6.7169
Guam	(US $)	1.5021	1	0.9365	0.9589
Guatemala	(Quetzal)	11.6263	7.7400	7.1919	7.3644
Guinea	(Fr)	2470.95	1645.00	1540.46	1577.41
Guinea-Bissau	(CFA Fr)	1052.18	700.470	655.957	671.688
Guyana	(Guyanese $)	271.129	180.500	169.029	173.083
Haiti	(Gourde)	28.3897	18.9000	17.6989	18.1234
Honduras	(Lempira)	22.1560	14.7500	13.8033	14.1343
Hong Kong	(HK $)	11.7036	7.7915	7.2964	7.4714
Hungary	(Forint)	416.683	277.400	259.771	266.002
Iceland	(Icelandic Krona)	117.269	78.0700	73.1087	74.8622
India	(Indian Rupee)	67.1026	44.6725	41.8336	42.8369
Indonesia	(Rupiah)	13060.8	8695.00	8142.44	8337.73
Iran	(Rial)(7)	2624.92o	1747.50	1636.45	1675.70
Iraq	(Iraqi Dinar)(1)	0.4670r	0.3109	0.2911	0.2981
Irish Rep	(Punt)	1.2633	0.8410	0.7876	0.8065
Israel	(Shekel)	6.1471	4.0923	3.8322	3.9242
Italy	(Lira)	3105.85	2067.67	1936.27	1982.71
Jamaica	(Jamaican $)	62.7878	41.8000	38.8627	39.7948
Japan	(Yen)	156.647	104.285	97.6577	100
Jordan	(Jordanian Dinar)	1.0680	0.7110	0.6658	0.6818
Kazakhstan	(Tenge)	214.530	142.820	133.744	136.952
Kenya	(Kenya Shilling)	116.413	77.5000	72.5749	74.3156
Kiribati	(Australian $)	2.5184	1.6766	1.5701	1.6077
Korea North	(Won)	3.3046	2.2000	2.0602	2.1096
Korea South	(Won)	1681.23	1119.25	1048.12	1073.26
Kuwait	(Kuwaiti Dinar)	0.4602	0.3064	0.2869	0.2938
Kyrgyzstan	(Som)	72.1538	48.0353	44.9827	46.0616
Laos	(New Kip)	11416.0	7600.00	7117.02	7287.72
Latvia	(Lats)	0.8994	0.5988	0.5607	0.5741
Lebanon	(Lebanese £)	2266.67	1509.00	1413.10	1447.00
Lesotho	(Maluti)	10.3325	6.8787	6.4416	6.5961
Liberia	(Liberian $)	1.5021o	1	0.9365	0.9589
Libya	(Libyan Dinar)	0.7521	0.5007	0.4689	0.4801
Liechtenstein	(Swiss Fr)	2.4893	1.6572	1.5519	1.5891
Lithuania	(Litas)	6.0099	4.0010	3.7468	3.8366
Luxembourg	(Lux Fr)	64.7067	43.0775	40.3399	41.3075
Macao	(Pataca)	11.9958	7.9860	7.4785	7.6579
Macedonia	(Denar)	96.6526	64.3450	60.2559	61.7011
Madagascar	(MG Fr)	9508.29	6330.00	5918.36	6060.32
Madeira	(Port Escudo)	321.581	214.087	200.482	205.291
Malawi	(Kwacha)	83.3667	55.5000	51.9731	53.2195
Malaysia	(Ringgit)	5.7080o	3.8000	3.5585	3.6439
	(Ringgit) (3)	5.7080	3.8000	3.5585	3.6439
Maldive Is	(Rufiya)	17.6046	11.7200	10.9752	11.2384
Mali Rep	(CFA Fr)	1052.18	700.470	655.957	671.688
Malta	(Maltese Lira)	0.6544	0.4356	0.4079	0.4177
Martinique	(Local Fr)	10.5218	7.0047	6.5596	6.7169
Mauritania	(Ouguiya)	362.292	241.190	225.863	231.280
Mauritius	(Maur Rupee)	39.0997	26.0300	24.3758	24.9604
Mexico	(Mexican Peso)	14.9925	9.9810	9.3467	9.5709
Moldova	(Leu)	18.8480	12.5478	11.7410	12.0226
Monaco	(French Fr)	10.5218	7.0047	6.5596	6.7169
Mongolia	(Tugrik)	1551.25	1032.72	954.168	977.053
Montserrat	(E Carib $)	4.0557	2.7000	2.5284	2.5891
Morocco	(Dirham)	15.8032	10.5207	9.8521	10.0884
Mozambique	(Metical)	24183.9	16100.0	15076.9	15438.5
Namibia	(Dollar)	10.3325	6.8787	6.4416	6.5961
Nauru Is	(Australian $)	2.5184	1.6766	1.5701	1.6077
Nepal	(Nepalese Rupee)	105.853	70.4700	65.9916	67.5744
Netherlands	(Guilder)	3.5349	2.3533	2.2037	2.2566
N'nd Antilles	(A/Guilder)	2.6738	1.7800	1.6669	1.7069
New Zealand	(NZ $)	3.1906	2.1240	1.9891	2.0368
Nicaragua	(Gold Cordoba)	19.0316	12.6700	11.8648	12.1494
Niger Rep	(CFA Fr)	1052.18	700.470	655.957	671.688
Nigeria	(Naira)	155.693m	103.650	97.0631	99.3911
Norway	(Nor. Krone)	13.1301	8.7412	8.1857	8.3820
Oman	(Rial Omani)	0.5783	0.3850	0.3606	0.3692

		£ STG	US $	EURO €	YEN (X 100)
Pakistan	(Pak. Rupee)	78.5148	52.2700	48.9483	50.1223
Panama	(Balboa)	1.5021	1	0.9365	0.9589
Papua New Guinea	(Kina)	3.6863	2.4541	2.2982	2.3532
Paraguay	(Guarani)	5264.86	3505.00	3282.26	3360.98
Peru	(New Sol)	5.2487	3.4943	3.2722	3.3507
Philippines	(Peso)	64.4401	42.9000	40.1737	41.1373
Pitcairn Is	(£ Sterling)	1	0.6657	0.6235	0.6384
	(NZ $)	3.1906	2.1240	1.9891	2.0368
Poland	(Zloty)	6.6802	4.4473	4.1646	4.2645
Portugal	(Escudo)	321.581	214.087	200.482	205.291
Puerto Rico	(US $)	1.5021	1	0.9365	0.9589
Qatar	(Riyal)	5.4680	3.6402	3.4089	3.4906
Reunion Is. de la	(F/Fr)	10.5218	7.0047	6.5596	6.7169
Romania	(Leu)	31855.8	21207.5	19859.8	20336.1
Russia	(Rouble)	42.2992m	28.1600	26.3705	27.0029
Rwanda	(Fr)	539.329	359.050	336.232	344.297
St Christopher	(E Carib $)	4.0557	2.7000	2.5284	2.5891
St Helena	(£)	1	0.6657	0.6235	0.6384
St Lucia	(E Carib $)	4.0557	2.7000	2.5284	2.5891
St Pierre & Miquelon	(F/Fr)	10.5218	7.0047	6.5596	6.7169
St Vincent	(E Carib $)	4.0557	2.7000	2.5284	2.5891
San Marino	(Italian Lira)	3105.85	2067.67	1936.27	1982.71
Sao Tome	(Dobra)	3571.99	2378.00	2226.88	2280.29
Saudi Arabia	(Riyal)	5.6336	3.7505	3.5121	3.5963
Senegal	(CFA Fr)	1052.18	700.470	655.957	671.688
Seychelles	(Rupee)	8.4388	5.6180	5.2675	5.3939
Sierra Leone	(Leone)	2672.23	1779.00	2090.30	2140.43
Singapore	($)	2.6017	1.7321	1.6220	1.6609
Slovakia	(Koruna)	67.8942	45.1995	42.3271	43.3423
Slovenia	(Tolar)	332.197	221.155	207.101	212.068
Solomon Is	($)	7.5952	5.0564	4.7351	4.8486
Somali Rep	(Shilling)	3935.50	2620.00	2453.50	2512.35
South Africa	(Rand)	10.3325	6.8787	6.4416	6.5961
Spain	(Peseta)	266.889	177.677	166.386	170.377
Spanish Ports in N Africa	(Sp Peseta)	266.889	177.677	166.386	170.377
Sri Lanka	(Rupee)	118.215	78.7000	73.6987	75.4663
Sudan Rep	(Dinar)	388.743	258.800	242.353	248.166
Surinam	(Guilder)	1215.95	809.500	758.056	776.238
Swaziland	(Lilangeni)	10.3325	6.8787	6.4416	6.5961
Sweden	(Krona)	13.3056	8.8580	8.2951	8.4940
Switzerland	(Fr)	2.4893	1.6572	1.5519	1.5891
Syria	(£)	78.8602	52.5000	54.7823	56.0963
Taiwan	($)	46.2144	30.7665	28.8113	29.5023
Tanzania	(Shilling)	1203.18	801.000	750.097	768.088
Thailand	(Baht)	58.6946	39.0750	36.5918	37.4694
Togo Rep	(CFA Fr)	1052.18	700.470	655.957	671.688
Tonga Is	(Pa'anga)	2.5184	1.6766	1.5701	1.6077
Trinidad/Tobago	($)	9.3731	6.2400	5.8434	5.9836
Tunisia	(Dinar)	2.0367	1.3559	1.2696	1.3002
Turkey	(Lira)	935455.4	622765.0	583188.3	597176.0
Turks & Caicos	(US $)	1.5021	1	0.9365	0.9589
Tuvalu	(Australian $)	2.5184	1.6766	1.5701	1.6077
Uganda	(New Shilling)	2374.83	1581.00	1480.53	1516.04
Ukraine	(Hryvna)	8.2465	5.4900	5.1412	5.2644
U A E	(Dirham)	5.5172	3.6730	3.4395	3.5220
United Kingdom	(£)	1	0.6657	0.6235	0.6384
United States	(US $)	1.5021	1	0.9365	0.9589
Uruguay	(Peso Uruguayo)	18.1304	12.0700	11.3030	11.5741
Uzbekistan	(Sum)	1164.13	775.000	725.749	743.156
Vanuatu	(Vatu)	204.136	135.900	127.264	130.316
Vatican	(Lira)	3105.85	2067.67	1936.27	1982.71
Venezuela	(Bolivar)	1022.55v	680.750	637.489	652.778
Vietnam	(Dong)	21158.6	14086.0	13190.8	13507.2
Virgin Is-British	(US $)	1.5021	1	0.9365	0.9589
Virgin Is-US	(US $)	1.5021	1	0.9365	0.9589
Western Samoa	(Tala)	4.6405	3.0893	2.8930	2.9624
Yemen (Rep of)	(Rial) (2)	233.464	155.425	145.548	149.039
Yugoslavia	(New Dinar)	18.2909	12.1769	11.4031	11.6766
Zambia	(Kwacha)	4641.50	3090.00	2893.63	2963.03
Zimbabwe	($)	57.6056	38.3500	35.9129	36.7742
Euro	(Euro)	1.6041	1.0679	1	1.0240
SDR	(SDR)	1.12930	0.751800	0.704000	0.720900

Fig. 12.4 FT guide to world currencies

rates. Many of these currencies are pretty obscure in terms of their role outside their countries of origin; many of them are fixed against the dollar or tied to important international or regional currencies; and many of them are very strictly controlled by the local monetary authorities, and are not openly dealt on world foreign exchange markets.

For the major currencies of the world, a daily table shows exchange cross-rates (see Figure 12.5a). This provides the reciprocal values for 16 of the world's principal trading currencies plus the euro, quoted in a grid displaying each currency's value in terms of the others. Half-yearly, the newspaper shows current and six-months-earlier values for 16 currencies in terms of dollars, euros and yen, as well as charts tracking the past six months' movements of the dollar against the yen and the euro and trade-weighted indices for the dollar, the yen and sterling.

Number of French francs per D-Mark

Number of D-Marks per 10 French francs

Number of Irish pounds per dollar

Number of euros per 100 yen

CROSS RATES AND DERIVATIVES

EXCHANGE CROSS RATES

Aug 3		BFr	DKr	FFr	DM	I£	L	Fl	NKr	Es	Pta	SKr	SFr	£	C$	$	Y	€
Belgium*	(BFr)	100	18.49	16.26	4.848	1.952	4800	5.463	20.19	497.0	412.5	20.93	3.832	1.499	3.324	2.242	242.2	2.479
Denmark	(DKr)	54.09	10	8.795	2.622	1.056	2596	2.955	10.92	268.8	223.1	11.32	2.073	0.810	1.798	1.213	131.0	1.341
France*	(FFr)	61.50	11.37	10	2.982	1.201	2952	3.360	12.42	305.6	253.7	12.87	2.357	0.922	2.044	1.379	149.0	1.525
Germany*	(DM)	20.63	3.813	3.354	1	0.403	990.0	1.127	4.165	102.5	85.07	4.317	0.790	0.309	0.686	0.462	49.96	0.511
Ireland*	(I£)	51.22	9.470	8.329	2.483	1	2459	2.798	10.34	254.6	211.3	10.72	1.963	0.768	1.703	1.148	124.1	1.270
Italy*	(L)	2.083	0.385	0.339	0.101	0.041	100	0.114	0.421	10.35	8.593	0.436	0.080	0.031	0.069	0.047	5.046	0.052
Netherlands*	(Fl)	18.31	3.384	2.977	0.888	0.357	878.6	1	3.696	90.97	75.50	3.832	0.701	0.274	0.608	0.410	44.34	0.454
Norway	(NKr)	49.52	9.156	8.053	2.401	0.967	2377	2.705	.10	246.1	204.3	10.37	1.898	0.742	1.646	1.110	120.0	1.228
Portugal*	(Es)	20.12	3.720	3.272	0.976	0.393	965.8	1.099	4.063	100	82.99	4.212	0.771	0.302	0.669	0.451	48.74	0.499
Spain*	(Pta)	24.24	4.482	3.942	1.175	0.473	1164	1.324	4.896	120.5	100	5.075	0.929	0.363	0.806	0.544	58.73	0.601
Sweden	(SKr)	47.77	8.833	7.768	2.316	0.933	2293	2.610	9.647	237.4	197.0	10	1.831	0.716	1.588	1.071	115.7	1.184
Switzerland	(SFr)	26.10	4.825	4.243	1.265	0.509	1253	1.426	5.269	129.7	107.6	5.462	1	0.391	0.867	0.585	63.21	0.647
UK	(£)	66.73	12.34	10.85	3.235	1.303	3203	3.646	13.48	331.6	275.2	13.97	2.557	1	2.218	1.496	161.6	1.654
Canada	(C$)	30.08	5.562	4.892	1.459	0.587	1444	1.643	6.075	149.5	124.1	6.297	1.153	0.451	1	0.674	72.87	0.746
USA	($)	44.60	8.247	7.253	2.163	0.871	2141	2.437	9.007	221.7	184.0	9.337	1.709	0.668	1.483	1	108.0	1.106
Japan	(Y)	41.29	7.633	6.713	2.002	0.806	1982	2.255	8.336	205.2	170.3	8.642	1.582	0.619	1.372	0.926	100	1.023
Euro	(€)	40.34	7.458	6.560	1.956	0.788	1936	2.204	8.146	200.5	166.4	8.444	1.546	0.605	1.341	0.904	97.71	1

Danish Kroner, French Franc, Norwegian Kroner, and Swedish Kronor per 10; Belgian Franc, Yen, Escudo, Lira and Peseta per 100. * EMU member.

Fig. 12.5a Exchange cross-rates

One last daily table headed "Other currencies" gives sterling and dollar buy and sell rates for a handful of second-rank currencies in which some sort of free market exists (see Figure 12.5b) or which are politically sensitive. In some of these cases, there may be a considerably higher degree of official exchange rate control than with front rank currencies.

■ OTHER CURRENCIES

Jun 16	£	$
Czech	Rp 56.8663 - 56.9358	37.5380 - 37.5690
Hungary	409.356 - 409.746	270.220 - 270.370
Iran	2629.39 - 2666.22	1735.00 - 1760.00
Kuwait	0.4636 - 0.4640	0.3060 - 0.3062
Peru	5.2643 - 5.2694	3.4750 - 3.4770
Poland	6.6921 - 6.7061	4.4175 - 4.4250
Russia	42.8414 - 42.8735	28.2800 - 28.2900
U.A.E.	5.5638 - 5.5664	3.6727 - 3.6730

Fig. 12.5b Other currencies

183

Saturday's newspaper adds a table of over 30 tourist rates against the pound in its Weekend Money section (see Figure 12.6). These are the rates at which individuals can buy the currencies.

Tourist rates

		Fri rate vs £
Australia	Dollars	2.43
Austria	Schillings	21.35
Barbados	Dollars	2.83
Belgium	Francs	62.53
Canada	Dollars	2.15
Cyprus	Pounds	0.89
Denmark	Kroner	11.56
Egypt	Pounds	4.83
Finland	Marks	9.22
France	Francs	10.18
Germany	Marks	3.04
Greece	Drachmei	521.28
Holland	Guilders	3.41
Hong Kong	Dollars	11.28
Ireland	Punts	1.22
Israel	Shekels	5.92
Italy	Lira	3003.00
Japan	Yen	152.41
Malaysia	Ringgit	5.41
Malta	Liri	0.62
New Zealand	Dollars	3.02
Norway	Kroner	12.72
Portugal	Escudos	311.28
Singapore	Dollar	2.50
South Africa	Rand	9.96
Spain	Pesetas	258.03
Sweden	Kronor	12.81
Switzerland	Francs	2.40
Thailand	Baht	54.39
Turkey	Lira	890941.00
United States	Dollars	1.46

Rates for deals up to £10,000.　　　　Source: NatWest

Fig. 12.6 Tourist rates

A final table on the foreign exchange markets gives an indication of the volatility or riskiness of three leading currencies – sterling, the euro and the yen – against the dollar (see Figure 12.7). The first column provides the latest reading for the volatility index, followed by the change on the previous reading, the reading for a month ago and the 52-week high and low. A "RiskGrade" of 100 corresponds to the average volatility of the international equity markets during "normal market conditions". So anything less than 100 is less volatile than global stock markets. In this example, the pound has clearly been less volatile against the dollar than either the euro or the yen. And all are less volatile than standard stock market volatility.

RISKGRADE VOLATILITY - FX markets

Currencies vs $	Aug 1	Day change	Month ago	52 wk high	52 wk low
Euro €	52	-1	57	65	40
£ Sterling	38	-1	43	46	30
Yen	47	-1	56	77	47

RiskGrades are calculated daily by RiskMetrics. They are designed to measure the riskiness of today's global market returns. A RiskGrade of 100 corresponds to the average volatility of the international equity markets during normal market conditions. Data shown is one day in arrears. More information is available at www.riskgrades.com

Fig. 12.7 RiskGrade volatility: FX markets

The money markets

The money markets are the markets in deposits and short-term financial instruments, places for money that is available for short periods and where money can be converted into longer period loans. It is a wholesale market for professionals only, though its operations have an impact on the price of money and liquidity generally. Its main functions are:

- those banks temporarily short of funds can borrow while those with a surplus can put it to work

- a source of liquidity

- banks can borrow wholesale funds as can companies and governments

- to correct imbalances between the banking system as a whole and the government.

FT reports describe monetary conditions and central bank money market intervention in a number of countries. The choice of market centres will depend on the amount of activity in each on the preceding day.

UK interest rates

The London money rates table (see Figure 12.8) provides details of interest rates for overnight deposits and other short-term instruments. These are representative interest rates taken by the newspaper from major market participants near the end of the London trading day, showing:

- **Loan period:** rates are given for a number of maturities, varying from overnight to one year, for a number of different instruments.

- **Interbank sterling:** this is a measure of short-term swings in rates; a constantly changing indicator of the cost of money in large amounts for banks themselves. For each maturity date, the first figure is the offer or lending rate, and the second figure the bid or borrowing rate. The interbank market exists to allow banks to lend and borrow surplus liquidity in substantial amounts; in practice, very large company depositors should be able to deal at or near interbank rates when they are placing money in the market. Rates for different maturities produce the yield curve; when interest rates might drop, the yield curve will be negative.

UK INTEREST RATES

LONDON MONEY RATES

Aug 17	Over-night	7 days notice	One month	Three months	Six months	One year
Interbank Sterling	$5\frac{3}{4}$ - $4\frac{7}{8}$	$5\frac{7}{8}$ - $5\frac{5}{8}$	6 - $5\frac{7}{8}$	$6\frac{3}{16}$ - $6\frac{1}{16}$	$6\frac{5}{16}$ - $6\frac{3}{16}$	$6\frac{1}{2}$ - $6\frac{3}{8}$
BBA Sterling LIBOR	-	6 -	$6\frac{1}{16}$ -	$6\frac{7}{32}$ -	$6\frac{5}{16}$ -	$6\frac{15}{32}$ -
Sterling CDs	-	-	6 - $5\frac{15}{16}$	$6\frac{1}{8}$ - $6\frac{3}{32}$	$6\frac{5}{16}$ - $6\frac{1}{4}$	$6\frac{17}{32}$ - $6\frac{15}{32}$
Treasury Bills	-	-	$5\frac{7}{8}$ - $5\frac{13}{16}$	6 - $5\frac{15}{16}$	-	-
Bank Bills	-	-	$5\frac{15}{16}$ - $5\frac{7}{8}$	$6\frac{3}{32}$ - $6\frac{1}{32}$	-	-
Local authority deps.	$6\frac{1}{2}$ - $6\frac{1}{2}$	$6\frac{1}{4}$ - 6	$6\frac{1}{8}$ - 6	$6\frac{1}{4}$ - $6\frac{1}{8}$	$6\frac{3}{8}$ - $6\frac{1}{4}$	$6\frac{9}{16}$ - $6\frac{7}{16}$
Discount Market deps	$5\frac{13}{16}$ - $5\frac{3}{4}$	$5\frac{7}{8}$ - $5\frac{5}{8}$	-	-	-	-

UK clearing bank base lending rate 6 per cent from Feb 10, 2000

	Up to 1 month	1-3 month	3-6 months	6-9 months	9-12 months
Certs of Tax dep. (£100,000)	$2\frac{1}{4}$	5	5	5	$5\frac{1}{4}$

Certs of Tax dep. under £100,000 is $2\frac{1}{4}$pc. Deposits withdrawn for cash $1\frac{1}{4}$pc.
Av. tndr rate of discount Jul 28. 5.4860pc. ECGD fixed rate Stlg. Export Finance. make up day Jul 31, 2000. Agreed rate for period Aug 26, 2000 to Sep 28, 2000, Scheme III 7.44pc. Reference rate for period Jul 1, 2000 to Jul 31, 2000, Scheme IV & V 6.192pc. Finance House Base Rate $6\frac{1}{2}$pc for August 2000. SONIA Aug 15: 5.6076

Fig. 12.8 London money rates

- **Sterling CDs:** certificates of deposit issued in sterling by UK banks and in which a secondary market exists. These carry a slightly lower rate than interbank loans.
- **Treasury and bank bills:** the rates at which various bills of exchange are discounted. Bills of exchange are securities issued by companies, banks or governments (in this case, the Treasury and banks) with a fixed maturity value. Discounting them means buying them at a discount from face value, with the discount rate being the difference between purchase price and face value as a percentage of the face value.
- **Deposits:** money lent to local authorities (offered rate for deposits), as well as the rates at which discount houses (the institutions with which the Bank of England carries out the bulk of its operations in the money market) accept the secured money from banks. Banks are required to maintain a certain amount of cash with the discount market, and these rates are generally below interbank levels.

World interest rates

The money rates table in Figure 12.9 lists representative interest rates from major money markets outside London, showing:

- **Loan period:** current overnight and one-, three-, six- and 12-month rates in the euro-zone, Switzerland, Japan and the United States.
- **Lombard intervention:** traditionally, the rate at which the central bank in Germany intervenes in the interbank market to manage day-to-day liquidity lending to German commercial banks. France, Belgium and Switzerland also have an official intervention rate of this kind.
- **Discount rate:** the rate at which central banks are prepared to buy bills of exchange from the discount houses, often known as the bank rate (or occasionally in the United

WORLD INTEREST RATES

DOMESTIC MONEY RATES

Jun 22	Over night	One month	Three mths	Six mths	One year	Lomb. inter.	Dis. rate	Repo rate
Euro-zone	4	4⅜	$4\frac{15}{32}$	$4\frac{21}{32}$	$4\frac{31}{32}$	-	-	4.25
Switzerland	3⅜	$3\frac{5}{16}$	$3\frac{13}{32}$	$3\frac{19}{32}$	$3\frac{29}{32}$	-	0.50	-
US	$6\frac{13}{32}$	$6\frac{21}{32}$	6¾	6⅞	$7\frac{5}{32}$	-	6.00	-
Japan	$\frac{1}{16}$	$\frac{3}{32}$	$\frac{5}{32}$	¼	⅜	-	0.50	-
$ Libor BBA fixing*								
Interbank Fixing	-	$6\frac{21}{32}$	6¾	$6\frac{29}{32}$	$7\frac{3}{16}$	-	-	-
US Dollar CDs	-	6.56	6.69	6.83	7.10	-	-	-
Euro Linked Ds	-	$4\frac{7}{16}$	$4\frac{17}{32}$	$4\frac{11}{16}$	$4\frac{31}{32}$	-	-	-
SDR Linked Ds	-	3⅜	$3\frac{17}{32}$	$3\frac{11}{16}$	$4\frac{1}{32}$	-	-	-
BBA Euro Libor	-	$4\frac{7}{16}$	$4\frac{17}{32}$	$4\frac{11}{16}$	$4\frac{31}{32}$	-	-	-
Euro Euribor	-	4.419	4.518	4.687	4.988	-	-	
EONIA	4.16	-	-	-	-	-	-	-
EURONIA	4.1708	-	-	-	-	-	-	-

* London interbank fixing rate (LIBOR) is the BBA London rate, fixed at 11am (London time).
Mid rates are shown for the domestic Money Rates, US$ CDs, Euro & SDR Linked Deposits (Ds).

INTERNATIONAL MONEY RATES

Jun 22	Short term	7 days notice	One month	Three months	Six months	One year
Euro	4⅛ - $3\frac{31}{32}$	$4\frac{13}{32}$ - $4\frac{5}{16}$	$4\frac{7}{16}$ - $4\frac{5}{16}$	$4\frac{17}{32}$ - $4\frac{13}{32}$	$4\frac{23}{32}$ - $4\frac{19}{32}$	$5\frac{1}{32}$ - $4\frac{29}{32}$
Danish Krone	4¾ - 4¼	4⅞ - $4\frac{25}{32}$	$4\frac{29}{32}$ - $4\frac{13}{16}$	5¼ - $5\frac{5}{32}$	$5\frac{11}{16}$ - $5\frac{19}{32}$	$5\frac{29}{32}$ - $5\frac{13}{16}$
Sterling	6¾ - 6⅝	6⅛ - 5⅞	$6\frac{1}{16}$ - $5\frac{15}{16}$	$6\frac{7}{32}$ - $6\frac{3}{32}$	$6\frac{11}{32}$ - $6\frac{7}{32}$	$6\frac{15}{32}$ - 6⅜
Swiss Franc	3½ - 3	$3\frac{11}{16}$ - $3\frac{9}{16}$	$3\frac{11}{32}$ - 3¼	$3\frac{7}{16}$ - $3\frac{11}{32}$	$3\frac{21}{32}$ - $3\frac{9}{16}$	$3\frac{31}{32}$ - $3\frac{13}{16}$
Canadian Dollar	$5\frac{13}{16}$ - $5\frac{11}{16}$	$5\frac{13}{16}$ - $5\frac{11}{16}$	$5\frac{13}{16}$ - $5\frac{23}{32}$	$5\frac{29}{32}$ - $5\frac{13}{16}$	$6\frac{1}{16}$ - $5\frac{15}{16}$	6¼ - 6⅛
US Dollar	6½ - 6⅜	6⅞ - $6\frac{25}{32}$	$6\frac{11}{16}$ - $6\frac{19}{32}$	$6\frac{13}{16}$ - $6\frac{11}{16}$	$6\frac{15}{16}$ - $6\frac{13}{16}$	$7\frac{7}{32}$ - $7\frac{3}{32}$
Japanese Yen	⅛ - $\frac{1}{16}$	⅛ - $\frac{1}{32}$	$\frac{5}{32}$ - $\frac{1}{16}$	$\frac{3}{16}$ - $\frac{3}{32}$	$\frac{5}{16}$ - $\frac{7}{32}$	$\frac{7}{16}$ - $\frac{11}{32}$
Asian $Sing	2 - 1¾	$2\frac{11}{16}$ - $2\frac{7}{16}$	2½ - 2¼	2⅝ - 2⅜	$2\frac{13}{16}$ - $2\frac{9}{16}$	3¼ - $2\frac{15}{16}$

Short term rates are call for the US Dollar and Yen, others: two days' notice.

Fig. 12.9 World interest rates

Kingdom, the base lending or minimum lending rate). Although often the most significant interest rate in domestic economies, they are not all strictly comparable: in some countries other market rates set by the central bank have more influence on the level of market interest rates than the bank rate itself.

- **Repo rate:** another rate at which central banks intervene in the market, this is the rate at which they will repurchase bills having sold them. It is an important rate in certain countries, notably the euro-zone where it is taken to be a key indicator of the central bank's intentions for monetary policy.
- **Interbank fixing:** these are one-, three-, six- and 12-month Eurodollar deposit rates representing the average of rates collected from four leading banks (Bankers Trust, Bank of Tokyo, Barclays and National Westminister) at 11am London time every trading day. The rates are intended to be used as a reference point by borrowers or lenders of floating rate money when the rate of interest is linked to Eurodollar LIBOR (London Inter-Bank Offered Rate). LIBOR, a major reference point for the international financial markets, is not calculated in any universal way or at a universally recognised time. These figures, published daily by the *Financial Times* since June 1980, are intended to fill this gap by providing an internationally acceptable standard rate. Rates are given for the last fixing and a week ago.

- **CDs:** rates are also quoted for US-dollar, euro-linked and SDR-linked certificates of deposit. These are, in essence, marketable bank deposits: a depositor who buys a three-month CD from a bank may sell it to a third party if liquidity is needed before the maturity date. Because CDs can be sold on, unlike ordinary deposits, they carry slightly lower interest rates.

- **BBA Euro Libor and Euro Euribor:** these are two interest rates battling to establish themselves as the euro-zone benchmark. BBA stands for the British Bankers' Association. This is the incumbent representing London as a key financial centre and is based on daily quotes from the 16 most creditworthy and internationally liquid banks. Euribor (the Euro Interbank Offered Rate), the challenger, is calculated from a panel of 57 mainly European banks from every member country of the euro-zone.

- **EONIA:** this benchmark (the Euro Overnight Index Average) indicates rates for overnight unsecured lending in the euro-zone interbank market. It is calculated by the European Central Bank drawing on the same banks as Euribor.

- **EURONIA:** this is the London equivalent of EONIA, the average interest rate, weighted by volume, of all unsecured overnight euro deposit trades arranged by eight money brokers in London.

- **International money rates:** interest rates on deposits in various currencies in markets outside their countries of origin, the so-called Euromarket rates. Outside the United States, for example, banks are not bound by any considerations of reserve requirements on their holding of dollars, and outside France, French francs are not affected by French controls. These then are free market rates at which banks lend and borrow money to and from each other. Interest rates are quoted for seven currencies and the so-called "Asian" dollar, that is, offshore dollars traded in the Far East before the European market opens.

The international money rates follow but do not necessarily match domestic rates. The key rate is the LIBOR, the heart of the interbank market, which is in turn the core of the money markets.

US interest rates

Another table relevant to both the money markets and the bond markets, and actually listed on the International Capital Markets pages, covers US interest rates (see Figure 12.10):

US INTEREST RATES

Latest		Treasury Bills and Bond Yields	
		One month .... -	Two year 6.46
Prime rate 9½		Two month .... -	Three year .... -
Broker loan rate 8¼		Three month 5.80	Five year 6.28
Fed.funds 6½		Six month 6.16	10-year 6.09
Fed.funds at intervention ... -		One year 6.12	30-year 5.95

Fig. 12.10 US interest rates

- **Rates:** the prime rate, the rate at which US banks lend to highly creditworthy customers, and the equivalent of the United Kingdom's base lending rate; and the Federal Funds rate, which is the overnight rate paid on funds lent between the member banks of the US Federal Reserve System. The latter is highly volatile and the most sensitive reflection of the day-to-day cost of money in the United States.
- **Treasury bills and bond yields:** these are yields on US government securities, the equivalent of UK Treasury bills and gilts. They range in maturity term from one month to the 30 years of the benchmark long bond, and in this case have a positive yield curve indicating that investors expect a premium for holding investments over the longer term.

Interest rates obviously play a critical role binding together the world's many financial markets, and strongly influencing companies' costs of borrowing and investors' likely returns. For the investor, the direction and relative importance of their effects on a given equity portfolio vary considerably. The immediate effect of a rise in interest rates in one country is that the dividend yield of a share will be relatively less attractive than the interest rate on a local deposit account. The yield will also be less appealing than that of a government bond in the same country, the price of which will have fallen so that its fixed coupon's yield corresponds to the interest rate. Investors with a portion of their assets in cash or other alternatives to equity should note these relative return movements.

A share's dividend yield may become even less desirable since the rate rise will probably increase the company's interest costs, reducing its profitability and perhaps leading it to cut dividends. The extent of the increased costs will hinge on the company's level of borrowing, and its skills at locking into fixed rate funding prior to the rate rise. Higher leverage and larger floating rate loans suggest greater potential damage to dividend yields from rising interest rates.

By the same token, much of the return sought on shares is from their potential for capital growth, and rate movements need not affect that. Interest rates tend to rise and fall in line with the level of economic activity. In a recession and the early stages of a recovery, they will generally be low and falling to encourage borrowing; while in the subsequent expansion and boom, they will rise as the demand for money exceeds the supply. As countries emerge from recession and move into boom, interest rates tend to rise, increasing capital costs. But, at the same time, growing economies should offer numerous opportunities for enhanced profitability. Over the longer term, the prospects for corporate profitability tend to have far more of an influence on share prices than interest rates. And those prospects are in turn powerfully affected by the growth potential and stability of the local economy.

Of course, rising interest rates may not necessarily signal the expansive phase of the business cycle. They could, for example, indicate excessive government budget deficits, which drive up the cost of borrowing. In that case, rate increases are unlikely to be promising for share values. Rate rises might also be a reflection of the need to restrain high or impending inflation. In a national context, this need not be disastrous since low inflation will benefit long-term corporate profitability, while high inflation at least implies low real interest rates. Within a global portfolio, however, company shares in relatively high inflation countries are eventually going to diminish in value when the currency in which they are priced devalues.

Equity returns are particularly affected by interest rates in firms and sectors where business revenues and costs are especially sensitive to rate changes, such as banks and life assurance companies. Even firms in industries dependent on household expenditure, such as the retail sector and breweries, may experience important changes in profits, as consumers shift their spending in response to the cost of credit. In addition, it is, as always, essential to note that as a result of investor expectations, the effects of changed interest rates could conceivably come before the change actually occurs. Financial markets often discount the future in this way, building into the prices of the assets traded on them all past, present and prospective information on their future values.

Interest rates also interact closely with currency rates: they are two of the most volatile features of world financial markets. To protect against their fluctuations and other price movements, many investors and companies employ a variety of risk management techniques which in turn offer speculative opportunities. This leads to the subject of the next chapter, the market for futures, options and other derivative assets.

"A derivative is like a razor. You can use it to shave yourself and make yourself attractive for your girlfriend. You can slit her throat with it. Or you can use it to commit suicide."

James Morgan

"Read Ben Graham and Phil Fisher, read annual reports, but don't do equations with Greek letters in them."

Warren Buffett

13

Futures and options

The derivatives markets

- **The international markets for derivatives** – futures and options become an integral part of the international capital markets
- **Options** – the right to buy or sell an underlying asset: reading the figures and using the information on LIFFE equity options
- **Financial futures** – agreements to buy or sell a standard quantity of an underlying asset at a future date: bond derivatives; interest rate derivatives; interest rate swaps; currency derivatives; stock index futures and options

The complexity of our modern lives and the numerous decisions we are able to take are only made possible by our ability to manage risks – the risk of house fire; the risk of losing a job; the risk to the entrepreneur who invests in a business; the risk to the farmer who plants a crop that will have an uncertain yield and be sold at an uncertain price in several months time; the risk to the investor in the stock market; and so on.

For each of these problems, society has found solutions. For example, most people agree that house insurance and unemployment insurance increase social well-being. The role of futures markets in insuring farmers against commodity price uncertainty is also understood to increase welfare. Equally, the role of the stock market in enabling the risks of businesses to be shared is now well understood – as indeed is the role of diversification in enabling investors to achieve the minimum risk for the returns generated on their portfolios.

But such widespread public acceptance is almost certainly not true of derivatives, and their role as a means for managing risk through the financial markets is frequently misunderstood. This may, in part, be due to the idiosyncratic nature of the instruments themselves, as illustrated by a number of controversial episodes: the failure of portfolio insurance in the 1987 stock market crash; their misuse in the cases of Barings, Gibson Greetings Cards, Metallgesellschaft, Orange County, California, and Procter & Gamble; and the near failure in 1998 of the hedge fund Long Term Capital Management, whose board included the pioneers of option pricing, 1997 Nobel Laureates for economics, Robert Merton and Myron Scholes.

Yet these instruments – futures, options and a multitude of variations on these themes – are packages of the basic components of risk: they more than anything else traded come close to the theoretically ideal instruments for the trading of risk. On the one hand, insurance can be a cost borne to eliminate a negative occurrence, accidental or structural, an outcome you cannot tolerate. On the other hand, it becomes a tool to shape a risk–return relationship, unique to each investor, from quite common investment alternatives. Derivatives can turn stocks into bonds and vice versa. And derivatives can pinpoint very precisely specific risks and returns that are packaged within a complex structure.

The standard definition of a derivative is an asset the performance of which is based on (derived from) the behaviour of the price of an underlying asset (often simply known as the "underlying"). Underlying assets (traded in what is known as the cash market) may be shares, bonds, currencies, interest rates or commodities, but in each case the assets themselves do not need to be bought or sold.

A derivative product can be either "exchange traded" where a contract is bought or sold on a recognised exchange, or it can be "over the counter" (OTC). An OTC instrument is "written" (sold) by a financial institution and tailored to suit the requirements of the client. Swaps where borrowers exchange the type of funds most easily raised for the type of funds that are required (based either on currency or interest rate considerations), usually through the medium of a bank intermediary, are a key OTC instrument.

■ The international markets for derivatives

Over the past 25 years or so, financial futures and options have established themselves as an integral part of the international capital markets. While futures and options originated in the commodities business, the concept was applied to financial securities in the United States in the early 1970s. Currency futures grew out of the collapse of the Bretton Woods fixed exchange rate system, and heralded the growth of a wide variety of financial instruments designed to capture the advantages or minimise the risks of an increasingly volatile financial environment. Now these products are traded around the world by a wide variety of institutions.

Financial Times' coverage of the derivatives markets focuses primarily on those products traded on exchanges such as the London International Financial Futures Exchange (LIFFE, pronounced "life") and the two oldest and biggest exchanges, the Chicago Mercantile Exchange (CME) and the Chicago Board of Trade (CBT). There are over 40 recognised, regulated exchanges worldwide.

The underlying cash instruments, be they bonds, equities, indices, interest rates or foreign exchange, are becoming ever more closely linked in price and trading patterns to the derivative instruments. In some markets, the turnover in derivatives is many times greater than turnover in the underlying products.

Essentially, futures and options provide alternative vehicles both for trading and for the management of a diverse set of financial risks. They are thus of benefit to financial market participants ranging from securities houses that are trading shares and government bonds for their own accounts, to multinational companies that wish to manage their foreign exchange or interest rate exposure.

Investment managers, for example, tend to use derivatives in two ways. One is in deciding on the appropriate allocation of assets within their portfolios. In this case, exposure to a particular market can be changed for a time at perhaps 5 or 10 per cent of the cost of dealing in the underlying cash market, making it economically viable to change exposure for short periods. The second role is in fund management where futures and options can be used to modify risk/return profiles, a form of insurance against a downturn in the market.

Other financial institutions tend to use derivatives as sources of income. In the Barings incident in February 1995, for example, it was, apparently, Nick Leeson's job to exploit small differences in prices by buying financial instruments on one Far East exchange and selling those same instruments on another exchange, the process of arbitrage. In fact, it appears he became involved in one-way speculation. In January and February 1995, he effectively took a one-way bet on Japanese equities through increasingly heavy purchases of Nikkei 225 futures contracts on both the Osaka and Tokyo exchanges. The bet became horribly unstuck due to a sustained period of weakness in the Japanese equity market. And it was this incident that brought derivatives to the attention of a wider public than narrow professional finance circles, leading them to be labelled "the wild card of international finance".

The rest of this chapter examines the various futures and options contracts on which data and analysis are published in the *Financial Times*. Readers seeking greater detail on the full range of derivative instruments, as well as examples of how they work in practice, are referred to Francesca Taylor's *Mastering Derivatives Markets* (Financial Times/ Prentice Hall) and to Lawrence Galitz's *Financial Engineering: Tools and Techniques to Manage Financial Risk* (Financial Times/Prentice Hall).

■ Options

Options are derivative securities: they derive their value from the value of underlying assets. In the case of financial options, these underlying assets may be bonds, interest rates, currencies, individual stocks or stock groupings, or indices such as the FTSE 100. An option on an asset represents the right to buy or sell that asset at a predetermined price (the striking, strike or exercise price) at a pre-determined future date (in the case of a European-style option) or by a predetermined future date (in the case of an American-style option). It is important to note that an option conveys the right, but not the requirement, to buy or sell.

The seller (generally known as the writer) of a put (an option to sell) or a call (an option to buy) receives a premium upfront from the option buyer. Other than this premium, there is no further exchange of money until and unless the option is exercised, either at or before expiration. If, say, over the life of a European-style call option, the price of the underlying asset rises above the striking price of the option, the option is said to be "in the money": the buyer can exercise the option at expiration and receive a profit equal to the difference between the option striking price and the actual price of the underlying assets, less the premium paid to the option writer. An in the money option is said to have intrinsic value.

If the call is "out of the money" or "at the money", that is, the underlying asset price is below or at the striking price, the option buyer will generally choose not to exercise the option. Nothing will be earned from the option position, and a loss will be incurred equal to the premium paid to the option writer. Before expiry, any option still has time value, the possibility that it will be worth exercising; at expiry, it only has intrinsic value left and if it is out of the money (or, as some analysts say, "under water"), then it has no intrinsic value.

On the other side of the transaction, the option writer receives the premium paid by the buyer. This represents clear profit if the option remains unexercised. However, the option writer also assumes the risk of having to sell the underlying asset at a striking price significantly below actual market price or to buy the underlying asset at a striking price significantly above the actual market price. In either of these cases, the loss suffered by the option writer at the exercise of the option can overwhelm any premium received for writing the option. It is potentially limitless.

LIFFE equity options

The LIFFE is the primary market for options and futures in the United Kingdom. It provides facilities for trading in derivatives contracts on stocks, stock indices, bonds, currencies and interest rates. Until 1992, the London Traded Option Market was a separate entity that dealt in equity option contracts, but it is now a part of the LIFFE. Nevertheless, the *Financial Times* continues to list price and trading data on equity and other financial derivatives separately. LIFFE equity options (traded options) are shown in Figure 13.1:

Closing price of the share in the stock market

Striking price for this line of options

Premiums for call options with an October exercise date

Premiums for put options with an October exercise date

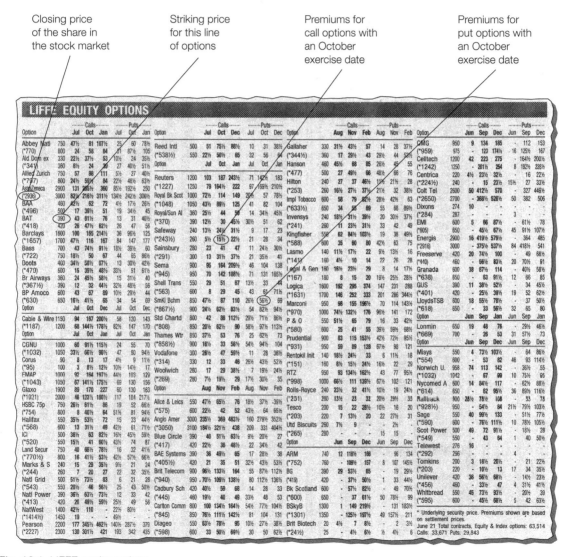

Fig. 13.1 LIFFE equity options

Reading the figures

- **Option:** the first column lists the security from which the options are derived and its closing price in the cash market on the previous day. For example, in this table, shares in Pearson closed at 2227 pence.

- **Striking price:** the second column gives the option series quoted. For Pearson, there are two series, one with a striking price of 2200 pence, the other with a striking price of 2300 pence. Thus, one is lower than the current cash market price, the other higher.

- **Calls:** the third, fourth and fifth columns give the price or premiums payable for call options that can be exercised on three different dates. For Pearson, the price of a 2200 pence call option that expires in October is $345\frac{1}{2}$ pence, while a 2300 option that expires in the same month costs $301\frac{1}{2}$ pence.

- **Puts:** the last three columns give the premiums payable for put options that can again be exercised on three dates in the future.

Using the information

The buyer of an option is willing to risk a limited amount (the premium) in exchange for an uncertain reward (the possibility of buying at some level below or selling at some level above the market price), whereas the option writer is willing to accept an offsetting, uncertain risk (having to sell at some level below or buy at some level above the market price) in return for a certain reward (the option premium).

Option contracts, like insurance policies, are used to protect the investor, whether writer or buyer, from unacceptable risk. The option buyer is in a position analogous to that of the owner of an insurance policy; the uncovered option writer is like the insurance underwriter who accepts risk in return for premium income.

For most investors and companies, options are protection against wide price fluctuations. For dealers and speculators, they are an opportunity for big profits.

As an investment, call options are highly geared so that a small change in the underlying asset value has a significant effect on the option value. Put options on the other hand are more of a hedging strategy protecting against the fall of stock or portfolio value by establishing a floor price below which they cannot fall.

As in the currency markets, it is important in the options markets to have liquidity, and so the *Financial Times'* reports often focus on the turnover in the option markets.

Financial futures

A financial futures contract is an agreement to buy or sell a standard quantity of a certain financial instrument or foreign currency at a future date and at a price agreed between two parties. Trades are usually executed on an exchange floor with buyers and sellers grouped together in a pit shouting at each other in what is termed "open outcry". Increasingly, exchanges are developing automated systems that allow trading to take place on computer screens. The financial guarantee is generally provided by a central clearing house, which stands between buyer and seller and guarantees the trade.

Futures and options are leveraged instruments. This means that for a relatively small down payment (margin for futures, premium for options), participants gain a disproportionately large exposure to price movements in the underlying cash market, hence their appeal as a trading vehicle. They are also used to a large extent as a hedging mechanism. For example, if a US multinational company incurs a significant exposure to the euro through the nature of its export markets, but also believes that the dollar will appreciate against the euro over coming months, the treasurer might wish to sell euro futures to cover the company's risk. Losses incurred by lower revenues should then be at least partially offset by gains from selling the future.

An investor might also use futures to hedge a portfolio, most commonly using index futures, which are futures on major market indices. For example, if the market is expected to fall, selling stock index futures can protect portfolio value: if the market does fall, the loss on the actual stocks is compensated by the profits of buying back the futures at a reduced price.

The relationship between the futures and cash markets is kept stable by the arbitragers who seek out discrepancies between the prices. Generally, futures trade a little above the cash price, reflecting the time and risk premiums. If, for example, there are expectations of a market rise and the future and cash prices are equivalent, money goes into the futures, driving up its price relative to the cash price.

Bond derivatives

The International Capital Markets and Currencies and Money pages of the *Financial Times* feature details of a wide range of commonly traded financial derivatives. For example, under World Bond Prices, there are prices for futures and options on French, German, Spanish, UK, US, Japanese and euro-denominated bonds (see Figure 13.2). For the most part, these are traded on the LIFFE, its French and Spanish equivalents (the MATIF and the MEFF), the Chicago Board of Trade and the Eurex, the new and rapidly growing German–Swiss electronic exchange, which has already overtaken LIFFE as the world's largest derivatives market.

BOND FUTURES AND OPTIONS
France

■ NOTIONAL EURO BOND FUTURES (MATIF) €100,000

	Open	Sett price	Change	High	Low	Est. vol.	Open int.
Sep	87.38	87.20	-0.06	87.38	86.86	244,382	490,784
Dec	-	86.65	-0.04	-	-		

Germany
■ NOTIONAL EURO BUND FUTURES (EUREX) €100,000 100ths of 100%

	Open	Sett price	Change	High	Low	Est. vol	Open int.
Sep	105.77	105.57	-0.09	105.77	105.26	712,412	579,396
Dec	105.41	105.28	-0.11	105.41	105.00	2,088	28,606

■ NOTIONAL EURO BUND (BOBL) FUTURES (EUREX) €100,000 100ths of 100%

	Open	Sett price	Change	High	Low	Est. vol	Open int.
Sep	103.25	103.13	-0.09	103.28	102.98	213,371	282,086

Spain
■ NOTIONAL SPANISH BOND FUTURES (MEFF) €100,000

	Open	Sett price	Change	High	Low	Est. vol.	Open int.
Sep	89.41	89.40	-0.06	89.50	89.12	2,543	12,758

UK
■ NOTIONAL UK GILT FUTURES (LIFFE)* £100,000 100ths of 100%

	Open	Close	Change	High	Low	Est. vol	Open int.
Sep	113.46	113.44	+0.04	113.63	113.04	12959	60506
Dec		113.20	+0.04			0	110

All Open interest figs. are for previous day.

■ LONG GILT FUTURES OPTIONS (LIFFE) £100,000 100ths of 100%

Strike Price	CALLS Sep	Oct	Nov	PUTS Sep	Oct	Nov
11250	1.31	1.40	1.67	0.37	0.70	0.97
11300	0.98	1.12	1.39	0.54	0.92	1.19
11350	0.71	0.87	1.15	0.77	1.17	1.45
11400	0.48	0.67	0.94	1.04	1.47	1.74
11450	0.30	0.50	0.75	1.36	1.80	2.05
11500	0.17	0.36	0.60	1.73	2.16	2.40

Est. vol. total, Calls 0 Puts 0. Previous day's open int., Calls 109 Puts 378

US
■ US TREASURY BOND FUTURES (CBT) $100,000 32nds of 100%

	Open	Sett price	Change	High	Low	Est. vol.	Open int.
Sep	99-02	99-12	+0-11	99-15	98-28	192,389	395,429
Dec	99-10	99-11	+0-11	99-13	99-03	2,996	10,963
Mar	99-11	99-10	+0-11	99-11	99-07	8	1,410

Japan
■ NOTIONAL LONG TERM JAPANESE GOVT. BOND FUTURES (LIFFE) Y100m 100ths of 100%

	Open	Sett price	Change	High	Low	Est. vol	Open int.
Sep	133.82	133.94	-	133.98	133.82	918	n/a
Dec	133.22	133.31	-	133.32	133.22	71	n/a

Euro
■ € 5 Year BOND FUTURES (MATIF) €100,000

	Open	Sett price	Change	High	Low	Est. vol.	Open int.
Sep	-	93.14	-	-	-	-	-

■ NOTIONAL EURO BUND OPTIONS €100,000 (EUREX)

Strike Price	CALLS Sep	Oct	Nov	PUTS Sep	Oct	Nov
104.5	1.30	1.39	1.61	0.15	0.46	0.67
105.0	1.01	-	1.30	0.28	-	0.89
105.5	0.64	0.75	1.04	0.47	-	1.12
106.0	0.39	0.60	-	0.71	-	-

Est. vol. total, Calls 26,517 Puts 27,702 . Previous day's open int., Calls n/a Puts n/a

■ NOTIONAL EFB SWAP FUTURES (LIFFE)* 5yr 4.0% €100,000 100ths of 100%

	Open	Sett price	Change	High	Low	Est. vol	Open int.
Sep		99.32	-0.03			0	0

■ NOTIONAL EFB SWAP FUTURES (LIFFE)* 10yr 4.5% €100,000 100ths of 100%

	Open	Sett price	Change	High	Low	Est. vol	Open int.
Sep		101.05	-0.14			0	0

* Listed on LIFFE CONNECT™. All open interest figs. are for previous day.

Fig. 13.2 Bond futures and options

- **Bond and date:** the name of the future indicates the underlying bond on which it is based, in the case of the UK bond future a notional UK gilt worth £100,000; the date in the first column of the bond futures is when the contract will be finally settled.

- **Face value and calibration:** for most bond futures, there is a nominal face value, in the case of the US Treasury bond future, $100,000. That price is a notional one, the owner paying (or receiving if the future price is below 100 per cent) only the difference between that and the futures contract price. The price on this future is calibrated in 32nds, that is, the price can move by a minimum of one 32nd of 100 per cent.

- **Opening, settlement price, change, high and low:** for bond futures, information on the price at which contracts began trading in the morning (not necessarily the same as the previous day's closing price); the current settlement price (yesterday's closing price, the price at which the contract would currently be settled); the change on the previous day's closing price; and highs and lows reached during the day's trading.

- **Estimated volume and open interest:** the estimated number of contracts actually exchanged during the day, and the number in which traders have expressed interest in buying or selling on the previous day. Not all contracts in which there is open interest are actually traded: they do not become part of estimated volume.

- **Options:** as with equity options, premiums for call and put options with a range of different striking prices and maturities, plus estimated volume and open interest details. Some of these options, like the UK long gilt futures option, are options to buy futures.

Interest rate derivatives

The Currencies and Money page carries similar tables for interest rate futures and options (see Figure 13.3), including futures and options on three-month Euribor and Euro LIBOR, Euroyen; Euro-Swiss francs, Eurodollars, US Treasury bills and three-month and short sterling. Interest rate derivatives can be used to cover any interest rate risk, from an overnight exposure to one lasting 25 years. Interest rate risk is either of increased funding costs for borrowers or of reduced yields for investors.

An example of how these contracts work, and one of particular interest to companies and financial institutions in the United Kingdom is the short sterling futures market. The short sterling futures contract is based on a notional three-month deposit transaction. Its price is equal to 100 minus whatever interest rate is expected by the market when the three-month contract expires. Hence the price of the contract rises when interest rates fall. The market also gives an indication of interest rate expectations, which is valuable for policy-makers and other forecasters.

Short sterling traders can use the market to protect themselves against possible interest rate movements, effectively fixing the interest rate at which they borrow or lend. For example, a lender who fears rate falls can buy short sterling contracts expiring in three months: if by then rates have not fallen the lender has lost nothing; if they have

■ THREE MONTH STERLING FUTURES (LIFFE) £500,000 100 - rate

	Open	Sett price	Change	High	Low	Est. vol	Open int.
Jul	93.730	93.730	-	93.740	93.730	757	3660
Dec	93.500	93.530	+0.020	93.540	93.490	8791	187557
Mar	93.410	93.450	+0.030	93.460	93.410	9379	106782
Jun	93.330	93.370	+0.030	93.380	93.320	3693	67284
Sep	93.260	93.310	+0.020	93.320	93.260	5119	63894

All Open interest figs. are for previous day.

■ SHORT STERLING OPTIONS (LIFFE) £500,000 100 - rate

Strike	CALLS			PUTS		
Price	Sep	Dec	Mar	Sep	Dec	Mar
93500	0.210	0.210	0.245	0.040	0.180	0.295
93625	0.125	0.150		0.080	0.245	
93750	0.060	0.100	0.140	0.140	0.320	0.440
93875	0.025	0.065		0.230	0.410	
94000	0.010	0.040	0.075	0.345	0.510	0.625
94125	0.005	0.025		0.460	0.620	

Est. vol. total, Calls 7211 Puts 1960. Previous day's open int., Calls 221905 Puts 230838

■ THREE MONTH EURODOLLAR (CME) $1m points of 100%

	Open	Sett price	Change	High	Low	Est. vol	Open int.
Sep	93.02	93.03	+0.01	93.04	93.02	48,161	625,718
Dec	92.79	92.83	+0.03	92.84	92.79	60,429	501,766
Mar	92.80	92.83	+0.04	92.83	92.78	51,823	374,107

■ US TREASURY BILL FUTURES (CME) $1m per 100%

	Open	Sett price	Change	High	Low	Est. vol	Open int.
Sep	93.94	93.91	+0.02	93.94	93.91	3	532

■ THREE MONTH EURIBOR FUTURES (MATIF)Paris Interbank offered rate

	Open	Sett price	Change	High	Low	Est. vol	Open int.
Sep	95.200	95.200	-0.016	95.200	95.186	215	8,621
Dec	94.850	94.876	-0.014	94.880	94.850	30	13,090

■ THREE MONTH EURIBOR FUTURES (LIFFE) €1m 100 - rate

	Open	Sett price	Change	High	Low	Est. vol	Open int.
Sep	95.200	95.200	-0.015	95.225	95.170	65303	357008
Dec	94.870	94.875	-0.015	94.905	94.840	46144	238666
Mar	94.820	94.805	-0.015	94.835	94.770	39057	168279
Jun	94.720	94.710	-0.020	94.740	94.670	23559	105866
Sep	94.650	94.645	-0.025	94.670	94.605	19841	99431
Dec	94.545	94.545	-0.025	94.565	94.500	7209	59789

■ THREE MONTH EURO LIBOR FUTURES (LIFFE) €1m 100 - rate

	Open	Sett price	Change	High	Low	Est. vol	Open int.
Sep		95.200	-0.015			0	40535
Dec		94.875	-0.015			0	15640

■ EURIBOR OPTIONS (LIFFE) €1m 100 - rate

Strike	CALLS				PUTS			
Price	Jul	Dec	Mar	Jun	Jul	Dec	Mar	Jun
95125	0.100	0.085			0.025	0.335		
95250	0.035	0.055	0.085	0.110	0.085	0.430	0.530	0.650
95375	0.010	0.030			0.185	0.530		
95500	0.005	0.020	0.040	0.060	0.305	0.645	0.735	0.850

Est. vol. total, Calls 15544 Puts 4787. Previous day's open int., Calls 432507 Puts 302190

■ THREE MONTH EURO LIBOR OPTIONS (LIFFE) €1m 100 - rate

Strike	CALLS				PUTS			
Price	Jul	Dec	Mar	Jun	Jul	Dec	Mar	Jun
95125	0.100	0.075			0.025	0.325		
95250	0.030	0.045	0.070	0.100	0.080	0.420	0.515	0.640
95375	0.005	0.025			0.180	0.525		
95500	0	0.015	0.030	0.050	0.300	0.640	0.725	0.840

Est. vol. total, Calls 0 Puts 0. Previous day's open int., Calls 0 Puts 0

■ THREE MONTH EURO SWISS FRANC FUTURES (LIFFE) SFr1m 100 - rate

	Open	Sett price	Change	High	Low	Est. vol	Open int.
Sep	96.200	96.260	+0.030	96.290	96.190	8562	58730
Dec	95.810	95.870	+0.020	95.890	95.810	3221	36393
Mar	95.850	95.900	+0.030	95.920	95.850	1523	17147
Jun		95.820	+0.030			0	5209

■ THREE MONTH EUROYEN FUTURES (LIFFE) Ұ100m 100 - rate

	Open	Sett price	Change	High	Low	Est. vol	Open int.
Sep		99.690	-0.005			0	n/a
Dec		99.570	+0.005			0	n/a
Mar		99.480	+0.005			0	n/a

■ EURO SWISS FRANC OPTIONS (LIFFE) SFr1m 100 - rate

Strike	CALLS			PUTS		
Price	Sep	Dec	Mar	Sep	Dec	Mar
96500	0.055	0.035	0.070	0.295	0.665	0.670
96625	0.030	0.020		0.395	0.775	

Est. vol. total, Calls 0 Puts 0. Previous day's open int., Calls 750 Puts 0

Fig. 13.3 Interest rate futures and options

fallen, the lower return on the investment is offset by a rise in the price of the futures contract. Similarly, a borrower fearing a rate rise could hedge the risk by selling short sterling futures: if rates do rise, the contracts can be bought back at a lower price, offsetting the higher interest costs. Speculators can use the markets for gambles on future rate movements.

The information provided in the tables for futures contracts includes the month in which the contract will finally be settled; the opening price of the contract on the latest day of trading; the settlement price, which is the closing price used for determining profits and losses for marking accounts to market; the change on the previous day's price; the day's high and low prices; the trading volume; and the open interest, the sum of outstanding long and short positions, which gives an indication of market depth.

The tables for options show the premiums for put and call options with a range of different striking prices and maturities

Interest rate swaps

Interest rate and currency swaps are a relatively recent innovation but they now dwarf other financial instruments. At the end of 1999, there was $46 trillion worth of swaps outstanding compared with $5.4 billion in international bond markets.

An interest rate swap is an agreement in which two parties (known as counterparties) agree to exchange periodic interest rate payments. The actual amount of the interest payments exchanged is based on a predetermined principal, called the notional principal amount. But the only money that is exchanged is the interest payments on this amount. In the most common type of swap, one party agrees to pay the other party fixed interest payments at designated dates for the life of the contract. The other party agrees to make interest payments that float according to an agreed index such as LIBOR.

Swaps are a useful tool. Banks, for example, can use them to match their assets and liabilities more closely. If they have lots of short-term floating rate liabilities such as savings accounts but long-term fixed rate assets such as loans, they can swap long-term assets into short-term ones. Similarly, companies can use swaps to convert fixed rate debt (which investors might prefer and which is therefore easier to raise) into floating rate debt.

A daily table published in the FT shows benchmark interest rates for swaps in five different currencies and for a range of different durations (see Figure 13.4).

Currency derivatives

The Currencies and Money page also contains listings for currency futures on euros, Swiss francs, yen and sterling and options on the sterling/dollar and euro/dollar exchange rates listed on the Philadelphia Stock Exchange (see Figure 13.5). These can be used for managing currency risk, the danger of receiving a smaller amount of the base currency than expected, or paying out more of the base currency to purchase a required

INTEREST RATE SWAPS

Aug 03	Euro-€ Bid	Ask	£ Stlg Bid	Ask	SwFr Bid	Ask	US $ Bid	Ask	Yen Bid	Ask
1 year	5.23	5.27	6.49	6.52	3.98	4.01	6.99	7.02	0.32	0.35
2 year	5.40	5.44	6.48	6.52	4.11	4.19	7.03	7.06	0.49	0.52
3 year	5.50	5.54	6.54	6.58	4.15	4.23	7.05	7.08	0.72	0.75
4 year	5.56	5.60	6.54	6.59	4.18	4.26	7.06	7.09	0.95	0.98
5 year	5.62	5.66	6.53	6.58	4.20	4.28	7.08	7.11	1.17	1.20
6 year	5.67	5.71	6.52	6.57	4.23	4.31	7.10	7.13	1.37	1.40
7 year	5.72	5.76	6.50	6.55	4.27	4.35	7.12	7.15	1.54	1.57
8 year	5.77	5.81	6.47	6.52	4.30	4.38	7.13	7.16	1.69	1.72
9 year	5.80	5.84	6.44	6.49	4.34	4.42	7.15	7.18	1.81	1.84
10 year	5.83	5.87	6.42	6.47	4.37	4.45	7.17	7.20	1.92	1.95
12 year	5.88	5.92	6.36	6.43	4.41	4.51	7.19	7.22	2.09	2.12
15 year	5.95	5.99	6.26	6.35	4.47	4.57	7.20	7.23	2.28	2.31
20 year	6.02	6.06	6.07	6.20	4.53	4.63	7.19	7.22	2.41	2.44
25 year	6.03	6.07	5.93	6.06	4.56	4.66	7.16	7.19	2.44	2.47
30 year	6.02	6.06	5.83	5.96	4.58	4.68	7.14	7.17	2.47	2.50

Bid and ask rates as of close of London business. US $ is quoted annual money actual/360 basis against 3 months Libor, £ and Yen quoted on a semi-annual actual/365 basis against 6 months Libor, Euro/Swiss Franc quoted on annual bond 30/360 basis against 6 month Euribor/Libor with the exception of the 1 year rate which is quoted against 3 month Euribor/Libor. Source: Garban-Intercapital plc

Fig. 13.4 Interest rate swaps

■ EURO € FUTURES (CME) €125,000 ($ per €)

	Open	Sett price	Change	High	Low	Est. vol	Open int.
Sep	0.9408	0.9430	+0.0019	0.9444	0.9343	9,433	54,954
Dec	0.9433	0.9482	+0.0019	0.9490	0.9433	2	628
Mar	-	0.9533	+0.0019	0.9535	0.9485	15	35

■ SWISS FRANC FUTURES (CME) SFr 125,000 ($ per SFr)

Sep	0.6077	0.6106	+0.0025	0.6118	0.6053	8,702	33,813
Dec	0.6127	0.6156	+0.0025	0.6165	0.6122	19	61
Mar	-	0.6204	+0.0025	-	-	8	1

■ JAPANESE YEN FUTURES (CME) Yen 12.5m ($ per Yen 100)

	Open	Sett price	Change	High	Low	Est. vol	Open int.
Sep	0.9707	0.9605	-0.0097	0.9740	0.9600	14,434	47,495
Dec	0.9770	0.9770	-0.0097	0.9770	0.9760	35	3,055
Mar	-	0.9932	-0.0097	-	-	25	46

■ STERLING FUTURES (CME) £62,500 ($ per £)

Sep	1.5032	1.5014	-0.0046	1.5056	1.4992	8,441	27,679
Dec	1.5060	1.5044	-0.0046	1.5060	1.5030	32	270
Mar	-	1.5068	-0.0046	-	1.5080	4	4

■ PHILADELPHIA SE £/$ OPTIONS £31,250 (cents per pound)

Strike Price	CALLS Jul	Aug	Sep	PUTS Jul	Aug	Sep
1.500	1.38	2.14	2.69	1.37	2.13	2.69
1.510	0.93	1.70	2.33	2.00	2.67	3.23
1.520	0.64	1.32	1.83	-	3.28	3.82

Previous day's vol., Calls 0 Puts 0 Prev. day's open int., Calls 1,295Puts 655

■ PHILADELPHIA SE EURO/$ OPTIONS €62,500 (cents per €)

Strike Price	CALLS Jul	Aug	Sep	PUTS Jul	Aug	Sep
0.920	2.23	2.84	3.48	0.37	0.85	1.28
0.940	0.99	1.74	2.36	1.07	1.69	2.12
0.960	0.34	0.97	1.51	2.39	2.83	3.26

Previous day's vol., Calls 11 Puts 31. Prev. day's open int., Calls 2,442Puts 413

Fig. 13.5 Currency futures and options

amount of foreign currency. Alternatively, they may be used by speculators aiming to buy and sell currencies for profit.

Stock index futures and options

Stock index futures and options began to be traded on the LIFFE in 1984. A stock index future is an agreement between two parties to compensate each other for movements in the value of a stock index over the contract period. The value of the stock index is defined as being the value of the index multiplied by a specific monetary amount, the index multiplier or amount per full index point.

A stock index option gives the holder the right but not the obligation to buy or sell an agreed amount of an equity index at a specified price on or before a specified date. A premium is paid for this right. One of the key principles behind stock index futures and options is cash settlement. This is the process used at expiry (or exercise) whereby a cash difference reflecting a price change is transferred, rather than a physical delivery of the underlying basket of shares.

As with all derivatives, both index options and futures can be used for either hedging or speculation. For example, a fund manager wishing to hedge the value of a portfolio when the stock market may fall will sell index futures. Being long in the cash market and short in the futures market will mean that if the market does fall, a nominal loss on the portfolio is compensated by a gain on the futures, which can be bought back at a lower price. A speculator expecting a market fall may sell futures without any underlying exposure, or sell call options on the index, profiting from the premium if the market does fall and the options expire out of the money.

The World Stock Markets page of the FT carries a daily round up of equity futures and options trading, focusing particularly on derivatives based on the FTSE 100 and FTSE 250 indices (see Figure 13.6):

- **Index futures:** as with bond futures, the table includes opening prices, settlement prices, price changes, daily highs and lows, estimated volume and open interest.

- **Index points:** pounds per full index point are a measure of the trading unit, for example, the FTSE 100 index future unit is £10 per index point. This means that when the index is at 6,500, a futures buyer is covering the equivalent of £65,000 of equities. If the index rises 200 points, the buyer can sell a matching contract and make a profit of £2,000.

- **Index options:** as with equity options, the table includes the current value of the underlying index, as well as the premiums for put and call options with a range of different striking prices and maturities.

- **European-style:** this option can only be exercised at the maturity date. Since this date is fixed, the premiums are typically a little lower than for more standard (American-style) options, which can be exercised at any point prior to maturity.

■ FTSE 100 INDEX FUTURES (LIFFE) £10 per full index point

	Open	Sett price	Change	High	Low	Est. vol	Open int.
Sep	6425.0	6477.0	+27.0	6506.0	6406.0	20846	249670
Dec	6529.0	6560.0	+27.0	6581.5	6529.0	24	1424
Mar		6619.5	+27.0			0	250

■ FTSE 250 INDEX FUTURES (LIFFE) £10 per full index point

		Sett price	Change			Est. vol	Open int.
Sep		6623.0	+53.0			0	946
Dec		6684.0	+53.0			0	0

■ FTSE 100 INDEX OPTION (LIFFE) (6405*) £10 per full index point   26 Jun

	6100		6200		6300		6400		6500		6600		6700		6800	
	C	P	C	P	C	P	C	P	C	P	C	P	C	P	C	P
Jul	379½	22½	293½	37½	218	61	150½	95	95½	143½	55	208½	27½	286½	12	379½
Aug	429½	67	353	92½	279	122	218	161½	158½	202	115	254½	75½	319	50½	396
Sep	479½	110	408	133½	331	165	274	202½	216	244½	169½	298½	130½	356½	95½	423
Oct	551	145	482	172	415½	203	361	241½	298	282½	243	334½	197½	397	153½	461
Dec†	638½	194	566	221	497½	254	438	292	382	331	324	374	277½	431½	228	485

Calls 217 ; Puts 776 .

■ EURO STYLE FTSE 100 INDEX OPTION (LIFFE) £10 per full index point   26 Jun

	6125		6225		6325		6425		6525		6625		6725		6825	
	C	P	C	P	C	P	C	P	C	P	C	P	C	P	C	P
Jul	349½	28	267	45	192½	70	129½	106½	79	155½	41½	217½	20	295½	8	383
Aug	396	71	324	98½	255½	128½	189	161½	137	208	94½	265	65	334½	38½	407
Sep	459	112	387	138½	320	170	258½	207½	205	252	157½	303	116½	361	83	426
Dec	619	197	549½	224½	483½	255½	421½	290½	363½	329½	310½	373½	261½	422	218	475
Mar†	739	266½	668½	292	604	323	542½	357	484½	394	428	433½	375½	476½	327½	523½

Calls 11,284; Puts 7,519 . * Underlying index value. Premiums shown are based on settlement prices. † Long dated expiry months.

Fig. 13.6 FTSE index futures and options

The UK market for index futures and options can be used in its own right for speculation, or as an overlay on a portfolio of UK securities in order to hedge its value or to expose it to greater risk and the potential for greater gain. Similarly, derivatives based on foreign market indices can be used to hedge an international portfolio or to gain exposure to those markets. One of the most important is of course the US market, and below the daily table of US indices are prices for futures contracts on a number of key market indices including the S&P 500 index, a series of futures very widely used for hedging and speculative purposes (see Figure 13.7):

EQUITY INDEX FUTURES

21 Aug		Open	Sett price	Change	High	Low	Est. vol.	Open int.
DJIA	Sep	11110.0	11130.0	+35.0	11180.0	11065.0	5,243	13,516
S&P 500	Sep	1501.10	1506.00	+5.20	1509.50	1497.10	37,527	368,364
Mini S&P 500	Sep	1501.00	1506.00	+5.25	1509.75	1497.25	49,751	46,519
Nasdaq 100	Sep	3839.00	3852.00	+16.50	3900.00	3796.00	11,084	33,164
Mini Nasdaq 100	Sep	3837.50	3852.00	+16.50	3900.00	3797.00	31,073	32,052
CAC-40	Aug	6617.0	6597.0	-22.0	6649.5	6550.0	27,761	243,281
DAX	Sep	7275.0	7213.0	-34.5	7275.0	7170.5	23,766	164,824
MIB 30	Sep	47250.0	47317.0	+207.0	47370.0	46880.0	7,804	21,329
AEX	Aug	687.00	691.50	+3.00	691.50	685.90	8,922	15,424
IBEX 35	Aug	11135.0	11104.2	-39.8	11250.0	11049.0	15,128	10,632
SMI	Sep	8292.0	8323.0	+48.0	8325.0	8231.0	10,728	130,953
FTSE 100	Sep	6573.5	6564.5	+2.5	6584.5	6508.0	30,555	281,704
Hang Seng	Aug	17340.0	17550.0	+210.0	17680.0	17340.0	13,361	32,736
Nikkei 225	Sep	16240.0	16040.0	-260.0	16260.0	15940.0	21,807	144,148
KOSPI 200	Sep	91.40	92.30	+0.50	92.75	91.15	74,622	54,090

Open interest figures for previous day.

Fig. 13.7 Equity index futures

Stock index futures of this kind offer a number of advantages to investors and fund managers. First, they permit investment in these markets without the trouble and expense involved in buying the shares themselves. Second, operating under a margin system, like all futures, they allow full participation in market moves without significant commitment of capital. Third, transactions costs are typically many times lower than those for share transactions. Fourth, it is much easier to take a short position. Lastly, fund managers responsible for large share portfolios can hedge their value against bear moves without having to sell the shares themselves.

A final table, carried on the FT's Euro Markets page, provides information on four futures contracts based on the new Eurotop 100, Eurotop 300 and €Stars indices, traded on the LIFFE, plus a European-style options contract on the Eurotop 100, traded on AEX or Amsterdam Exchanges (see Figure 13.8). Amsterdam Exchanges, the result of a merger between the Amsterdam Stock Exchange and the European Option Exchange, is the central Dutch market for trading in stocks, bonds, options and futures.

■ **FTSE EUROTOP 300 INDEX FUTURES** (LIFFE) €20 per full index point

	Open	Sett price	Change	High	Low	Est. vol	Open int.
Sep		1597.0	-21.0			0	0

■ **FTSE EUROTOP 300 EX UK INDEX FUTURES** (LIFFE) €20 per full index point

	Open	Sett price	Change	High	Low	Est. vol	Open int.
Sep		1752.0	-16.0			0	0

■ **FTSE EUROTOP 100 INDEX FUTURES** (LIFFE) €20 per full index point

	Open	Sett price	Change	High	Low	Est. vol	Open int.
Sep	3762.5	3733.5	-46.5	3762.5	3733.0	115	9352

■ **EURO STYLE FTSE EUROTOP 100 INDEX OPTION** (AEX) €10 per index point

	355		360		365		370		375		380		385		390	
	C	P	C	P	C	P	C	P	C	P	C	P	C	P	C	P
Jul	21	3	17	4	13	5	10	7	7	9	5	12	3	15	2	19
Aug	-	-	20	7	-	-	14	10	11	13	8	15	7	18	5	22

Est vol total:0 . Prev day's open interest total: 6,222 . Premiums shown are based on settlement prices.

■ **FTSE €STARS INDEX FUTURES** (LIFFE) €10 per full index point

	Open	Sett price	Change	High	Low	Est. vol	Open int.
Sep		4288.0	-27.0			0	80

Fig. 13.8 Eurotop index derivatives

A typical report on the UK equity futures and options market looks like this, an analysis of a key index future:

Furious technical trading dominated derivatives activity as dealers wrestled with the biggest ever open interest in Footsie futures. Almost 60,000 lots changed hands in the September contract on the Footsie, which expires next Friday. Half of the business represented traders rolling forward positions into December. September, which has an estimated fair value premium to cash of 8.3, ended 30 higher than the cash market. It was also out of line with its fair value spread to December, which is calculated at 84. By the end of after-hours dealing, the two contracts were 94 points apart.

(*Financial Times*, 7 September 2000)

The report indicates the impact of the underlying cash markets and the direct relationship between the FTSE 100 future and the cash instrument, the index itself. A future is generally assumed to be at a fair value premium, the correct reflection of its value as determined by the time to maturity and the risk. Here it is above fair value, suggesting it might go down, perhaps as arbitragers sell it and buy the index.

Economic news and other financial markets are crucial in determining futures market behaviour. Similarly, their ability to spread risk and deliver exceptional profits makes the derivatives markets increasingly central to financial activity and a major influence on the world economy.

"Gold, the barbarous relic."

John F Kennedy

"Gold, part of the apparatus of conservatism."

John Maynard Keynes

14

Primary products

The commodities markets

- **London spot markets** – commodities available for immediate delivery
- **Commodity futures markets** – opportunities for hedging and speculation in the markets for "softs": cocoa, coffee and sugar; other commodities, including oil
- **Metals** – precious and base metals: the London Metal Exchange; reading the figures and using the information on gold and the London bullion market; other metals
- **Other key commodity markets** – London traded options; the markets in New York and Chicago; commodity price indices

Commodities are basic raw materials, primary products and foodstuffs that are homogeneous and generally traded on a free market. Commodity contracts may represent cash transactions for immediate delivery, or, more commonly, forward contracts for delivery at a specified time in the future. The bulk of such contracts are bought and sold on a commodities exchange by dealers and commodity brokers or traders. Their homogeneity, coupled with fast communications and an efficient system of quality grading and control, means that they can be traded without an actual transfer of the goods. This allows enormous scope for hedging and speculative activity as traders buy and sell rights of ownership in spot and futures markets. Commodities were in fact the origin of the derivatives markets discussed in the previous chapter.

As in all free markets, the prices of commodities are determined by the forces of demand and supply. And because of the nature of the conditions of demand and supply for commodities, their prices tend to swing more violently than prices of manufactured goods. A small but persistent surplus of the supply of, say, tin, over demand can cause a dramatic slump in prices; similarly, disastrous weather conditions and a poor harvest can drive up a crop price.

Commodities are primarily of interest to industrial users. Oil is the one with the most widespread potential impact since almost all businesses have some energy needs, but there are plenty of other examples. Prospective cocoa prices, for instance, are critical to chocolate makers, while certain metal prices will affect such companies as producers of cars, ships and manufactured goods, as well as the construction industry.

Companies whose profitability is partly dependent on the cost of their raw materials will naturally seek protection from potential surges in primary commodity prices. It is this need to hedge that gives rise to the futures markets.

For investors, commodities offer the potential for exceptionally high returns but a very high degree of risk. In addition, investing in physical commodities is rarely possible given the problem and costs of storage. Indeed, few private investors play even the commodities futures markets except through various managed funds, which diversify their risks across a variety of commodities, or by investing in companies in oil, gold mining and other extractive and exploratory industries. The majority of the players in the primary commodity markets are professional speculators who take the opposite side of hedgers' positions. For this small group, the commodity sector is ultimately high risk for high reward.

The *Financial Times*' Commodities and Agriculture page appears from Tuesday to Friday with the upper section devoted to reports on the markets and the lower section to a presentation of the previous day's trading and price data from markets in London, New York and Chicago. The lower section also appears on Saturday with a review of the week in the markets. The commodities markets are dominated by a limited range of players but are important to all markets and the wider economy particularly as a leading indicator of trends and expectations in inflation and equity and bond prices.

London spot markets

Price coverage begins with the London markets for spot goods – commodities available for delivery within two days. Generally, these figures represent the cost of actual physical material, exceptions being the London daily sugar prices and the cotton index, which are guide prices based on a selection of physical price indications. An example of spot markets is shown in Figure 14.1:

LONDON SPOT MARKETS

■ CRUDE OIL FOB (per barrel) +or-

Dubai	$28.42-8.53x	+1.035
Brent Blend (dated)	$30.30-0.35	+0.79
Brent Blend (Jul)	$31.53-1.57	+0.91
W.T.I.	$32.53-2.57x	+1.05

■ OIL PRODUCTS NWE prompt delivery CIF (tonne)

Unleaded Gasoline	$379-381	+1
Gas Oil*	$243-244	+5
Heavy Fuel Oil	$137-139	
Naphtha	$273-275	+2
Jet fuel	$276-277	+4
Diesel ■	$271-274	+3.5

■ NATURAL GAS (Pence/therm)

NBP ‡ (Jul)	16.525-6.725	+0.13

Petroleum Argus. Tel. London 020 7704 4700

■ OTHER

Gold (per troy oz)♣	$290.15	+4.05
Silver (cents per troy oz)♣	508.75	+7.75
Platinum (per troy oz.)	$551.00	+5.00
Palladium (per troy oz.)	$663.00	+21.0
Copper	68.0c	
Lead (US prod.)	45.00c	
Tin (Kuala Lumpur)	19.94r	
Tin (New York)	258.5c	+5.00
Cattle (live weight)	92.65p	+1.21*
Sheep (live weight)	99.61p	-2.67*
Pigs (live weight)†	78.71p	-1.20*
Lon. day sugar (raw)	$206.20	
Lon. day sugar (wte)	$237.50	
Barley (Eng. feed)	Unq	
Maize (US No3 Yellow)	£96.00	
Wheat (US Dark North)	£126.00	+2.00
Rubber (Jul)♥	50.25p	+0.50
Rubber (Aug)♥	50.75p	+0.50
Rubber (KL RSS No1)	261.50m	+1.00
Coconut Oil (Phil)§	$435.00y	-5.00
Palm Oil (Malay.)§	$315.00	+5.00
Copra (Phil)§	$288.00y	+6.00
Soyabeans (US)	153.00	-4.00
Cotton Outlook'A' index	59.35	-0.70
Wooltops (64s Super)	309p	

£ per tonne unless otherwise stated. p pence/kg. c cents/lb. r ringgit/ kg. m Malaysian cents/kg. z Feb/Mar. y May/Jun. x Jul. ♥London Physical. § CIF Rotterdam. ♣ Bullion market close. * Change on week. ‡ National Balancing Point quoted from March 8th. †Based on 2,849 head of pigs sold.*Correction for 7/6/2000 229-230

Fig. 14.1 London spot markets

- **Prices and changes in price from the previous trading day:** figures are given for the principal crude oils, oil products, natural gas, metals, meat, sugar, grains, rubber, vegetable oils and oilseeds, cotton and wool.

■ **Weekly price changes:** Saturday's newspaper adds figures on prices at the close of trading for the week, the change on the previous week, prices one year ago and the highs and lows for the year to date (see Figure 14.2). Half-yearly, the newspaper summarises current prices in key commodity markets as well as prices six months and a year previously.

WEEKLY PRICE CHANGES

	Latest prices	Change on week	Year ago	.... 2000 .... High	Low
Gold per troy oz.	$284.45	+4.20	$259.95	$309.50	$272.00
Silver per troy oz	333.13p	+5.15	316.74p	335.58p	312.15p
Aluminium 99.7% (cash)	$1460.5	+19.5	$1311.5	$1741.5	$1428.5
Copper Grade A (cash)	$1720.0	-25.5	$1414.0	$1850	$1637.5
Lead (cash)	$421.5	+4.00	$496.5	$489	$404.0
Nickel (cash)	$9495	-90	$5170	$10620	$8240
Zinc SHG (cash)	$1094.5	-15.50	$1004.0	$1215	$1080
Tin (cash)	$5462.5	+74.75	$5295	$6105	$5305
Cocoa Futures Jul	£629	-2	£760	£666	£554
Coffee Futures Jul	$923	-31	$1394	$1231	$906
Sugar (LDP Raw)	$199.40	+4.90	$150.0	$194.50	$128.10
Barley Futures Sep	£65.50	+0.50	£72.00	£74.90	£65.50
Wheat Futures Jul	£71.10	+2.10	£81.25	£76.15	£67.75
Cotton Outlook A Index	60.05c	-0.65	59.00c	61.55c	44.00c
Wool (64s Super)	309p	-6	309p	315p	270p
Oil (Brent Blend)	$29.22x	-0.04	$15.625	$29.41	$22.58

Per tonne unless otherwise stated. p Pence/kg. c Cents lb. x Jul

Fig. 14.2 Weekly price changes

■ Commodity futures markets

As indicated, futures markets are chiefly used by consumers of physical commodities to avoid the risks of adverse price movements during the periods between contracting purchases and receiving deliveries. This hedging involves the opening of parallel but opposite futures contracts when physical orders are made, so that physical "profits" or "losses" made by the time the commodity is delivered will be cancelled out by losses or profits on the futures markets.

The futures markets are basically paper markets, not to be confused with forward physical prices, which are simply quotations for physical material for delivery some time in the future. Speculators take on the risk consumers wish to avoid in the hope of accruing the potential profits that the consumer has relinquished.

■ Coffee, cocoa and sugar

The main UK futures market for "soft" commodities (foodstuffs) is the London International Financial Futures and Options Exchange (LIFFE). Its core commodity contracts are in coffee, cocoa and sugar, but it also features other agricultural products (wheat, barley and potatoes), a freight futures contract previously traded on the Baltic Exchange, and some traded options (see below). LIFFE prices for coffee, cocoa and sugar are shown in Figure 14.3, plus prices for softs quoted elsewhere. The table has information on:

- **Contract size and pricing:** after the name of the commodity and the exchange on which it is traded is the size of the contract (how many tonnes, pounds, gallons or bushels of the commodity in a single contract) and the manner of pricing (for example, dollars or pounds per tonne).

- **Date:** the first column lists the expiry dates for the futures contracts currently in issue.

- **Settlement price:** the second column indicates the closing offer prices in the brokers' bid/offer spreads, the price at which they are prepared to sell a specific futures contract in these commodities. As usual with a spread, the bid prices will have been somewhat lower.

- **Day's change:** the third column indicates the change over closing offer prices on the preceding trading day.

- **High and low:** the fourth and fifth columns show the highest and lowest levels at which trades were executed during the day. It is possible for prices to close outside these ranges because they may move further near the end of the day without any business actually being done.

- **Volume:** the sixth column shows the actual number of lots or trading units that changed hands during the day.

- **Open interest:** the last column shows the number of lots of trading units up for sale or purchase during the day, not all of which will have actually been bought or sold.

- **ICCO and ICO:** indicator prices calculated by the International Cocoa Organisation and the International Coffee Organisation. These are related to price support systems, affecting changes in export quotas and buffer stock sales or purchases. Cocoa indicator prices are denominated in Special Drawing Rights (see Chapter 12) to prevent them from being too susceptible to currency movements.

- **Sugar futures:** the market for white (refined) sugar operates on an automated trading system, in which dealers operate from their offices via screens linked to a central computer. This contrasts with the open outcry "ring dealing" system of most other commodity markets.

A typical report on these soft commodity markets looks like this:

> Coffee futures traded on LIFFE hit an eight-year low because of worries about surplus supplies from the main exporter. Vietnam, the world's biggest producer of robusta, has started to harvest its new crop and analysts forecast a return far greater than the 600,000 tonnes seen in the current year.　　　(*Financial Times*, 1 September 2000)

SOFTS

■ COCOA LIFFE (10 tonnes; £/tonne)

	Sett price	Day's change	High	Low	Vol	Open int
Jul	629	+5	638	624	1,239	25,024
Sep	650	+5	659	646	1,305	33,647
Dec	684	+5	693	680	372	38,377
Mar	700	+5	708	698	124	28,759
May	714	+5	723	710	471	18,051
Jul	728	+5	737	737	12	5,396
Total					3,523	177,957

■ COCOA CSCE (10 tonnes; $/tonnes)

Jul	846	-4	866	845	4,999	15,803
Sep	878	-4	899	877	4,893	33,758
Dec	911	-4	931	910	713	21,542
Mar	945	-5	952	952	93	7,930
May	972	-2	990	976	46	5,753
Jul	997	-2	1008	1008	38	7,065
Total					10,703	111,663

■ COCOA (ICCO) (SDR's/tonne)

Jun 9	Price	Prev. day
Daily	700.09	704.19

■ COFFEE LIFFE (5 tonnes; $/tonne)

Jul	891	-19	911	890	2,837	26,486
Sep	909	-17	927	905	2,957	23,094
Nov	923	-17	940	920	562	7,264
Jan	938	-17	954	942	101	2,784
Mar	953	-17	970	960	108	910
May	968	-16	980	980	30	609
Total					6,573	61,147

■ COFFEE 'C' CSCE (37,500lbs; cents/lbs)

Jul	90.80	-0.35	91.35	89.10	5,043	20,523
Sep	94.15	-0.35	94.75	92.70	3,550	21,828
Dec	98.55	-0.30	98.60	97.50	434	6,446
Mar	103.30	-0.05	102.75	102.25	166	2,768
May	105.80	-0.05	106.00	105.00	51	361
Jul	108.30	-0.05	107.50	107.50	36	112
Total					9,204	52,088

■ COFFEE (ICO) (US cents/pound)

Jun 12	Price	Prev. day
Comp. daily	66.25	66.63
15 day average	68.16	68.30

■ WHITE SUGAR LIFFE (50 tonnes; $/tonne)

Aug	239.9	+2.9	240.5	236.2	3,904	22,064
Oct	239.7	+2.9	240.3	236.1	1,128	11,994
Dec	239.7	+2.6	240.2	238.5	296	3,535
Mar	238.8	+2.4	239.5	237.0	154	4,954
May	236.5	+2.3	237.8	237.7	11	971
Aug	233.5	+2.0	235.0	232.7	145	2,138
Total					5,709	46,727

■ SUGAR '11' CSCE (112,000lbs; cents/lbs)

Jul	8.72	+0.23	8.78	8.52	15,859	64,962
Oct	8.80	+0.15	8.84	8.69	12,048	74,859
Mar	8.60	+0.17	8.64	8.48	2,462	39,731
May	8.53	+0.17	8.54	8.41	385	6,589
Jul	8.45	+0.16	8.45	8.33	147	7,135
Oct	8.37	+0.16	8.40	8.25	272	8,627
Total					31,173	205,297

■ COTTON NYCE (50,000lbs; cents/lbs)

Jul	56.98	+0.33	57.95	56.15	6,871	15,510
Oct	60.50	+0.70	60.80	59.50	459	2,737
Dec	61.06	-	62.40	60.90	6,514	22,306
Mar	62.38	-	63.55	62.30	313	3,799
May	63.02	+0.08	63.06	62.92	341	2,158
Jul	63.84	-0.96	63.90	63.84	47	634
Total					14,627	47,717

■ ORANGE JUICE NYCE (15,000lbs; cents/lbs)

Jul	82.40	+0.35	83.20	82.20	983	8,859
Sep	82.50	+0.30	83.00	82.30	829	8,323
Nov	82.60	+0.55	82.80	82.25	23	3,843
Jan	82.60	+0.55	82.90	82.50	15	1,691
Mar	82.75	+0.05	83.50	82.75	11	1,397
May	83.10	+0.10	84.00	84.00	-	256
Total					1,911	24,651

Fig. 14.3 Softs

In this case, the futures prices for coffee have suffered from the likelihood of future surplus of this commodity. The prices are following the simple laws of supply and demand: as supply rises, the price falls.

Other commodities

The *Financial Times* also carries information on the International Petroleum Exchange (IPE) and its futures contracts in crude oil and gas oil. Indeed the North Sea oil price features daily on the front page of the newspaper in its key market summary. This is because of the critical importance of oil prices to the world economy. High and rising prices are typically an indicator of bad times ahead. At the "macro" level, there is the threat to inflation and economic growth. The OECD rule of thumb warns that a $10 increase sustained for a year adds half a percentage point to inflation and knocks quarter of a percentage point off growth. This in turn demands higher interest rates, with their typically negative effects on corporate profitability and share values.

High priced oil also has a direct "micro" effect on profits since it is a significant input in many industries and eventually discourages firms from investing for the future. Airlines are the most obvious victims of the cost of jet fuel increases, but chemical producers that rely on oil as a raw material also suffer. And even service sector companies make some use of energy, whether for travel or simply running their offices. Understandably, the trebling of the price of oil in 2000 was a major news story:

> The price of oil jumped to a 10-year high on Monday as traders predicted this weekend's meeting of the Organisation of Petroleum Exporting Countries would fail to halt market turmoil. In London, the October futures contract for Brent blend finished at $32.80 a barrel, a gain of 95 cents on the day and its highest close since 1990, when prices were buoyed by Iraq's aggression towards Kuwait. Saudi Arabia, the world's leading oil producer, has been under increasing pressure from the US and other oil consumers, to engineer lower crude prices. Oil prices have been rising in recent months because of evidence that the stockpiles of oil in the US, the world's largest consumer of the commodity, are at their lowest for more than 20 years.
>
> (*Financial Times*, 4 September 2000)

Many analysts were extremely concerned by these developments. The last three times oil went over $22 a barrel – in 1973, 1979 and 1990 – the fall in profits tipped the western economies into recession. Of course, there are some beneficiaries: companies in the oil sector itself, plus some of the electricity and gas firms that have both reduced their dependence on oil-powered plant and diversified into oil exploration and production. If alternative energy sources once again become important, companies developing solar, wind and hydro-power may also benefit.

The Commodities and Agriculture page also provides coverage of certain minor markets: tea on Wednesdays, nuts and seeds on Thursdays, wool on Fridays and spices on Saturdays.

■ Metals

■ The London Metal Exchange

The main non-ferrous metals (aluminium, copper, lead, nickel, tin and zinc) are traded on the London Metal Exchange (LME). Although it has always operated as a futures market, the LME has traditionally had a closer relationship with the physical trade than other London markets. It is claimed to account for 70 to 80 per cent of its turnover. Only in 1987 did new investor protection legislation force the LME to abandon its cherished principal trading system in favour of the central clearing system used by the other commodity futures markets. Figure 14.4 shows the LME listing from the commodity prices section of the *Financial Times*. The list of commodity indices (see below) adds a table of LME warehouse stocks of the metals, showing:

- **Close and previous, high and low:** these are price indicators as on the LIFFE, except that for close and previous, both bid and offer prices are shown. The prices are for immediate delivery and for delivery in three months. The futures price is for a standard contract of metal of a defined grade. It is generally higher than the spot price, a phenomenon known as "contango" or "forwardation". The reverse, where the spot price stands at a premium over the futures price, is called "backwardation".

- **AM official:** these are the values of the metals at the end of the morning "ring". The ring opens at 11.50am and closes at 1pm with a ten-minute interval starting at 12.20pm. It is followed by 25 minutes of after-hours dealing, known as the kerb session because it used to be conducted on the street outside the exchange. Prices at the close of the official ring are widely used for industrial supply contract pricing.

- **Kerb close:** the afternoon "unofficial" ring begins at 3.20pm and ends at 4.30pm. Kerb trading continues until 5pm with each metal phasing out from 4.45pm. This column carries the final prices from this session.

- **Open interest:** the number of trading lots that remain to be covered by opposite transactions or physical delivery. Lot sizes are 25 tonnes, except for nickel which is six tonnes.

- **Total daily turnover:** the number of trading lots traded that day.

- **Closing:** the last line of the LME table gives the sterling/dollar rates published by the exchange at the unofficial close. This can be used to translate LME prices for contract purposes.

■ Gold

Twice a day, at 10.30am and 3pm, representatives of the major bullion dealers meet at the offices of NM Rothschild to set the fixing price of a troy ounce of gold, and a substantial number of transactions tends to take place at the fixing sessions. Figure 14.5 shows the London bullion market listing.

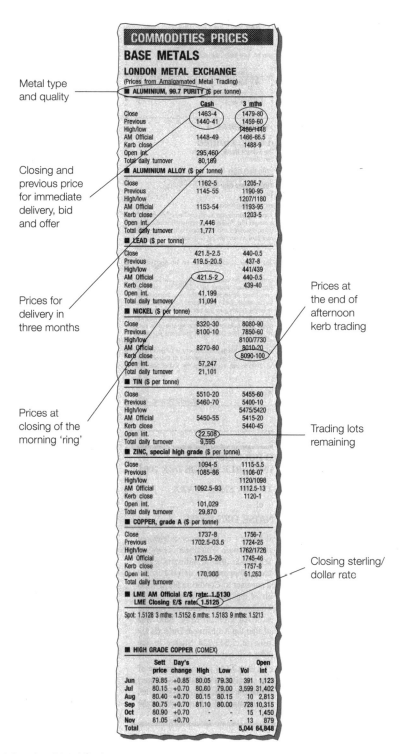

Metal type and quality

Closing and previous price for immediate delivery, bid and offer

Prices for delivery in three months

Prices at closing of the morning 'ring'

Prices at the end of afternoon kerb trading

Trading lots remaining

Closing sterling/dollar rate

COMMODITIES PRICES

BASE METALS

LONDON METAL EXCHANGE
(Prices from Amalgamated Metal Trading)

■ **ALUMINIUM, 99.7 PURITY** ($ per tonne)

	Cash	3 mths
Close	1463-4	1479-80
Previous	1440-41	1459-60
High/low		1466/1448
AM Official	1448-49	1466-66.5
Kerb close		1488-9
Open int.	295,460	
Total daily turnover	80,169	

■ **ALUMINIUM ALLOY** ($ per tonne)

Close	1162-5	1205-7
Previous	1145-55	1190-95
High/low		1207/1180
AM Official	1153-54	1193-95
Kerb close		1203-5
Open int.	7,446	
Total daily turnover	1,771	

■ **LEAD** ($ per tonne)

Close	421.5-2.5	440-0.5
Previous	419.5-20.5	437-8
High/low		441/439
AM Official	421.5-2	440-0.5
Kerb close		439-40
Open int.	41,199	
Total daily turnover	11,094	

■ **NICKEL** ($ per tonne)

Close	8320-30	8080-90
Previous	8100-10	7850-60
High/low		8100/7730
AM Official	8270-80	8010-20
Kerb close		8090-100
Open int.	57,247	
Total daily turnover	21,101	

■ **TIN** ($ per tonne)

Close	5510-20	5455-60
Previous	5460-70	5400-10
High/low		5475/5420
AM Official	5450-55	5415-20
Kerb close		5440-45
Open int.	22,508	
Total daily turnover	9,595	

■ **ZINC, special high grade** ($ per tonne)

Close	1094-5	1115-5.5
Previous	1085-86	1106-07
High/low		1120/1098
AM Official	1092.5-93	1112.5-13
Kerb close		1120-1
Open int.	101,029	
Total daily turnover	29,870	

■ **COPPER, grade A** ($ per tonne)

Close	1737-8	1756-7
Previous	1702.5-03.5	1724-25
High/low		1762/1726
AM Official	1725.5-26	1745-46
Kerb close		1757-8
Open int.	170,900	61,263
Total daily turnover		

■ **LME AM Official £/$ rate: 1.5130**
LME Closing £/$ rate: 1.5125

Spot: 1.5128 3 mths: 1.5152 6 mths: 1.5183 9 mths: 1.5213

■ **HIGH GRADE COPPER** (COMEX)

	Sett price	Day's change	High	Low	Vol	Open int
Jun	79.85	+0.85	80.05	79.30	391	1,123
Jul	80.15	+0.70	80.60	79.00	3,599	31,402
Aug	80.40	+0.70	80.15	80.15	10	2,813
Sep	80.75	+0.70	81.10	80.00	728	10,315
Oct	80.90	+0.70	-	-	15	1,450
Nov	81.05	+0.70	-	-	13	879
Total					5,044	64,848

Fig. 14.4 London Metal Exchange

PRECIOUS METALS
■ LONDON BULLION MARKET
(Prices supplied by N M Rothschild)

Gold(Troy oz)	$ price	£ equiv	€ equiv
Close	289.90-290.40		
Opening	292.50-293.00		
Morning fix	293.00	193.553	305.686
Afternoon fix	291.50	192.435	303.298
Day's High	293.75-294.25		
Day's Low	289.40-289.90		
Previous close	285.90-286.30		

Loco Ldn Mean Gold Lending Rates (Vs US$)
1 month ....6.07 6 months 6.03
2 months ....6.07 12 months 5.87
3 months 6.05

Silver Fix	p/troy oz.	US cts equiv.
Spot	336.030	508.75

Silver Lending Rates
1 month ....5.75 6 months 4.75
2 months ....5.50 12 months 3.50
3 months 5.00

Gold Coins	$ price	£ equiv.
Krugerrand	289-294	190-192
New Sovereign	66-70	43-45

Fig. 14.5 London bullion market

Reading the figures

- **Gold:** morning and afternoon fixing prices in dollars per troy ounce (with sterling and euro conversions), as well as early and late prices for the London market. As with currency markets, there is no official close although the word is used to describe the late price.

- **Loco London mean gold lending rates:** familiarly known as "Gold Libor", these are the interest rates at which large gold holders, principally central banks, will lend gold held in their reserves to approved borrowers, principally miners, who repay the loans from future production. The low rates on offer reflect the highly secure nature of the loans and the extra cost to the borrower of the spread between the bid and offer price on the gold market, usually about $2.50 an ounce.

- **Silver fix and silver lending rates:** prices at the morning silver fix in pence per troy ounce, with US cents equivalents; and interest rates at which silver holders will lend silver.

- **Gold coins:** prices for a representative selection of gold coins. Gold coin prices are for large quantities and are exclusive of value added tax.

Using the information

The gold market can be attractive for some investors and speculators. The price of gold is affected by a wide range of factors, moving up and down with bond yields, interest rates and exchange rates. Gold does not pay interest, and so its price is likely to be higher with lower interest rates. Gold is often a safer asset when there is upward pressure on inflation. But it is also a currency risk for non-US investors since its price is always denominated in dollars. Given the relatively small number of players in the gold markets, the price can be significantly influenced by individuals.

Enthusiasts for gold are known as "goldbugs". They see the yellow metal as nature's own store of value, which is far superior to the corrupt paper money churned out on high speed printing presses controlled by politicians. But for the 20-year period from 1980 to 2000, a time of booming markets for equities and many other assets, goldbugs have suffered: the price of gold has declined by 70 per cent.

Other metals

On Tuesday, the *Financial Times* lists minor metals prices, covering what are known as the strategic metals (because of their importance in high-technology and military applications). The metals are antimony, bismuth, cadmium, cobalt, mercury, molybdenum, selenium, tungsten ore, uranium and vanadium. There are also regular price listings for gold and silver on the US market, and for two other precious metals: platinum and palladium.

A typical report on the metals markets looks like this, an indication of the effects of the markets on the actual users of commodities as inputs in their production processes, as well as on the broader economy:

> Platinum and palladium prices surged yesterday amid continued concern about supplies and rising demand for the precious metals from carmakers. Spot markets in London and Tokyo saw palladium reach record highs of more than $840 an ounce, while platinum jumped to 12-year highs of above $600. Both metals are drawing support from fears about deliveries from Russia and the inability of South African mines to meet platinum demand.　　　　(*Financial Times*, 3 August 2000)

Other key commodity markets

London traded options

Traded options appear in a number of commodity futures contracts. Options confer on holders the right, but not the obligation, to trade at a predetermined price, the striking price, within a pre-set timespan. For this, they pay a non-returnable premium. Since the premium is the only money the investor can lose, options represent a relatively low risk way of speculating in commodities.

Traded options differ from straight options only in that they can be bought and sold rather than just operated by the original buyer. Figure 14.6 gives the FT traded options listing:

■ **Puts and calls:** current call (buy) and put (sell) premiums (prices) for options maturing in specified months with three different striking prices for each commodity.

LONDON TRADED OPTIONS				
Strike price $ tonne	···· Calls ····		···· Puts ····	
■ ALUMINIUM				
(99.7%) LME	Jul	Oct	Jul	Oct
1450	47	83	13	40
1500	20	57	36	63
1550	6	38	72	92
■ COPPER				
(Grade A) LME	Jul	Oct	Jul	Oct
1750	33	83	35	70
1800	14	60	67	96
1850	5	43	108	128
■ COFFEE LIFFE	Jul	Sep	Jul	Sep
900	21	76	30	67
950	9	56	68	97
1000	4	45	113	136
■ COCOA LIFFE	Jul	Sep	Jul	Sep
650	11	51	32	51
675	5	40	51	65
700	2	32	73	82
■ BRENT CRUDE IPE	Aug	Sep	Aug	Sep
2950	145	134	110	186
3000	118	115	133	217
3050	97	97	162	249

Fig. 14.6 London traded options

■ The markets in New York and Chicago

The *Financial Times* also covers commodities futures markets in the United States. These are of interest to many readers, including traders in the commodities and outside speculators following the markets on both sides of the Atlantic. These markets are also, of course, the original futures markets and are still very influential because of that. Extracts from the New York and Chicago exchanges are shown in Figure 14.7.

In New York, the exchanges covered are:

■ **The Commodity Exchange (Comex):** for copper, silver and gold. The price of gold on the Comex is a widespread reference, and is noted daily on the front page of the newspaper.

■ **The New York Mercantile Exchange (Nymex):** for platinum, palladium, crude oil, natural gas, unleaded gasoline and heating oil.

■ **The Cocoa, Sugar and Coffee Exchange (CSCE).**

■ **The Cotton Exchange (NYCE):** this also trades frozen concentrated orange juice.

Precious Metals

GOLD COMEX (100 Troy oz.; $/troy oz.)

	Sett price	Day's change	High	low	Vol	Open int
Jun	285.5	-1.0	290.5	286.0	21	153
Jul	286.7	-1.0	285.0	285.0	2	2
Aug	288.1	-1.0	296.5	286.8	17,145	75,125
Oct	291.1	-1.0	299.0	290.8	14	4,309
Dec	294.1	-1.0	303.5	293.1	646	21,446
Feb	296.8	-1.0	306.5	296.5	265	9,692
Total					18,099	138,740

PLATINUM NYMEX (50 Troy oz.; $/troy oz.)

	Sett price	Day's change	High	low	Vol	Open int
Jul	541.1	-2.9	549.9	539.0	719	8,803
Oct	528.6	-0.9	538.0	531.0	121	1,719
Jan	513.6	-0.9	-	-		31
Total					840	10,553

PALLADIUM NYMEX (100 Troy oz.; $/troy oz.)

	Sett price	Day's change	High	low	Vol	Open int
Jun	666.30	+20.55	-	-	6	60
Sep	667.30	+20.05	673.00	650.25	40	1,855
Dec	665.30	+20.05	645.00	645.00	1	114
Total					46	2,029

SILVER COMEX (5,000 Troy oz.; Cents/troy oz.)

	Sett price	Day's change	High	low	Vol	Open int
Jun	500.5	-1.5	-	-	-	-
Jul	502.5	-1.7	514.0	501.5	7,800	50,243
Sep	507.2	-1.7	518.5	506.0	1,671	9,657
Dec	513.2	-1.8	525.0	512.5	167	8,740
Jan	515.2	-1.8	-	-	2	60
Mar	517.4	-1.8	528.0	527.5	22	917
Total					9,671	74,633

MEAT AND LIVESTOCK

LIVE CATTLE CME (40,000lbs; cents/lbs)

	Sett Price	Day's change	High	Low	Vol	Open int
Jun	69.075	-0.100	69.325	69.050	3,176	11,062
Aug	68.400	-0.225	68.700	68.350	5,903	45,348
Oct	70.375	-0.175	70.750	70.175	2,316	26,798
Dec	72.200	-0.050	72.300	72.025	651	9,084
Feb	73.700	-	73.750	73.400	249	4,657
Apr	75.525	-0.075	75.575	75.250	166	4,713
Total					12,569	104,145

LEAN HOGS CME (40,000lbs; cents/lbs)

	Sett price	Day's change	High	Low	Vol	Open int
Jun	69.625	-0.750	70.000	69.375	3,506	7,388
Jul	67.900	-1.150	68.350	67.250	5,543	16,231
Aug	68.050	-0.875	68.150	67.300	3,848	16,592
Oct	58.925	-0.575	59.100	58.400	564	8,342
Dec	55.550	-0.725	56.150	55.350	298	6,097
Feb	56.725	-0.225	57.225	56.450	62	1,680
Total					13,834	56,962

PORK BELLIES CME (40,000lbs; cents/lbs)

	Sett price	Day's change	High	Low	Vol	Open int
Jul	85.725	-1.975	86.900	85.300	1,122	3,777
Aug	83.275	-1.650	84.500	83.050	341	1,869
Feb	73.150	-0.800	74.350	72.850	11	106
Mar	75.500	-	75.600	-	4	11
Total					1,472	5,764

ENERGY

CRUDE OIL NYMEX (1,000 barrels. $/barrel)

	Sett price	Day's change	High	Low	Vol	Open int
Jul	32.56	+0.82	32.85	31.65	76,201	103.0k
Aug	31.20	+0.77	31.40	30.35	51,195	106.1k
Sep	30.16	+0.63	30.40	29.45	16,741	38,547
Oct	29.41	+0.56	29.60	28.85	8,371	24,584
Nov	28.83	+0.53	28.93	28.40	5,006	20,583
Dec	28.30	+0.50	28.45	27.90	9,452	39,680
Total					170,629	485,246

CRUDE OIL IPE ($/barrel)

	Sett price	Day's change	High	Low	Vol	Open int
Jul	31.49	+0.28	31.70	30.90	31,335	51,976
Aug	29.85	+0.52	30.05	29.25	48,160	87,364
Sep	28.98	+0.58	29.05	28.28	16,322	31,175
Oct	28.30	+0.46	28.25	27.69	4,086	17,182
Nov	27.80	+0.39	27.76	27.25	1,222	12,344
Dec	27.27	+0.38	27.25	26.72	3,754	32,183
Total					110,000	298,525

HEATING OIL NYMEX (42,000 US galls.; c/US galls.)

	Sett price	Day's change	High	Low	Vol	Open int
Jul	78.51	+0.64	79.20	77.05	16,788	28,367
Aug	78.53	+0.74	79.00	77.45	7,595	16,950
Sep	78.68	+0.74	79.20	77.90	2,680	10,281
Oct	78.88	+0.69	79.40	78.00	538	7,688
Nov	79.13	+0.69	79.35	78.40	387	11,373
Dec	79.18	+0.69	79.50	78.30	645	18,109
Total					29,855	121,315

GAS OIL IPE ($/tonne)

	Sett price	Day's change	High	Low	Vol	Open int
Jul	238.00	+4.00	238.50	234.00	12,399	38,987
Aug	237.00	+3.75	237.25	233.75	10,134	15,697
Sep	237.50	+3.50	237.50	34.00	2,273	7,716
Oct	238.50	+4.00	238.50	234.50	1,959	7,737
Nov	237.50	+3.75	238.00	233.25	897	3,016
Total					27,000	106,734

NATURAL GAS IPE (1,000 therms; pence per therm)

	Sett price	Day's change	High	Low	Vol	Open int
Jul	16.670	+0.140	16.750	16.530	760	7,595
Aug	17.350	+0.340	17.350	17.000	245	2,315
Total					n/a	/a

NATURAL GAS NYMEX (10,000 mmBtu.; $/mmBtu.)

	Sett price	Day's change	High	Low	Vol	Open int
Jul	4.158	-0.054	4.265	4.115	27,545	47,554
Aug	4.142	-0.056	4.250	4.100	10,552	36,682
Sep	4.120	-0.053	4.220	4.085	1,870	27,122
Oct	4.105	-0.055	4.210	4.075	3,508	26,898
Nov	4.168	-0.047	4.260	4.130	1,168	16,417
Dec	4.240	-0.040	4.315	4.210	1,501	24,987
Total					57,313	341,925

UNLEADED GASOLINE NYMEX (42,000 US galls.; c/US galls.)

	Sett price	Day's change	High	Low	Vol	Open int
Jul	106.22	+1.82	106.90	103.70	18,150	35,936
Aug	101.73	+1.89	102.00	99.40	9,050	20,573
Sep	95.33	+1.63	95.35	93.40	3,858	17,335
Oct	87.83	+1.63	87.30	86.00	1,241	10,142
Nov	82.83	+1.43	82.60	81.00	262	5,376
Dec	80.13	+1.38	79.40	79.00	204	2,213
Total					33,129	93,817

GRAINS AND OIL SEEDS

WHEAT LIFFE (100 tonnes; £ per tonne)

	Sett price	Day's change	High	Low	Vol	Open int
Jul	72.75	+0.75	72.75	72.25	41	759
Sep	64.25	+0.30	64.25	64.25	10	658
Nov	66.25	+0.45	66.25	66.25	15	3,406
Jan	68.05	+0.35	68.05	67.95	185	1,240
Mar	69.80	+0.30	69.75	69.75	10	543
May	71.15	+0.25	71.25	71.25	65	290
Total					326	6,896

WHEAT CBT (5,000bu min; cents/60lb bushel)

	Sett price	Day's change	High	Low	Vol	Open int
Jul	264.75	-1.00	268.25	264.25	17,280	56,729
Sep	276.75	-0.75	280.75	276.00	6,494	32,902
Dec	293.25	-0.75	296.75	292.25	3,714	28,941
Mar	304.75	-1.50	309.00	304.50	1,486	9,192
May	312.00	-1.00	314.00	312.00	29	158
Jul	316.50	+0.50	318.50	315.00	24	4,553
Total					29,029	132,886

MAIZE CBT (5,000 bu min; cents/56lb bushel)

	Sett price	Day's change	High	Low	Vol	Open int
Jul	207.75	-0.50	210.00	207.50	69,730	176,751
Sep	216.75	-0.50	218.75	214.75	22,742	89,592
Nov	223.50	-0.75	225.50	223.50	432	1,120
Dec	228.00	-0.50	230.25	227.50	33,286	155,720
Jan	231.25	-0.75	233.50	231.00	68	93
Mar	238.00	-0.50	239.75	237.50	2,979	20,501
Total					131,764	461,623

BARLEY LIFFE (100 tonnes; £ per tonne)

	Sett price	Day's change	High	Low	Vol	Open int
Sep	65.25	-	-	-	-	10
Nov	67.25	-	-	-	-	204
Jan	68.75	-	-	-	-	5
Mar	70.25	-	-	-	-	4
May	71.75	-	-	-	-	-
Total						213

SOYABEANS CBT (5,000bu min; cents/60lb bushel)

	Sett price	Day's change	High	Low	Vol	Open int
Jul	510.50	-	514.50	506.50	47,594	61,056
Aug	506.50	-2.25	511.25	505.00	8,122	17,365
Sep	505.00	-3.25	510.50	503.00	5,149	15,112
Nov	509.00	-2.00	514.50	506.00	22,889	59,026
Jan	517.00	-3.50	523.00	515.50	1,297	6,179
Mar	525.00	-3.50	531.00	523.50	139	4,701
Total					85,896	175,039

SOYABEAN OIL CBT (60,000lbs; cents/lb)

	Sett price	Day's change	High	Low	Vol	Open int
Jul	16.11	-0.19	16.42	16.08	12,252	44,281
Aug	16.30	-0.19	16.62	16.28	2,191	22,743
Sep	16.52	-0.17	16.81	16.51	2,105	15,935
Oct	16.68	-0.23	17.04	16.68	1,582	10,222
Dec	17.07	-0.23	17.43	17.03	6,274	29,391
Jan	17.41	-0.23	17.60	17.43	108	9,461
Total					24,554	144,575

SOYABEAN MEAL CBT (100 tons; $/ton)

	Sett price	Day's change	High	Low	Vol	Open int
Jul	176.8	+1.5	178.5	175.7	16,487	46,730
Aug	170.4	+0.4	171.2	169.5	6,315	18,303
Sep	166.7	-0.9	168.0	166.0	2,012	10,424
Oct	164.1	-1.5	166.3	164.2	905	7,053
Dec	165.4	-1.1	167.3	165.0	7,837	28,692
Jan	165.9	-1.8	167.3	165.8	192	2,993
Total					34,151	120,013

POTATOES LIFFE (20 tonnes; £ per tonne)

	Sett price	Day's change	High	Low	Vol	Open int
Nov	84.5	-	-	-	-	-
Mar	87.0	-3.5	-	-	-	-
Apr	99.5	-3.5	100.0	98.0	31	926
May	109.5	-3.5	-	-	-	-
Jun	119.5	-3.5	-	-	-	-
Total					31	926

FREIGHT (BIFFEX) LIFFE ($10/index point)

	Sett price	Day's change	High	Low	Vol	Open int
Jun	1605	-	-	-	10	20
Jul	1465	-	-	-	-	96
Oct	1520	-	1520	1520	-	57
Jan	1520	-	-	-	-	-
Apr	1590	-	-	-	-	-
Total					1	173

	Close	Prev
Baltic Panamax Index (BPI)	1,599	1,593

PULP AND PAPER

PULPEX OMLX (US$; 24 air dry tons)

	Sett price	Day's change	High	Low	Vol	Open int
Jun	729.50	-27.50	-	-	-	-
Sep	730.00	-27.50	-	-	-	-
Total						1,053

FUTURES DATA
All futures data supplied by CMS.

Fig. 14.7 Commodity prices on New York and Chicago exchanges: precious metals, meat and livestock, energy, grains and oil seeds, pulp and paper

In Chicago, prices are quoted from:

- **The Chicago Mercantile Exchange (CME or Merc):** for live cattle, live hogs and pork bellies.
- **The Chicago Board of Trade (CBT):** for maize, wheat, soyabeans, soyabean meal and soyabean oil.

The many other US markets are not covered because they are too small or primarily of interest to domestic US consumers.

Commodity indices

The last item in the commodities section of the newspaper is a record of three indices plus LME warehouse stocks (see Figure 14.8):

INDICES

■ **Reuters** (Base: 18/9/31 = 100)

Jun 13	Jun 12	month ago	year ago
1375.7	1377.7	1388.4	1355.7

■ **CRB Futures** (Base: 1967 = 100)

Jun 12	Jun 9	month ago	year ago
224.58	224.99	-	-

■ **GSCI Spot** (Base: 1970 = 100)

Jun 9	Jun 8	month ago	year ago
n/a	224.36	212.69	158.95

LME WAREHOUSE STOCKS (tonnes)

Aluminium	-3,000	to	568,850
Aluminium alloy	+380	to	95,920
Copper	-1,800	to	584,900
Lead	-75	to	191,450
Nickel	-48	to	21,600
Zinc	-1,550	to	236,050
Tin	-	to	9,675

Fig. 14.8 Commodity price indices

- **Reuters:** this index is calculated from sterling prices for 17 primary commodities, weighted by their relative importance in international trade. Values are given for the last two days, a month ago and a year ago.
- **CRB Futures:** an index of 21 commodity futures prices compiled by the New York-based Commodities Research Bureau. Each commodity gets equal weight; and the index is dominated by food prices with a weight of 57 per cent.
- **GSCI Spot:** a commodity spot price index produced by Goldman Sachs.

PART 3

Understanding
the economies

"Economists don't know very much. And other people know even less."

Herbert Stein

"An economist is an expert who will know tomorrow why the things he predicted

yesterday didn't happen today."

Laurence J Peter

15

UK economic indicators

- **Gross domestic product** – the country's national accounts: consumption and investment; government policy and the business cycle; output by market sector

- **Production and employment** – key indicators of real economic performance: industrial production and manufacturing output; retail sales and consumer confidence; the labour market

- **Inflation** – rates of price changes: the retail prices index; inflation versus unemployment; competitiveness

- **Money and finance** – the money supply; interest rates and equity market yield

- **External trade** – the balance of payments

- **The economy and the markets** – the impact of interest rates

In addition to the regular coverage of the financial markets, the *Financial Times* also reports on the progress of other key markets. These include the product and labour markets, as well as the overall economies of the United Kingdom, Europe and the world. Almost every day sees publication of new facts and figures for one economic indicator or another: consumer credit, industrial production, retail sales, unemployment, inflation, the balance of payments, and so on. These indicators all interact with, and have effects on, the financial markets and, as a result, it is vital to understand their implications when making key business and investment decisions.

For the UK economy, FT coverage is particularly intense. Each month a wealth of figures is produced by the Office for National Statistics (ONS), the government department responsible for compiling economic statistics. These official figures, many with track records that go back decades, together throw light on the state of the economy, indicating to businesses, consumers and the government whether the economy is in recession, growing or at a turning point. The *Financial Times* tracks most of these monthly and quarterly data, together with unofficial but longstanding and widely regarded economic surveys produced by bodies such as the Confederation of British Industry (CBI).

The data compiled by the ONS usually refer to the previous month's economic activity. They are collected through nationwide surveys with the results analysed by teams of statisticians. By the time the figures are announced to the public, they have generally been "smoothed" to take account of seasonal patterns and to give a clearer picture of the underlying trend. For example, average earnings figures are "seasonally adjusted" for the extra hours worked in retailing and postal services in the period before Christmas.

Many of the figures are presented as indices, assuming constant prices from a given date, usually 1995=100. The reference date is arbitrary and merely provides a convenient landmark for comparison. What matters is not the index numbers themselves but the change from one period to the next. Figures for such key economic indicators as unemployment, inflation, output and gross domestic product (GDP) are especially likely to make the headlines, particularly when the monthly or quarterly changes are sharp.

Economic news reports appear in the first section of the *Financial Times* the day after they are released by the ONS. For easy reference, a table of UK economic figures appears on Thursday. The economic indicators table gathers together a range of key economic statistics to give an instant overview of activity in the UK economy (see Figure 15.1). Thursday's "The economy at a glance" and Saturday's "Preview" provide additional information. The following are the indicators, detailed in these tables and elsewhere, that are most likely to be reported in the press as well as to provoke public interest.

■ Gross domestic product

Each quarter, the newspaper presents figures on the National Accounts of the six biggest economies in the Organisation for Economic Cooperation and Development (OECD), the club that comprises 30 industrialised countries of the world. The economies covered are those of the United States, Japan, Germany, France, Italy and the United Kingdom.

	Real GDP (%)*	RPI**	RPIX change (%)*	Earnings growth (%)*	Manuf. output***	Unemploy. rate (%)
					Economic indicators	
1997	3.5	157.5	2.8	4.2	101.7	5.5
1998	2.6	162.9	2.7	5.1	102.0	4.7
1999	2.1	165.4	2.3	4.7	101.9	4.3
Q3 1998	2.4	163.7	2.6	5.3	102.4	4.6
Q4	2.1	164.4	2.6	4.7	101.4	4.6
Q1 1999	1.7	163.7	2.6	4.6	101.1	4.5
Q2	1.7	165.5	2.3	4.5	101.4	4.4
Q3	2.2	165.6	2.2	4.7	102.9	4.2
Q4	2.8	166.8	2.2	5.1	103.2	4.1
Q1 2000	3.0	167.5	2.1	5.9	102.8	4.0
Q2	3.2	170.6	2.1	4.6	103.2	3.8
Feb 2000	n.a.	167.5	2.2	6.0	102.6	4.0
Mar	n.a.	168.4	2.0	5.7	103.1	3.9
Apr	n.a.	170.1	1.9	5.1	102.8	3.8
May	n.a.	170.7	2.0	4.6	103.3	3.8
Jun	n.a.	171.1	2.2	4.1	103.5	3.8
Jul	n.a.	170.5	2.2	n.a.	n.a.	3.7

* GDP, RPIX, underlying earnings: percentage growth over same period in previous year
** RPI Index Jan 1987=100   *** Manufacturing output index 1995=100

Fig. 15.1 Economic indicators

Gross domestic product measures overall economic activity in a country and is calculated by adding together the total value of annual output of goods and services. GDP can also be measured by income to the factors producing the output (essentially capital and labour) or expenditure by individuals, businesses and the government on that output. The first column of Figure 15.1 shows the growth rate of real GDP and Figure 15.2 charts it over the late 1990s. Real GDP means that the figures are adjusted for the effects of inflation from what is known as nominal GDP. The growth rate is the percentage change over the corresponding point in the previous year. Figure 15.2 also shows the growth rate of output in the service industries.

GDP can be broken down into four components:

- **Private consumption:** the percentage of GDP made up of consumer spending on goods and services. These figures typically include imputed rents on owner occupied housing, but not interest payments, purchases of buildings or land, transfers abroad, business expenditure, buying of second-hand goods or government consumption. Figure 15.3 charts the growth rate of consumption

- **Total investment:** the percentage of GDP made up of capital investment (as opposed to financial investment) by both the private and public sectors. This is spending on new factories, machinery, equipment, buildings, roads, accommodation, raw materials, etc. "Gross domestic fixed capital formation", as investment is sometimes termed, is a key component of current growth of GDP as well as a critical foundation for future expansion. Obviously, investment in machines has greater potential for future output than that of houses, though the contribution of infrastructure such as roads may be harder to assess. Figure 15.4 charts the growth rate of investment.

231

■ **Government consumption:** the percentage of GDP made up of consumer spending by the public sector. Government spending on such items as infrastructure is accounted in these figures under total investment, though in some presentations of GDP, government spending encompasses both consumption and investment.

■ **Net exports:** the percentage of GDP made up of the difference between the value of national exports of goods and services and that of imports. In current prices, this balance of trade in goods and services (the current account of the balance of payments) in the United Kingdom is typically negative, with the value of imports exceeding that of exports.

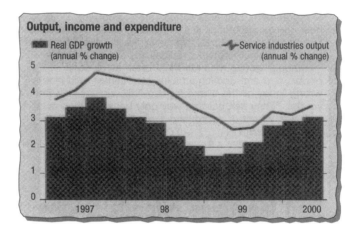

Fig. 15.2 Output, income and expenditure

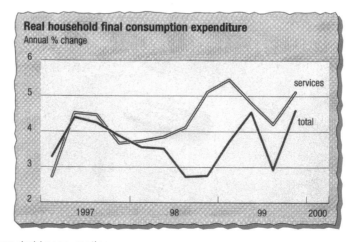

Fig. 15.3 Household consumption

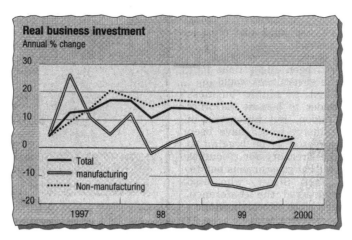

Fig. 15.4 Business investment

A month after the end of each quarter the ONS produces a provisional estimate of GDP based on output data, such as industrial production and retail sales (see below). A month later the ONS provides a further estimate taking account of income and expenditure data. Finally, one month after that, the full national accounts are produced based on complete information. As well as revisions to the provisional GDP figures, the national accounts show a full breakdown of economic activity during the previous quarter by sector, and identify trends in such key GDP components as personal disposable income, personal consumption and savings, and fixed investment and stock building. The ONS publication that contains the annual UK national accounts is known as the *Blue Book*.

When the level of GDP falls compared with the previous quarter, the economy is said to be contracting. Two consecutive quarterly falls, and it is said to be in recession. When GDP rises quarter to quarter, the economy is expanding. The movement of GDP from slump to recovery to boom to recession to slump again is known as the business cycle. Government macroeconomic policy is often aimed at smoothing this cycle, easing the pain of recession and applying restraint when the economy is in danger of overheating. This would typically be done through fiscal policy (boosting public expenditure and cutting taxes, or the reverse) or monetary policy (loosening or tightening the money supply, perhaps through lowering or raising interest rates).

Private consumption is a function of personal disposable income, the amount of income available to households after payment of income taxes and national insurance contributions. The other side of this coin is personal savings, the difference between consumer income and consumer spending. This can be either actual savings held in a deposit account or repayments of debt. The savings ratio is the proportion of income that is saved expressed as a percentage of personal disposable income.

Investment is also the twin of savings. By definition, investment equals savings: leaving exports and imports out of the picture, if consumption plus savings equals total income, income equals expenditure, and consumption (household and government) plus investment (private and public) equals expenditure, then investment and savings are equivalent. What happens is that income saved rather than consumed is available for investment: savings and investment are both about deferring current consumption for future prospects of consumption.

The fourth element of total GDP arises from the fact that the economy is open to international trade and financial flows. Exports contribute to growth; in contrast, imports can stifle it, reducing increases in national output relative to growth in demand. For example, increasing imports might suggest that demand is outstripping what can be provided by domestic output. Longer-term increases in imports might imply declining competitiveness on the part of national industries. If the level of imports is consistently and substantially higher than that of exports, and the deficit is not balanced by net inflows of interest, profits, dividends, rents and transfer payments, the current account balance stays in deficit. This can be financed in the capital account temporarily, but longer term a deficit leads to exchange rate problems, as discussed in Chapter 12.

In terms of the state of the economy, growth in personal consumption often leads a general recovery from recession, encouraging manufacturers to invest. Accounting for around 60 per cent of total GDP in most industrialised countries, it is clearly a critical target of government macroeconomic policy. But if consumption grows faster than productive capacity, imports are sucked into the national economy. This can have adverse implications both for the balance of payments and for domestic inflation, where prices of imported goods drive up the general price level.

Government policy and the business cycle

Clearly a vital component of GDP is government spending on both consumption and investment. As shown in Chapter 4, this is financed by taxation of individuals and corporations. The difference between government revenues and income is known as the public sector net cash requirement. Forecasts for this and other key elements of the economy are published by the Treasury at the time of the annual government budget in March in what is known as the *Red Book*.

Monthly figures for the public sector net cash requirement show how much the government has borrowed or paid back in one month. When tax revenues are weak and government spending high, for example in a recession, the deficit is likely to grow. It will narrow once the economy picks up and tax revenues rise again as more people find jobs. Thus, the state of public sector finances is, in part, dependent on the state of economic activity: this part of the deficit is referred to as the "cyclical" deficit. However, governments also incur persistent debts by systematically spending more than they collect in tax revenues: this part of the deficit, which exists regardless of economic activity, is referred to as the "structural" deficit.

Government policy on the public sector net cash requirement has two basic effects on the economy. The first is through fiscal policy: if the deficit is increased in times of stagnant or falling output and high unemployment, the directly higher spending of the government and/or the indirectly higher spending of consumers resulting from their lower taxes and greater disposable incomes stimulate demand. Through various multiplier effects, this can lead to recovery, increased output, reduced unemployment and growth. However, the second effect may temper this: high, persistent and/or growing annual deficits may drive up the cost of borrowing, discouraging both consumption and investment. Governments are frequently torn between the conflicting effects of the macroeconomic policies at their disposal.

The pattern of the business cycle, whether influenced by government policy or not, is shown by cyclical indicators, produced once a month by the ONS. These monitor and predict changes in the UK economy; based on series that are good leading indicators of turning points in GDP, such as business and consumer confidence surveys, they provide early indications of cyclical turning points in economic activity. In addition to these and the Treasury's predictions for the UK economy, hundreds of other private and public bodies produce their own forecasts, ranging from City analysts to independent think-tanks. The OECD also produces a forecast for the UK economy.

Output by market sector

In addition to the breakdown of GDP by consumption, investment, government activity and international trade, the ONS produces a breakdown by output of various market sectors. The key sectors can be analysed by comparing their percentage change over a period with the percentage change in overall GDP: relatively faster growing sectors, for example, are making a more substantial contribution to overall growth. A given percentage change in a dominant sector naturally has a larger effect on total activity than that of a less important sector. This point is particularly important to bear in mind when comparing the relative importance of certain sectors in different countries, and the changes of those sectors' importance. For example, a shifting balance from the manufacturing sector to the services sector is often noted in mature economies. Developing countries in contrast are more likely to be starting with agriculture and shifting to manufacturing.

Production and employment

The overall national accounts figures give a broad historic picture of the state of the economy while the output figures break it down by market sector. Figures for production and employment included in the international economic indicators table (see Figure 15.5) focus on key indicators of national economic performance that generally appear in advance of detailed GDP figures. These too are often leading indicators of the prospects for the economy. Comparative figures for retail sales volume, industrial production, the unemployment and vacancy rates, as well as a composite leading indicator for the six leading economies of the OECD are included in the table. Retail sales, industrial production and the vacancy rate are all indices based on 1995=100. The unemployment rate is a percentage of the total labour force.

■ UNITED KINGDOM					
	Retail sales volume	Industrial production	Unemployment rate	Vacancy rate indicator	Composite leading indicator
1990	93.0	94.1	7.1	92.2	86.1
1991	91.7	90.9	8.9	63.6	90.8
1992	92.4	91.3	10.0	65.0	93.9
1993	95.3	93.3	10.5	71.5	99.2
1994	98.8	98.3	9.6	87.6	102.6
1995	100.0	100.0	8.7	100.0	101.8
1996	103.2	101.1	8.2	122.9	104.9
1997	108.6	102.1	7.0	151.5	106.4
1998	111.8	102.7	6.4	156.1	104.1
1999	115.4	103.2	6.2	164.3	113.2
2nd qtr.1999	2.8	−0.5	6.0	158.6	109.9
3rd qtr.1999	3.3	0.9	5.9	163.3	111.9
4th qtr.1999	4.8	1.8	5.9	176.3	113.2
1st qtr.2000	5.1	1.5	5.8	178.8	112.5
June 1999	4.0	−0.7	5.9	159.8	109.9
July	2.9	0.4	5.9	161.1	110.4
August	3.5	1.0	5.9	164.6	111.2
September	3.6	1.3	5.9	164.4	111.9
October	4.7	1.7	5.9	173.0	112.3
November	4.2	1.9	5.9	175.6	112.7
December	5.5	1.8	5.9	180.4	113.2
January 2000	6.2	1.9	5.8	178.1	113.2
February	4.6	1.1	5.8	178.3	113.1
March	4.5	1.5	5.7	180.1	112.5
April	4.7	2.3		184.8	111.7
May	3.6			183.6	

Fig. 15.5 International economic indicators: production and employment

Each month the ONS estimates the output of UK manufacturing industry (quoted in Figure 15.1) and the level of energy production in the previous month. These come together as the index of output of the production industries (see Figure 15.6). The two components are usually quoted separately because oil and gas output is often erratic and can easily distort the underlying performance of manufacturing industry. Repairs to oil installations in the North Sea, for example, can bring energy production sharply down in one month.

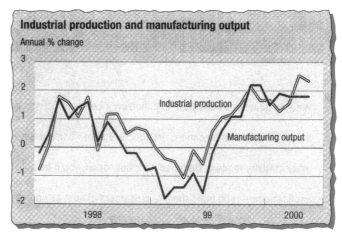

Fig. 15.6 Industrial production and manufacturing output

As well as monthly rises in output, the ONS compares output with the levels of a year ago and output in the latest three months (compared with the previous three months) to give a better idea of underlying trends. Industrial production is strongly indicative of the state of the economic cycle, since the output of industries producing capital goods and consumer durables is most reduced during a recession. While the monthly net output of physical goods in the United Kingdom represents only a quarter of total output, industrial production remains an important monthly indicator of the overall level of activity in the economy. Retail sales is also a leading indicator, functioning as a proxy for consumer spending in the eventual GDP figures.

Of all the monthly economic indicators the ONS pumps out, the statistics for industrial output are probably the most useful for evaluating particular equity investments. They offer precise data on the performance of the various sectors that constitute the production industries: the four categories that make up manufacturing – durable goods such as cars; non-durables like clothing and footwear, and food, drink and tobacco; investment goods such as electrical equipment; and intermediate goods like fuels and materials – plus mining and quarrying, which includes oil and gas extraction; and electricity, gas and water.

A number of surveys, produced by bodies such as the CBI, supplement the regular FT reporting of UK economic statistics. One of the most important is the CBI's quarterly industrial trends survey of manufacturers. This gives a strong indication of future trends in manufacturing output. By questioning up to 1,300 manufacturing companies about their recent and anticipated output, orders, employment, investment, exports, prices and costs, the survey provides a comprehensive "bottom-up" view of changing business expectations. With each variable, firms are asked whether they expect the direction of change to be up, down or the same over the coming four months. The results are summarised as a "balance" – the percentage of firms reporting up, less the percentage reporting down (see Figure 15.7):

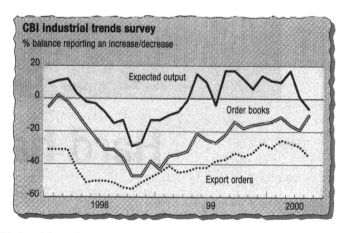

Fig. 15.7 CBI industrial trends survey

The British Chamber of Commerce also carries out a quarterly economic survey of its members (see Figure 15.8): unlike the CBI industrial trends survey, this includes the service sector. The CBI also does a monthly inquiry into the state of the distributive trades sector (mainly wholesalers and retailers) that supplements official information on retail sales.

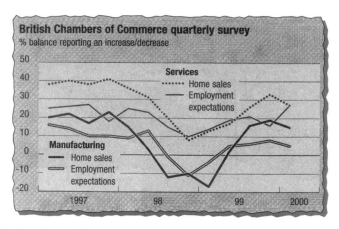

Fig. 15.8 British Chambers of Commerce survey

■ Retail sales and consumer confidence

The level of retail sales is another important leading indicator, and one that receives considerable media attention. Encompassing up to a half of all consumer spending in the eventual figures for GDP (most of the rest is spent in the service sector and on accommodation), the volume and value of retail sales are key indicators of consumer confidence and demand (see Figure 15.9). For example, a significant upturn in retail sales will typically lead to higher wholesale sales, to more factory orders and eventually to increased production. Figures for retail stocks and retail orders will also give some indication of the pace of demand.

The pattern of retail sales is influenced by a wide range of factors, many of which affect different sectors in different ways, according to the characteristics of the products. For example, seasonality is very important with some goods: off-licences will expect to see sales volume jump at Christmas or during a long hot summer; grocers, however, can expect fairly consistent demand throughout the year.

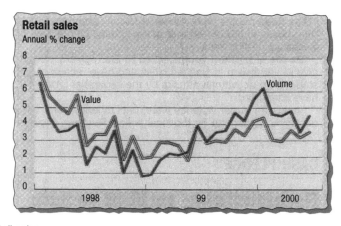

Fig. 15.9 Retail sales

Figures on retail sales should be examined very carefully by the companies that support and supply retailers. For example, the results of the CBI's distributive trades survey of over 500 retailers, wholesalers and motor traders will indicate whether consumer demand for their products is growing or declining. Since the data are available relatively quickly, supplying companies are able to adjust their output quite flexibly.

A related indicator is the UK "consumer confidence barometer", published monthly for the European Commission by market researchers GfK, who survey a representative sample of over 2,000 consumers (see Figure 15.10). These people are asked about the economy and their own financial situations, both looking back over the last 12 months and forward to the next 12, and including their expectations for employment and inflation and whether they intend to make any major purchases.

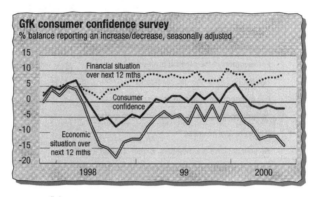

Fig. 15.10 Consumer confidence

The responses generate an overall indicator of consumer sentiment, which subtracts those feeling pessimistic about the future from those feeling optimistic. Since GfK launched the survey, the monthly average is minus 1 with a peak of plus 10 in August 1997, when the post-election "feel-good factor" was accompanied by the windfalls from many building societies converting into banks.

The labour market

The production and employment table (see Figure 15.5) also includes two important indicators of the state of the labour market: the unemployment rate and the vacancy rate. Variants of these measures also appear regularly:

■ **Registered unemployment:** the total number of people (in thousands, and excluding school leavers) who were out of work and claiming unemployment benefit in the previous period. The figure is seasonally adjusted to take account of annual fluctuations, such as at the end of the academic year when school leavers flood the jobs market.

■ **Unfilled vacancies:** vacancies (in thousands) notified to Department of Education and Employment job centres, about one-third of the total vacancies in the economy. The change in the number of vacancies is seen as an important indicator of future employment trends.

Figures for unemployment and vacancies, as well as average earnings and unit wage costs, are provided by the Department of Education and Employment. The measure of unemployment, known as the claimant count, is often criticised for excluding large numbers of people who cannot find jobs but who are not eligible for unemployment benefit. Thus women seeking to return to work, the self-employed and 16- and 17-year-old school leavers do not show up in the official count.

There are clearly more people unemployed than the official figures suggest. Every quarter, the Department of Education and Employment carries out a survey of the labour force, designed to capture those unemployed people who are left out of the claimant count. The Labour Force Survey (LFS) uses the International Labour Office measure of unemployment, an internationally recognised definition. It refers to people who were available to start work in the two weeks following their LFS interview and had either looked for work in the four weeks prior to interview or were waiting to start a job they had already obtained.

There is often a difference between the unemployment total revealed by the claimant count measure and the total arrived at by the LFS. The discrepancy between the two measures is usually greatest at a time of economic expansion when people feel encouraged to go out and look for work.

Department of Education and Employment statistics cover very detailed aspects of the labour market, including breakdown of unemployment by age, sex and region of the country. One example of the implications of such breakdowns is that a drop in the number of young unemployed men is usually regarded as a sign of economic recovery.

■ Inflation

Rates of change of prices in the UK economy feature in the weekly UK economic indicators table (see Figure 15.1). A number of different measures of UK inflation are published by the ONS, but by far the most popular and widely covered is the retail prices index (RPI):

- **Retail prices index:** an index of the average change in the prices of millions of consumer purchases represented by a "basket" of goods. This is the most widely quoted index of inflation, sometimes referred to as the headline rate of inflation.

- **RPIX change:** the essential element to note is the change in the RPI year to year: if inflation is 4 per cent, this means that the RPI has risen by 4 per cent since the same month of the previous year; the average basket of goods is 4 per cent more expensive. RPIX excludes mortgage interest payments.

- **Earnings growth:** the monthly labour market statistics for growth in average earnings cover the whole economy, including both the service and manufacturing sectors. In addition to basic wages, earnings also include overtime payments, grading increments, bonuses and other incentive payments. For this reason, earnings increases usually exceed settlement increases and wage claims.

The retail prices index

The ONS says it gets more queries from the public about the RPI than any other statistic, a reflection of the influence inflation has on everyone's life. For example, inflation determines the real value of savings, affects increases in pensions and other state benefits and plays an important part in wage bargaining.

The index is compiled by tracking the prices of a "basket" of goods, which represents spending by the typical UK family. All types of household spending are represented by the basket apart from a handful of exceptions, including savings and investments, charges for credit, betting and cash gifts. Indirect taxes such as value-added tax (VAT) are included, but income tax and national insurance payments are not: direct taxes are sometimes accounted for in a separate index, the tax and price index.

The average change in the price of the RPI basket is calculated from the findings of government price collectors. Each month, they visit or telephone a variety of shops, gathering about 130,000 prices for different goods and services. They go to the same places and note the prices of the same things each month so that over time they compare like with like. Information on charges for gas, water, newspapers, council rents and rail fares are obtained from central sources. Some big chain stores, which charge the same prices at their various branches, help by sending information direct from their headquarters to the ONS.

The components of the RPI are weighted to ensure that the index reflects average household spending. Thus housing expenditure has a much greater weighting than cinema tickets; the biggest weightings currently go to housing, food and motoring. The weights are obtained from a number of sources but mainly from the Family Expenditure Survey. For this, a sample of 7,000 households across the country keep records of what they spend over a fortnight plus details of big purchases over a longer period. The spending of two groups of people is excluded on the grounds that their pattern of spending is significantly different from most people's: families with the top 4 per cent of incomes and low income pensioners who depend mainly on state benefits.

Every year the components and the weightings of the RPI are reviewed to take account of changing spending habits. Over the past few years, microwave ovens, video recorders and compact discs have been introduced, while black and white televisions were dropped when sales declined.

In addition to the "all-items" index, the ONS publishes the RPI excluding mortgage interest payments (RPIX), an underlying measure of inflation favoured by the Treasury. It does this because a cut or rise in interest rates automatically influences mortgage interest payments. These have a higher weighting than any other component of the RPI and, as a result, have a strong bearing on the direction of the index. Excluding mortgage interest payments from the standard index prevents interest rate changes obscuring the underlying pattern of price changes, as Figure 15.11 illustrates. The chart also shows a third measure of inflation, the harmonised index of consumer prices, which allows better comparisons across countries:

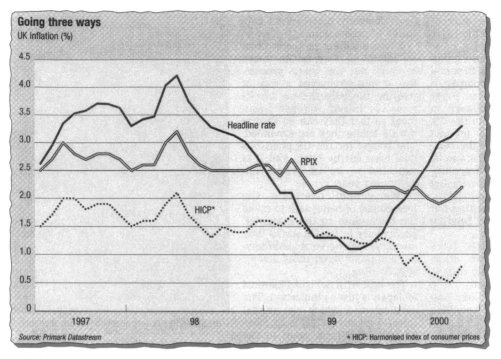

Going three ways
UK inflation (%)

Headline rate

RPIX

HICP*

1997   98   99   2000

Source: Primark Datastream   * HICP: Harmonised index of consumer prices

Fig. 15.11 UK inflation

■ Inflation versus unemployment

A key economic debate is over the causes of, and relationship between inflation and unemployment; in particular, whether there is a trade-off between them. This trade-off begins with the questions of which is worse, economically, socially and politically, and which therefore should be the primary goal of economic policy. Over the past decade, western governments have tended to argue that it is the control of inflation that should come first, traditionally the viewpoint of the political centre-right. Inflation makes it hard to distinguish between changes in relative price rises and general price rises, distorting the behaviour of individuals and firms and reducing efficiency; since it is unpredictable, it causes uncertainty and discourages investment; and it redistributes wealth unjustly, from creditors to borrowers, from those on fixed incomes to those on wages, and from everyone to the government.

Certainly inflation is damaging to the performance of the real economy, but so is high unemployment. It is an incredible waste of productive resources, it is expensive in terms of government benefits, and it is miserable for all the individuals who experience it. Along with substantial earnings differentials, and tax policies that favour the better off, it can cause drastic disparities in the distribution of income and potentially disastrous social disruption. Concerns about the consequences of high global unemployment in the 1990s have seen a resurgence of interest in the pursuit of full employment, traditionally a key policy goal of the centre-left. This raises the central issue of how unemployment and inflation are connected, and what full employment might mean.

It used to be believed that there was a simple trade-off between the two variables: what is called the Phillips curve, after its progenitor, suggested that in order to reduce inflation, society had to tolerate higher unemployment, and vice versa. This inverse relationship did in fact exist in the US economy among others through the 1960s; it subsequently broke down irretrievably as later years witnessed both high inflation and high unemployment, what became known as stagflation. Such times led to the coining of a new economic indicator, the misery index, the combination of the rates of consumer price inflation and unemployment (an alternative misery index adds together inflation and interest rates).

Nowadays, the consensus of economic opinion seems to be that there is some level of output and employment beyond which inflation rises. For example, there is always a gap between the actual level of output and the potential level, a measure of the amount of slack in the economy called the output gap. If this gap is closed too far, supply cannot rise to meet any increased demand, thus forcing up prices; there exist what economic reports often call bottlenecks or supply constraints. This might be called a situation of excess demand: spending power, perhaps arising from tax cuts, increased consumer borrowing or a bigger money supply, exceeds the availability of goods and services, bidding up their prices.

Similarly, it is argued that beyond a certain unemployment rate, what has been called the natural or non-accelerating inflation rate of unemployment, higher demand becomes inflationary. At such a point, the supply and demand for labour are in balance; beyond it, higher demand for labour supposedly drives up wage costs, which feed through to retail price inflation, which in turn encourages demands for higher wages, and so on in an inflationary spiral.

Estimates vary of what that rate of unemployment really is and arguments continue about whether it should be regarded as the "full employment" unemployment rate. It is assumed to depend on such factors as the level of minimum wages, benefits, employment taxes, unionisation, the age structure of the labour force and other demographic factors, and these are now the issues of much economic and political debate.

Financial markets' perception of the natural rate is reflected when news of an increase in the jobless figures is greeted enthusiastically by the markets, with stock and bond prices surging in response to lengthening dole queues. Contrariwise, the impact of falling unemployment can be bad for share prices, especially if the economy is "overheating". Falling unemployment is, after all, characteristically a lagging indicator of the business cycle. But longer term, depending on the sectors and regions in which a portfolio is invested, more jobs and lower unemployment should mean better returns.

▪ Competitiveness

A monthly table of international economic indicators for prices and competitiveness (see Figure 15.12) gives details of indices for consumer prices, producer prices, earnings, unit labour costs and the real exchange rate for six leading OECD countries. Yearly figures are shown in index form with the common base year of 1985=100. The real exchange rate is an index throughout; the other quarterly and monthly figures show the percentage change over the corresponding period in the previous year:

UNITED KINGDOM				
Consumer prices	Producer prices	Earnings	Unit labour costs	Real exchange rate
1989 121.8	113.9	137.2	107.0	100.6
1990 133.3	121.0	151.1	113.3	101.9
1991 141.2	127.5	162.9	118.8	104.8
1992 146.4	131.5	173.6	118.9	101.4
1993 148.7	136.7	181.6	118.7	93.7
1994 152.4	140.1	190.7	118.4	94.6
1995 157.6	145.7	199.1	122.9	91.1
1996 161.5	149.6	207.8	129.1	94.2
1997 166.5	151.0	216.5	133.7	109.6
1998 172.2	151.8	226.3	140.6	112.3
1999 174.9	153.6	235.6	141.1	111.7
2nd qtr.1999 1.4	1.0	3.5	0.8	111.8
3rd qtr.1999 1.2	1.4	4.0	−0.8	111.8
4th qtr.1999 1.5	2.1	5.2	−0.5	113.9
1st qtr.2000 2.3	2.4			
May 1999 1.3	1.0	3.5	0.4	112.0
June 1.3	1.0	3.4	0.8	112.6
July 1.3	1.1	3.6	−0.2	111.5
August 1.1	1.3	4.1	−0.8	111.2
September 1.1	1.7	4.4	−1.3	112.6
October 1.2	1.9	4.6	−0.7	113.2
November 1.4	2.1	4.9	−1.1	113.7
December 1.8	2.3	6.0	0.3	114.7
January 2000 2.0	2.4	5.8	0.7	116.4
February 2.3	2.4		0.0	
March 2.6	2.4			
April	2.2			

Fig. 15.12 International economic indicators: prices and competitiveness

- **Consumer prices:** indices of consumer prices that are not seasonally adjusted. These are equivalents of the UK RPI.

- **Producer prices:** indices of producer prices that again are not seasonally adjusted, and use varying measures of output.

- **Earnings:** indices of non-seasonally adjusted earnings. These are compiled from surveys of the gross wages and salaries paid to employees in the private and public sectors.

- **Unit labour costs:** seasonally adjusted indices of labour costs per unit of output, measured in domestic currencies. Unit labour costs reflect labour costs and productivity.

- **Real exchange rate:** calculated by JP Morgan as indices of relative national costs or prices expressed in a common currency. These real effective exchange rates are calculated against a composite of 18 industrial countries' currencies, adjusted for changes in the relative wholesale prices of domestic manufactures (a measure of inflation). A fall in the index indicates improved international competitiveness.

National competitiveness is a difficult and controversial concept to define. One attempt is that it is the degree to which a country can produce goods and services that meet the tests of international markets while simultaneously maintaining and expanding the real incomes of its people over the long term. This depends on changes in costs and prices relative to comparable changes in countries with which trade is conducted, adjusting for movements of the exchange rate. It is generally accepted that greater competitiveness of a country's output can be achieved through some combination of reasonable productivity growth and an appropriately valued exchange rate.

Each of these indicators gives some guide to national competitiveness. The first two are measures of domestic rates of inflation: for each country, they can be used to assess changes in the general price level and inflationary prospects. In effect, they can be interpreted in the same way as all the earlier figures for inflation in the United Kingdom. However, when they are compared internationally, they become indicative of countries' ability to sell their exports abroad; they show relative consumer and producer prices. For example, if UK consumer prices are rising faster than French ones, without compensating movements in the euro/sterling exchange rate, UK exports to France are more expensive than they were, and hence less competitive.

Earnings and unit labour costs focus on the relative costs side of comparisons of international competitiveness. Earnings measure total labour costs; unit labour costs measure labour costs divided by output, and are therefore a function of productivity. Earnings and unit labour costs are an important indicator of inflationary pressures in an economy: if labour costs increase faster than productivity, then unit labour costs rise. Used to compare countries, they reveal cost competitiveness: higher unit labour costs, without compensating movements in the exchange rate, make it harder for companies to price their goods competitively on the international market and maintain their profit margins.

Real exchange rates are effective exchange rates between countries' currencies that have been adjusted to take account of differential rates of inflation. The inflation indicator might be wholesale prices, as in the table, or unit labour costs. Either way, the real exchange rate is an excellent indicator of national competitiveness, incorporating changes in the exchange rate, the relative rates of inflation and the relative growth of productivity. Its importance was illustrated by the particularly decisive shift in the value of this indicator for the United Kingdom in the last quarter of 1992 when the pound left the EMS.

The combination of devaluation and productivity growth gave the United Kingdom a strong low cost advantage over other EU countries, though not against North America or Japan. For companies exporting to the EU, competing with EU imports, or considering either of these options, this was good news. They were able to price their goods very competitively, and still earn quite attractive profits. Thus competitiveness on a national scale and as a corporate concern become intertwined.

Money and finance

One or two of the financial indicators discussed earlier in this book, as well as monetary indicators such as the money supply, appear in the money and finance version of the international economic indicators of the six leading economies of the OECD (see Figure 15.13). These focus on measures of narrow and broad money, short- and long-term interest rates and equity market yield:

UNITED KINGDOM					
	Narrow Money (M0)	Broad Money (M4)	Short Interest Rate	Long Interest Rate	Equity Market Yield
1990	5.3	15.9	14.82	11.56	5.07
1991	2.4	7.9	11.58	10.08	4.97
1992	2.4	5.1	9.74	9.09	4.91
1993	4.9	3.5	5.99	7.40	4.01
1994	6.4	5.1	5.57	8.01	3.94
1995	5.9	7.3	6.77	8.16	4.15
1996	6.7	9.9	6.11	7.79	4.08
1997	6.1	11.2	6.94	7.02	3.59
1998	6.1	9.7	7.41	5.52	3.03
1999	7.2	5.2	5.51	4.98	2.44
2nd qtr.1999	6.7	6.6	5.24	4.76	2.31
3rd qtr.1999	7.5	3.7	5.25	5.32	2.35
4th qtr.1999	9.4	3.6	5.95	5.39	2.34
1st qtr.2000	9.8	3.8	6.18	5.51	2.36
June 1999	7.4	5.4	5.16	5.02	2.29
July	7.6	3.6	5.14	5.20	2.27
August	7.7	4.3	5.21	5.24	2.37
September	7.1	3.0	5.40	5.53	2.41
October	7.4	3.3	6.00	5.70	2.45
November	8.9	3.5	5.82	5.17	2.31
December	11.8	3.9	6.02	5.31	2.23
January 2000	12.7	3.2	6.12	5.73	2.36
February	8.5	3.2	6.21	5.55	2.46
March	8.3	5.1	6.20	5.27	2.27
April	8.4	4.7	6.25	5.24	2.31
May	7.9	5.0	6.26	5.33	2.33

Fig. 15.13 International economic indicators: money and finance

■ **M0:** also known as "narrow money" or the monetary base, this measure consists almost entirely of notes and coins in circulation. Growth in M0 indicates that consumer spending is buoyant; a contraction in M0 suggests consumers are behaving more cautiously.

■ **M4:** known in the United Kingdom as "broad money", this measure comprises M0 plus bank and building society retail and wholesale deposits.

■ **Short interest rate:** this is the rate payable on money lent for three months. For example, for the United Kingdom, the figure is three-month LIBOR, and for the United States, it is the rate payable on 90-day commercial paper.

■ **Long interest rate:** the yield on ten-year benchmark government bonds.

■ **Equity market yield:** the gross dividend yield on the national index measure by the FTSE world series.

Every month the Bank of England publishes figures showing the amount of money in circulation in the UK economy, and the year-to-year percentage changes. The total value of money in circulation depends on the definition of the money supply. In the United Kingdom there are two main measures, one broad and one narrow. Sometimes monetary authorities choose to target growth in the money supply as part of an anti-inflationary strategy. Rapid growth in the amount of money circulating in the economy is often taken to be a sign that inflationary pressures are building up.

External trade

Each month the ONS publishes figures showing how much the United Kingdom imported and exported in the previous month and consequently how much the country is in deficit or surplus with the rest of the world. These are reported in the monthly table of international economic indicators covering balance of payments for the six main economies of the OECD. The figures it provides for exports, visible trade and current account balances, and euro and effective exchange rates are examined in Chapter 17.

Monthly ONS figures are mainly concerned with trade in visible items or merchandise goods. Trade in visible items is measured both in current values and in volume terms with adjustments made for erratic components, such as aircraft and precious stones, that are likely to distort the underlying trend. Visible trade is simpler to measure than invisible trade in services, and financial transactions such as transfer payments, interest payments, profits and dividends.

The volume of exports is determined by the demand from overseas, which in turn depends on the state of the importing economies, the price of the exports (a function of relative inflation levels and the exchange rate) and, of course, the quality of the products. Like export volume, import volume depends on relative prices arising from relative inflation and exchange rates, as well as the state of the UK economy. When the economy is growing, imports generally increase.

The balance of trade is the net balance in the value of exports and imports of goods in billions of pounds (see Figure 15.14). When the United Kingdom imports more visible items than it exports, a perennial national problem, it is said to have a "trade gap". This may be of no particular concern provided it is offset by surpluses elsewhere on the balance of payments, such as in invisible items.

The current balance is the balance of trade in both goods and services plus net interest, profits, dividends, rents and transfer payments flowing into the United Kingdom from

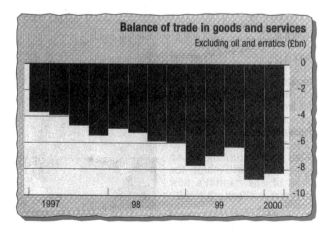

Fig. 15.14 Balance of trade

countries overseas in billions of pounds (see Figure 15.15). A deficit on the current account balance must be made up in the capital account of the overall balance of payments through net investment into the country, loans from abroad or depletion of the official reserves. A persistent deficit puts pressure on the currency (as discussed in Chapter 12), encouraging devaluation to increase the price competitiveness of exports and decrease that of imports.

By bringing together the balances in visible and invisible trade, the ONS provides the current account. Adding in the capital account provides a complete statement of the United Kingdom's trade and financial transactions with the rest of the world. This full picture is known as the balance of payments and is published every quarter. A publication known as the *Pink Book* gives detailed balance of payments data, including the City of London's contributions to the United Kingdom's overseas earnings, total transactions with the rest of the European Union and details of the UK's overseas assets and liabilities.

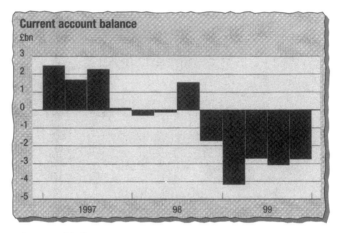

Fig. 15.15 Current account balance

■ The economy and the markets

The economy is one of the most important drivers of the stock market. The central economic force of interest rates, plus the assorted effects of exchange rates, inflation, public spending and taxation, will eventually have a say in overall valuations, whatever the temporary investment craze. At the same time, the stock market has a major impact on the economy, both as a forward indicator and determinant of consumer sentiment, and as a vital mechanism in the management of risk, encouraging the innovation and entrepreneurship that drive economic growth.

Shares and bonds provide the essential capital that enables companies to take the risks inherent in business. From their origins in mediaeval Italy, through increasing size and sophistication in 17th- and 18th-century Amsterdam, 19th-century London and 20th-century New York, the stock markets in which these assets traded have meant that the business risks of new projects can be shared – from building the rail, road and aviation infrastructure of the 19th- and 20th-century economies to building the electronic infrastructure of the 21st-century economy. Such risk-sharing has transformed the potential for economic growth and, in the latter part of the last century, as more and more people have got involved in the investment process, changed fundamentally our understanding of the relationship between risk and return.

For most of financial market history, debt finance was dominant. Until as late as the 1950s, shares were largely in the hands of wealthy individuals. Buying and owning shares was considered far too risky by the less well off and even by the institutions that now dominate the investment scene; instead, they held portfolios of high-grade, long-term bonds. But this arrangement has been swept aside in the last few decades, as investors of all kinds have sought better returns, companies have seen the hugely increased financing opportunities of the equity markets, and economic growth has made enormous improvements in living standards in the developed world.

Of course, there have been bad times in the past half-century and the stock market has been a good leading indicator of future economic gloom. For example, the closing of the period 1950–73 – often described as the "golden age" of economic growth in western Europe and the United States – was clearly foretold in the disastrous crash of 1973–4, when markets fell by over 50 per cent. The bear market of the early 1970s clearly reflected the ominous economic events of that unfortunate decade: sky-rocketing oil prices, the breakdown of the Bretton Woods agreements for managing international monetary affairs, and the emergence of persistent inflationary forces.

Many feared that these collapsing share valuations would lead to economic disaster, just as the Great Crash of 1929 was thought to have led to the Great Depression of the 1930s. Certainly, speculative manias or "bubbles" that culminate in self-feeding panics and eventual crashes can have widespread and undesirable consequences in the real economy. Clearly, too, a booming market boosts consumer sentiment, encouraging spending, reducing saving and increasing debt, and adding further fuel to a raging economy.

But economic policy itself has a major impact on the interaction between share values and the economy. In the 1990s, for example, cheap and easily available money sustained the market's upward trend. And in both the United States and the United Kingdom, the crashes of 1987 had marginal effects on economic performance since the monetary policy authorities in both countries were quick to cut interest rates to increase liquidity. Similarly, the US Federal Reserve's rate-cutting response to the global crisis of 1997–8 seemed to be successful in restoring the good times.

◼ The impact of interest rates

But what about the influence of the economy on the stock market? In the short term, it can be hard to discern a clear relationship as markets often rise in a recession and fall or go sideways in a boom. Share valuations clearly react to economic news but the market's moves can often seem perverse, appearing to be happening more in response to how the figures compare to prior forecasts and expectations than to their actual values.

Over the longer term, the relationship becomes clearer. At base, investors are looking for the likely impact of any economic indicator on the future course of interest rates. If inflation is rising, it might mean the Bank of England will raise rates; if output is falling, it might mean a recession in which case rates will be cut; and so on.

And what makes interest rates so important? Interest rates are one of the two key variables – along with corporate profitability – that affect investment results. They act on share valuations like gravity: the higher the rate, the greater the downward pull. In simple terms, this is because the returns investors need from their assets is directly linked to the risk-free return they can earn on government bonds. So, other things being equal, if the government rate rises, the prices of all other investments must adjust downwards to bring their expected returns into line.

The huge impact of interest rates on the market has been starkly demonstrated by the celebrated US investor Warren Buffett, best known for his incredible stockpicking success and consistent outperformance of US market indexes over at least three decades. Buffett notes that, in the 17-year period 1964–81, the US economy grew by a massive 370 per cent, yet the Dow Jones Industrial Average moved hardly a jot. In contrast, in the following 17-year period, 1982–99, the economy grew far less strongly – under 200 per cent – yet the Dow went up to over ten times its starting value, an annual return on shares of 19 per cent.

Of course, all sorts of factors influence these contrasting market performances, but Buffett ascribes interest rates the leading role. In the 1964–81 period, US interest rates went from 4 per cent to over 15 per cent, while in the 1982–99 period, they went from 15 per cent to 5 per cent. At the turning point of 1981, corporate profits were below par and interest rates were sky high, and so investors placed a low value on the market. In 2000, profits were above par and interest rates low, and so shares were highly valued.

What does this all mean going forward? Investors seem to be expecting double-digit average annual real returns on their shares to continue. But according to Buffett's history lesson, this requires profits to take an even larger slice of national income, which seems unlikely; and/or interest rates to fall even further, which is possible but improbable on current trends. Buffett's conclusion is that returns for the next 17 years are more likely to go back to their average level over the eight decades since the 1920s: 4 per cent a year.

Might the investment opportunities of the information economy save the day for the skilful technology stockpicker? Buffett is sceptical, making the comparison between the impact of the internet and the impact of cars and planes: all three industries have had a transformational effect on the economy but in the end, very few of the firms that were in there at the start made money. With the stock market playing an invaluable role, innovators and entrepreneurs have driven economic growth; but the forces of competition mean that over the long term, there are no great gains for investors. The economy ultimately makes itself felt.

"I want the whole of Europe to have one currency; it will make trading much easier."

Napoleon Bonaparte

"The path to European monetary union will not be a stroll; it will be hard and thorny."

Karl Blessing,
Bundesbank President, 1963

16

The European economy

Market integration and monetary union

- **The European economy** – exchange rates and the European Monetary System (EMS); currency market volatility in 1992 and 1993

- **Launching the euro** – economic and monetary union (EMU); the early weakness of the single currency; EMU and European capital markets

- **Enlargement** – expanding European Union membership

National economies like that of the United Kingdom can no longer be examined in isolation. Increasingly, international flows of goods, services and capital are making economies more and more interdependent and, with an almost global consensus on the positive effects of free trade, this movement can only go further. Countries' economies interact in a number of ways, generally facilitating each other's progress, and certainly having important effects on and being in turn affected by the national and international financial markets. Nowhere is this more evident than in the European Union (EU). This chapter explores the basics of the European economy.

■ The European economy

The European Union is on its way to representing one-third of world output, compared with one-quarter for the United States and one-sixth for Japan. As a market comprising 15 countries, the Union accommodates over a quarter of all world commerce within its frontiers. Furthermore, it is the world's most substantial source of foreign direct investment, its most important provider and consumer of services and the largest global supplier of aid.

The European Union has been through a number of transformations in its history. One of the most economically significant was the "1992" project, the creation of a single market. On 1 January 1993 that single market came into effect: in principle and to a large extent in practice, the remaining obstacles to the free flow of goods, services, capital and labour between the then 12 member states of the EU were removed, and the Union moved significantly closer to its goal of becoming a genuine "common market".

In the face of serious upheavals in European currency markets, notably in the latter halves of 1992 and 1993, the EU's long-term goal became the establishment of a full economic union, involving a close harmonisation of member countries' general economic policies, the centralisation of fiscal and monetary control procedures and a single currency. The single market had already produced a number of benefits for European consumers and businesses, and it was anticipated that there were many more to be reaped from the process of "ever closer union".

One of the most important steps towards that full economic and monetary union (EMU) was taken in 1979, when the then European Community set about creating a "zone of currency stability" known as the European Monetary System (EMS). The Treaty on European Union, agreed at Maastricht in 1991 and signed the following year, established a timetable for further advancement of the EMU goal, which was ultimately achieved on 1 January 1999 when 11 EU members launched the single currency.

■ Exchange rates and the European Monetary System

The idea behind the European Monetary System was to achieve currency stability through coordinated exchange rate management. This would facilitate intra-Union trade and set the stage for a single currency. The exchange rate mechanism (ERM), a system of fixed but flexible exchange rates, was the central plank of the EMS. Countries participating in the ERM would keep the value of their currencies within margins of 2.25 per cent either side of agreed central rates against the other currencies in the mechanism. Sterling, the peseta and the escudo, all of which joined the ERM several years after its inception, were allowed to move within margins of 6 per cent.

The ERM worked by requiring members to intervene in the foreign exchange markets in unlimited amounts to prevent currencies breaching their ceilings or floors against the other currencies. For example, if the peseta fell to its floor against the D-Mark, the Bank of Spain was required to buy pesetas and sell D-Marks. Other members could help by intervening on behalf of the weak currency. This, in theory, would prop up the peseta before it fell through its floor.

Second, the country whose currency was under fire could raise its short-term interest rates to make its currency more attractive to investors. If intervention on the foreign exchanges and adjustment of short-term rates failed to stop a currency from sliding too low or rising too high, an absolute last resort was a realignment of the central rates to relieve the tensions in the system.

In the early years of the ERM, there were several realignments but from 1987 until 1993, when the ERM was effectively suspended, there was none. Many economists argue that it was the failure of the mechanism to realign in response to the strength of the D-Mark that led to the tensions of the autumn of 1992 and the summer of 1993.

Currency market volatility in 1992 and 1993

After five years of relative calm, the currency markets of Europe erupted in a sequence of dramatic market events. The explanation for these events lay in German reunification at the end of the 1980s. To pay for unification, the German government had to borrow substantial amounts of money, which forced up the cost of borrowing in Germany. High German interest rates coincided with low US interest rates and the result was strong international demand for D-Marks, forcing German rates even higher.

This happened just as the rest of Europe, heading into recession, needed lower interest rates to stimulate economic activity. However, since all the other currencies were committed to maintaining their central rates against the D-Mark, they were forced to keep their interest rates at levels that were damaging their economies. So long as Germany's rates were high, countries like the United Kingdom and France were unable to lower their lending rates without causing a run on the pound and the franc.

In the case of the United Kingdom, the tensions became too much for the system in September 1992. The country was suffering its longest recession since the 1950s yet had interest rates of 10 per cent. With inflation low, the real cost of borrowing was exceptionally high. The markets took the view that such high lending rates at a time of recession were unsustainable. Pressure on the pound mounted over August, but the UK government, mindful of the hardship being caused by the high cost of borrowing, was unwilling to raise rates further in order to protect the pound. Its only weapons were intervention on the foreign exchanges and repeated assurances by ministers that there would be no devaluation.

Events came to a head on 16 September 1992, Black Wednesday (or White Wednesday to "Eurosceptics", delighting at its negative implications for future UK participation in Europe), when sterling and the Italian lira were forced out of the mechanism. Speculative investors, losing confidence in the currencies and seeing the opportunity for significant profits, shifted vast funds out of sterling and the lira into the D-Mark. Many, for example, sold the pound short, expecting to be able to buy it back at a much reduced rate.

The effect of all this selling was to drive the pound down. On the day, the UK government tried to save it by buying large quantities of pounds, and by announcing an increase in interest rates to 15 per cent. But this was not enough to stem the flow against sterling: effectively, the Bank was transferring its reserves to the short selling speculators. After a steady drain on reserves, the government pulled out. Both sterling and the lira sank well below their ERM floors as soon as the authorities gave up the struggle to keep them within their old bands.

For the next 11 months, relative calm returned to what was left of the mechanism. However, in August 1993, tensions arose once more, this time centred on the French franc. The problems were familiar: France was in a recession with high unemployment yet was unable to cut its very high interest rates. One solution would have been for Germany to ease its lending rates, but the Bundesbank, the German central bank, would not contemplate such a move for fear of encouraging inflation at home. According to the German constitution, the prime duty of the Bundesbank is to monitor domestic monetary policy. Thus it was required by law to put the need for low German inflation before the travails of the ERM.

As pressure mounted, EU finance ministers met to find a solution. The answer was to widen the currency bands for all except the D-Mark and the Dutch guilder to 15 per cent. The bands were so wide that although the ERM survived in name, the currencies were effectively floating. With the new bands a currency could theoretically devalue by 30 per cent (from its ceiling to its floor) against another member, without falling out of the system. That was the system of the ERM until the launch of the euro.

▩ Launching the euro

On 1 January 1999, the currencies of 11 members of the EU (all bar Denmark, Greece, Sweden and the United Kingdom) were irrevocably locked together and the euro was launched. Prices in euro-zone countries are still quoted in the national currency as well as euros but the exchange rate is fixed. Eventually, the national currencies will disappear as euro notes and coins are introduced.

Monetary policy in the euro-zone is managed by the European Central Bank (ECB) in Frankfurt, which operates with a high degree of independence from political interference. The ECB has been given the responsibility for maintaining price stability through setting short-term interest rates in the euro-zone. It is not required also to consider employment when setting policy.

Fiscal policy remains the preserve of national governments since there is no necessary connection between a single currency and a unified fiscal policy. Nevertheless, there is considerable policy coordination between finance ministries through the "euro-11", a regular meeting of euro-zone finance ministers.

The early weakness of the single currency

The *Financial Times* gives prominent coverage to the progress of the euro, in particular publishing its exchange rate against other leading currencies on the front page of Monday's edition (see Figure 16.1). The chart shows movements of the euro against sterling, the dollar and the yen since its launch, plus the latest rates against the dollar, the yen, the Swiss franc and the four currencies of EU countries that remain outside the euro-zone – sterling, the Swedish krona, the Danish krone and the Greek drachma.

The big story since the euro's launch has been its weakness against other leading currencies. There is no question that its more than 20 per cent fall against the dollar since the beginning of 1999 has been a setback for advocates of the benefits of a single currency, particularly those in Germany, a country that always took pride in the strength of the D-Mark. But such declines are not irreversible and there is every chance that the euro will come bouncing back strongly in due course.

International financial markets have a number of signs that the euro will soon stand alongside the dollar as a dominant world currency. For example, equity and corporate bond issuance denominated in euros is growing exponentially; there is a progressive shift of central banks' reserves from dollars into euros; and the euro is increasingly important as a peg for other currencies. So why has it started out so poorly?

The main reason for the euro's weakness has been the relative strength of the US economy compared to the euro-zone, notably the former's continuing combination of dynamic growth with low inflation. This has been compounded by substantial net capital outflows from the euro countries, partly due to low inward investment and partly to foreign investors unwinding excessively bullish early positions in euro-zone assets. But

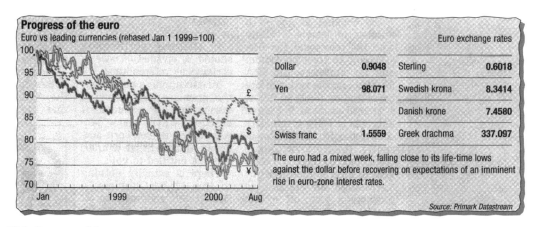

Fig. 16.1 Progress of the euro

these things will probably change as European growth gathers pace. Despite high-profile political interventions in the economy, the structural economic change Europe needs is starting to happen. And the macroeconomic picture is very promising: inflation is low; unemployment is falling; and the current account is strongly in surplus. What is more, the euro's relatively low level is good news for European businesses selling overseas.

Part of the problem may lie in the ECB's oft-criticised communication strategy. The monetary framework as presently configured is poorly equipped to deal with conflicting signals. For example, the widely advertised, self-imposed ceiling of 2 per cent for inflation makes the ECB more vulnerable to temporary overshooting than the more pragmatic Federal Reserve, which manages US monetary policy.

Europe's monetary architecture is unfinished, and this may further raise uncertainty. The Maastricht Treaty is unclear on who is in charge of the exchange rate: the ECB or national governments. Foreign exchange market intervention is controversial, which encourages prudence but only up to a point. With unclear attribution of responsibilities, neither party may be willing to take a risk. What is more, governments are likely to take different views among themselves as they face diverging economic conditions.

In the end, however, the euro's early weakness may simply be yet another instance of vagaries in the foreign exchange markets. Freely floating exchange rates are known to fluctuate wildly with little link to the fundamentals. In the face of such fluctuations, a policy of "benign neglect" may be the best option.

Despite the early weakness of the single currency, there is much talk of the "out" members of the EU joining it. As of late 2000, Greece was very keen to join and seemed to be fulfilling the Maastricht "convergence criteria". Denmark's referendum, however, ended up against adoption.

In the United Kingdom, the great Europe debate continued to rage but it seemed likely that there would be a referendum on the single currency at some point following the election in 2001.

In the meantime, the FT publishes a daily table on the Currencies and Money page, showing the relationship between the euro and the "out" currencies (see Figure 16.2):

ERM EURO RATES

Jun 20	Euro cen. rates	Rate against Euro €	Change on day	% +/- from cen. rate	% spread v weakest	Div. ind.
Greece	340.75	336.55	-0.05	-1.23	1.19	8
Denmark	7.46038	7.4564	-0.0013	-0.05	0.00	0
NON ERM MEMBERS						
UK	0.653644	0.63260	-0.0047	-3.22	3.27	

Euro central rates set by the European Central Bank. Sterling central rate set by the European Commission. Percentage changes are for Euro; a positive change denotes a weak currency. Divergence shows the ratio between two spreads: the percentage difference between the actual market and Euro central rates for a currency, and the maximum permitted percentage deviation of the currency's market rate from its Euro central rate.

Fig. 16.2 ERM euro rates

■ **Euro central rates:** the basic rates of national currencies against the euro around which they may fluctuate. These are set by the ECB or, in the case of sterling, the European Commission.

- **Rate against euro and change on day:** the current market rates of the national currencies against the euro, and the changes in those rates from the day's starting rates.

- **Percentage deviation from the central rate:** percentages by which the current market rates are above or below the central rates. The percentage differences are for the euro against the national currencies: a negative difference indicates that the currency has strengthened against the euro.

- **Percentage spread over the weakest currencies:** percentages by which currencies are spread against the weakest currency in the system.

- **Divergence index:** ratios between two spreads, the percentage deviation of actual market rates from euro central rates, and the maximum permitted percentage deviation of currencies' market rates from their euro central rates.

- **Non-ERM members:** sterling has still not sought re-entry to the ERM but for the purpose of tracking convergence between all countries of the EU, the newspaper calculates its exchange rate against the euro.

EMU and European capital markets

One of the hopes for the single currency is that it will eventually lead to pan-European capital markets. EMU offers the possibility of creating a domestic financial market to rival that of the United States. In 1995, for example, the combined value of outstanding equities, bonds and bank assets in the 11 countries in the euro-zone was $21,084 billion, compared to $22,865 billion in the US market. The key question is to what extent this arithmetic is likely to translate into economic reality. While a single currency is a necessary condition for the emergence of pan-European capital markets, it is by no means a sufficient one.

The assessment of many economists is that the impact of the euro on European capital markets is very favourable. On almost all counts, EMU has either already drastically changed the financial landscape of Europe or has the potential to do so in the future. This success is all the more surprising given the euro's early weakness against the dollar.

Europe's capital markets have undergone a remarkable transformation since the euro was launched. A euro-denominated corporate bond market has emerged with issuing activity in 1999 in excess of that in the dollar market. Primary issues in European equity have reached record highs. Europe-wide indices have been established and portfolios have begun to be allocated along pan-European sectoral lines rather than on a country basis. Eurex, the German–Swiss exchange founded in 1998, has overtaken the Chicago Board of Trade to become the world's largest derivative exchange. Banks all over Europe have merged or formed alliances on an unprecedented scale, dramatically changing national banking environments and beginning to create international firms and networks. And cross-border mergers in all industries have increased strongly, giving rise to record volumes in Europe's M&A industry.

Some of these developments could have been expected as consequences of the "direct effects" of the euro. These effects comprise standardisation and transparency in pricing; shrinking of the foreign exchange market; elimination of currency risk; elimination of currency-related investment regulations; and homogenisation of the public bond market and bank refinancing procedures. But the euro also has indirect effects on the cost of cross-country transactions within the euro-zone; the liquidity of European financial markets; and the diversification opportunities available to European investors.

In the first instance, EMU had little direct effect on transaction costs, but it clearly made the existing obstacles and inefficiencies more visible. Within Europe, cross-border payments and securities settlements are more expensive, lengthier, riskier and less standardised than equivalent domestic transactions. What is more, the euro-zone has 18 large-value systems (compared to two in the United States), 23 securities settlement systems (compared to three in the United States) and 13 retail payments systems (again, compared to three in the United States). Differences in taxation, legislation and standards create further obstacles.

EMU has prompted a renewed urgency among policy makers to address these problems. The establishment of TARGET and EURO1 – the settlement systems for large transactions for the European System of Central Banks and the European Banking Association, respectively – and the implementation of the European Commission's Directive on cross-border credit transfers are the most visible steps taken in this direction.

Despite the problem of transaction costs, by eliminating currency risk, EMU has put traders in foreign euro-denominated assets on an equal risk base with domestic traders. Together with the increase in transparency resulting from the single currency, this has greatly reduced the barriers to trading such assets. In this sense, EMU has increased the demand side of the market for every asset traded in the euro-zone. And to the extent that expanded markets give rise to increased trading, this should reduce liquidity risk.

A second potential benefit of increased market size is the opportunity for greater diversification. EMU fosters market integration not just by eliminating foreign exchange risk, but by improving information flows and by reorientating traditional international asset allocation methods from a country basis to a pan-European industry basis.

■ Enlargement

The issue of the single currency has dominated the European Union in recent years. But an equally important issue is that of expanding EU membership. The Helsinki summit at the end of 1999 launched accession negotiations with five East European countries plus Malta and Turkey. This brought to 13 the number of potential new EU members in the first decade of the new century. Can this possibly be good news for the European economy?

Many people are understandably dubious about the economic benefits of an EU enlargement involving Turkey, although the political benefits are probably substantial.

But eastern enlargement to encompass several of the formerly communist countries now undergoing "economic transition" looks like offering extraordinary growth opportunities for western European companies and investors.

Economic integration almost invariably improves growth: by opening the west's markets to eastern agricultural and lower-tech manufacturing goods, incomes will be substantially raised in the east, increasing demand for the higher-tech products and services of western companies. At the same time, the latter can invest more easily in the east, often making more productive use of their capital.

Here lies one of the key benefits of enlargement, not only for these companies but also for investors: EU membership locks countries into well-defined property rights, sound policies and open capital markets. These mean investors can put money in and out easily, making investment substantially less risky but still with very promising returns.

Members and potential members of the European Union

Original members

Belgium
France
Germany
Italy
Luxembourg
Netherlands

First enlargement

Denmark
Ireland
United Kingdom

Second enlargement

Portugal
Spain

Third enlargement

Greece

Fourth enlargement

Austria
Finland
Sweden

Candidates for future accession

The Visegrad countries
Czech Republic
Hungary
Poland
Slovakia

From the Balkans
Romania
Bulgaria
Slovenia

From the Mediterranean
Malta
Cyprus

The Baltic states
Estonia
Latvia
Lithuania

Plus
Turkey

"No nation was ever ruined by trade."

Benjamin Franklin

"When your neighbour loses his job, it's a slowdown; when you lose your job, it's a recession; when an economist loses his job, it's a depression."

Anon

17

The world economy

Trade, growth and international institutions

- **The world economy** – the main regional groupings: North America, the European Union, and east Asia; the rest of the world

- **Global economic institutions** – the key international forums: the IMF; World Bank; G7; OECD; EBRD

- **Economic growth and development** – export orientation, sequencing, aid and debt; migration, the environment and economic transition

- **International trade** – comparative advantage and the gains from trade; trade liberalisation

- **Exchange rates and international finance** – the role of central banks

Business and investment decisions are increasingly made in an international context. Global flows of goods, services and capital are making national economies more and more interdependent, and this trend appears unlikely to be reversed. First, there seems to be a consensus on the positive effects of liberal trade policies whereby barriers to trade between nations are reduced and removed. Second, national product markets are increasingly dominated by powerful multinational corporations, companies that cut across national boundaries and are eager to produce and sell their output wherever they can do so profitably. And third, as the second part of this book discussed, there are the international financial markets (for debt and equity capital, for cash and currencies, and for commodities and derivative products), in which borrowers seek the cheapest funds available, and investors and speculators chase the highest possible returns.

Economic globalisation is having increasingly important effects on national economies, on local financial markets and on individual companies. In making business and investment decisions, it is no longer advisable simply to take account of the domestic economy, either with regard to particular markets or at the aggregate level. Even if a business tends to rely on domestic suppliers or sell primarily to the home market, or if investors restrict their portfolios to the local exchanges, it is still useful to consider international trade and financial flows, and economic developments elsewhere in the world. These can affect any business, adding an international dimension to economic considerations.

Alongside the process of globalisation are the processes of market integration and regionalisation, pursued by national governments. The countries of western Europe are well advanced on the path to integrating their economies, as well as coordinating their economic policies, and many other regions of the world are following their example. These processes, too, interact with the business of exporting and importing, with running a business more generally, and with national and international asset markets. It is valuable to understand them and their coverage in the *Financial Times* in order to make more informed business and investment decisions.

■ The world economy

The world economy breaks down into a number of key regional or other economic groupings based on standards of living, levels of output and trade, and historical or geographical connection. The three most powerful blocs are North America (the United States and its partners in the North American Free Trade Agreement or NAFTA, Canada and Mexico), the 15 member states of the European Union (EU) and east Asia centred on Japan. While the United States remains the world's dominant economy, representing a quarter of global output and a third of the industrialised countries' output, the other two blocs are certainly threatening its position. This post-communist balance is sometimes described as the tripolar world.

Japan and the NAFTA and EU countries, plus 11 other industrialised countries, primarily located in western Europe, form the Organisation for Economic Cooperation and

Development (OECD), the "rich countries' club". The leading countries of the OECD (the United States, Japan, Germany, France, Italy, the United Kingdom and Canada) make up the Group of Seven (G7), which as a whole accounts for two-thirds of world output. Then there are the "newly industrialised countries" (NICs) of south-east Asia, the mainly Middle Eastern nations of the Organisation of Petroleum Exporting Countries (OPEC), the ex-communist countries of eastern Europe and the former Soviet Union, and the developing countries of Latin America, Africa and the rest of the world.

1973 is often seen as the turning point of the post-war period, marking the end of the high growth, low inflation, full employment, and fixed exchange rate years, and the beginning of the more uncertain times since. The problems of the latter period were launched by the floating of the dollar and the consequent chaos in the international financial markets; and by the oil crises, when the price of oil quadrupled within the space of three months.

The collapse of communism at the end of the 1980s was expected to usher in a new era of prosperity. But the countries of eastern Europe are finding that the struggle to make the transition from a command economy to a market economy is far more difficult than expected. Worse still is the position of the former Soviet Union: Russia's economic reform efforts have run into ever greater problems, while the disintegration of the Comecon trading bloc has greatly increased the adjustment problems of all the former communist states. Africa continues to lag economically behind the rest of the globe.

Although economic statistics from outside the United Kingdom are reported by the *Financial Times* on a less systematic basis than the UK figures, a broad range of figures are published throughout the year. For the world, the most regular and reliable statistics are collated by the IMF in its monthly publication *International Financial Statistics* and its annual *World Economic Outlook*. Another useful source of statistical information is the OECD, in particular its annual country reports and the twice yearly *Economic Outlook*.

On Tuesday, the newspaper includes a table of international economic indicators comparing key variables for the six main economies of the OECD: the United Kingdom, the United States, Japan, Germany, France and Italy. In rotation, these cover monthly figures for production and employment, prices and competitiveness, money and finance, and balance of payments (see Figure 17.1), plus a quarterly presentation of figures for national accounts. For countries outside the OECD, especially in Latin America, Africa and Asia, the most detailed economic coverage, in addition to IMF statistics, is often the FT special survey of the country, published once a year.

Global economic institutions

A number of international fora exist to discuss global economic issues, and the newspaper reports on most of their activities. The main ones are:

■ **The International Monetary Fund:** set up by the Bretton Woods agreement of 1944 and coming into operation in March 1947, this institution was established to encourage international cooperation on monetary issues. The aim of the Fund is to tide members over temporary balance of payments difficulties. It does this by making hard-currency loans to members while trying to enforce structural adjustment of their economies. The Fund has more than 140 members who pay subscriptions according to the size of their economies. They pay 75 per cent of the quota in their own currency and 25 per cent in international reserve assets. Members are then given borrowing rights with the Fund, which they can use to help finance a balance of payments deficit. Countries in difficulty can also negotiate standby credit on which they can draw as necessary. Members are required to repay their drawings over a three- to five-year period.

■ **The World Bank:** established at the same time as the IMF, and originally intended to finance Europe's post-war reconstruction, this institution has subsequently concentrated on loans to poor countries to become one of the largest single sources of development aid. The Bank has traditionally supported a wide range of long-term investments, including infrastructure projects such as roads, telecommunications and electricity supply. Its funds come mainly from the industrialised nations, but it also raises money on international capital markets. The Bank operates according to business principles, lending at commercial rates of interest only to those governments it feels are capable of servicing and repaying their debts.

■ **Group of Seven (G7):** a grouping that dates back to 1975 when the French president, Valéry Giscard d'Estaing, invited the leaders of the United States, West Germany, Japan and the United Kingdom to discuss economic problems following the first oil price shock. Since then, the summits have grown to include political and foreign issues, which form the subject of a political declaration issued on the penultimate day of talks. The sixth and seventh members are Italy and Canada. Since the disintegration of the Soviet Union, Russia has also participated in many of the discussions.

■ **Organisation for Economic Cooperation and Development:** sometimes referred to as the rich countries' club, this organisation's membership consists of the 30 industrialised nations of the world (Slovakia being the most recent new member, joining in 2000) with a secretariat based in Paris. It too goes back to the end of the war when it was set up to organise Europe's recovery. It is now more of a think-tank to discuss economic issues of mutual interest, but it is a particularly valuable source of publications. Its annual surveys of the member countries and twice yearly *Economic Outlook* provide a useful overview of prospects for the industrialised world.

■ **European Bank for Reconstruction and Development (EBRD):** a development bank set up in 1990 to help the countries of eastern Europe develop market economies. An EU initiative, it resembles existing multinational regional development banks, such as the African Development Bank and the Inter-American Development Bank, and was the first institution specifically designed to coordinate western economic help for eastern Europe in the wake of the collapse of their communist regimes. EU states and institutions have a 53.7 per cent stake; most other European countries are also shareholders and the United States has the biggest single stake of 10 per cent. Japan's 8.5 per cent shareholding matches those of the United Kingdom, Germany, France and Italy.

Economic growth and development

All countries pursue economic growth, an increase in their output of goods and services, and an increase in their incomes to purchase those goods and services as well as those produced abroad. For countries outside the industrialised world, this is generally termed development. Numerous different policies have been tried since the war to achieve this goal, but nowadays it is typically pursued through a combination of encouraging production of goods for export, attracting foreign direct investment, borrowing from banks and international institutions, aid from overseas, macroeconomic stabilisation policy, and market liberalisation. Much debate centres on the appropriate "sequencing" of economic policies for development, meaning which ones should come first.

The economies of south-east Asia have been the most successful at development, becoming the "newly industrialised countries", or NICs. Much of that success may have resulted from high export orientation as measured by exports as a proportion of GDP, what is known as export-led growth. Many of the countries of eastern Europe, Latin America, Africa, and elsewhere in Asia (notably India and China), are eager to follow the progress of the NICs, and, as a consequence, it is important for the markets of the developed world to be open to their products.

Part of such development can be funded by foreign aid. Some is in the form of bilateral grants and loans, as opposed to contributions to multilateral institutions. The remainder is tied to the purchase of goods and services from donor countries. This kind of aid is less beneficial to poor countries since it forces recipients to pay higher prices for imports, encourages them to invest in vast capital projects, and does little for the relief of poverty, one of the most pressing problems of the developing world.

Another notable problem for developing countries has been the debt crisis, when numerous governments defaulted on their loans from western banks. Until early 1995, this had eased considerably since the late 1980s when Latin American countries particularly had very high debt service ratios, the proportion of export revenues taken up by debt repayment. It was re-ignited at that point when Mexico was plunged into a deep financial crisis with implications for the rest of the continent and other emerging markets.

The World Bank discerns five major development challenges for the future. These are the promotion of economic reforms likely to help the poor, perhaps in contrast to the inequitable "structural adjustment" (somewhat extreme free market) programmes of the past; increased investment in people, particularly through education, health care and family planning; protection of the environment; stimulation of private sector development; and public sector reform that provides the conditions in which private enterprise might flourish.

Migration, the environment and economic transition

Alongside the longstanding issues of economic development in the "third world" are the more recent development problems of the formerly planned economies of eastern Europe and the ex-Soviet Union. The transition of these countries to democratic market economies has thrown up many new questions about the appropriate sequencing of economic policies and the extent to which market reforms (including price liberalisation, trade liberalisation, privatisation, establishment of capital markets and the institution of a legal and regulatory framework) should be implemented suddenly as "shock therapy". There is also concern in the traditional developing world about the diversion of industrialised nations' attention, aid, trade preferences and capital.

A major issue in both developing and ex-communist countries is the environment, and whether the goals of expanded trade and development, and protection and preservation of the environment, are compatible. For example, should developing countries adopt less strict regulations on pollution by "dirty" industries than the developed world in order to attract investment by firms in those industries? At the heart of this debate is the concept of "sustainable development", whether there are policies that promote both economic growth and an improved environment. This is a highly contentious issue: many developing countries ask why environmental concerns should hinder their progress when the industrialised countries had ignored such concerns in their own development.

Another issue high on the international agenda is also very contentious, that of migration. Flows of goods, services and capital are well covered by the institutions of global capitalism, but there is little policy on the treatment of international flows of people. Indeed, there is much hypocrisy among believers in the free market system, demanding "free markets, free trade and free enterprise", but at the same time, strict immigration controls. If trade and finance can flow freely, why not labour, some ask. Such considerations have stressed the importance of free trade and foreign investment to discourage mass migration: by investing directly in the poorer parts of the world and providing open markets to their products, the industrialised countries will not experience so much migratory pressure from those places.

■ International trade

International trade is a central driving force of global economic growth and development, and the general trend since the war has been for it to increase. Today, the United States is the biggest exporter, while Germany and Japan are neck and neck for second place. The trade figures for these and three other leading European countries (France, Italy and the United Kingdom) are published monthly in the *Financial Times* (see Figure 17.1), showing:

■ **Exports:** the level of exports of merchandise (that is, trade in physical goods, not services) in billions of euros.

■ **Visible trade balance:** the difference between the value of merchandise exports and imports in billions of euros. The value of imports can be derived by subtracting the visible trade balance from exports.

INTERNATIONAL ECONOMIC INDICATORS: BALANCE OF PAYMENTS

Trade figures are in billions of Euros. The exchange rate shows the number of national currency units per Ecu up to end 1998 and per Euro thereafter. The nominal effective exchange rate is an index with 1990=100.

UNITED STATES

	Exports	Visible trade balance	Current account balance	Ecu/Euro exch. rate	Effective exch. rate
1989	330.2	−99.3	−94.6	1.1017	104.9
1990	309.0	−79.3	−62.2	1.2745	100.0
1991	340.5	−53.5	3.5	1.2391	98.5
1992	345.9	−65.2	−39.1	1.2957	96.5
1993	397.3	−98.7	−72.9	1.1705	99.4
1994	432.3	−127.0	−102.6	1.1857	97.6
1995	452.3	−122.8	−87.8	1.2928	91.7
1996	499.0	−135.9	−103.2	1.2526	96.6
1997	609.4	−159.6	−126.9	1.1309	104.4
1998	607.5	−204.6	−196.4	1.1229	109.4
1999	651.7	−309.4	−317.7	1.0667	106.8
3rd qtr.1999	108.0	−83.4	−85.4	1.0492	107.3
4th qtr.1999	175.5	−88.7	−92.7	1.0378	104.7
1st qtr.2000	188.9	−102.3	−103.7	0.9869	107.2
2nd qtr.2000				0.9339	110.1
July 1999	55.4	−29.0	n.a.	1.0357	109.8
August	55.8	−27.4	n.a.	1.0612	107.0
September	57.3	−27.1	n.a.	1.0508	105.1
October	56.1	−28.2	n.a.	1.0698	104.0
November	58.1	−30.2	n.a.	1.0323	104.9
December	61.4	−30.3	n.a.	1.0112	105.3
January 2000	60.6	−32.0	n.a.	1.0124	105.4
February	63.0	−33.2	n.a.	0.9835	108.0
March	65.4	−37.2	n.a.	0.9649	108.0
April	66.7	−38.1	n.a.	0.9466	108.6
May	69.2	−40.0	n.a.	0.9051	112.1
June			n.a.	0.9501	109.3

JAPAN

	Exports	Visible trade balance	Current account balance	Ecu/Euro exchange rate	Effective exchange rate
1989	246.6	74.7	60.1	151.87	110.9
1990	221.3	54.9	35.7	183.94	100.0
1991	249.4	77.9	57.8	166.44	108.4
1992	256.4	96.0	86.3	164.05	113.7
1993	300.1	118.2	111.1	130.31	136.6
1994	324.8	121.2	109.9	120.99	147.1
1995	331.5	101.4	86.2	121.43	154.6
1996	319.8	66.6	52.9	136.24	134.1
1997	361.7	89.8	83.4	136.84	126.2
1998	333.6	109.6	107.1	146.69	118.3
1999	376.6	115.0	102.8	121.40	138.4
3rd qtr.1999	97.4	29.0	26.3	118.80	139.5
4th qtr.1999	105.8	28.8	25.0	108.44	151.4
1st qtr.2000	115.4	33.7	34.6	105.65	150.5
2nd qtr.2000	124.7	35.0	34.9	99.59	154.4
July 1999	31.1	9.5	9.5	123.72	132.7
August	32.3	9.2	8.7	120.29	138.6
September	34.1	10.3	8.0	112.40	147.1
October	33.6	10.9	9.9	113.40	147.3
November	35.7	8.7	7.9	108.04	151.3
December	36.8	9.1	7.1	103.87	155.2
January 2000	37.2	12.1	12.0	106.72	151.1
February	38.5	12.2	14.2	107.64	147.2
March	39.8	9.4	8.3	102.58	152.8
April	42.0	13.6	12.8	99.99	154.8
May	41.0	10.1	11.4	98.01	154.0
June	41.6	11.2	10.8	100.76	154.5

GERMANY

	Exports	Visible trade balance	Current account balance	Ecu/Euro exchange rate	Effective exchange rate
1989	*327.9*	*68.8*	*54.7*	*2.0681*	*95.9*
1990	340.6	54.0	40.6	2.0537	100.0
1991	340.4	11.8	−15.6	2.0480	99.1
1992	343.2	17.3	−11.7	2.0187	102.1
1993	321.3	30.1	−8.3	1.9337	106.1
1994	353.1	36.4	−19.8	1.9198	106.4
1995	383.2	43.6	−15.2	1.8509	111.9
1996	403.4	50.3	−6.1	1.8844	108.9
1997	454.3	59.7	−2.5	1.9584	103.9
1998	488.4	64.4	−4.1	1.9728	104.1
1999	505.1	63.7	−19.6	1.9558	102.0
3rd qtr.1999	129.7	15.5	−8.9	1.9558	101.6
4th qtr.1999	132.4	16.9	−5.0	1.9558	100.5
1st qtr.2000	140.2	15.9	−3.2	1.9558	99.3
2nd qtr.2000	146.4	15.1		1.9558	98.0
July 1999	43.4	6.5	−1.8	1.9558	101.8
August	43.1	3.5	−4.6	1.9558	102.0
September	43.2	5.5	−2.6	1.9558	101.1
October	42.6	5.0	−1.8	1.9558	101.4
November	45.9	5.8	−0.1	1.9558	100.4
December	43.9	6.1	−3.0	1.9558	99.7
January 2000	45.5	4.1	−7.9	1.9558	99.7
February	46.2	6.1	0.8	1.9558	99.5
March	48.5	5.7	3.9	1.9558	98.7
April	46.8	4.7	−1.7	1.9558	97.9
May	49.7	4.3	−3.0	1.9558	97.3
June	49.9	6.1		1.9558	98.6

FRANCE

	Exports	Visible trade balance	Current account balance	Ecu/Euro exchange rate	Effective exch. rate
1989	171.3	−10.6	−3.8	7.0169	95.9
1990	176.0	−12.2	−7.6	6.9202	100.0
1991	182.3	−9.6	−5.2	6.9643	98.3
1992	185.6	−0.3	3.0	6.8420	101.5
1993	177.8	8.2	8.1	6.6281	105.0
1994	196.8	6.7	5.4	6.5659	104.5
1995	215.3	8.3	8.3	6.4460	109.2
1996	223.4	11.2	16.0	6.4068	109.1
1997	257.8	23.9	34.8	6.5925	105.6
1998	274.4	21.9	36.4	6.6137	106.1
1999	282.2	17.2	34.3	6.5596	104.6
3rd qtr.1999	73.0	5.4	11.4	6.5596	104.2
4th qtr.1999	73.4	2.9	8.2	6.5596	103.4
1st qtr.2000	76.4	2.1	7.3	6.5596	102.3
2nd qtr.2000				6.5596	101.3
July 1999	24.6	2.6	2.3	6.5596	104.3
August	24.1	1.0	4.5	6.5596	104.5
September	24.3	1.9	4.6	6.5996	103.9
October	24.7	1.8	3.7	6.5596	104.1
November	24.5	1.0	3.0	6.5596	103.3
December	24.1	0.2	1.5	6.5596	102.7
January 2000	25.2	0.7	1.6	6.5596	102.7
February	25.6	0.7	0.2	6.5596	102.4
March	25.6	0.7	2.5	6.5996	101.9
April	25.2	0.2	1.5	6.5996	101.2
May	27.6	1.9	3.9	6.5996	100.7
June				6.5996	101.9

ITALY

	Exports	Visible trade balance	Current account balance	Ecu/Euro exchange rate	Effective exchange rate
1989	99.6	−8.8	−8.4	1509.2	98.5
1990	105.1	−7.3	−10.1	1523.2	100.0
1991	108.3	−8.3	−15.2	1531.3	98.6
1992	113.3	−6.5	−18.6	1591.5	95.5
1993	137.5	17.2	8.3	1836.7	80.4
1994	159.1	18.5	11.8	1908.6	76.9
1995	196.9	23.5	22.6	2106.4	69.3
1996	200.8	34.9	32.7	1932.1	75.7
1997	208.8	26.8	28.6	1924.0	76.3
1998	217.8	25.2	18.4	1947.3	76.0
1999	214.2	13.1	11.1	1936.3	74.6
3rd qtr.1999	52.8	5.3	4.8	1936.3	74.4
4th qtr.1999	58.3	2.3	−1.0	1936.3	73.8
1st qtr.2000	56.8	−0.4	−1.8	1936.3	73.0
2nd qtr.2000				1936.3	72.3
July 1999	21.1	3.9	3.9	1936.3	74.4
August	13.3	1.8	1.6	1936.3	74.6
September	18.4	−0.5	−0.7	1936.3	74.1
October	20.4	1.5	1.3	1936.3	74.3
November	19.5	1.1	−0.5	1936.3	73.7
December	18.5	−0.1	−1.7	1936.3	73.3
January 2000	15.0	−1.2	−1.7	1936.3	73.3
February	19.4	0.0	−0.3	1936.3	73.1
March	22.4	0.7	0.2	1936.3	72.7
April	19.3	−0.3	−0.9	1936.3	72.3
May	22.4	−0.6	−1.1	1936.3	71.9
June				1936.3	72.7

UNITED KINGDOM

	Exports	Visible trade balance	Current account balance	Ecu/Euro exchange rate	Effective exchange rate
1989	137.6	−36.7	−34.9	0.6728	102.3
1990	143.1	−26.2	−27.3	0.7150	100.0
1991	148.4	−14.6	−12.0	0.7002	100.8
1992	146.6	−17.7	−13.7	0.7359	97.0
1993	156.9	−17.1	−13.6	0.7780	89.0
1994	174.8	−14.3	−1.9	0.7736	89.2
1995	187.7	−14.3	−4.6	0.8190	84.8
1996	208.6	−16.3	−0.7	0.8026	86.3
1997	248.8	−17.2	9.6	0.6906	100.6
1998	242.2	−30.3	−1.0	0.6775	104.0
1999	250.7	−40.4	−19.4	0.6591	103.8
3rd qtr.1999	66.4	−8.7	−4.1	0.6549	103.9
4th qtr.1999	67.5	−11.3	−2.4	0.6364	106.0
1st qtr.2000	72.6	−10.7	−6.5	0.6142	108.5
2nd qtr.2000				0.6092	107.7
July 1999	21.3	−3.5	n.a.	0.6577	103.5
August	22.4	−2.9	n.a.	0.6602	103.4
September	22.7	−2.3	n.a.	0.6469	104.8
October	22.1	−3.4	n.a.	0.6456	105.4
November	22.7	−3.8	n.a.	0.6367	105.8
December	22.7	−4.2	n.a.	0.6268	106.8
January 2000	23.3	−4.2	n.a.	0.6172	100.5
February	24.2	−3.3	n.a.	0.6148	108.5
March	25.1	−3.2	n.a.	0.6106	108.5
April	24.8	−4.4	n.a.	0.5977	110.1
May	25.5	−4.3	n.a.	0.6004	108.6
June			n.a.	0.6296	104.7

The trade figures for the USA, Japan and the UK have been converted using the Ecu exchange rate up till end 1998 and the Euro rate thereafter. The figures for Germany, France and Italy are in Euros throughout. All trade figures are seasonally adjusted, except for the Italian series and the German current account. Imports can be derived by subtracting the visible trade balance from exports. Export and import data are calculated on the FOB (free on board) basis, except for German and Italian imports which use the CIF method (including carriage, insurance and freight charges). German data up to and including June 1990, shown in italics, refer to the former West Germany. The nominal effective exchange rates are period averages of Bank of England trade-weighted indices. Data supplied by Datastream and WEFA from national government and central bank sources.

Fig. 17.1 International economic indicators: balance of payments

- **Current account balance:** the balance of trade in goods and services in billions of euros.
- **Ecu/euro exchange rate:** the number of national currency units per ecu up to the end of 1998 and per euro after that.
- **Effective exchange rate:** a nominal average exchange rate against a trade-weighted basket of currencies presented as an index based on 1990=100. Effective exchange rates do not take account of differential rates of inflation, and are therefore not a useful guide to national competitiveness. They are, however, a valuable way of expressing the equivalent of a currency's movements against all other key currencies in one figure.

The interaction of national economies through international trade increases world output by allowing countries to specialise in the production of those goods and services that they can produce most efficiently. Countries could cut themselves off from the rest of the world, and seek to provide for all their needs domestically. However, if, for example, their industries are particularly good at making high-quality, low-cost computers, and not so efficient at growing rice, it makes sense to focus their energies on the manufacture of computers, and, in effect, trade them for rice with other countries. Even if those other countries are not more efficient at rice-growing, but agriculture is still their most effective industry, specialisation in production followed by free trade should still be beneficial to all parties.

It is generally accepted that specialisation (to some degree) and free trade allow all countries to develop more rapidly, and expand global output and incomes. However, there are many obstacles to their working out in practice. These arise from the interests of particular groups within countries (including managers, investors and employees), and play out in governments' trade and commercial policies, in recurrent trade disputes between countries and trading blocs, and in the great debate between free trade and protectionism.

A number of arguments for protection are advanced. For example, companies in declining or internationally uncompetitive industries sometimes demand protection in order to avoid going out of business. Their managers might argue for the "national interest", the importance of producing their goods domestically, the unemployment their failure would cause (here they would be backed by their workforce), and the "cheating" strategies their foreign competitors adopt.

Similarly, firms in "infant industries" (often new, high-technology, sectors) might claim they need protection because they are as yet too young, small and weak to compete effectively at the international level. Governments themselves might pursue strategic protection of industries they believe it might be dangerous for foreigners to control.

The trade policies of the EU, for example, are the outcome of three conflicting compulsions: the liberal commitment to the idea of free trade, as reflected in multiple global trading initiatives; the protectionist desire to shield some domestic producers from foreign suppliers; and what is known as a "pyramid of preferences", which ranks various trading partners, often on the basis of historical connection. The protectionist element of these policies has predominantly been directed at manufactured imports from other industrialised countries, but, increasingly, they also affect goods produced by competitive suppliers in less developed countries.

▪ Trade liberalisation

The growth of international trade is frequently hampered by barriers erected to keep out imports and protect domestic industries. These might take the form of tariffs, quotas, duties, limits, "voluntary export restraints" and a host of other schemes. Since the end of the war, big advances have been made in reducing these barriers to the free flow of goods and services, but there is still a long way to go. The world recession of the early 1990s threatened a renewed bout of protectionism as countries looked inwards to deal with their own problems.

The main forum for addressing trade issues was the General Agreement on Tariffs and Trade (GATT), a multinational institution set up in 1947 to promote the expansion of international trade through a coordinated programme of trade liberalisation. The GATT's primary two-pronged approach was to eliminate quotas and reduce tariffs. It supervised several conferences (or "rounds") on tariff reductions and the removal of other barriers to trade, and, in late 1993, brought to completion the Uruguay Round of trade discussions. Part of the final agreement was that it should become the World Trade Organisation.

The Uruguay Round (1986–93) was an attempt by the international community to renegotiate the world trading system. With the participation of over 100 countries, it aimed both to repair the old GATT and to extend it to many new areas: it was the first negotiating round in which developing countries pledged themselves to substantive obligations; it was the first application of liberal trading principles to the services sector, foreign direct investment, and intellectual property rights; and it re-integrated into the GATT system two important sectors, textiles and agriculture.

The success of the Uruguay Round centres on, among other things, an enormous cut in tariffs. This, coupled with more transparent and orderly trading rules, gave a powerful boost to the world economy, stimulating competition and offering developing countries new opportunities for integration into international markets. The accords of the Final Act, agreed on 15 December 1993, came into force in 1995 following ratification by all member countries.

The Uruguay Round introduced a series of institutional innovations to back up the new rules: a semi-judicial dispute settlement system, a trade policy review mechanism and the new World Trade Organisation. The principal change is that the old GATT has lapsed: the new system as it results from the Final Act of the Uruguay Round is a very different and legally distinct institution.

At ministerial meetings in Seattle in late 1999, the WTO tried to launch a new round of talks on trade liberalisation – the so-called "Millennium Round". But there was strong opposition to these latest globalisation efforts from an alliance of environmentalists, trade unionists and assorted human and consumer rights activists. The eventual failure of the meeting reflected several negative forces: the parties' widely disparate positions; the lukewarm attitude of many governments towards further trade liberalisation; and the difficulties experienced by the WTO as an institution.

It is generally felt that if the WTO is to recover from Seattle, it will need to bring the developing countries much more securely into the trading system. After all, developing countries comprise a large majority of WTO membership and account for an increasing share of world trade and the bulk of its growth. At present, they feel frustrated about the difficulties of implementing the Uruguay Round and by the unsympathetic attitude of the developed countries towards their aspirations.

Having torn the fabric of the world trading system, it will be impossible to put it together again without the active enthusiasm of a majority of its members. But restoring the system's legitimacy in the eyes of a majority of its members is not mere charity: rather, it is a matter of self-interest for the developed countries. They still have much to gain from both the further liberalisation of world trade and the disciplines that an effective WTO imposes on domestic policy discretion.

Alongside the process of trade liberalisation across the globe is that of market integration. This process typically begins with a free trade agreement, an arrangement between countries (usually in the same geographical region of the world) to eliminate all trade barriers between themselves on goods and services, but in which each continues to operate its own particular barriers against trade with the rest of the world. It may develop into a customs union or common market where arrangements for trade with the rest of the world are harmonised, subsequently into a single market like the EU, and perhaps on to full economic and monetary union.

A number of regional free trade agreements exist, most notably the NAFTA and the Association of South East Asian Nations (ASEAN), which includes Brunei, Indonesia, Malaysia, the Philippines, Singapore, Thailand and Vietnam. Such initial efforts at market integration are spreading rapidly, including, for example, the Mercosur in Latin America, incorporating Brazil, Argentina, Uruguay and Paraguay.

■ Exchange rates and international finance

The cross-border exchange of goods and services is made possible by the fact that it is possible to convert one national currency into another. Thus, a UK company wishing to buy a US product (priced naturally in the local currency, dollars) can make the transaction by buying dollars with its pounds. The price it pays for those dollars in sterling is the exchange rate, and the markets on which it buys them are the international currency markets.

When these markets are allowed to work freely, with the price of currencies in terms of other currencies fluctuating according to demand and supply, it is known as a floating exchange rate system. That, for example, is the kind of system currently in place between the dollar and the yen. The opposite is to have rates set by governments with occasional devaluations and revaluations: a fixed rate system, such as the one that operated in the post-war world up to 1973. In practice, systems are typically somewhere in between, with rates allowed to fluctuate to some extent, but managed by national monetary authorities.

As well as providing the means for companies and countries to conduct trade across borders, exchange rates also allow various forms of international investment and speculation. Broadly characterised, there are three types: first, there is speculation by owners of large quantities of "hot money", constantly moving their funds around the world in pursuit of the best return, and going in and out of money market accounts in response to minuscule shifts in relative interest rates. "Hot money" flows in and out of countries in response to the pursuit of short-term gain and without any considerations of longer-term issues of economic development of product markets or national economies. It moves simply on the basis of movements or expected movements of exchange rates and relative interest rates.

Second, there is portfolio investment in international asset markets by investors. This flow of cross-border financial investment is growing substantially as investors place larger portions of their portfolios in international equities and bonds. As with all portfolio investment, this might be short- or long-term investment, depending on the goals of the investors, immediate profit or longer-term financial goals. It is reflected particularly in the increasing enthusiasm for the emerging markets (see Chapter 9).

Third, there is international capital investment by companies, seeking low-cost production facilities and/or access to new markets, and by governments and financial institutions. In the case of the private sector, this is called foreign direct investment (FDI); from governments, it might be in the form of loans, or conditional or unconditional aid. Such investment might also come from major global organisations such as the World Bank. Given the difficulties of planning such investments, they typically have long-term ambitions in mind.

The role of central banks

The forces of globalisation and liberalisation have led to major changes in the way central banks go about their principal tasks. Markets have become much more powerful: they discipline unsustainable policies; and they give participants ways to get round administrative restrictions on their freedom of action. This means that central banks have to work with rather than against market forces. Maintaining low inflation requires the credibility to harness market expectations in its support. And effective prudential supervision involves "incentive-compatible" regulation.

In monetary policy, attempts to exploit a supposed trade-off between inflation and unemployment have given way to a focus on achieving price stability as the best environment in which to pursue sustainable growth. The intermediate goals of monetary policy have also changed. Monetary targets and exchange rate pegs have proved difficult to use in practice, and an increasing number of countries have adopted inflation targets, backed up by transparency in the policy-making process and independence of action for central banks.

The objective of financial stability has acquired much more prominence in recent years, following various high-profile mishaps at individual institutions and severe problems in some financial systems. It has become harder to segment different types of financial activity or to apply restrictions to the activities of individual institutions. Systemic stability requires ensuring that financial institutions properly understand and manage the risks they acquire, and hold an appropriate level of capital against them.

The international monetary system has been through a major transformation in the past 25 years. The Bretton Woods system developed at the end of the Second World War was "government-led": official bodies decided on exchange rates and the provision of liquidity, and oversaw the international adjustment process. Now, the system is "market-led": major exchange rates are floating; liquidity is determined by the market; and the adjustment mechanism operates through market forces. The job of central banks is to see that market forces work efficiently and that any instability is counteracted. This seems to mean stable and sustainable macroeconomic policies, and, where possible, action to ensure that inevitable changes in the direction and intensity of capital flows do not destabilise financial systems.

PART 4

Beyond the financial pages

"I am a better investor because I am a businessman,

and a better businessman because I am an investor."

Warren Buffett

"Because there is so much noise in the world, people adopt rules of thumb."

Fischer Black

18

Company and investor lives

The key performance ratios

by Ken Langdon

- **Key financial ratios** – what to look for in annual reports: gearing; income gearing; return on capital employed; pre-tax profit margin

- **Key shareholder ratios** – what to look for in the financial pages: yield; price/earnings ratio; dividend cover

- **The life of a growth stock** – four stages in the history of a telecommunications company: the annual report; changes in the key financial and shareholder ratios

Ken Langdon is co-author of *Smart Things to Know About Business Finance* (Capstone) and works with businesses and investors to improve understanding of financial information. For further details, contact (01628) 782193.

Any person in business has two, three or at most four financial ratios by which he or she measures performance. These ratios are very specific to each individual. The head of a consultancy will be concerned with the ratio of days billed to days available. A sales manager will be worried about orders taken to date as a proportion of the budget or target for that period of time. And a self-employed one-man company in the building trade will probably focus simply on what money is owed to him, what money he owes to his suppliers, what his bank balance is, and the amount and timing of his next tax bill. These financial ratios are by no means the only indicators of the health of a business, but they are chosen by their owners because of their crucial importance to achieving success.

Investors are never in the position of a manager in a business of knowing intimately how it is doing, but there are some ratios that allow them to make well-informed assessments. Two of the most crucial ratios are reported daily in the *Financial Times* (**dividend yield** and the **price/earnings ratio**), and a third on a weekly basis: **dividend cover**, which is published in the London share service in Monday's newspaper.

The next source of information available to investors is the company's annual report. This offers some consistency of key indicators, since they are regulated by law and accountancy standards. Using these, investors can make relevant comparisons of one company with another, particularly if the companies are in the same industry sector. Company reports are notorious for what they hide as well as what they reveal. It is possible, at least in the short term, for creative accountants and their boardroom employers to produce figures that more accurately reflect their aspirations for the company rather than its actual performance. However, this does tend to disappear with time: as the business continues to perform in a certain way, so the accountants will eventually force the board to be more frank with the shareholders.

Despite this caveat, the annual report does give some very useful information. For the small private investor, generally the most usable of these ratios are **return on capital employed**, **gearing**, **income gearing** (or interest cover) and **pre-tax profit margin**. Armed with these seven ratios, investors are in a better position to make decisions. The problem is that for many private investors this is too time-consuming and they either take decisions based on less information than this, or trust their money to the professionals who charge royally for the privilege.

This chapter endeavours to describe a quick method of getting to these figures, and then, by the example of a company going through a 30-year life cycle, to show how the mix of investor or shareholder ratios and the company's key financial or management ratios paint a picture of the health and prospects of potential investments. If investors add a judicious reading of the chairman's statement to discover the board's intentions for the future, they are as well prepared as is possible without becoming a full-time company watcher.

■ Key financial ratios

The four company ratios provide an effective check on progress and are reasonably easy to calculate. They should always be done for the two years in the report so that changes over time are reflected. The chairman's statements can then be checked to see if they comment on changes that an investor may regard as significant. Frequently, the report will include "facts for shareholders" or "five-year record", which include some calculated ratios. The advantage of these is that they remove the need to do any extrapolation or calculation. Unfortunately, there are two disadvantages that make them much less useful. The first is that the published ratios are calculated in a way that suits each company: they will tend to use figures that are not misleading or inaccurate, but which give a gloss on performance that the truly objective investor wishes to avoid.

The second problem is connected: since companies use ratios that suit themselves, they do not use the same ones. So, for the sake of consistency, it is better for an investor to become very familiar with four ratios and to work them out for him or herself. An investor can also build a personal database of examples, offering various benchmarks for examining and comparing any company. This is particularly true if studying only one or a limited number of business sectors.

The rules of thumb quoted in the next few sections are useful to an investor as he or she learns to appreciate the significance of the ratios. They are only guides, however, and as the following company history suggests, their significance varies depending on the business the company is in and the stage of its lifecycle it has reached.

Gearing

Gearing (or balance sheet gearing, as it is often called to distinguish it from other forms of gearing) compares the amount of money in shareholders' funds with the amount of external liabilities that the company has. High gearing is more risky than low gearing, but could mean that the company is pushing hard for expansion and needs high levels of debt to finance that growth. It is possible to calculate gearing in a number of ways, but one of the easiest is also one of the harshest measures of a company's exposure to the perils of high levels of debt and creditor dependence.

The ratio is a comparison between the total debt liabilities of a company with its shareholders' funds. The higher the ratio, the more likely it is that debt will become a burden. The more debt, the more interest, the lower the profits and therefore the worse the potential for paying dividends.

The calculation is as follows: find the current liabilities in the annual report, often called "liabilities: amounts falling due within one year". Add "creditors: amounts falling due after more than one year", ensuring that everything is included, to find total debt liabilities. Find the figure for total shareholders' funds, but do not include minority interests. Divide total debt liabilities by total shareholders' funds and multiply by 100 to arrive at a percentage figure.

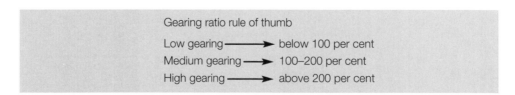

Gearing ratio rule of thumb

Low gearing ⟶ below 100 per cent
Medium gearing ⟶ 100–200 per cent
High gearing ⟶ above 200 per cent

■ Income gearing

The total debt liabilities to shareholders' funds ratio has the limitation that it includes all current liabilities as well as all debt. It is often valuable therefore to have another ratio that indicates the company's ability to service its debt. Income gearing (and its reciprocal, interest cover – see Chapter 2) provides this information. It is the ratio of interest payable to the profits out of which interest is paid. It takes a little more calculation than the other ratios, but has the merit of being impossible to fudge. Many investors regard it as the key gearing ratio.

To calculate income gearing: find the interest payable for the year, often a detail in the notes. The figure on the balance sheet is "net interest", which is interest payable minus interest receivable, not the figure needed here. Find the earnings, or profit, before interest and tax. Often this must be calculated by adding interest payable to the pre-tax profit shown on the profit and loss account. Divide interest payable by profit before interest and tax and multiply by 100 to express it as a percentage.

Income gearing ratio rule of thumb

Low income gearing ⟶ below 25 per cent
Medium income gearing ⟶ 26–75 per cent
High income gearing ⟶ above 75 per cent

■ Return on capital employed (ROCE)

This measure is a key indicator of managerial performance, relating pre-tax profit to the long-term capital invested in the business. It is a good guide as to whether sufficient return is being generated to maintain and grow dividends and avoid problems of liquidity. Unfortunately, it is prone to being misrepresented: there are a number of areas where boards can make this simple measure lead an investor away from the company's problems rather than towards them. Nevertheless, over time it does reveal what is necessary to know about the health of a company measured by profits. Many investors regard it as the key profitability ratio.

To calculate ROCE: capital employed is equivalent to total assets minus current liabilities and this figure is often given on the balance sheet. If not, calculate it as long-term debt, plus provisions for liabilities and charges, plus any other long-term liabilities, plus shareholders' funds, plus minority interests. Divide pre-tax profit by capital employed and multiply by 100 to express it as a percentage.

Return on capital employed rule of thumb

Low profitability ⟶ below 10 per cent
Medium profitability ⟶ 10–20 per cent
High profitability ⟶ above 20 per cent

Pre-tax profit margin

This indicator reveals the profits earned per pound of sales and therefore measures the efficiency of the operation. This ratio is an indicator of the company's ability to withstand adverse conditions such as falling prices, rising costs or declining sales.

To calculate pre-tax profit margin: take the pre-tax profit figure on the profit and loss account. Divide it by the total sales revenues, often known in UK reports as "sales turnover", and multiply by 100 for a percentage.

> Pre-tax profit margin rule of thumb
>
> Low margin ———➤ below 2 per cent
> Medium margin ——➤ 4–8 per cent
> High margin ———➤ above 8 per cent

Key shareholder ratios

Chapter 5 explains the following indicators of company and share performance and where they can be found in the *Financial Times* listings of share price information. The following is a brief refresher before examining how these ratios, along with the financial ratios explored earlier, may change over the life of a company.

Yield

This is the percentage return on investment that a shareholder receives in dividend compared to the current share price. It is listed daily in the newspaper, along with the average for all the industry sectors. Generally, investors looking for income will pick shares with an above-average yield. However, long-term investors will also look for yield, particularly when they are investing in a tax efficient way, as for example with an ISA. Here the tax advantage magnifies the growth available in a high yielding share.

Price/earnings ratio

Also known as the multiple, the p/e ratio reflects the market's valuation of a company expressed as a multiple of past earnings (profits). It is listed daily in the newspaper, along with the average for all the industry sectors. Investors looking for capital growth will look for shares that have a high p/e. If the market has made a correct prediction, an investor in such a share should expect to see growth of sales and profits in the company.

■ Dividend cover

This ratio of the profits to gross dividends is another useful indicator for investors. Many private investors recognise the long-term benefits of a growing income stream from dividends. If they are investing for the long term, therefore, they may very well look for shares that are out of favour with the market and which, as a result, have a high yield. It is quite likely that the capital growth of such a share may be very limited in the short or even medium term. But this slow growth at the early stage is less important if the dividend payments are worth having.

The problem arises where a high yielding share has insufficient profits to continue to increase or even maintain its dividend. The chances of its being able to keep the payments up are indicated by the number of times the dividend is covered by the profits.

■ The life of a growth stock

There is no such thing as a typical company. Their different products, markets and management styles make each enterprise unique. It is possible, however, to use the following example as a benchmark of the characteristics and ratios of a company over a long period of time. For each of the four stages, there is an indication of the kind of information the annual report may provide, and the likely financial and shareholder ratios.

■ Stage 1: inception to ten years old

Turn back the clock to the time when telecommunications was in its first meteoric growth phase. The imaginary sample company, Phoneco, was created by a flotation from its parent where it had been a non-core business. The newly floated company in the early stages has the ability to generate very rapid growth of sales. The market is eager for the new service and sales are there for the taking for any company that can lay down a telecommunications network.

Phoneco is very aggressive at this stage. It needs volume to cover its voracious appetite for cash as it invests millions of pounds in infrastructure. This makes its competitiveness very sharp. To a considerable extent, it will sacrifice profit for market share. It hires a salesforce of "hunters", salespeople who enjoy the challenge of getting new business quickly. These salespeople are good at closing business and handling objections. If they do not close business fast, they go elsewhere. It is to be expected that there is high morale in the company as the business and consumer markets flock to the upstart.

The annual report

The chairman's statement will reflect this growth. Extracts may include such comments as the following: "May saw another milestone when the new connections rate for residential customers signing up with Phoneco reached 30,000 per month"; "Our sales growth last year exceeded 50 per cent, and although this is likely to prove exceptional, Phoneco is confident of its ability to take further advantage of the expanding market over the next few years." The report's tone will reflect the excitement and enthusiasm of the fledgling, which is discovering success for the first time.

The financial ratios

The board is running Phoneco by its cash flows rather than by its profit and loss account. It needs huge amounts of cash for capital investment and will probably have very high levels of borrowing. This high gearing will show itself in both of the gearing ratios, with a high percentage of debt and very little profit left over once interest is deducted. Profitability will be relatively low measured by both return on capital employed and the profit margin.

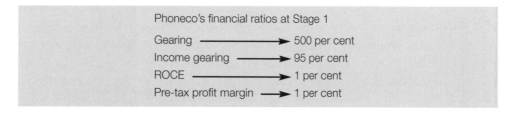

Phoneco's financial ratios at Stage 1

Gearing ──────────▸ 500 per cent
Income gearing ──────▸ 95 per cent
ROCE ──────────▸ 1 per cent
Pre-tax profit margin ──▸ 1 per cent

The shareholder ratios

Investors will find that the market only sees Phoneco as long-term potential, resting in the high risk part of their portfolios. It is undesirable for the company to pay large amounts in dividend, since it needs all its cash to fund its expansion. Hence, the yield will be low. The p/e will be very high as the market calculates future profit streams for the company as it gets into a position to exploit its assets. The dividend cover may very well be high, not because the profits are huge but because the dividend is low.

Phoneco's shareholder ratios at Stage 1

Yield ──────────▸ 0.3
Price/earnings ──────▸ 35
Dividend cover ──────▸ 13

▪ Stage 2: 10 to 20 years old

Phoneco has come of age. It has survived the heady days of 30 per cent year-on-year growth and shown itself to be competitive. The company is now well into the FTSE 250 list of companies. It has a viable market share in the areas where it already operates and is looking for new opportunities to make further investment either in new markets, such as overseas, or in new product areas, such as telephone equipment.

This diversified growth will still cost a great deal of money, but the business now generates a healthy cash flow and is profitable. There is still a fair amount of risk in the company. It is vulnerable to making mistakes as it moves into new activities. No matter how good the prospects, it is always more risky to take old products into new markets or new products into old markets than to keep doing more of the same.

The annual report

The chairman's statement may now see more talk of consolidation of the company's current affairs, although the emphasis of the report will still be on growth, and possibly on new initiatives. Extracts from the statement for a Stage 2 company may include such remarks as, "Our earnings per share before exceptional items grew by 22 per cent"; "Our strengthening financial position allows us to explore new areas seeking basic telephone services, while at the same time consolidating our strategy to focus on those parts of the world where we are already strong and where our returns will be the greatest."

The financial ratios

The debt ratios are still high. Almost certainly by this time, Phoneco will have been back to its investors for more cash through a rights issue. This, of course, radically reduces the debt to equity ratio, but it will rise again to reflect continued investment. Profitability has improved to what could be described as fairly safe levels. This means that the current business will produce reliable profits, and it is only in the new areas of activity that there is still high risk.

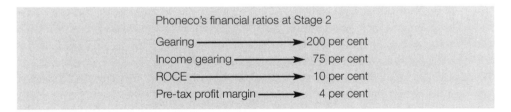

Phoneco's financial ratios at Stage 2

Gearing ⟶ 200 per cent
Income gearing ⟶ 75 per cent
ROCE ⟶ 10 per cent
Pre-tax profit margin ⟶ 4 per cent

The shareholder ratios

Phoneco wants to pay out some dividend of real worth. It probably had to make promises in this area when it made its cash call and it sees dividend as a sign of impending "respectability". Nevertheless, the yield is still well below the sector average, as the price of the share is buoyed by the market's expectation of further growth. The p/e is also still very high. It is probably less than other new entrants in Stage 1 of their lifecycles, but it will be well above the industry average. The dividend is stretching cover much more than in the first phase. Investors are starting to ask when the return to their money will start to come through, and there is no room for the very high dividend cover of the earlier stage.

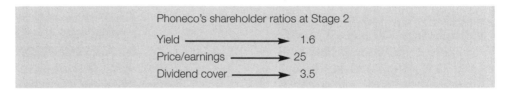

Phoneco's shareholder ratios at Stage 2

Yield	1.6
Price/earnings	25
Dividend cover	3.5

Stage 3: 20 to 30 years old

The company has achieved respectability. It is now at the bottom end of the FTSE 100 companies. It is a complex company and the analysts are looking for good statements of strategy, which prove that the current management can run a cruiser, having been very successful in managing fast patrol boats and destroyers. The company's share price will vary with the changes in the industry. A bad regulatory change, for example, could endanger profit growth significantly. Long-term planning is no longer a luxury, but a vital responsibility of the board and its advisers.

The company will have some "big names" on its board with the possibility of an ex-cabinet minister among its numbers. Risk has changed in its nature. The company could now afford to make some mistakes without threatening its actual life. The market sees the risk as comparative with other stocks in the sector. Investors will see reports of sell-offs of one share in the sector and swaps into other companies in the same sector being recommended.

The annual report

It is unlikely that the annual report will claim that everything is rosy. Shareholders expect more circumspect statements with admissions of error and promises of remedy. A careful look at the ratios on which the chairman reports can be revealing. For example, if he produces a graph showing that the past 25 years of share price appreciation has consistently outperformed the market index, he is probably trying to reassure the market that there is still plenty of growth potential there. He does not want the growth in share price to stall, although it will certainly have slowed.

Like the professionals, the private investor should look for a confident statement of comprehensive and long-term goals and strategies. Extracts from the chairman's statement for a Stage 3 company may say: "We see alliances with other companies as an important contributor to our vision to be the supplier of choice for people seeking high levels of features combined with international coverage"; "New technologies offer enormous opportunities to broaden the services available to our current customers. The convergence of voice, music, graphics, video and data will radically alter the way we conduct our lives"; "The reorganisation, which we completed during the year, has ensured that we can carry through our promises of presenting a global image and relationship with our key accounts worldwide."

The financial ratios

The ratios have now reached the mature end of industry averages. Gearing is at the low-risk end and less than a third of profits are required to pay the interest bill. The measure of return on capital employed is as meaningful and reliable as any other large company's, and reflects the kind of return expected from the whole sector as opposed to the rapid growth part of the sector. The relatively high pre-tax profit margin shows the built-in profitability of the telecommunications sector, which can exploit its expensive invest-ments in infrastructure for many, many years.

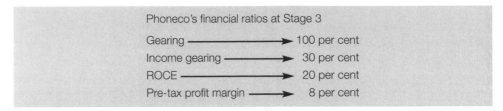

Phoneco's financial ratios at Stage 3

Gearing ⟶ 100 per cent
Income gearing ⟶ 30 per cent
ROCE ⟶ 20 per cent
Pre-tax profit margin ⟶ 8 per cent

The shareholder ratios

The dividend is an important part of large investors' portfolio plans. The yield will there-fore tend to be around the average for the sector and even for the whole market. The p/e is similarly near the average for the sector. The dividend cover has gone sharply down as investors start to make the returns they were expecting at this stage in Phoneco's lifecycle.

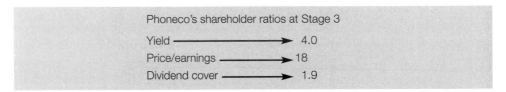

Phoneco's shareholder ratios at Stage 3

Yield ⟶ 4.0
Price/earnings ⟶ 18
Dividend cover ⟶ 1.9

■ Stage 4: Over 30 years old

The board is now commanding a battleship or a stately galleon. Shareholders have stopped looking for excitement in the share and want long-term promises on dividends and the delivery of these promises. The company is in the top 20 of the FTSE 100 and has a high-profile chairman and non-executive directors. The chairman will be frequently heard on the television and radio talking about the company's performance, the economic situation, the regulatory environment and other current affairs.

Representatives of the company now have a lot of power over standards bodies and supplier policies. Someone from Phoneco will be one of the panel in any debate with a telecommunications context, from virtual reality shopping to home working. The salesforce now comprises more "farmers" than "hunters". The company has well-founded key account management techniques in place to develop and protect market share.

The chairman will probably be found complaining about the view that the stock market takes of Phoneco's shares. The company likes to think it is a growth and innovation enterprise, while the market sees it as primarily a utility, with limited opportunities for the sort of growth that will make a significant difference to its profit stream.

The annual report

The chairman's statement will include an emphasis on benefits to customers. The company takes very seriously its dominant place in a number of markets, and is anxious to show that it is not exploiting this. Phoneco will boast of new offerings to its customers, lower prices and generally better service. Extracts from the chairman's statement for a Stage 4 company may include: "Steady growth of sales at 4 per cent and earnings at 5.5 per cent demonstrate our progress towards meeting the expectations of both our shareholders and our customers"; "Against this economic and competitive background, Phoneco's strategy remains clear. We will develop vigorously in our traditional markets and at the same time establish ourselves in new markets for advanced services both in our traditional and new parts of the world."

The financial ratios

The ratios are all safer than the industry average and are at the top end of the benchmark. There is no question in the short term that the company can maintain its market and profit growth, limited though that is. Investors will be wary for any signs of decline. Regulations and new competitors represent the biggest risk. Phoneco has already shown good control of costs, but this needs to be a continuing phenomenon and reflected in the profit margin.

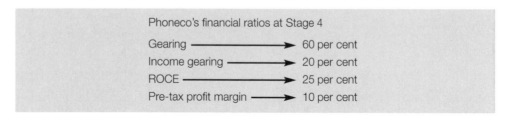

Phoneco's financial ratios at Stage 4

Gearing ⟶ 60 per cent
Income gearing ⟶ 20 per cent
ROCE ⟶ 25 per cent
Pre-tax profit margin ⟶ 10 per cent

The shareholder ratios

The share is now in almost all pension and private portfolios. The expectation is for dividend progress rather than capital growth, and the yield and dividend cover show it. The yield is well above the average and cover is at a low level. Dividend cover probably wants to stay around here except if there is an exceptional item affecting profits. The p/e is the sign of the stately galleon.

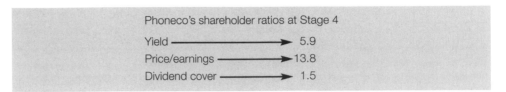

Phoneco's shareholder ratios at Stage 4

Yield ⟶ 5.9
Price/earnings ⟶ 13.8
Dividend cover ⟶ 1.5

"Anyone who is not intimately involved with the internet and the web does so at extreme peril."

Bill Gates

"Cyberspace is where your money is."

John Perry Barlow,
co-founder of the Electronic Frontier Foundation

19

Finance on the internet

Using the electronic financial pages

- **Reading the electronic pages** – Reuters, Bloomberg and Bridge; FT.com

The *Financial Times* provides a globally used reference point for financial data, but the newspaper medium obviously has the limitation of being published only once a day. For readers needing to supplement the newspaper's overview of the news and markets with more sophisticated real-time data, there are other media, notably the internet and private online services. The growing versatility of computers, their increased power, larger memories, faster modems and interconnectedness all mean that the options for accessing information on financial markets (as well as trading online) have never been greater than they are today. A very brief introduction to a variety of electronic information sources is the subject of this chapter. Much more advice can be found in the newspaper, particularly the Saturday edition, as well as in a wide variety of investment publications and books like David Emery's *The Good Web Guide to Money* and Alpesh Patel's *Net-Trading: Get Online with the New Trading Strategies* (Financial Times/Prentice Hall).

Reading the electronic pages

For the professional investment community, the global information product suppliers – Reuters, Bloomberg and Bridge – remain essential tools. These companies deliver news services, markets reports and price quotations to customer screens in most financial institutions. They provide constant real-time datafeeds on currencies, stocks, bonds, futures, options and other instruments across a range of countries and markets. The services also provide software to analyse the data, graphical displays and asset price analysis, allowing the user to retrieve historic news and price quotations.

These companies also offer transaction products that enable traders to deal from their keyboards. Reuters, for example, has an equity trading mechanism called Instinet, which allows traders to negotiate deals directly but anonymously via a computerised "bulletin board", where traders place their bids and offers of shares, and deals are matched automatically.

Electronic sources of financial information like these have been around for some time, but never has the market been so competitive, the quality of what is provided so high or the range of products so varied. For market participants, the difficult decision is over how to make the trade-off between data quality and cost. Most of the databases are essential tools of investing for professionals dealing in equities and other instruments. The needs of the individual investor, unless a very active trader with an extremely large personal portfolio, probably run to something less complete and less expensive.

What is more, computers are now bridging the divide between the large investing institutions, traditionally close to the markets, and individual investors, previously far from the action and at a considerable disadvantage. The primary force behind this development is, of course, the internet. Numerous websites now offer relatively easy access to real-time prices and the ability to chart them with historical prices. They also provide the opportunity to research background information on companies, market and economies; to give trading orders directly, with the advantages of speed and savings on telephone charges; and to integrate all of these into a personal finance and/or portfolio management software package.

Reading the online FT

The *Financial Times* was one of the first newspapers to launch an online edition, starting in May 1995. In early 2000, the website was relaunched as a "global business portal". The site has seven "channels", covering everything from business news to leisure, and some excellent web tools. From the point of view of tradition, the most important channels are News and Analysis and Markets and Portfolio. These draw on the newspaper's established strengths, in reporting, analysis and access to data.

But the newspaper now publishes not only its flagship website, FT.com, which seeks to reach a wide range of business users, but also two other sites with more specific aims. One of these, FTYourMoney, seeks to provide financial planning tools for the general public. The other, FTMarketWatch, is a site for active individual investors across Europe, providing up-to-the-minute market news and comment with a speed and immediacy that allows the site's users to be intimately connected with the ebb and flow of prices and sentiment. The site also offers a set of powerful tools for understanding market trends. For example, users can construct their own charts, plotting an individual company's share price against an index or a competitor and choosing whatever time period they wish. This sort of tool was previously only available at a high monthly fee.

As an example of how to make sense of the FT's electronic pages, a couple of screens for equities from FT.com provide a good introduction. The best place to start is to call up a particular company by typing its name or symbol into the "company view" box on the top left-hand side of the website's home page. This then brings up a list of markets where the stock (or derivatives based on it) is quoted, from which it is generally best to pick LSE (London Stock Exchange). This then leads to a host of market information (see Figure 19.1) plus links to detailed background information on the company's financial position, access to annual reports and analysts' estimates and a FTSE discussion forum on the company:

- **Quotes:** the first box on the left-hand side provides a latest quote on the share price, the time at which that price was quoted, the percentage change in price on the previous day's closing price, the net volume of shares traded and the price at which the share opened that day. Prices are usually updated every 15 minutes so they do not necessarily reflect prices at which it is possible to trade.

- **Location:** the box below indicates in which country and on what exchange the share is traded as well as its symbol.

- **Fundamentals:** the third box down provides price highs and lows over the past 12 months, the latest dividend payment, when it was paid and the date the share went ex-dividend. It also shows the company's market capitalisation, dividend yield, price/earnings ratio and earnings per share.

FTSE discussion forum

PEARSON

Quotes	03Jan2001
Price	1596.00 p
Time	10:52 GMT
% Change	-0.8%
Net Volume	303,034
Open	1589.00 p

Location	
Country	UK
Exchange	LSE
Symbol	PSON

Fundamentals	
52 Wk High	2573
52 Wk Low	1548
Dividend	9.2 p
Div Date	11 Aug2000
Ex Date	07 Aug2000
Ex/Cum	0
Market Cap	12.83B
Div Yield	1.43
P/E Ratio	33.38
EPS	48.2

PEARSON 3M closing prices

Click here for interactive charting

Share Price for the last 5 days			
Date	Close	Net Change	% Change
01 Jan2001	0	0	-
29 Dec2000	1590	-11.00	-0.68%
28 Dec2000	1601	-23	-1.41%
27 Dec2000	1624	+29.00	+1.81%
22 Dec2000	1595	+10.99	+0.69%

view latest PEARSON news

interactive charting
Compelling graphics and intuitive navigation to make your research experience productive

analyst estimates
Consensus Recommendations and Analyst Forecasts from BARRA Global Estimates

Fig. 19.1 Electronic share price information

- **Closing prices:** the chart on the top right shows the ups and downs of the share price over recent weeks. An "interactive charting" tool allows the viewer to alter the period shown and compare the movements against an index or other shares.
- **Share prices for the last five days:** the final box carries the closing price for the last five trading days and the changes on the previous days, in terms of both cash and as a percentage.

Broader equity market data can be obtained via the Markets button at the top of the website. For example, going to Markets: world indices brings up the latest values of a range of key indices, including the S&P 500, the Dow and the Nasdaq Composite, plus a chart showing the movements of the FTSE 100 index over the past year (see Figure 19.2).

equities home

View full list: World Indices | FTSE World Indices Series | World Closing

World Indices Summary			3 Jan 2001
Index	**Rate**	**Time**	**% Change**
S&P	1283.27	16:59 EST	-2.8%
DJIA	10646.10	16:31 EST	-1.3%
NASDAQ	2291.86	17:16 EST	-7.2%
FTSE 100	6138.60	10:54 GMT	-0.6%
CAC 40	5733.21	11:38 CET	-1.1%
DAX	6249.22	11:39 CET	-0.6%
HANG SENG	14589.50	Close	-1.9%
NIKKEI 225	13785.60	Close	-1.2%

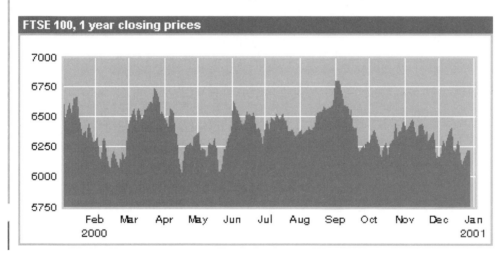

Fig. 19.2 Electronic index information

This is only a tiny flavour of the range of financial information available to investors on the internet. Much more is available via company websites and online financial publications, as well as a growing number of facilities for investors to trade shares online.

"You may not get rich by using all the available information,

but you surely will get poor if you don't."

Jack Treynor

"I know you believe you understand what you think I said,

but I am not sure you realise that what you heard is not what I meant."

Alan Greenspan

20

Sources of information

A brief guide

■ **Information sources** – newspapers; magazines; reference books; radio and television; institutional advice; annual reports, newsletters, tip sheets and City publications

■ **Using the information** – reading between the lines of company and market commentary: Marks & Spencer, Dell Computer and Lufthansa as examples in Lex

■ **Reading the *Financial Times*** – a brief reiteration of where to find the key information

The *Financial Times* is essential reading for anyone involved or interested in money and the financial markets. But there are plenty of other sources of information: not just the electronic datafeeds and internet services discussed in the previous chapter, but a variety of newspapers, magazines, newsletters and other publications as well as broadcast media. An information consumer requires three skills to avoid being overwhelmed by the deluge of information available: an ability to select the best sources; a filter to focus only on relevant information; and an understanding of how to read between the lines of financial reporting and comment, and carefully to distinguish it from sales promotion by interested parties. This chapter aims to be a rough guide to what is available and how to go about reading it. It closes by returning to the *Financial Times* itself with a brief reiteration of how to find your way through the newspaper and get to the information you need.

■ Information sources

The US equivalent of the *Financial Times* is *The Wall Street Journal*, which is available in European and Asian editions, though their international coverage is to some degree at the expense of the extremely detailed coverage of the US markets carried by its regular edition. Other good newspaper sources of business and financial information for the United States include *The New York Times* and *Investor's Business Daily*. In the United Kingdom, there is good coverage of the local, European and international markets in all the quality daily and Sunday newspapers, but nowhere near the depth of financial market data or company news carried by the *Financial Times*.

The key magazines for the investor are, in the United Kingdom, *Investors' Chronicle*, and in the United States, *Barron's*. *The Economist* also provides excellent broad coverage of international business and finance. Other magazines that cover financial issues include *Investor's Week* and *Shares*; the UK personal finance publications, such as *Moneywise*, *Inside Money* and *Money Observer*; US business magazines, such as *Forbes*, *Fortune* and *Business Week*; magazines for financial intermediaries, such as *Money Management*; the international banking magazine, *The Banker*; *International Financing Review* for corporate financiers; and *Euromoney* for those involved in the Euromarkets.

There are numerous reference publications on the markets, which can supplement the real-time information available electronically and the news coverage and data of papers and magazines. Good UK examples include the *Stock Exchange Yearbook*, which provides detailed history and financial information on all securities listed on the London exchange; the *Hambro Company Guide*, which also provides data on all fully listed companies; the *Estimate Directory*, which contains individual UK brokers' forecasts and composite forecasts for hundreds of companies; and the *Handbook of Market Leaders*, which includes data on contract details, share prices, up to five years of financial information, activity analysis, and graphic share-price analysis.

In the United Kingdom, radio and television offer a limited number of programmes covering financial and business issues apart from the daily news. The notable ones are the weekly Radio 4 programme *Money Box* with its wide-ranging discussions of personal finance, and BBC 2's business forum, *The Money Programme*. However, both television data services, CEEFAX and Teletext, provide share and option prices updated four times daily plus financial market headlines; and FT Cityline and Teleshare offer telephone services with real-time share prices, updated constantly. The United States is far better served by its broadcast media; indeed, at least one mainstream channel, CNBC, is devoted to business and finance.

For further details on the UK market for financial information, Proshare, an organisation committed to encouraging wider share ownership, publishes a useful guide to information sources for the private investor.

■ Institutional advice

On top of the generally objective information and analysis provided by the press, there is a host of rather less disinterested material from the major players in the markets. Company reports are of course the single most important source of information on individual companies, containing all financial information and official statements from the company for the last financial year. All shareholders receive a copy of the annual report as of right and non-shareholders can apply to the company secretary for a free copy. The *Financial Times* also offers a free company report service for a wide selection of companies: the relevant companies are indicated in the London share service. How to start analysing the information provided by annual reports is discussed in Chapter 18 of this book.

A secondary source of information for investors comes from newsletters or, as they are sometimes more disparagingly known, tip sheets. There are newsletters for every occasion and every investment style, particularly in the United States where estimates of the number published range from 800 to several thousand. In the United Kingdom, there are significantly fewer, perhaps only 20 of any substance, which is partly a result of the extensive coverage of the markets in the national press. It is also perhaps partly due to fear of their writers using the format to push stocks for their own advantage, and certainly investors should be aware of possible lack of objectivity. They should also examine a newsletter's track record before following its advice automatically.

The attraction of newsletters is that they offer ideas, data, analysis and a point of view that are not going to duplicate regular sources. Most are small operations centred on one individual, their editor–adviser, and their whole purpose is for investors to find information that others may not have, and to learn about opportunities both to sell and buy stocks before the mainstream investment community. Essentially, there are three main types of newsletter: company-specific tip sheets, providing recommendations on specific stocks; market-related newsletters, which cover the markets themselves and often involve sophisticated technical analysis; and political and/or socio-economic newsletters, which, rather than focusing on specific investment advice, offer alternative views and analysis of what is happening in the world and how events may shape markets. The *Hulbert Financial Digest*, published in the United States, offers an objective source for the performance analysis of investment advisory newsletters.

Other subjective sources of information are the publications of major brokers and investment houses. Many financial institutions offer information sheets and/or newsletters of some kind to their clients, and these are frequently driven by the need for sales. The UK regulatory bodies, for example, demand that when brokers and tip sheet writers publish investment recommendations, they must be researched and able to be substantiated, but it is best to be sceptical.

With brokers' advice, it is vital to remember that their primary interest is in transactions rather than their clients' portfolio performance. This creates a bias towards activity or "churning" of the account. There is an additional bias towards encouraging purchases rather than sales. One reason for this is that the former have more commission-generating power since everyone is a potential buyer. The dominance of buy over sell recommendations may also be more likely because analysts can be reluctant to express pessimistic opinions: for effective research on their chosen industry sector, they need open lines of communication with companies' management. The outcome of this bias to the positive is that they frequently overestimate stocks' potential success.

Lastly, it is worth remembering that there is an awkward paradox at the heart of any published investment advice. If the advice is obvious, the markets will have already taken it into account. If it is not obvious, but still correct, the markets will react to it instantaneously so that most advisers will have already acted. The best kind of investment advice, therefore, is often general, not specific, and it is about spotting trends rather than discrete events.

Using the information

Newspapers like the *Financial Times* pride themselves on dealing in fact rather than speculation, and on the accuracy, authority and objectivity of their information and analysis. But even their reporting and comment must be interpreted: while the highly regarded FT Lex column, for example, does not make investment recommendations as such, it is still necessary to try to understand the underlying view and its implications. The following examples from the column, coverage of the UK retailer Marks & Spencer the US computer firm Dell and the German airline Lufthansa published in 2000, may provide some indication of how to "read between the lines" of any writing about companies and markets. They also show the kind of performance ratios that are seen as important by leading commentators on the market. The reader may still want to look at other hard facts of company and share price performance.

Marks & Spencer

If only managing a retail business were like managing market expectations. Yesterday, Marks & Spencer shares were the FTSE 100's top performer with an 18 per cent leap as the company announced pre-tax profits lower than last year but ahead of analysts' downgraded forecasts. Even so, the stock has underperformed throughout the past 12 months, despite the odd outbreak of bid speculation.

Luc Vandervelde, the new executive chairman, spoke forcefully about the need for the group both to embrace globalisation and to ensure that stores responded to local customers' needs. But this is talk from a company that has had difficulties meeting much less ambitious aims over the year being reported. There have been moments when M&S has struggled to get stock into its stores; its sales are flat; and cutting back on loss-making international activities has produced an exceptional charge of £62m.

M&S has made improvements over the past year. It has increased gross margins and cut costs. The decision to accept credit cards is already lifting sales, and an advertising push this autumn should give a boost going into the critical pre-Christmas trading period. This is welcome, though much of it is just overdue common sense. Mr Vandervelde has pledged to improve performance within two years and yesterday's results will help the comparison. But despite upwardly revised forecasts for 2001, the shares, on ten times enterprise value to earnings before tax, interest, depreciation and amortisation, do not look cheap. *(Financial Times,* 24 May 2000)

Dell Computer

When a momentum stock like Dell Computer shows signs of mortality, investors flee. They did so again yesterday, knocking a tenth off the shares after second-quarter sales grew 25 per cent rather than the expected 30 per cent. With the stock now having fallen nearly a third in less than a month it is time to reassess the group's prospects.

First, a slowdown in revenues is inevitable – it is simply a function of Dell's increasing size. On top of that, the personal computer market itself is sluggish. However, the group is still growing at twice the rate of its ten largest rivals. Second, Dell is becoming increasingly profitable. A higher mix of notebooks, servers and service revenues pushed gross margins up to 21 per cent and Dell still claims a 10–15 per cent cost advantage over the competition. The fact that the group holds just seven days' worth of inventory and produces a 294 per cent return on invested capital is an elegant testimony to its efficiency. Earnings are expected to grow 40 per cent this year and 30 per cent next.

The clinching argument is value. Dell's rating has fallen far more rapidly over the past 18 months than its growth rate, with the stock's forward price/earnings ratio down from nearly 100 to 32. At this point it is trading at barely a 30 per cent premium to the S&P 500 index, although it is growing more than twice as fast. That looks a bargain. *(Financial Times,* 12–13 August 2000)

Lufthansa

Lufthansa is cruising. While other European airlines have had a torrid time, its operating profits rose 18 per cent in the first half. The German carrier is forecasting 15 per cent growth for the year. That is not particularly exciting, bearing in mind it is in the take-off part of its cycle. But the management is being conservative after last year's racier approach backfired. The share price wobble yesterday reflects fears about rising fuel costs as much as anything else – and Lufthansa is hedged better than most.

Limited exposure on North Atlantic and Asian routes means that Lufthansa has not suffered the problems that have afflicted British Airways and others. Nor has it been hit as hard by low-cost competition in Europe. The weakness of the euro has also provided a boost, though at least a bit – say a fifth – of the increase in yields in the first half reflects higher prices. And after shooting itself in the foot in 1999, Lufthansa is now keeping a lid on capacity.

Turbulence should not be a problem, therefore. But nor is Lufthansa poised for the kind of cyclical upswing that others, including BA, may be heading towards. Indeed, if BA's strategy of concentrating on premium traffic pays off, it will offer greater excitement. The danger is that BA ends up overpaying for a tie-up with KLM that turns out to be little more than a distraction. Lufthansa is trading at a hefty discount to BA. For those content with a steady ride, Lufthansa offers better value.

(*Financial Times*, 24 August 2000)

■ Reading between the lines

A significant proportion of press coverage is about the profits companies earn and their prospective future profits. In these cases, the companies have just published results and while all have been good, not all have had a positive impact on the share price. The key is how the results compare with what analysts are expecting: M&S beat expectations of the pre-tax profits it would announce even though the actual performance was worse than the previous year; while Dell's sales fell below expectations even though profits were very strong. This meant that the former's share price rose while the latter's fell. Lufthansa seems to have beaten profit expectations but its shares have been marked down because of the potential impact of higher oil prices on future profitability.

The comments on the share prices of M&S and Dell refer to their performance relative to the relevant market, the FTSE 100 for the former and the S&P 500 for the latter. Lufthansa's valuation is compared with British Airways rather than a national market index, a reflection of the growing European interest in making comparisons of companies within pan-European industry sectors rather than relatively narrow national stock markets.

Each story focuses on the markets in which the companies operate, and on the industry-specific indicators that should be added to the all-purpose financial ratios (of profitability, yield, etc.) when assessing their performances. For M&S, sales in the

Christmas season are crucial; for Dell, sales growth and the level of inventory seem to be important; and for Lufthansa, passenger numbers relative to capacity and the yields on those passengers are clearly key factors.

The current and future prospects for the three markets and the degree of competition these companies face are also very important considerations. Dell faces a market that is growing more slowly than it has in the past, but by undercutting its rivals, it is taking a substantial share of that market. Lufthansa is operating on routes that appear to be less competitive than some that its rivals face. And M&S is in a relatively mature domestic market and has not been particularly successful in moving into overseas markets.

The final paragraph of each piece returns to relative share valuations and the essential question of whether the prices are too high or two low. Dell's price/earnings ratio is compared to the market's and although it is at a premium, the suggestion is that the company's growth rate implies that it should be at an even higher premium. This is a growth or momentum stock.

Lufthansa's valuation is compared to that of a close competitor against which it is trading at a discount. Again, the implication is that the company is underrated and that the share price will, or should rise.

For M&S, the opposite view is taken. Here, the analysis compares enterprise value, which is the combined market value of the company's equity (market capitalisation) and net debt, to a particular measure of profitability, and comes to the conclusion that the ratio is too high. In contrast with the views taken on Dell and Lufthansa, this comment could be taken by investors as indicating that they should get out of the stock or at least not get into it.

Comments in widely read publications, like these three examples, can easily have an impact on the markets as investors follow their implicit advice to buy or sell. They can also be seen as forecasting future price movements. There is no doubt that good financial reporting has a reasonable track record of predicting price movements of individual stocks, though they certainly are unable to forecast turning points for the market as a whole. Similarly, economic forecasters can often be read for their thoughts on the speed with which a given indicator will continue to move in one direction, though they rarely spot the key turning points of the business cycle when slump turns into recovery or boom into recession. But with all of these commentators, it is vital to cut through the jargon, the kind of terminology spoofed below:

Today's stock market report

Helium was up. Feathers were down. Paper was stationery.

Fluorescent tubing was dimmed in light trading. Knives were up sharply.

Cows steered into a bull market. Pencils lost a few points.

Hiking equipment was trailing.

Elevators rose, while escalators continued their slow decline.

Weights were up in heavy trading.

▶

Light switches were off.

Mining equipment hit rock bottom. Diapers remained unchanged.

Shipping lines stayed at an even keel.

The market for raisins dried up.

Coca-Cola fizzled.

Caterpillar stock inched up a bit.

Sun peaked at midday.

Balloon prices were inflated.

And, Scott Tissue touched a new bottom.

■ Reading the *Financial Times*

The Lex column, carried on the back page of the *Financial Times*' first section (with additional Lex comments sometimes to be found close to the relevant news in different editions) is often the first item readers turn to. Where else in the newspaper can a reader find the information he or she needs? The following is a brief overview.

The main news and equity price information on companies and markets is to be found in the second section of the newspaper on Tuesday to Friday (and in the first section on Saturday). The first few pages focus on UK company news (results, key personnel, financing arrangements, takeovers, etc.) followed by similar news for overseas companies. The back page reports on the London Stock Exchange with a full market report, comments on individual stock movements and tables of market information including "Market at a glance". Inside the back page comes the London share service: price and key ratio details for all stocks for which there is a reasonably liquid market.

Moving back through the newspaper, there is a collection of commentaries on other leading international stock markets, more data on London equities and two pages of data for individual shares and indices from a range of world stock markets. This is preceded by five pages of the FT managed funds service, details on a variety of unit trusts and other pooled investments.

Since the second section of Monday's newspaper has rather less financial market news from the previous couple of days, it provides more of a survey of what has happened the previous week and what to look forward to. The London share service, for example, includes some longer-term data on the listed shares, as well as dialling instructions for real-time share prices from FT Cityline. There is also a Markets Week page on the week's prospects for the equity and bond markets plus a companies diary of expected announcements.

On Saturday, the format is also a little different. The first section carries the company news and equity market data plus a table of dealings in less liquid London shares. The Money section carries the managed fund service plus a wealth of articles, tables and charts relating to issues of personal finance and investment: the previous week in the markets, saving and borrowing rates, investing for growth and for income, pensions, financial planning, ISAs, annuities, and the performance of unit trusts and investment trusts.

Markets other than the equity markets receive daily coverage in the middle of the newspaper's second section. The Euro Markets page covers equity indices, derivatives, currencies, money and bonds in the euro-zone and elsewhere in Europe. The International Capital Markets page covers fixed income securities, including government and corporate bonds plus bond derivatives and interest rate swaps; the Commodities and Agriculture page covers the markets for gold and other metals, energy, "soft" food commodities, etc.; and the Currencies and Money page covers the money markets, the foreign exchange markets and the currency and interest rate derivatives markets. Equity and equity index futures and options are listed on the page with World Stock Markets and Other London Market Data.

For the key data on the economy, Tuesday's first section carries one of five tables of international economic indicators for six leading OECD countries (France, Germany, Italy, Japan, the United Kingdom and the United States). Thursday's first section carries the latest UK economic indicators in "The economy at a glance". Monday's front page has the latest euro exchange rates, and on the back page of Monday's second section is an economic diary of key international economic statistics due to be released in the coming week.

Appendix 1
The key ratios guide

Key financial ratios

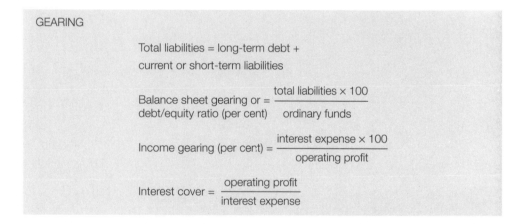

PROFITABILITY

$$\text{Pre-tax profit margin (per cent)} = \frac{\text{pre-tax profit} \times 100}{\text{turnover}}$$

$$\text{Return on capital employed (per cent)} = \frac{\text{pre-tax profit} \times 100}{\text{capital employed}}$$

$$\text{Earnings per share} = \frac{\text{after tax profit}}{\text{number of shares}}$$

GEARING

Total liabilities = long-term debt +
current or short-term liabilities

$$\text{Balance sheet gearing or debt/equity ratio (per cent)} = \frac{\text{total liabilities} \times 100}{\text{ordinary funds}}$$

$$\text{Income gearing (per cent)} = \frac{\text{interest expense} \times 100}{\text{operating profit}}$$

$$\text{Interest cover} = \frac{\text{operating profit}}{\text{interest expense}}$$

Key shareholder ratios

YIELD

$$\text{Dividend yield (per cent)} = \frac{\text{gross dividend per share} \times 100}{\text{share price}}$$

PRICE/EARNINGS

$$\text{Price/earnings ratio} = \frac{\text{share price}}{\text{earnings per share}}$$

DIVIDEND COVER

$$\text{Dividend cover} = \frac{\text{earnings per share}}{\text{gross dividend per share}}$$

Appendix 2

The key indices guide

■ The FT Ordinary Share index (FT 30)

■ The original constituents in 1935

Associated Portland Cement	Hawker Siddeley
Austin Motor	Imperial Chemical Industries
Bass	Imperial Tobacco
Bolsover Colliery	International Tea Co.'s Stores
Callenders Cables & Const.	London Brick
Coats (J&P)	Murex
Courtaulds	Patons & Baldwins
Distillers	Pinchin Johnson & Associates
Dorman Long	Rolls-Royce
Dunlop Rubber	Tate & Lyle
Electrical & Musical Industries	Turner & Newall
Fine Spinners and Doublers	United Steel
General Electric	Vickers
Guest Keen & Nettlefolds	Watney Combe & Reid
Harrods	Woolworth (FW)

■ The current constituents

Allied Domecq	Imperial Chemical Industries
BG	Invensys
Blue Circle Industries	Lloyds TSB
BOC	Marconi
Boots	Marks & Spencer
BP Amoco	P&O Steam Navigation
British Aerospace	Prudential
British Airways	Reuters
British Telecom	Royal & Sun Alliance
Cadbury Schweppes	Royal Bank of Scotland
Diageo	Scottish Power
EMI	SmithKline Beecham
GKN	Tate & Lyle
Glaxo Wellcome	Tesco
Granada Compass	Vodafone

The FTSE 'Footsie' 100

The original constituents in 1984

Allied–Lyons	GKN
ASDA Group	Glaxo Holdings
Associated British Foods	Globe Investment Trust
Barclays Bank	Grand Metropolitan
Barratt Developments	Great Universal Stores
Bass	Guardian Royal Exchange
BAT Industries	Hambro Life Assurance
Beecham Group	Hammerson Prop. Inv. & Dev.
Berisford	Hanson Trust
BICC	Harrisons & Crossfield
Blue Circle Industries	Hawker Siddeley
BOC	House of Fraser
Boots	Imperial Chemical Industries
Bowater	Imperial Cont. Gas Association
BPB Industries	Imperial Group
British & Commonwealth	Johnson Matthey
British Aerospace	Ladbroke
British Elect. Traction	Land Securities
British Home Stores	Legal & General
British Petroleum	Lloyds Bank
Britoil	Magnet & Southerns
BTR	MEPC
Burton Group	MFI Furniture Group
Cable & Wireless	Marks & Spencer
Cadbury Schweppes	Midland Bank
Commercial Union Assurance	National Westminster Bank
Consolidated Gold Fields	Northern Foods
Courtaulds	P&O Steam Navigation
Dalgety	Pearson
Distillers	Pilkington
Eagle Star	Plessey
Edinburgh Investment Trust	Prudential
English China Clays	Racal Electronics
Exco International	Rank Organisation
Ferranti	Reckitt & Colman
Fisons	Redland
General Accident	Reed International
General Electric	RMC

Rowntree Mackintosh
Royal Bank of Scotland
Royal Insurance
RTZ Corporation
Sainsbury
Scottish & Newcastle
Sears Holdings
Sedgwick Group
Shell
Smith & Nephew
Standard Chartered
Standard Telephone & Cables

Sun Alliance
Sun Life Assurance Society
Thorn EMI
Tarmac
Tesco
Trafalgar House
Trusthouse Forte
Ultramar
Unilever
United Biscuits
Whitbread
Wimpey

The constituents as of January 2001

3i
Abbey National
Alliance & Leicester
Allied Domecq
AMVESCAP
Anglo American
ARM Holdings
Associated British Foods
AstraZeneca
Autonomy
BAA
BAE
Bank of Scotland
Barclays Bank
Bass
BAT Industries
BG
Billiton
Blue Circle Industries
BOC
Boots
BP Amoco
British Airways
British Sky Broadcasting
British Telecom
Cable & Wireless
Cadbury Schweppes

Canary Wharf
Capita
Carlton Communications
Celltech
Centrica
CGNU
CMG
Colt Telcom
Daily Mail & General Trust
Diageo
Dimension Data
Dixons
Electrocomponents
EMI
Energis
Exel
GKN
Glaxo Wellcome
Granada Compass
Granada Media
Great Universal Stores
Halifax
Hays
Hilton
HSBC
Imperial Chemical Industries
Imperial Tobacco

International Power
Invensys
Kingfisher
Land Securities
Lattice
Legal & General
Lloyds TSB
Logica
Marconi
Marks & Spencer
Misys
National Grid
Nycomed Amersham
Old Mutual
Pearson
Powergen
Prudential
Railtrack
Reckitt Benckiser
Reed International
Rentokil Initial
Reuters
Rio Tinto

Rolls-Royce
Royal & Sun Alliance
Royal Bank of Scotland
Safeway
Sage Group
Sainsbury
Schroders
Scottish & Southern Energy
Scottish Power
Shell Transport & Trading
Shires Pharmaceuticals
SmithKline Beecham
Smiths Group
South African Breweries
Spirent
Standard Chartered
Telewest Communications
Tesco
Unilever
United News & Media
United Utilities
Vodafone
WPP

The Dow Jones Industrial Average

The 12 original constituents in 1897

American Cotton Oil

American Spirit

American Sugar

American Tobacco

Chicago Gas

General Electric

Laclede Gas

National Lead

Pacific Mail

Standard Rope & Twine

Tennessee Coal & Iron

US Leather

The 30 constituents in 2001

Aluminium Company of America

American Express

AT&T

Boeing

Caterpillar

Citigroup

Coca-Cola

Du Pont

Eastman Kodak

Exxon Mobil

General Electric

General Motors

Home Depot

Honeywell International

Hewlett-Packard

IBM

Intel

International Paper

Johnson & Johnson

JP Morgan

McDonald's

Merck

Microsoft

Minnesota Mining & Manufacturing

Philip Morris

Procter & Gamble

SBC Communications

United Technologies

Wal-Mart Stores

Walt Disney

Index

THE FINANCIAL TIMES

GUIDE TO

USING THE FINANCIAL PAGES

FINANCIAL TIMES
Prentice Hall

In an increasingly competitive world, it is quality
of thinking that gives an edge – an idea that opens new
doors, a technique that solves a problem, or an insight
that simply helps make sense of it all.

We work with leading authors in the fields of
management and finance to bring cutting-edge thinking
and best learning practice to a global market.

Under a range of leading imprints, including
Financial Times Prentice Hall, we create world-class
print publications and electronic products giving readers
knowledge and understanding which can then be
applied, whether studying or at work.

To find out more about our business and professional
products, you can visit us at **www.business-minds.com**

For other Pearson Education publications, visit
www.pearsoned-ema.com

Pearson
Education